S0-DUU-489

THE STATE OF
THE ENVIRONMENT

ORGANISATION FOR ECONOMIC CO-OPERATION AND DEVELOPMENT

NATURAL HISTORY MUSEUM
OF LOS library
ANGELES COUNTY

Hc
79
.E5
S72
1991

Pursuant to Article 1 of the Convention signed in Paris on 14th December 1960, and which came into force on 30th September 1961, the Organisation for Economic Co-operation and Development (OECD) shall promote policies designed:

— to achieve the highest sustainable economic growth and employment and a rising standard of living in Member countries, while maintaining financial stability, and thus to contribute to the development of the world economy;
— to contribute to sound economic expansion in Member as well as non-member countries in the process of economic development; and
— to contribute to the expansion of world trade on a multilateral, non-discriminatory basis in accordance with international obligations.

The original Member countries of the OECD are Austria, Belgium, Canada, Denmark, France, Germany, Greece, Iceland, Ireland, Italy, Luxembourg, the Netherlands, Norway, Portugal, Spain, Sweden, Switzerland, Turkey, the United Kingdom and the United States. The following countries became Members subsequently through accession at the dates indicated hereafter: Japan (28th April 1964), Finland (28th January 1969), Australia (7th June 1971) and New Zealand (29th May 1973). The Commission of the European Communities takes part in the work of the OECD (Article 13 of the OECD Convention). Yugoslavia takes part in some of the work of the OECD (agreement of 28th October 1961).

Publié en français sous le titre :

L'ÉTAT
DE L'ENVIRONNEMENT

© OECD 1991
Applications for permission to reproduce or translate
all or part of this publication should be made to:
Head of Publications Service, OECD
2, rue André-Pascal, 75775 PARIS CEDEX 16, France

The Organisation for Economic Co-operation and Development, in fulfilling its goal of promoting economic development in Member countries, is concerned with the qualitative and quantitative aspects of economic growth, and related sustainable development.

This report was prepared by the OECD Secretariat but its successful completion depended upon significant efforts by many individuals in Member countries who have contributed to it personally or officially, as well as the active support of the Group on the State of the Environment and of the Environment Committee.

The report and its conclusions were reviewed by Environment Ministers of the OECD countries at their meeting in Paris on 30-31 January 1991.

This report is derestricted under the authority of the Secretary-General.

Also available

OECD ENVIRONMENTAL DATA – COMPENDIUM 1989 (Bilingual)
(97 89 03 3) ISBN 92–64–03223–1   FF220   £26.50   US$46.50   DM91

Forthcoming

OECD ENVIRONMENTAL DATA – COMPENDIUM 1991 (Bilingual)

Prices charged at the OECD Bookshop.

*The OECD CATALOGUE OF PUBLICATIONS and supplements will be sent free of charge
on request addressed either to OECD Publications Service,
2, rue André–Pascal, 75775 PARIS CEDEX 16, or to the OECD Distributor in your country.*

GENERAL OUTLINE OF THE REPORT

Part I

THE STATE OF THE ENVIRONMENT: PROGRESS AND CONCERNS

Part II

A CHANGING ECONOMIC CONTEXT

Part III

MANAGING THE ENVIRONMENT: TOWARDS SUSTAINABILITY

DETAILED TABLE OF CONTENTS

Part I
THE STATE OF THE ENVIRONMENT: PROGRESS AND CONCERNS

LIST OF INSETS

LIST OF FIGURES

LIST OF TABLES

TRANSPORT

16. Selected Environmental Effects of Principal Transport Modes
17. Transport and the Environment: Selected Indicators

ENERGY

18. Selected Environmental Effects of the Energy Sector
19. Energy and the Environment: Selected Indicators

SOCIO-DEMOGRAPHIC CHANGES

20. Structure of Households' Consumption Expenditures

ECONOMIC ASPECTS

21. Pollution Abatement and Control (Pac) Expenditures
22. Types of Charge Systems

INTERNATIONAL ASPECTS

23. List of Multilateral Conventions
24. Public Opinion on Environmental Problems

Data included in the report are those received before the 15th September 1990. All references in the report to Germany consequently concern *western Germany* (Federal Republic of Germany before the unification of Germany).

The following signs and abbreviations are used in Figures and Tables :

..	: not available
—	: nil or negligible
·	: decimal point
billion	: thousand million
G7	: Canada, United States, Japan, France, Germany, Italy and United Kingdom.
OECD-Europe	: All European Member countries of OECD, i.e. countries in EEC plus Austria, Finland, Iceland, Norway, Sweden, Switzerland and Turkey.
OECD-Pacific	: Australia, Japan, New Zealand.
OECD-Total	: All Member countries of OECD, i.e. countries of OECD-Europe plus Canada, United States, Japan, Australia and New Zealand.

INTRODUCTION

The third *OECD Report on the State of the Environment* is presented here. It aims at:

- Assisting Member countries in the definition, implementation and evaluation of environmental policies;
- Helping them to incorporate environmental concerns into economic decision-making in order to progress towards sustainable development;
- Providing environmental information to the public.

This report reviews the environment today to assess the *progress achieved over the past two decades*, that is to say, the lifetime of environmental policies and institutions in most Member countries. It also identifies the remaining problems, which provide a full *agenda for the 1990s*, concerning global atmospheric issues, air, inland waters, the marine environment, land, forest, wild life, solid waste and noise. (See Chapters in Part I)

The relationship emphasizes the *relationship between the state of the environment and economic growth and structural changes* in OECD countries. (Figure 1) Over the past two decades, GDP grew by 72 per cent in the OECD area as a whole. Industrial production increased by 72 per cent, road traffic by 86 per cent and energy use by 30 per cent. The state of the environment is shaped by the pressures from human activities in such sectors as agriculture, industry, transport and energy, as well as socio-demographic changes. But these activities in turn depend on the environment for their sustainable development. (See Chapters in Part II and Chapter on Economic Responses in Part III)

While the report focuses on the environment in OECD countries, it places its analysis in the *context of world ecological and economic interdependence*. OECD countries represent only 16 per cent of the world's population and 24 per cent of its land area; but they also account for about 72 per cent of world gross product, 78 per cent of all road vehicles, and 50 per cent of global energy use. They generate about 76 per cent of world trade, and provide 95 per cent of bilateral assistance. The environmental and economic state of OECD countries influences and is influenced by non-OECD countries. (See in particular the Chapter on International Responses in Part III)

The report draws on the OECD's environmental database, as well as other evidence and scientific expertise accumulated by OECD. It also builds on information from national reports on the state of the environment and from national environmental yearbooks now available in most Member countries.

The report is issued under the responsibility of the Secretary-General of the OECD, but its successful completion depended largely upon significant personal or official contributions by many individuals in Member countries, as well as the active work and support of the OECD Group on the State of the Environment and OECD Environment Committee. The report was presented to *Environment Ministers of the OECD countries* at their meeting in Paris on 30th and 31st January 1991.

Figure 1. **SCOPE AND FRAMEWORK OF THE REPORT**

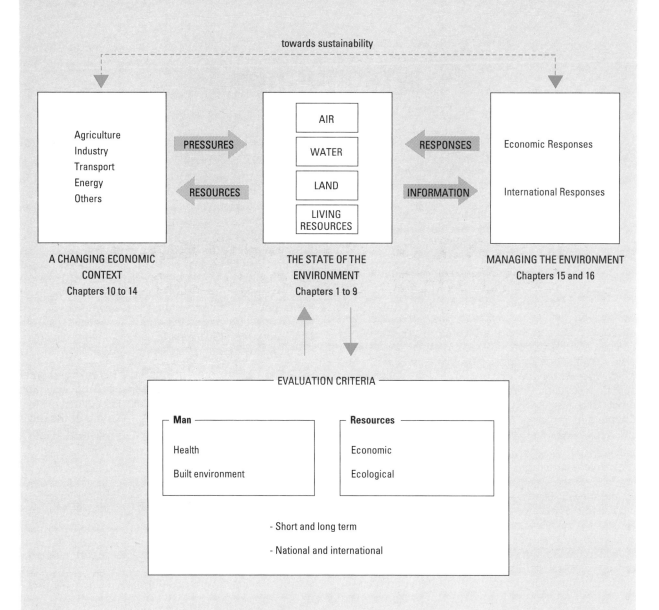

The state of the environment interacts with the state of the economy: human activities impose pressures on the environment (e.g. pollution, waste, environmental restructuring) and depend on it for natural resources inputs (e.g. water, marine, forest, land resources). The state of the environment also depends on its management through responses from economic and environmental agents to environmental changes: environment policies based so far on national regulations and technological progress have economic and international dimensions. Environmental changes can be evaluated with two types of criteria relating to man and to natural resources (from an economic and ecological point of view). However, achieving sustainable development nationally and internationally requires also bringing about changes in OECD economies.

Part I

THE STATE OF THE ENVIRONMENT: PROGRESS AND CONCERNS

Chapter 1

GLOBAL ATMOSPHERIC ISSUES

Concern over the ways in which human activities can alter the global atmosphere has increased dramatically during the past 25 years. It is now clear that the atmospheric composition is changing and that the consequences of these changes, both those observed so far and those expected in the future, are serious. This chapter looks in particular at three major issues:

- Stratospheric ozone depletion;
- The greenhouse effect;
- The global spread of air pollution.

These global issues are linked in a number of ways. The growth of the global population and the subsequent increased demand for energy, food and water is one specific cause of these problems. Other links are also of interest, especially to those involved in developing policies in response to the problems. Stratospheric ozone depletion and the greenhouse effect are linked because chlorofluorocarbons (CFCs), which play a major role in the destruction of stratospheric ozone, are also very potent greenhouse gases. Moreover, the stratospheric cooling which is expected as a result of the greenhouse effect will alter stratospheric chemistry and as a consequence ozone depletion rates. There are other causal links between the global atmospheric issues. For instance, fossil fuel combustion not only adds greenhouse gases to the atmosphere, but also emits other pollutants which can be transported long distances in the atmosphere, giving rise to transboundary pollution.

This chapter examines the observations made during the past 20 years, the scientific understanding of the nature and magnitude of the problems and projections of possible changes in the near future. The concluding section discusses the necessary scientific and political responses to these issues between now and the end of the century.

1. STRATOSPHERIC OZONE DEPLETION

Background

During the past 10 years the number of studies of the processes that control atmospheric ozone has increased, following research in the 1970s showing that human activities could modify the total column amount and vertical distribution of atmospheric ozone. The underlying reason for concern is that ozone is the only gas in the atmosphere that prevents the most harmful solar ultraviolet radiation from reaching the surface of the earth. An increase in the amount of ultraviolet radiation reaching the earth's surface would have potentially harmful effects on human health (melanoma and non-melanoma skin cancer, eye damage, and suppression of the immune response system) and on the productivity of aquatic and terrestrial ecosystems. Changes in the vertical distribution of ozone could alter the distribution of temperature in the atmosphere and lead to regional and global climatic change.

Global ozone trends

Since the concentration of ozone in the atmosphere has large natural temporal and spatial variations, it is difficult to determine global ozone trends. Moreover, observations of both the total column content and the vertical distribution of ozone have been made for several decades, using networks of different measurement techniques with acknowledged limitations. In 1986 NASA in conjunction with the Federal Aviation Administration (FAA), the National Oceanic and Atmospheric Administration (NOAA), the World Meteorological Organization (WMO) and the United Nations Environment Programme (UNEP), started a major review of all ozone data. Over one hundred scientists participated in this assessment of whether the chemical composition and physical structure of the stratosphere had changed.

Figure 2. TRENDS IN OZONE CONCENTRATIONS

Changes in ozone concentration profiles, 1979-1987 (20-50° latitude)

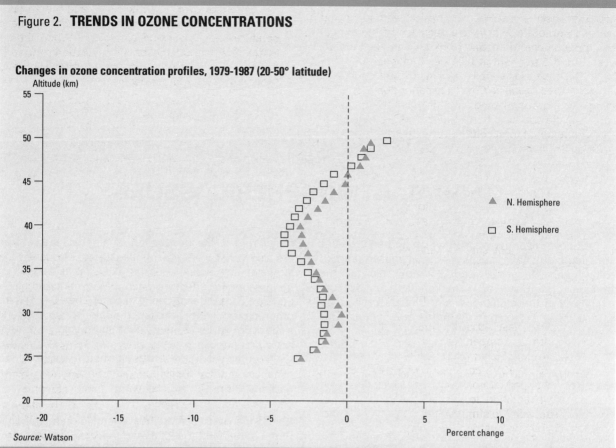

Altitude (km)

Percent change

Source: Watson

October mean monthly ozone concentrations, 1960-1988 (Halley Bay, Antartica)

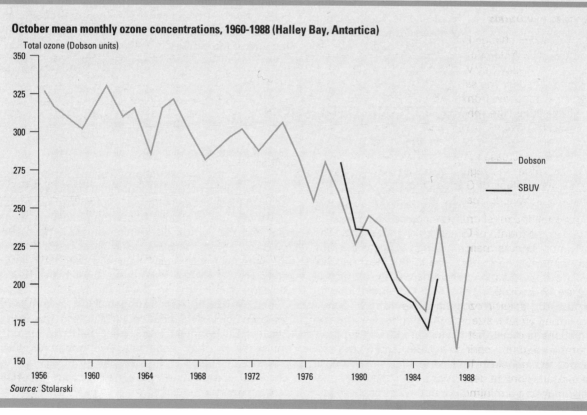

Total ozone (Dobson units)

Source: Stolarski

Analysis of data from ground-based instruments, after the effect of natural geophysical variability had been accounted for, showed a decrease of the annual average total column ozone from 1969 to 1988 of between 3 and 5 per cent at latitudes between 30°N and 64°N. The decreases were largest in the winter months. Trends in total ozone column data cannot be estimated using such ground-based data for the tropics, subtropics or the southern hemisphere outside Antarctica. Measurements of total column ozone have been made by satellite instruments since October 1978. Normalised data from this source show a decrease of the column ozone total, averaged between 53°S and 53°N, of about 2.5 per cent between October 1978 and October 1985. Theoretical calculations suggest, however, that the decrease of solar activity during this period may have contributed to the observed ozone decrease. The present satellite data sets are not yet long enough, however, for definitive studies of long-term trends.

Analysis of satellite and ground-based data since 1979 shows that the largest decrease in ozone concentration occurred near 40 km altitude in both hemispheres. (Figure 2) Temperatures in the stratosphere between 45 km and 55 km have decreased globally by about 1.7°C since 1979, consistent with the observed decreases in upper stratospheric ozone of less than 10 per cent. In addition to global trends in the total amount of ozone in the atmosphere, there are observations of the changing vertical distribution of ozone.

Antarctic ozone trends

A significant change in the springtime total ozone content over the Antarctic was first reported from the station data at Halley Bay with a smaller change found at Argentine Islands. The satellite data not only confirm the decrease observed from the ground-based data but demonstrate that the phenomenon is on a large regional scale. (Figure 2) Maps of total ozone in the southern hemisphere for October in the years 1979 - 1986 show the decrease in the October mean values of total ozone within the region of the ozone minimum. The maximum values of October mean total ozone at about 55-60°S have decreased.

Although the most dramatic decreases have been observed in the month of October, the development of the minimum occurs mainly during September when the sun rises over the polar region. The decreases in total ozone were progressively larger in the 1980s than during the 1960s or 1970s, reaching 50 per cent or more loss of the total column ozone in September 1987 over an area roughly the size of the Antarctic continent. Observations showed that the ozone depletion in the southern hemisphere spring in 1989 was as large as the record-setting hole in 1987. From early August 1989 the total ozone content decreased by about 1.5 per cent per day, reaching a minimum value of ozone of 45 per cent by October 5.

The size of the "ozone hole" and the amount of depletion vary from year to year depending on the temperature and polar wind conditions. When the polar vortex (the strong atmospheric circulation centred over the polar area) is undisturbed and temperatures are especially cold, a larger decrease occurs.

The ozone losses are concentrated in the lower stratosphere between about 12-25 km. The decrease in total ozone stops in early October, but the residual low values of ozone persist until the final breakup of the polar vortex in November, at which point air that has more ozone is introduced from more temperate latitudes.

Causes of the Antarctic ozone hole

Major observation campaigns in 1986 and 1987 showed that the unique meteorology during winter and spring over the Antarctic sets up the special conditions of an isolated air mass (the polar vortex) with cold temperatures required for the observed chemical perturbation. Moreover, there are strong indications that chlorine species resulting from human activities are primarily responsible for the observed decrease in ozone within the polar vortex. The chlorine comes primarily from the breakdown in the stratosphere of chlorofluorocarbons (CFCs). The CFCs are released at the earth's surface and are transported upwards into the stratosphere without undergoing any changes. The sources of CFCs are discussed in Section 2. Polar stratospheric clouds (PSCs) are thought to play a key role in the formation of the Antarctic ozone hole. Satellite data show that the frequency of occurrence of PSCs is higher in the Antarctic stratosphere than anywhere else in the stratosphere. The abundance of the reactive chlorine compounds is observed to be elevated by a factor of 50 to 100 in the springtime. The persistence of PSCs was observed to increase in 1985 and 1987.

Global implications

An important reason for concern about the Antarctic ozone hole is that the processes that appear to be significant in the polar environment could be important at other latitudes and contribute to a global ozone reduction. These processes are neither fully understood nor included in atmospheric models. There is, in fact, already evidence of ozone depletions in winter at mid- and high-latitudes in the northern hemisphere, that are larger than those predicted by photochemical models. Observations also show that ozone has decreased not only over the Antarctic but also by more than 5 per cent at all latitudes south of 60°S throughout the year since 1979.

The Scientific Assessment in 1989 reported that chemical perturbations in the Arctic similar to those observed in the Antarctic have been found. Studies in

January and February 1989 showed that the abundances of reactive chlorine were enhanced by a factor of 50-100. These changes could lead to ozone depletion in the Arctic.

Prediction of ozone depletion

Models are used to simulate the effects of human activities on ozone concentrations. One-dimensional models are used to predict the changes in the column content of ozone and the vertical distribution of ozone and temperature but cannot be used to predict distributions according to latitude, longitude, or season. Two-dimensional models on the other hand compute the ozone and temperature distributions as a function of latitude and season. Three-dimensional models that look at the coupling between the chemical, radiative and dynamic processes controlling the distributions of ozone and temperature are being developed.

One-dimensional model studies have examined the effects of increases of the carbon dioxide (CO_2), methane (CH_4) and nitrous oxide (N_2O) concentrations at their current rates and various assumed rates of increase of the emissions of chlorine- and bromine-containing chemicals. The results of such calculations show the strong chemical coupling between these gases. Because of this coupling, even when the column ozone changes in the models are small, there are large changes in the vertical distribution of ozone and temperature. Such changes could result in significant climatic changes: model results show a decrease of the ozone amount in the middle to upper stratosphere, mainly as a result of the increasing concentrations of CFCs, and an increase in the lower stratosphere as a result of the increasing concentrations of CH_4; the reductions in the ozone at 40 km lead, in the models,

to a local cooling of about 5°C, which could affect the earth's climate.

Two-dimensional models, which do not include a dynamic feedback with ozone change, predict a significant variation in the ozone column decrease with latitude; the greatest depletions occur at high latitudes. Seasonal effects are smaller than the latitudinal differences found in the two-dimensional model results. In general, two-dimensional models show somewhat larger ozone depletion than one-dimensional models for the same trace gas scenarios.

In reviewing the reliability of the models used to predict ozone change, it has been noted that the models predict the distribution of chemical constituents of the atmosphere quite well but that the measurements are not adequate for critical testing of photochemical models. Intercomparisons show that modelled ozone concentrations are typically 30 to 50 per cent lower than measured ozone concentrations in the upper stratosphere and such disagreements reduce the confidence in model reliability. The reduction of total column ozone since 1969 at northern mid-latitudes appears to be greater than predicted. As a result, the predictions made using models are also uncertain. Some of the causes of the discrepancies between models and observations are known and could be removed through intensive research, including theoretical modelling, laboratory studies and measurements.

Major shortcomings of available models include poor representation of polar meteorology and lack of inclusion of heterogeneous processes (i.e. the chemical reactions in PSCs). Also, only a few models include the influence of increasing CO_2 concentrations and decreasing ozone concentrations on temperature, which itself influences the rate of ozone destruction.

2. THE GREENHOUSE EFFECT

The greenhouse effect is best described in terms of the annual global average radiative energy budget of the earth-atmosphere system. The earth-atmosphere system radiates about 236 Watts per square meter (long-wave radiation) to space and this amount balances the incoming short-wave radiation from the sun. With a temperature of 15°C the earth's surface radiates about 390 Watts per square meter. The reduction of the long-wave radiation to space as a result of the intervening atmosphere is referred to as the greenhouse effect. The most important atmospheric constituents contributing to the greenhouse effect are water, carbon dioxide, and clouds. Calculations show that without the greenhouse effect, but with the same amount of incoming solar radiation and the same albedo, the global average surface temperature would be about −19°C. With greenhouse gases in the atmos-

phere, the long-wave radiation from the earth's surface is partly absorbed and then re-emitted by the gases at the temperature of the air at their level. This has the effect of raising the effective emitting level to several kilometres above the surface, where the temperature is about 30°C lower than near the earth's surface. As a result the earth's surface temperature can be higher by about this amount (the global average surface temperature is about 15°C). The earth and atmosphere together emit the same amount of radiation to space as in the absence of greenhouse gases.

In recent decades this balance has been disturbed by the addition of gases to the atmosphere that increase the greenhouse effect. These are referred to, accordingly, as greenhouse gases. An increase in the atmospheric concentration of a greenhouse gas

Figure 3. **GREENHOUSE EFFECT**

Contribution to Annual Net Emissions of Greenhouse Gases[a]

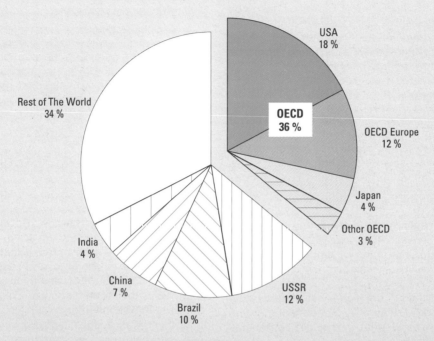

Note: a) This index developed by WRI is based on annual emissions of the three major greenhouse gases (CO_2, CFCs, and CH_4) and the heat-trapping potential of each gas. The CO_2 emissions are net emissions because they take into account the effect of deforestation on the CO_2 flux into the atmosphere. The index is expressed in CO_2 equivalents (tonnes of Carbon).

	Contribution of greenhouse gases by sector (%)					
	CO_2	CFC	CH_4	O_3	N_2O	Total
Energy	35	..	4	6	4	49
Deforestation	10	..	4	..	..	14
Agriculture	3	..	8	..	2	13
Industry	2	20	..	2	..	24
% warming by gas	50	20	16	8	6	100

Source: WRI

changes the radiative energy balance, and this leads to both an increase in the temperature of the earth's surface and lower atmosphere and a decrease of the temperature in the upper atmosphere. Calculations made with models of the climate system have shown that a doubling of the concentration of CO_2 from its pre-industrial value would lead to an increase of the global average annual surface temperature of 1.5-4.5°C. The range of uncertainty is a result of uncertainties about the various feedbacks in the climate system that amplify or reduce the temperature change resulting from the shifts in the radiative energy balance.

The greenhouse gases

The atmospheric concentrations of a number of greenhouse gases (GHGs) have been increasing as a result of human activities. Despite their low concentrations, these gases, especially carbon dioxide (CO_2), methane (CH_4), chlorofluorocarbons (CFCs), nitrous oxide (N_2O) and tropospheric ozone (O_3), can change the earth-atmosphere radiation balance significantly.

Rough estimates can be made for the percent of global warming between 1980 and 2030 arising from each gas and sector, assuming current trends. (Figure 3) Some useful conclusions can be drawn. First, if current trends were to continue, CO_2 would continue to contribute roughly half of the global warming over the next 40 years. Second, when the contributions by the various sectors are considered, energy use contributes about half of the increased greenhouse effect, deforestation and agriculture together contribute in the region of 25 per cent and industry the remaining 25 per cent. The latter figure, however, depends on the assumption that current trends of CFC emissions continue. Full implementation of the Montreal Protocol would reduce the CFC contributions to global warming by half of the projected value by 2030.

Recent analyses have made it possible to calculate a "greenhouse index" for 50 countries for 1987, including the carbon dioxide heating equivalents of the annual increases in the atmosphere of CO_2, CH_4, and CFCs. The total contribution of each country and the percentage contribution to the global total have also been calculated. It is clear that responsibility for greenhouse gas emissions is spread widely around the world.

Global and regional climatic changes

The globally averaged surface temperature is a useful indicator of the magnitude of the effect of changes of the GHG concentrations. However, for many purposes more detailed forecasts of regional changes of temperature, precipitation amount and other climatic variables are required. As a result of shortcomings in climate models, uncertainties in the forecasts of regional climatic changes are greater than those in the forecasts of the global temperature change. There is a relatively high degree of confidence in the estimates of global changes of temperature, sea-level, precipitation, and evapotranspiration. The estimates of regional changes of these and other climatic variables are made, on the other hand, with medium or low confidence levels. Changes in the interannual variability of all of these elements are uncertain.

Greenhouse gas emissions

Carbon dioxide

The atmospheric concentration of CO_2 has increased by about 25 per cent since industrialisation began. The human activities that have added CO_2 to the atmosphere are the combustion of fossil fuels, deforestation and changes of land use. It has been estimated that in the period between 1860 and 1984 a cumulative total of about 183 billion tonnes of carbon was emitted as a result of fossil fuel combustion and about 150 billion tonnes of carbon from deforestation and land use changes.

The emissions for the world as a whole increased from 4.8 billion tons of carbon in 1971 to about 6 billion tonnes of carbon in 1988. (Figure 4) During the same time period there was only a slight increase in CO_2 emissions due to energy use in OECD countries. The curves for both the OECD and the world between 1980 and 1981; that reduction was clearly a result of a decrease in oil consumption at the time. In OECD countries there was a significant drop in oil consumption between 1980 and 1983 and since 1985 emissions of CO_2 from oil use have again been increasing. CO_2 emissions from coal use in OECD countries have risen since 1975, while those from natural gas use climbed by only a small amount between 1971 and 1988. (Figure 4)

When fossil fuels are burned, carbon is oxidised and CO_2 is released into the atmosphere. When burned, the various fuels produce different amounts of CO_2 for a given release of thermal energy: coal releases about 20 per cent more CO_2 than oil, which in turn releases more than natural gas.

The other source of CO_2 emissions as a result of human activities is terrestrial ecosystems. When forests or grasslands are converted into farmland, organic matter is oxidised and emitted as CO_2 into the atmosphere. The present annual emissions from deforestation and land use changes are not accurately known since they depend on uncertain estimates of the annual area undergoing deforestation or land use change as well as uncertain estimates about the net release of CO_2 per unit area when deforestation/land use changes occur. It has been estimated that the annual emissions from deforestation and land use changes are in the range of 1.6 billion tonnes of carbon per year, which is considerably smaller than the annual rate of emissions from fossil fuel combustion (about 6 billion tonnes of carbon in 1987).

The major reservoirs of carbon are the atmosphere, the terrestrial biosphere including soils, the

Figure 4. TRENDS IN MAN-MADE ^{a} CARBON DIOXIDE EMISSIONS

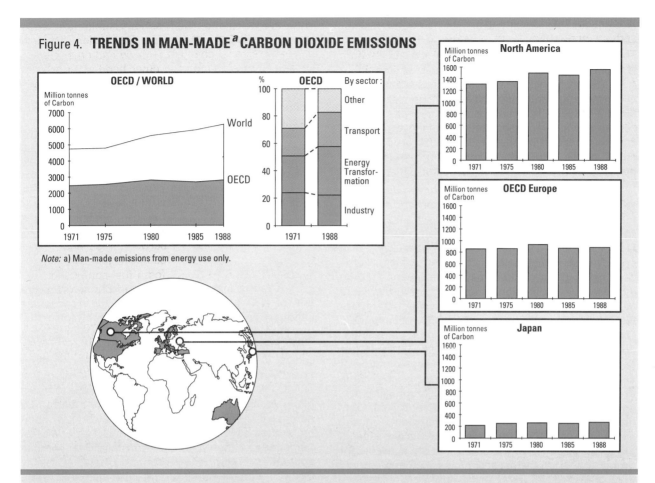

Note: a) Man-made emissions from energy use only.

	Million tonnes of Carbon				
	1971	1975	1980	1985	1988
Canada	94	109	124	115	124
USA	1 209	1 240	1 369	1 339	1 433
Japan	217	252	261	253	272
France	126	126	139	109	103
Germany ^{a}	208	198	219	200	198
Italy	92	97	106	101	108
UK	187	170	167	159	163
North America	1 302	1 349	1 493	1 453	1 557
OECD Pacific	270	312	330	325	350
OECD Europe	855	860	934	870	886
Non-OECD					
Africa	141	162	202	256	273
America	195	233	289	305	334
Asia	266	308	386	458	538
Eastern Europe	322	360	424	444	452
Middle East	60	70	102	144	169
USSR	691	800	907	960	1 025
People's Republic of China	276	356	460	584	670
OECD	2 427	2 522	2 756	2 648	2 793
World	4 750	4 811	5 528	5 802	6 256

Note: Data refer to man-made emissions from energy use only.
　　　a) Includes western Germany only.
Source: OECD-IEA

oceans and reserves of fossil fuels. There is considerable uncertainty about reservoir sizes and transfers. The total amount of carbon stored in the atmosphere is about 725 billion tonnes, in the biota plus soils about 2 180 billion tonnes, and in the oceans about 38 400 billion tonnes. Of the estimated 7 billion tonnes of carbon that are added to the atmosphere each year as a result of human activities, about half remains in the atmosphere and the other half is transferred to the ocean. The magnitude of the natural fluxes of carbon is much larger than that of the fluxes due to human activities.

Clearly, if each reservoir were to take up the CO_2 released by human activities in proportion to its size, then the increase in the atmosphere would be very small. However, in the case of the oceans there are two factors that dramatically reduce their capacity to take up CO_2. First, there is a chemical buffering factor of the carbonates in the ocean water, which means that the increase in concentration of total carbon in the water at equilibrium is about one order of magnitude less than the increase in atmospheric CO_2 concentration. Therefore, the change in atmospheric CO_2 concentration by about 25 per cent over the last 100 years has been associated with a change in the concentration of dissolved inorganic carbon in the ocean surface waters of only 2-2.5 per cent to maintain equilibrium. The second factor is that the oceans are poorly mixed. Only the upper layers of the ocean participate in the exchanges of CO_2 on the decadal time scale. Indeed, the upper 50-100 m of the ocean that are available for taking up CO_2 on the decadal time scale have roughly the same effective size as the atmospheric reservoir — and for this reason the current rate of increase of the atmospheric CO_2 concentration is about half of that which would occur if all of the CO_2 released by human activities were to remain in the atmosphere.

The atmospheric concentration of carbon dioxide has increased steadily as a result of the emissions from fossil fuel combustion and deforestation/land use changes. (Figure 5) Seasonal fluctuations in the northern hemisphere are a result of photosynthesis in plants in the spring and of the decomposition of organic matter in autumn and winter.

Methane

In the middle latitudes of the northern hemisphere, there was an average annual increase of about 1.1 per cent in the concentration of methane in the atmosphere in recent years. Longer term trends can be obtained from the analysis of air bubbles trapped in the ice sheets of Greenland and Antarctica. These data show an approximately exponential increase in atmospheric CH_4 concentration over the past 300 years.

Methane is produced by microbial activities during the mineralisation of organic carbon under strictly anaerobic conditions, e.g. in waterlogged soils and in the intestines of herbivorous animals. There is considerable uncertainty about the natural and anthropogenic

sources of methane. The following numbers, however, give the orders of magnitude:

Anthropogenic Sources (in millions of tonnes per year)		Natural Sources (in millions of tonnes per year)	
Enteric fermentation (cattle, etc.)	75±35	Enteric fermentation (wild animals)	5±3
Rice paddies	70±30	Wetlands	110±50
Biomass burning	70±40	Lakes	4±2
Natural gas and mining losses	50±25	Tundra	3±2
Solid waste	30±30	Oceans	10±3
		Termites and other insects	25±20
		Other	40±40

Nitrous oxide

A recent increase in the atmospheric concentration of N_2O has been observed in the troposphere, although the rate of increase is considerably lower than that of methane. Samples collected between 1976 and 1980 showed an annual increase of 0.2 per cent - 0.3 per cent. N_2O is reduced in the stratosphere and there are no known significant tropospheric sinks. The emissions of N_2O into the atmosphere are primarily due to microbial processes in soil and water and are a part of the nitrogen cycle. There is considerable uncertainty about the emissions due to human activities, especially the magnitude of the emissions from fossil fuel combustion. Other anthropogenic sources of N_2O emissions include biomass burning, and cultivated soils, especially with the intensive use of fertilizers.

Tropospheric ozone

The concentration of atmospheric ozone varies considerably both in space and in time as a result of interactions between atmospheric motions and chemical reactions. The concentration of tropospheric ozone is increasing due to photochemical processes. Methane, carbon monoxide and other hydrocarbons and nitrogen oxides play important roles in this context. Their increasing concentrations and reactions with the hydroxyl (OH) radical are important for the ozone chemistry of the troposphere.

Because of the spatial variations of the atmospheric ozone concentration, it is difficult to assess the global changes. An increase has, however, clearly taken place at middle and high latitudes of the northern hemisphere in the last 20-30 years, particularly during the summer months. The present rate of change is estimated to be 1-2 per cent per year.

Chlorofluorocarbons

CFCs have been produced for a variety of uses, such as solvents, foaming agents, refrigerator fluids and spray can propellants. Atmospheric measurements are available for only about 15 years but past concen-

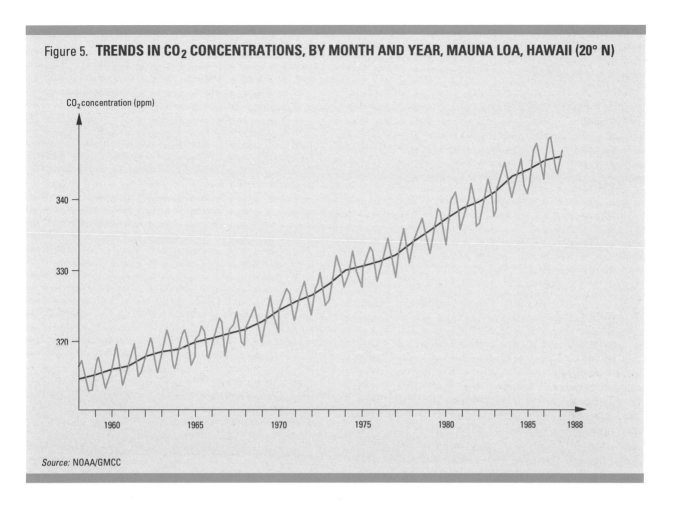

Figure 5. TRENDS IN CO$_2$ CONCENTRATIONS, BY MONTH AND YEAR, MAUNA LOA, HAWAII (20° N)

CO$_2$ concentration (ppm)

340

330

320

1960   1965   1970   1975   1980   1985   1988

Source: NOAA/GMCC

trations can be estimated with reasonable accuracy on the basis of production and emission figures from the Chemical Manufacturing Association. A rapid increase in the emissions of the most important CFCs, CFC-11 and CFC-12, until about 1970 changed to a decline during the latter part of the 1970s as a result of restrictions on the use of CFCs introduced by some countries in view of the possible threat of CFCs to stratospheric ozone. Since the late 1970s the non-propellant uses of CFCs have continued to increase by about 4 per cent per year, while the propellant use decreased from 56 per cent to 34 per cent of total CFC production.

CFCs are photochemically decomposed almost entirely in the stratosphere. At the beginning of the 1980s the atmospheric concentrations of CFC-11 and CFC-12 were increasing at about 6 per cent per year. An International Convention for the Protection of the Ozone Layer was drawn up in 1985 and a Protocol requiring signatories to regulate the production of CFCs was signed in Montreal in 1987. The 1987 protocol stipulated a 50 per cent reduction in CFC production by 1999. At a meeting in London in June 1990, signatories to the 1987 protocol agreed to revise the agreement leading to the *elimination* of CFC production by 2000 and also to that of methyl chloroform (by 2005) and

carbon tetrachloride (by 2000), that were not included in the 1987 protocol. Hydrogen-based CFCs (or HCFCs) would be restricted to applications where less ozone-destructive alternatives are not available and phased out by 2040 at the latest.

Projected emissions and temperature changes

Numerous studies have made projections of the emissions of greenhouse gases during the next hundred years, the resulting atmospheric concentrations of greenhouse gases and the consequences for global surface temperature. Since it is not possible to predict greenhouse gas emissions, because these depend on social, political, technical and economic factors that are not well understood, and since the predictions of global temperature are also based on models that have recognised shortcomings, the results of such analyses must be considered as "realistic scenarios" which illustrate the orders of magnitude of changes that could occur. Recent assessments suggest that if emissions continue to increase as they have in the recent past, global temperature will increase during the next century by 0.3°C/decade. This would give an increase of global mean temperature of about 1°C

25

Figure 6. **CHANGES IN GLOBAL SURFACE TEMPERATURE**

Global surface air temperature

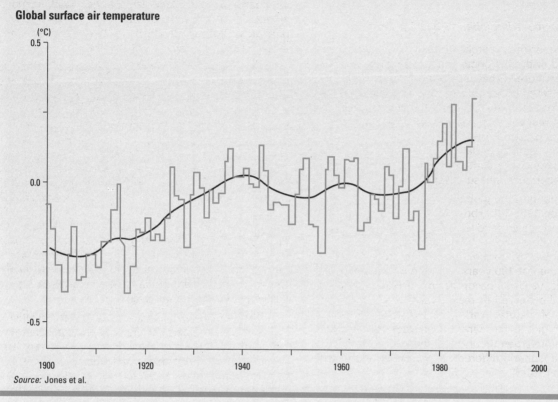

Source: Jones et al.

Scenarios of changes in globally averaged surface temperature

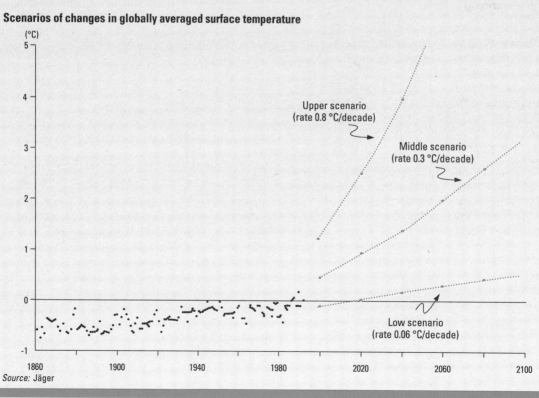

Source: Jäger

above the present value by 2025 and 3°C before the end of the next century. On the other hand, emission reduction measures could reduce the rate of change of global surface temperature to about 0.1°C/decade.

Observed changes in globally averaged temperature

A number of research groups around the world have looked at the historical changes in globally averaged temperature. Since each group has used the same basic set of observations, there are considerable similarities between the results of the analyses. Differences are a result of the analysis schemes (interpolation, averaging, data homogenisation, etc.) and of the types of data used: only data from land-based meteorological stations or a combination of land and ocean surface temperature measurements.

In computing the global surface air temperatures for the period 1901-1987, both land-based air temperature data and sea surface temperature data were used to calculate the averages. (Figure 6) The data show a general increase of temperature of the order of 0.3 to 0.6°C over the last 100 years, with the five global-average warmest years all occurring in the 1980s. Some of the changes observed in recent years are likely to be the result of natural variations: whilst the recent changes in global temperature are not inconsistent with greenhouse gas theory, the changes, particularly the interhemispheric differences, cannot be explained by this factor alone.

Effects of global warming

It is not possible to predict with any reliability the future emission rates of greenhouse gases, their future concentrations in the atmosphere or the global and regional climate changes that would follow changes in atmospheric composition. The uncertainties about the magnitudes of feedbacks within and between the physical, chemical and biological systems increase the difficulties in evaluating the potential effects of climatic change. Present knowledge provides the basis for developing scenarios that describe plausible pictures of the future. It is equally difficult to forecast the consequences of climatic change, for example, on agriculture, forestry, the energy sector, water systems, and so on; instead scenarios are developed to describe the kinds of changes that could occur.

Half of humanity lives in coastal regions and for this reason considerable attention has been given to potential changes in sea level as a result of global warming. Observations show that global sea level has risen by about 10 cm during the past 100 years. Calculations indicate that global warming induced by greenhouse gases will accelerate this sea-level rise, giving an increase of about 20 cm by 2030 and 65 cm by the end of the next century. These changes would be a result of thermal expansion of the sea water and melting of land ice. The rate of increase of sea level could be 3-10 times greater than the 0.01 m per decade long-term average observed during the past century. The effects of sea-level rise will include erosion of beaches and coastal margins, land-use changes, wetlands loss, changes of the frequency and severity of flooding, damage to coastal structures and port facilities, and damage to water management systems.

Agriculture will experience major transformations in the coming decades, some linked to climate and others to fundamental technological, socio-economic, and environmental changes. Since no detailed predictions can be made of regional changes in climate as a result of the increasing greenhouse effect, it is not possible to make forecasts of climate-induced changes in agriculture. Instead, studies so far have concentrated on looking at the sensitivity of agricultural systems in particular regions to climatic change. It is agreed that climatic changes associated with global warming will cause intra-regional shifts in agricultural productivity. For all but the most rapid warming, adaptation based on agricultural research should permit general maintenance of total global food supplies with some local disruptions. A rapid rate of warming could lead to more erratic reductions in food availability.

The effects of climatic change on relatively unmanaged ecosystems could be very significant. For example, if the rate of climatic change were very fast, it has been estimated that major effects on forests in the mid-latitudes would begin around the year 2000, with forest dieback as a result of climatic change beginning between 2000 and 2050. On the other hand, with a rate of temperature change of about 0-1°C/decade, species extinction, reproductive failure and large-scale forest die-back would not occur before the year 2100.

Changes in the tundra and the northern limit of the boreal forest will include both a stimulation of growth and carbon fixation and rapid decay of organic matter. The overall effect on carbon storage is not predictable. However, in both the high and middle latitude, there is the possibility of a large net release of carbon dioxide and methane from soils, tundra, melting permafrost, forest dieback and ecosystem changes. Such releases would further increase the greenhouse effect.

Strategies for responding to climatic change are generally divided into two categories: adaptation strategies adjust the environment or the ways it is used to reduce the consequences of a changing climate; limitation strategies control or stop the growth of greenhouse gas concentrations in the atmosphere. A prudent response to climatic change should consider both limitation and adaptation. Even if a very concerted effort were made now to implement limitation strategies, some adaptation would still be necessary because of the climatic changes resulting from the greenhouse gases that have already been emitted into the atmosphere. Both adaptation and limitation strategies would involve large expenditures.

POTENTIAL SEA-LEVEL RISE IN RELATION TO CLIMATE CHANGE: A DUTCH CASE STUDY

Rising concentrations of carbon dioxide and certain trace gases in the atmosphere have led to predictions that global temperatures will increase in the years ahead. Of all potential impacts resulting from human-induced climate change, a global rise in sea levels may be the most dramatic, since a large part of the world's population and food production are situated in low-lying coastal areas.

Although predictions vary significantly, some cite an average rate of global sea-level rise of about 6 centimetres per decade in the next century. By 2030 this would result in a rise of about 20 cm, and by the end of the twenty-first century 65 cm. The principal causes would be thermal expansion of seawater, retreat of mountain glaciers and melting of polar icecaps. However, there will be significant regional variations.

Numerous Adverse Impacts

The impacts of a rise in sea level will be most severe in the deltaic areas of the world because such areas are generally densely populated and highly productive. Small, low-lying nations like the Maldives are vulnerable and their very existence may be threatened. A rise in sea level will inundate wetlands and other lowlands, accelerate coastal erosion, increase the risk of severe flooding, create problems with drainage and irrigation systems and increase saltwater intrusion into groundwater, rivers and farmland.

Furthermore, the forced abandonment of agricultural land and certain coastal developments, and the need in some areas to build new coastal defences, will cause heavy economic losses and social disruption. In the Netherlands, the current value of land threatened by inundation is approximately ECU 25 000 per hectare.

Responding to Sea-level Rise

Sea-level rise can best be dealt with through a comprehensive strategy which addresses climate change as a whole. The three main response options are:

- Reducing greenhouse gas emissions;
- Minimising the effects of sea-level rise through measures which protect and stabilise coastal areas at risk;
- Taking no action and thus adapting to the situation as it evolves.

A reduction of greenhouse gas emissions would reduce the rate of global warming and consequently slow sea-level rise and its effects. However, coastal protection measures will most likely be required as well since a certain amount of global warming is inevitable. Taking no action would entail abandonment of many existing coastal areas and the movement inland of marine ecosystems. This choice can be motivated by forecasts that protection would entail excessive economic or environmental impacts. In extreme cases, entire areas may be abandoned.

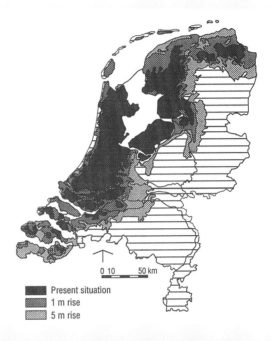

Present situation
1 m rise
5 m rise

0 10   50 km

Economics of Coastal Protection Measures

Studies in the Netherlands have estimated the costs to coastal countries and to the world of coastal defences required to combat a one-metre rise in sea levels. This would require some 360 000 km of coastal defences at a total cost of roughly US $500 billion over the next 100 years. Present coastal defence needs, impacts of saltwater intrusion and flooding of unprotected areas are not included in these estimates.

The per capita costs of coastal defences for the 181 coastal countries considered amount to about US $103. The annual cost as a fraction of the Gross National Product (GNP) of these countries is 0.037 per cent. For the small islands and island groups in the Pacific and Indian Oceans, these costs are much higher: 0.75 per cent and 0.91 per cent of GNP, respectively.

However, the responses to accelerated sea-level rise must be based on more than a simple cost-benefit ratio; many important considerations cannot be expressed in simple monetary terms. Each area at risk must be examined on a site-specific basis, as there is significant variation in both environmental and cultural factors. It may be necessary to retreat from the eroding shore in some areas while fortifying and even reclaiming land in others. Clearly, a global response is required in that international research and co-operative efforts represent the only reasonable approach.

Contribution from the Netherlands

3. OTHER GLOBAL ATMOSPHERIC POLLUTION

Transboundary pollution results from the atmospheric circulation which transports pollutants from one region to another. (See Chapter on Air) This section examines the extent to which such pollution has become a global issue.

Aerosols are particles of smoke, dust and sea spray that are larger than molecular size. There are five major aerosol types:

– Coarse mechanically produced mineral dust;
– Coarse oceanic sea-salt particles;
– Fine directly-produced soot;
– Fine- and medium-sized products of gas-to-particle conversion;
– Volcanic ash of varying composition.

While volcanic ash and sea salt particles are added to the atmosphere as the result of natural processes, mineral dust can result from either natural processes (e.g. wind erosion) or human activities (e.g. ploughing) and the other two main aerosol types are added to the atmosphere primarily as a result of human activities (in particular, combustion). The residence time of the aerosols in the atmosphere is short. Therefore, the global and temporal distribution is very variable. Although it is known that local and regional changes of aerosol concentration have occurred, it is not certain whether there have been global changes as a result of human activities. The relative magnitude of production rates from major sources of aerosols can be estimated. There are clearly uncertainties. The length of time that the aerosols remain in the atmosphere depends on the particle size, the height at which they are injected and condensation processes that wash aerosols out.

Long distant transport of aerosols has been documented in a number of cases. The transport of Saharan dust over the Atlantic has been traced in satellite pictures as far as to the Caribbean and Europe, and dust from Texan deserts has been traced to Europe. Aerosol particles that clearly come from automobile and diesel exhaust and industrial operations at midlatitudes have been collected in winter in the North Polar region.

Arctic haze contains large amounts of anthropogenic components like carbon soot and sulphuric acid and has a substantial impact on the springtime solar heating rates. Under clear sky conditions, the haze layer can enhance the heating rate by as much as 50 per cent. The Arctic haze concentrations are greatest between December and April because south-north airmass movements are stronger and more frequent at this time and the pollutants are less readily removed, due to the low cloudiness and stability of the Arctic atmosphere. In addition to altering the absorption of solar radiation, the soot particles can reduce the albedo (reflectivity) of the snowpack and can thereby accelerate the rate of snowmelt. Observations from an ice cap in Ellesmere Island suggest a marked post-1950 increase in Arctic pollution; the Arctic cannot be regarded as having a pristine atmospheric environment.

4. CONCLUSIONS

This chapter has discussed three global issues that have received increasing attention in the past 20 years. In each case human activities are changing the global atmosphere. There are clear links between the issues and these interactions must be considered when developing responses.

Stratospheric ozone depletion leads to an increase of the amount of ultraviolet radiation reaching the earth's surface and this has potentially harmful effects on human health, and on the productivity of aquatic and terrestrial ecosystems. There was a decrease in the annual average total column ozone from 1969 to 1988 of between 3 and 5 per cent at latitudes between 30°N and 64°N. Satellite data show a decrease of the total column ozone of about 2.5 per cent between October 1978 and 1985 between 53°S and 53°N. A significant change in the springtime total ozone content over the Antarctic was first reported from the station data at Halley Bay. Satellite data confirm the ground-based data.

The second global issue considered in this chapter is the greenhouse effect. The effect itself is undisputed: certain gases absorb and emit the long-wave radiation coming from the earth's surface and thus warm the surface and the lower atmosphere. Also undisputed are the observed increases of the atmospheric concentrations of some of these gases: carbon dioxide, methane, CFCs, nitrous oxide and tropospheric ozone, in particular. These increases are generally a result of human activities. In the 1980s about half of the increased greenhouse effect was attributable to carbon dioxide and the other gases together contributed the other half.

It is generally agreed that a doubling of the atmospheric carbon dioxide concentration from its pre-industrial value (or changes of the other greenhouse gases that would have the same radiative effect) would lead to an increase of the globally averaged annual surface temperature by 1.5-4.5°C.

Observed data show that there has been a general increase in the globally averaged temperature of about 0.5 K in the last 100 years and that the 1980s had a number of very warm years. There is still scientific dispute about whether the observed temperature increase can be attributed to the increased greenhouse effect. It is clear, however, that if emissions of greenhouse gases continue to rise at the rates observed during the past 20 years, the rate of increase of global temperature over the next 50 years will be larger than historical rates of change.

The third issue examined in this chapter is that of long distance transport of aerosols. During the past 20 years there has been growing evidence that atmospheric pollutants are being transported over large distances by global atmospheric circulation. In particular, aerosol particles that clearly come from automobile and diesel exhaust and industrial operations in the middle latitudes have been collected in winter in the North Polar Region. Observations show a marked increase in Arctic pollution since 1950. Clearly, there are strong links between the problems of the long distance transport of aerosols and the greenhouse effet, in particular since the combustion of fossil fuels is a major cause of both.

In the case of stratospheric ozone depletion the international response has already included the 1985 Vienna Convention and the 1987 Montreal Protocol. The latter requires signatories to reduce CFC production to 50 per cent of their 1986 level by the year 2000. Furthermore, the recognition that the reductions required by the Montreal Protocol are not large enough to prevent further stratospheric ozone depletion led the signatory nations to agree to important revisions of the Protocol in London in June 1990.

Concern about air pollution led to the signing of a Convention on Long- Range Transboundary Air Pollution by 34 states and the European Economic Community in November 1979. The Convention had the form of a framework agreement, recognising the problems of air pollution and the responsibility of the signatories for solving them. The Convention came into force in March 1983 after the requisite number of states had ratified it. A Protocol on Sulphur Emissions was signed in July 1985 and came into force in September 1987. The signatories undertake to reduce national emissions of sulphur dioxide – or their transboundary fluxes – by at least 30 per cent by 1993 at the latest (with 1980 emission levels as the basis). The Protocol on NOx emissions was signed in 1988. Any agreements reached on the reduction of CO_2 emissions could also be instrumental in reducing emissions of air pollutants, such as SO_2 and NOx.

The Intergovernmental Panel on Climate Change was formed in November 1988 by the World Meteorological Organization and the United Nations Environment Programme to evaluate the scientific background of the global warming issue, potential impacts and response strategies. International conferences, in particular the one in Toronto in 1988 and the Ministerial Conference in Noordwijk in 1989, have emphasised the need for industrialised countries to limit or reduce their greenhouse gas emissions, especially CO_2 emissions from energy use. Indeed, some OECD countries have now made plans to reduce emissions by the beginning of the next century by 20 per cent or more from their current level. The Montreal Protocol provides a mechanism for reducing the emissions of one type of greenhouse gas (CFCs) and it is expected that negotiations on a Climate Convention will begin after the publication of the IPCC report in 1990 and the Second World Climate Conference (Geneva, 29th October - 9th November 1990).

In the coming decade the responses to these issues will continue to be varied and to differ as a function of time and place. Policy development will have to consider both the measures needed to limit the problems and measures to reduce their impacts. Policy development will also have to consider linkages between the issues of global atmospheric change problems. As pointed out in Chapter 2 of this report, for example, more rigorous efforts to conserve energy would avert both air pollution problems and global climatic changes. Scientific research must continue to improve the understanding of the processes involved in each of these issues through theoretical modelling, detailed observation programmes and laboratory studies. The last 10 years have witnessed a growing awareness of the linkages between global environmental issues and of the interactions on many scales between the atmosphere, the oceans, the biosphere, and the earth's surface. Programmes such as the IGBP (International Geosphere-Biosphere Programme) are beginning to look at these interactions. It is within such a global context that the issues of atmospheric change will have to be addressed during the coming decade.

SAVING STRATOSPHERIC OZONE - THE MONTREAL PROTOCOL

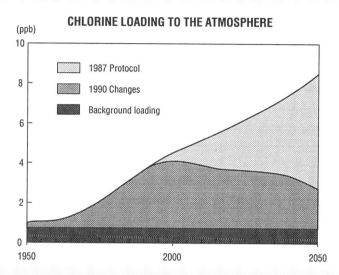

CHLORINE LOADING TO THE ATMOSPHERE

(ppb)

- 1987 Protocol
- 1990 Changes
- Background loading

The Threat to the Ozone Layer

In 1974, a landmark scientific paper pointed out that chlorine-containing substances called chlorofluorocarbons (more commonly known as CFCs) pose a threat to the ozone layer. Ozone is found in a diffuse atmospheric layer at stratospheric altitudes, between 20 and 40 kilometres, and acts as a shield against harmful solar ultra-violet radiation.

Since then, evidence has mounted that ozone decreases are occurring. In the Antarctic, major and unanticipated ozone holes have been detected during the spring; ozone depletions exceeding 50 per cent have been measured. Evidence that the same processes are occurring in the Arctic is also accumulating.

The Montreal Protocol

CFC use as a propellant in most aerosol spray cans was restricted in Scandinavia and North America in the 1970s. Throughout the late 1970s and the 1980s, public pressure grew to extend limitations on use. The United Nations Environment Programme initiated a series of international negotiations. On 22nd March 1985 the Vienna Convention for the Protection of the Ozone Layer was signed, laying the groundwork for control measures. Negotiations culminated in the signing by 24 countries, on 16th September 1987, of the Montreal Protocol on Substances that Deplete the Ozone Layer. It came into force on 1st January 1989.

As originally formulated, the control measures set out in Article 2 of the Protocol applied to two groups of ozone depleting substances: CFCs (11, 12, 113, 114, 115) and Halons (1211, 1301, 2402). Each party to the Protocol agreed to reduce consumption of controlled substances on the basis of the 1986 level. The Protocol aimed to hold consumption at or below that level. After mid-1993, consumption of controlled CFCs was to be limited to 80 per cent of the 1986 level, and after mid-1998 it was to be further reduced to 50 per cent of the 1986 level.

A Strengthened Montreal Protocol

In the three years following the signing of the Montreal Protocol, scientists established the link between emissions of CFCs (and other ozone-depleting substances) and ozone depletion with much-increased confidence. On 28th June 1990, at a meeting of the parties to the Protocol in London, attended by almost 100 countries, agreement was reached to eliminate consumption of the five CFCs in the 1987 agreement completely by the year 2000. This will be achieved through intermediate-step reductions of 20 per cent, 50 per cent and 85 per cent on 1 January 1992, 1995 and 1997 respectively. The same schedule was also agreed to concerning elimination of other CFCs -- substances that have been used only in very low volume, if at all. It was also agreed to phase out the use of halons by the year 2000, starting with a 50 per cent reduction in 1995. The agreement left some scope for exemptions for essential uses of halons in high-hazard situations.

Controls on other ozone-depleting chemicals were introduced. Carbon tetrachloride, with the exception for its use as a feedstock in the production of other substances, will be phased out in the year 2000, with an intermediate cut of 85 per cent in 1995. Methyl chloroform, again with exemptions for feedstock uses, will be cut by 30 per cent in 1995 and 70 per cent in 2000 and eliminated in 2005.

Assistance for Developing Countries

One of the major achievements at the London meeting was to put in place a mechanism for enabling developing countries to meet their obligations under the Protocol. This includes provision for transfer of technologies needed by developing countries and arrangements to meet incremental costs incurred in moving away from ozone-depleting technologies and substances. Delegations from India and China, the world's two most populous countries, indicated that on this basis they would be able to recommend their countries' participation in the Protocol.

Contribution from Canada

Chapter 2

AIR

Man's pursuit of development has caused air pollution problems on various scales: locally, especially in urban areas; regionally, often beyond national frontiers; globally, affecting the planet as a whole. (See Chapter on Global Atmospheric Issues) In this chapter only local and regional problems are reviewed. Problems do not only occur when layers of brown haze obscure our cities and larger regions: polluted air affects our lives in many different ways. Not only does it bring unpleasant odours and decreased visibility, but it can also cause adverse health effects and, in some cases, even death. Since most atmospheric pollutants enter the body by inhalation, the greatest effect of air pollution is on the respiratory system, and in particular the lungs. There are, however, pollutants that affect other parts of the body; cadmium, for instance, is harmful to the kidneys, benzene is a carcinogen that affects the blood, and mercury impairs the central nervous system. Air pollution can also cause damage to our natural environment, as well as to our cultural heritage through, for example, acid rain.

These effects can have substantial economic and social consequences, ranging from added costs of medical care and building restoration to reduced agricultural output, widespread forest damage, and a generally lower quality of life.

Worldwide, fuel combustion is the principal cause of man-made air pollution problems. Energy demand and the combustion of fuels have risen as population and industrial activity have increased. Since the middle of the last century, energy production has expanded more than 20 times, following a tripling of world population and average annual growth of 2 to 4 per cent in economic output. At the same time air pollution problems have dramatically intensified.

Starting in the 1950s and 1960s, individual countries became increasingly aware of the existing problems; since the 1970s, many OECD countries have passed laws and regulations to stabilise, or even reverse, the deterioration in the quality of the air. Also in the 1970s, many countries realised that air pollution travelled long distances across national borders, and that action on a supra-national scale was required to protect one of the earth's most important natural resources.

1. LOCAL AND URBAN AIR POLLUTION

Since the last century, air pollution in cities and other densely populated areas has been of prime interest because these are the areas, firstly, where most man-made sources of pollution are located and, secondly, where most people live and breathe the polluted air.

Traditional air pollutants

The most common air pollutants – those that occur in the greatest quantities and whose effects on human health and the natural environment were acknowledged the earliest – include sulphur dioxide (SO_2), nitrogen oxides (NOx), carbon monoxide (CO), ozone (O_3) in the lower atmosphere, lead (Pb) and particulate matter (PM). All of these, with the exception of ozone, are emitted directly into the air from human and industrial activities and, to a certain extent, from natural sources. Worldwide, fuel combustion is the major man-made source of these traditional air pollutants. Ozone – the main component of photochemical smog – is formed in the lower atmosphere wherever emissions of NOx and volatile organic compounds (VOC) are present to react in sunlight. The ozone produced in this way is not to be confused with ozone in the stratosphere, where it occurs naturally and protects life on earth from receiving excess ultraviolet radiation. (See Chapter on Global Atmospheric Issues)

Figure 7. MAN-MADE EMISSIONS OF AIR POLLUTANTS, late 1980s

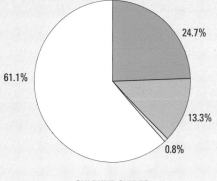

SULPHUR OXIDES

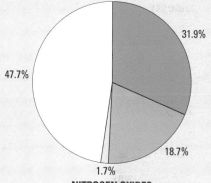

NITROGEN OXIDES

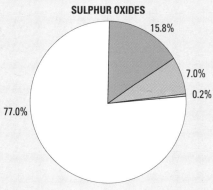

PARTICULATE MATTER

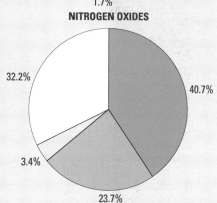

CARBON MONOXIDE

■ North America   ▨ OECD Europe   □ Japan   □ Rest of the World

	Sulphur Oxides	Nitrogen Oxides	Particulates	1000 tonnes Carbon Monoxide
Canada	3 800	1 943	1 709	10 781
USA	20 700	19 800	6 900	61 200
Japan	835	1 176	101	..
France	1 335	1 766	298	6 198
Germany *a*	1 306	2 872	532	8 738
Italy	2 070	1 570	413	5 571
Netherlands	256	560	95	1 057
Norway	65	226	25	607
Sweden	199	316	170	1 754
UK	3 664	2 513	533	5 508
North America	24 500	21 700	9 000	72 000
OECD Europe	13 200	12 700	4 000	42 000
OECD	39 900	36 600	13 000	125 000
World	99 000	68 000	57 000	177 000

Note: a) Includes western Germany only.
Source: OECD - IEA

Figure 8. MAN-MADE EMISSIONS OF AIR POLLUTANTS PER UNIT OF GDP, late 1980s

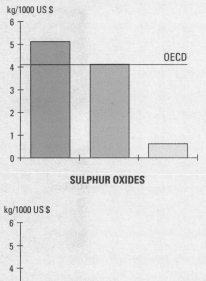

SULPHUR OXIDES

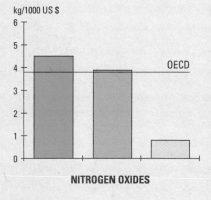

NITROGEN OXIDES

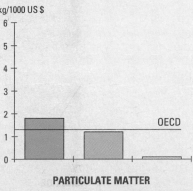

PARTICULATE MATTER

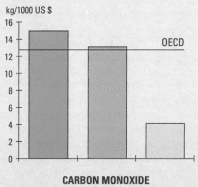

CARBON MONOXIDE

■ North America   ■ OECD Europe   □ Japan

	Sulphur Oxides	Nitrogen Oxides	Particulates	Carbon Monoxide
				kg/1000 US$ [a]
Canada	9.7	4.9	4.3	27.4
USA	4.7	4.5	1.6	13.8
Japan	0.6	0.8	0.1	..
France	2.4	3.1	0.5	11.0
Germany [b]	1.9	4.3	0.8	13.0
Italy	4.4	3.4	0.9	11.9
Netherlands	1.9	4.2	0.7	7.9
Norway	1.0	3.6	0.4	9.6
Sweden	1.8	2.9	1.6	16.2
UK	7.0	4.9	1.0	10.7
North America	5.1	4.5	1.8	14.9
OECD Europe	4.1	3.9	1.2	13.1
OECD	4.1	3.8	1.3	12.8
World	7.3	5.0	4.2	13.1

Notes: a) GDP values refer to 1985 prices and exchange rates.
　　　　b) Includes western Germany only.

Source: OECD

Most of the traditional air pollutants affect the respiratory and cardiovascular systems. The severity of the effects depends on exposure levels; it is the very young and the elderly, as well as people already affected by respiratory diseases, who are most at risk. *Sulphur dioxide* aggravates respiratory diseases, corrodes metals and stone, can reduce plant growth, and through acidification, injures aquatic life. *Nitrogen dioxide* (NO_2) also affects the respiratory system. Both NO_2 and nitrogen monoxide (NO) together with VOC are involved with the formation of photochemical oxidants, such as ozone; and they contribute, together with SO_2, to the formation of acidic compounds that can harm plants and animals. *Carbon monoxide* has immediate health effects because it reduces the blood's capacity to carry and circulate oxygen; these effects range from slowed reflexes and drowsiness to eventual death at very high exposure levels. *Photochemical oxidants* such as *ozone* can impair breathing, cause headaches, and irritate the eyes, nose and throat; furthermore, they can reduce visibility, deteriorate organic materials, and damage trees and crops. *Lead* inhibits haemoglobin synthesis in red blood cells in the bone marrow and disturbs the function of red blood cells; it harms the liver and kidneys, and may cause neurological damage. *Particulate matter* irritates the human respiratory system and can contribute to acute respiratory illness. It may increase both the incidence and the severity of chronic respiratory disease. It may provide reaction sites for other pollutants and facilitate acid formation.

Emissions of traditional pollutants

During the past two decades, many OECD countries have passed legislation calling for emission control over most of the traditional air pollutants. Regulations have been introduced to a) restrict the use of certain fuels, b) limit the sulphur and lead contents of fuels, c) require flue gas treatment after combustion from stationary sources such as power plants, and d) require automobiles to meet certain emission standards. These measures have substantially reduced emissions of some air pollutants in many countries, despite the growth in economic activity and energy consumption. There are, however, significant variations in pollutant emissions among countries (Figures 7 and 8).

Trend analysis shows that SO_2, CO, lead and particulate emissions have generally decreased in the OECD region compared to 1970 levels. In general, these decreases are due to:

- Stricter emission regulations;
- The two world oil crises in the 1970s that caused a temporary reduction in energy use;
- Changes in energy structures and fuel prices;
- The introduction of more efficient technologies; and
- The economic slowdown, for instance, in the first part of the 1980s in Europe.

As regards man-made *sulphur dioxide* emissions, energy production by utilities is the predominant source in almost all OECD countries, followed by industrial combustion and industrial processes which on average together account for less than 10 per cent. In OECD countries, natural emissions of SO_2 – mainly from volcanic activity – and of H_2S and its subsequent oxidation to SO_2 – mostly from decaying organic matter – probably make up less than 10 per cent of the total. Globally, natural and anthropogenic sources add roughly equal amounts of sulphur compounds to the atmosphere.

Compared with 1970, lower SO_2 emissions in most OECD countries today are the result of a) environmental policies based on tighter regulations regarding the average sulphur content of fuels, b) energy policies based on conservation and a shift away from oil to sulphur-free energy sources, such as natural gas and nuclear energy, and c) structural changes in OECD economies. National and international commitments in the 1980s have decreased emissions in many countries below 1980 levels. (Figure 9)

As far as *carbon monoxide* is concerned, it is emitted in OECD countries from incomplete combustion of fossil fuels – up to 90 per cent of it by road traffic and by industry. On a global scale, natural sources, chiefly decomposition of organic matter, and biomass burning, including forest fires, make up around 65 per cent of total CO emissions.

There has been a continuous decline in CO emissions in many, but not all, OECD countries since about 1970. The downward trend reflects both the decreased use of solid fuels in domestic heating and small industries and the introduction of controls on automobiles. However, since the early 1980s automobile traffic has been growing rapidly in many countries, and the trend in CO emissions has depended on whether or not emission limits have become progressively more stringent to offset the growth in mileage travelled. This has been the case in the United States, Canada and western Germany where total man-made CO emissions fell by more than 25 per cent between the mid-1970s and the late 1980s.

Lead is emitted into the air from a variety of man-made sources; road traffic is by far the largest source of lead in air where and when leaded gasoline is used. Emissions have been reduced, particularly in the 1980s in most OECD countries, as a result of regulations limiting the maximum allowable lead content in gasoline or prohibiting lead content altogether. Emissions decreased most sharply – by over 80 per cent – in North America between the mid-1970s and mid-1980s. In Europe, emissions started to be reduced significantly rather later, mainly in the late 1980s, and the reductions have been more modest, ranging from 45 per cent in the Netherlands to 60 per cent in the United Kingdom.

Particulate matter (PM) emissions arise from man-made and natural sources; fine particulate matter

Figure 9. **TRENDS IN MAN-MADE SULPHUR OXIDE EMISSIONS**

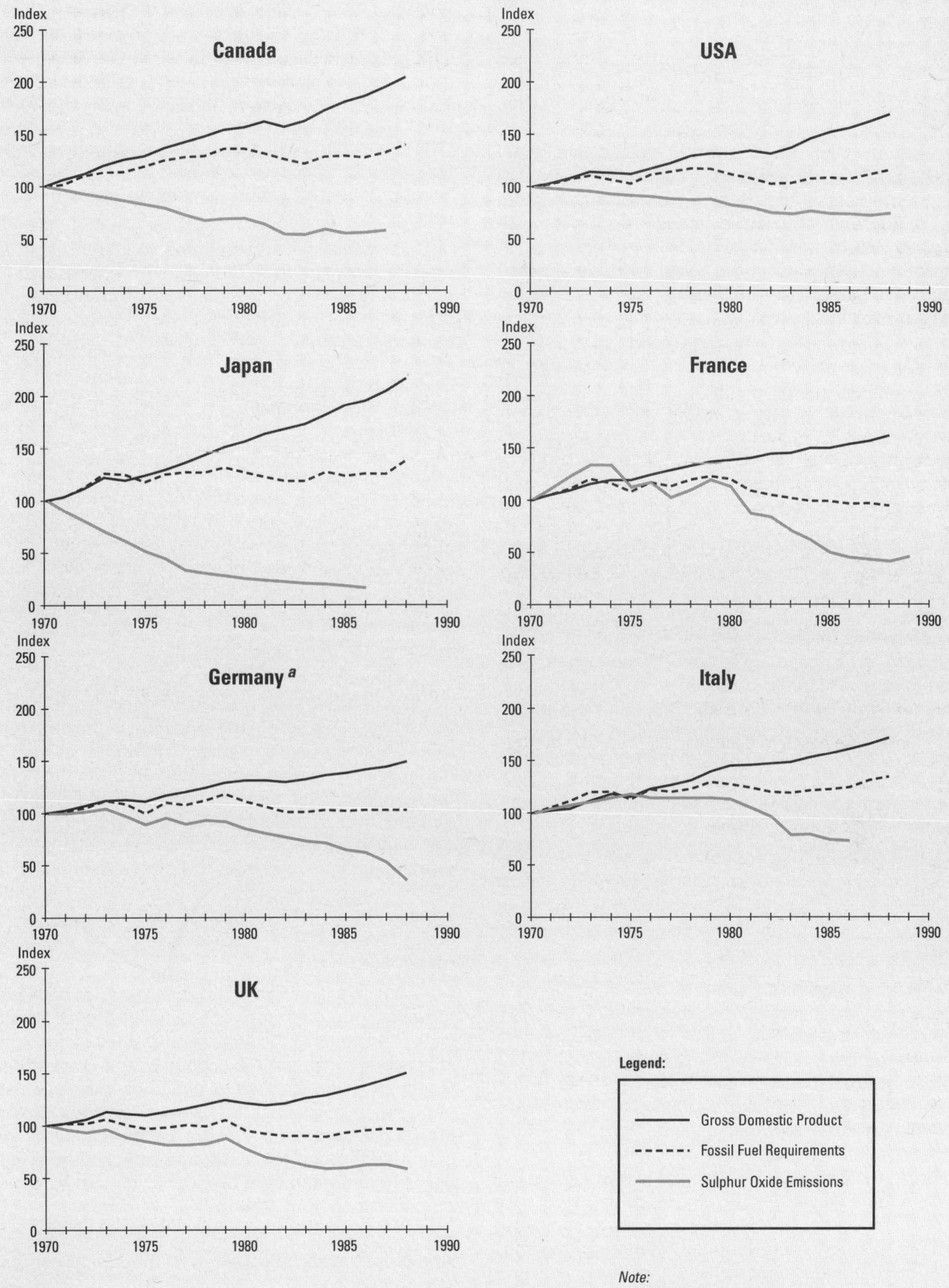

Canada
USA
Japan
France
Germany a
Italy
UK
Index
250
200
150
100
50
0
1970
1975
1980
1985
1990
Legend:
Gross Domestic Product
Fossil Fuel Requirements
Sulphur Oxide Emissions

Source: OECD

Note:
a) Includes western Germany only.

in the atmosphere forms by agglomeration and chemical transformation of gaseous emissions. Whereas natural particulate matter is mainly in the form of dust, man-made particulate emissions are often toxic and therefore of greater concern to human health. The combustion of fuels is the largest source in most OECD countries; in the European Community, it is estimated to be responsible for 95 per cent of man-made particulate emissions.

A substantial reduction in PM emissions in many OECD countries has been attributed to reduced coal burning in industry and the domestic sector since the late 1960s, as well as to the installation of dust removal equipment in coal-fired utilities. In some cases, however, lower emissions in these areas are being offset by growing PM emissions from the increased use of diesel-powered vehicles.

In contrast to these general decreases, NOx and VOC emissions have continued to increase or, at best, have remained stable, mainly due to the growth in automobile traffic and total mileage driven since 1970. Although traffic volume leveled off to some extent in many countries during and after the two oil crises, a general increase is again occurring in most OECD countries. (See Chapter on Transport)

Nitrogen oxides comprise a wide range of gases of which the most important ones in the atmosphere are nitrogen dioxide (NO_2), nitric oxide (NO), and nitrous oxide (N_2O). About 50 per cent of all man-made NOx emissions in OECD countries — mostly in the form of NO and, on average, up to about 10 per cent as NO_2 — come from road traffic, followed by power plants and industrial combustion. Emissions of natural nitrogen oxides — mainly from the decomposition of organic matter in the soil and from natural fires — may be significant, but they are to a large extent in the form of N_2O, which is non-reactive in the lower atmosphere. N_2O, however, contributes to global warming.

Emissions of NOx are not falling, with the exception of Japan; they are even rising somewhat in most OECD countries. (Figure 10) An increasing fraction of NOx emissions in most countries now comes from the mobile source sector.

Volatile organic compounds (VOCs) comprise a wide variety of hydrocarbon and other substances, many of which are highly reactive and have considerable environmental and health implications. At a global scale, the most abundant atmospheric volatile hydrocarbon is methane, which is produced mainly by such natural processes as organic matter decomposition. Because of its relatively low reactivity, its local or regional environmental significance is low. Less abundant but more volatile are the organic compounds, such as ethylene oxide, formaldehyde, phenol, phosgene, benzene, carbon tetrachloride, chlorofluorocarbons and polychlorinated biphenyls. All of these are produced mainly by human activities, and they are almost all known, or suspected, carcinogens. Several, also, are

possible mutagens or teratogens (i.e. substances which increase the incidence of congenital malformations). As well as their direct effects on human health, many organic compounds have more widespread environmental implications: they react with compounds such as nitrogen oxides and oxygen in the presence of sunlight to produce ozone and other oxidants; these, in turn, contribute to the formation of smog and aerosol pollution, and may have a number of toxicological effects, including eye, throat and lung irritation. In addition, they are believed to inhibit plant growth and to encourage deterioration of rubber and other compounds.

Emissions of non-methane volatile organic compounds stem first from natural sources, predominantly coniferous forests and wetlands. The importance of the different types of VOC compounds in ozone formation depends not only on the magnitude of emissions but also on their individual reactivity. The magnitude of the VOC emissions from forests varies greatly in OECD countries; in Scandinavia they make up more than half of all VOCs. Emissions of non-methane VOC also stem from man-made sources such as traffic, the production and use of organic chemicals, the transport and processing of crude oil and the use and distribution of natural gas. Of the man-made emissions in OECD countries, about half come from road traffic and a third from the use of solvents in industry and households. Another probably major anthropogenic, but less quantified, source of VOCs to air are waste disposal sites and waste water treatment plants.

Although another VOC, methane (CH_4), is a relatively unreactive gas, it too is of importance in ozone formation, especially in the long term in the free troposphere. Methane is also a major contributor to increases in the average global temperature through the "greenhouse effect". Its most important emission sources globally are: *a)* anaerobic decay of organic matter in rice paddies, natural wetlands and landfills; *b)* enteric fermentation in ruminants; *c)* biomass burning; and *d)* coal mining operations. In industrialised countries, leakage from natural gas distribution systems and emissions from cattle breading may be the biggest man-made sources.

Emissions of VOCs in OECD countries have either remained broadly stable or increased over the past decade. In general, the proportion emitted by road traffic is increasing, with the exception of the United States, where emission regulations up to now have been strict enough to counteract the growth in traffic volume. Emissions from industry have been reduced in many countries through the installation of recovery systems because of the inherent economic value in VOCs.

Ambient concentration levels of traditional pollutants

People are exposed to air pollution throughout the day, whether indoors or outdoors. The particular

Figure 10. **TRENDS IN MAN-MADE NITROGEN OXIDE EMISSIONS**

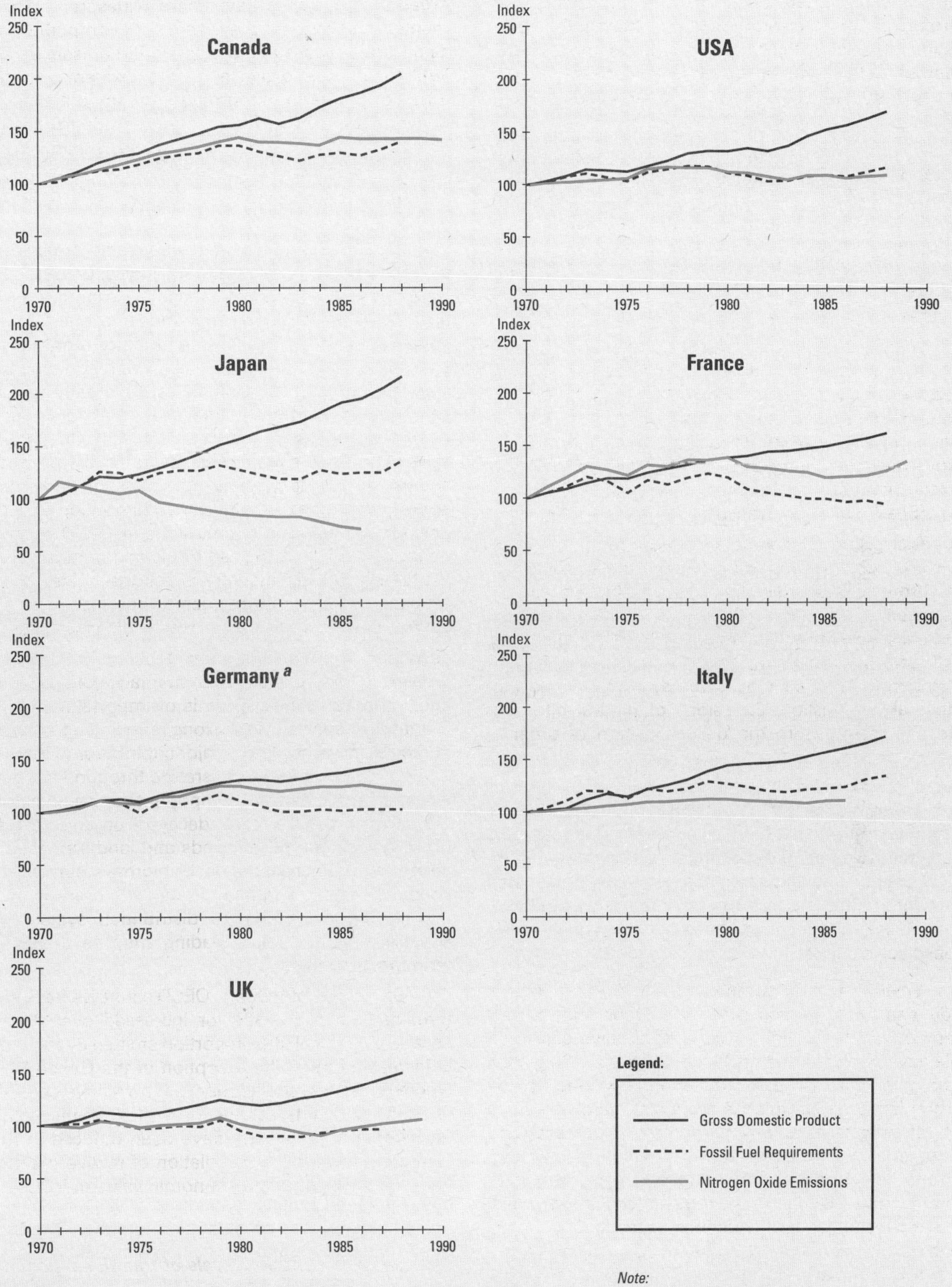

Canada
USA
Japan
France
Germany a
Italy
UK
Index
250
200
150
100
50
0
1970
1975
1980
1985
1990
Legend:
Gross Domestic Product
Fossil Fuel Requirements
Nitrogen Oxide Emissions

Source: OECD

Note:
a) Includes western Germany only.

mix and concentration of air pollutants vary considerably from location to location and from day to day. The most important determinants of air quality at any given time and place are the combination of emissions intensity, location of sources and weather conditions.

A number of OECD countries, including the United States, Canada, Japan, and the European Community, have promulgated ambient air quality standards for at least some of the traditional air pollutants in order to protect human health and the general environment. Moreover, the World Health Organization published a series of air quality guidelines in the late 1970s and most recently in 1987.

Changes in ambient air quality in OECD countries during the past two decades have to some extent reflected the emission reductions, or increases, that have taken place. For all traditional air pollutants, with the exception of ozone and nitrogen dioxide, improvements have been observed in most OECD countries since the early 1970s. These improvements are reflected in lower average long-term and short-term concentrations, and in the decline of the number of days or hours exceeding any air quality guidelines. There are, however, exceptions, and there has been a reversal of this trend in many countries in the last couple of years.

Between 1975 and the late 1980s, annual average *sulphur dioxide* concentration levels declined by 60 per cent in Japan, where the maximum allowable daily concentration of 100 $\mu g/m^3$ is exceeded in less than half of 1 per cent of all cases. Levels declined by about 45 per cent in Canada and the United States between the mid-1970s and the late 1980s, the number of areas not attaining the US national ambient air quality standard diminishing by more than 40 per cent. In the United Kingdom, ambient levels declined by 52 per cent. These reductions in concentration levels are significantly larger than the emission reductions that took place over this period. Since there has been a trend in OECD countries towards building large new power stations with higher stacks away from densely populated areas, SO_2 emissions may have become much more dispersed, leading to lower concentrations in urban air.

Concentrations of SO_2 have declined most in urban areas and in those cities where levels were highest in the early 1970s. (Figure 11) But in many cities in southern Europe in particular, the European Community's air quality guideline of 130 $\mu g/m^3$ (daily mean during winter) is still exceeded to a great extent.

The highest levels of *carbon monoxide* occur in urban areas, especially in the vicinity of highways and at busy intersections. Concentrations may vary between 1.0 and 100 mg/m^3. Average national trends have shown substantial declines in many countries.

Particulate matter in ambient air has declined in all OECD countries, and especially in urban air where the impact of man-made emissions is highest. In many countries this trend was most pronounced in the 1970s,

when a large reduction in solid fuel burning for domestic heating took place. It has since levelled off. The installation of dust removal equipment in industry in the 1970s also contributed to this decline.

In North America the annual average PM levels in the mid-1980s were 25 to 35 per cent lower than in the mid-1970s, with concentrations now ranging around 60 $\mu g/m^3$. That is below the US ambient air quality standard of 75 $\mu g/m^3$. It is estimated, however, that over 40 million people still live in areas in the United States where that standard is exceeded. In Europe concentrations are considerably lower, recently averaging around 20 to 25 $\mu g/m^3$, compared with levels of between 50 and 100 $\mu g/m^3$ some 20 years ago. In Japan the annual average PM levels decreased from 60 $\mu g/m^3$ in the early 1970s to below 40 $\mu g/m^3$ in 1985, but the ambient air quality standard of 100 $\mu g/m^3$ is met at only about 50 per cent of all monitoring stations. Although the amount of total particulate matter has decreased substantially almost everywhere in the OECD region, it should be noted that no significant decline of the fine fraction (i.e. smaller than 10 m), which is inhalable, has yet taken place.

Lead levels have fallen substantially in many OECD countries as a result of lower emissions from road traffic. The sharpest decrease has been achieved by North America — more than 85 per cent between the mid-1970s and the late 1980s. In some European countries the decline started in the mid-1970s after regulations had been introduced to limit the lead content of gasoline. The concentration reductions have been greatest in the urban environment; in Frankfurt, Brussels and Paris, for example, ambient levels fell by about 50 per cent over a 5-year period. The mean annual air quality standards of 1.5 $\mu g/m^3$ in the United States and 2 $\mu g/m^3$ in European Community countries are generally met. In Dublin, for example, they were between 1.5 $\mu g/m^3$ in the city centre and 0.2 $\mu g/m^3$ in the suburbs. As leaded gasoline is now being phased out altogether in Europe, the declining trend is expected to continue.

Average *nitrogen dioxide* levels in many OECD countries do not show a clear trend over the past 20 years. In some countries, such as the United States, average annual values for 1988 were somewhat below those for 1977; in other countries, such as western Germany and Japan, average NO_2 levels in 1988 were higher than or close to those in the early 1970s. Recent increases can be explained by the increasing number of motor vehicles and the higher speeds driven. Concentrations of NO_2 in urban areas show large variations over time, with peak levels often several times higher than the average. In Japan, for example, the national environmental quality standard for NO_2 of 115 $\mu g/m^3$ (daily average) was exceeded in more than 20 per cent of all roadside monitoring stations in 1985.

At one time it was thought that only the outside air was polluted, but numerous measurements now show that *indoor pollution* may be equally unhealthy,

Figure 11. TRENDS IN SULPHUR DIOXIDE CONCENTRATIONS

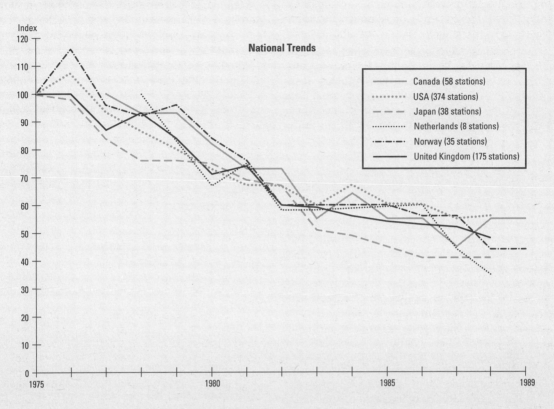

National Trends

Legend:
- Canada (58 stations)
- USA (374 stations)
- Japan (38 stations)
- Netherlands (8 stations)
- Norway (35 stations)
- United Kingdom (175 stations)

Index (y-axis): 0 to 120
X-axis: 1975, 1980, 1985, 1989

Urban Trends

		Base 1975 µg/m³	1970	1975	1980	1985	Late 1980s
				Index 1975 = 100			
CANADA	Montreal (Queb.)	40.3	..	100	101	50	40
USA	New York (N.Y.)	43.1	..	100	87	85	75
JAPAN	Tokyo	60.0	182	100	80	42	33
BELGIUM	Bruxelles	99.0	162	100	63	34	32
DENMARK	Copenhagen	45.0 (1976)	..	..	69	58	47
FINLAND	Tampere	103.0	..	100	57	40	7
FRANCE	Paris	115.0	106	100	77	47	38
	Rouen	63.0	..	100	111	59	56
GERMANY	Berlin (West)	95.0	..	100	95	71	64
ITALY	Milano	244.0	106	100	82	36	23
LUXEMBOURG	National Network	61.0	..	100	61	31	28
NETHERLANDS	Amsterdam	34.0	224	100	74	47	41
NORWAY	Oslo	48.0	..	100	75	31	27
PORTUGAL	Lisboa	36.2	..	100	122	86	119
SWEDEN	Gothenburg	41.0	..	100	59	54	32
	Stockholm	59.0	..	100	71	36	24
UK	London	116.0	..	100	60	36	34
	Newcastle	112.0	128	100	62	36	32

Note: Annual Average Daily Concentrations are given here as example to illustrate general trends over the past two decades. Methods of measurement are not strictly comparable among cities. Cities include cities in which a notable portion (5-10%) of the national population is concentrated; or industrial cities in which a significant number of inhabitants are considered to be exposed to a comparatively high level of pollutants in 1980.

Source: OECD

or even worse. A specific example is NOx emissions from unvented gas cookers. They are now of particular concern because NO_2 concentrations in kitchen air can frequently exceed recommended ambient concentration levels.

Photochemical pollution by *ozone* and other compounds like *peroxyacetyl nitrate* (PAN) is a phenomenon which was first identified in Los Angeles in the 1950s. Since then it has been observed in most large cities around the globe. Ozone and other photo-oxidants such as PAN are typically formed in the lower atmosphere from NOx and VOC emissions in the presence of sunlight during stagnant high-pressure weather conditions. This occurs most often during summertime, and leads to the well-known photochemical smog episodes characterised by a thick layer of brown haze.

Ozone concentrations in OECD countries have not shown a clear trend; the principal reason is that they depend largely on prevailing weather conditions, which can change considerably from year to year. In many OECD countries, ozone levels exceed recommended standards. In the United States, for example, the maximum daily one-hour average is higher than the limit of 235 $\mu g/m^3$. No major urban area, with the exception of Minneapolis, meets this health-related standard and it is estimated that about 75 million people are exposed to higher levels. In Japan the same ozone limit is also exceeded on a few days in the year, mostly in the Tokyo and Osaka areas. In Europe mean concentrations of ozone appear to be below 50 $\mu g/m^3$ in cities and below 100 $\mu g/m^3$ in rural areas. The peak concentrations exceed 200 $\mu g/m^3$ in urban as well as in rural areas.

Expectations in the 1990s

In spite of some of the improvements described above, many OECD countries are still determined to reduce the emission levels of the traditional pollutants. Because of economic growth and further increases in traffic volume in the coming decade, current regulations may be insufficient to halt the rise in emissions and air concentration levels.

Emissions of CO, VOC, and NOx are of particular concern, because episodes of photochemical smog, as well as urban "hot spots" of high CO levels, remain problems in many cities. The main cause of these problems is undoubtedly automobile traffic. In addition, emissions of SO_2, NOx, and VOC remain the target of further reductions because they are responsible for large-scale air pollution problems, as discussed below. To secure substantial reductions, it may be necessary to change countries' energy infrastructures considerably, so that they incorporate strict energy conservation and sustainable energy systems.

Toxic trace pollutants

In contrast to the traditional air pollutants, which are few in number, have by now been thoroughly studied and are relatively well controlled, toxic trace pollutants are numerous, not as well known and not systematically controlled. Many of these pollutants are emitted from specific industries and thus present an ambient air problem in the vicinity of these industrial complexes as well as an occupational exposure problem. A large number of toxic trace pollutants are, however, emitted from a great variety of other sources, including industrial by-products, incomplete combustion of certain fuels and wastes, or the use of contaminated materials. Cadmium, for example, originates from sources as diverse as metal smelting, waste and coal incineration, natural volcanic particles, pigments in plastics, and fertilizer use. Moreover, several toxic pollutants present an indoor air pollution problem, as in the case of radon and formaldehyde.

Toxic trace pollutants can be grouped into four major categories:

- Heavy *metals*, such as beryllium, cadmium, mercury, etc.;
- *Organic compounds*, such as benzene, polychlorinated dibenzo-dioxins and -furans, formaldehyde, vinyl chloride, etc.;
- *Radioactive particles and gases*, such as radionuclides and radon; and
- *Fibres*, such as asbestos.

People may be exposed to toxic trace pollutants through inhalation, contact with skin, and ingestion. The health effects of toxic trace pollutants are probably more diverse than those of the traditional air pollutants because many of them are of remarkably higher toxicity and, due to their excellent lipid solubility, affect a much wider range of organs in the human body. (Tables 1 and 2) Many of them may cause hormonal disturbances, cancer, birth defects, and other reproductive effects as do, for example, coplanar polychlorinated biphenyls (PCB). As in the case of heavy metals, toxic air pollutants may be transferred from the atmosphere to other environmental media, where they can cause additional damage to man and the natural environment.

Assessment of toxic trace pollutant emissions

Many sources emit toxic trace chemicals into the atmosphere: incinerators, industrial and manufacturing processes, solvent use, sewage treatment plants, hazardous waste handling and disposal sites, and motor vehicles. Metal refining and processing plants as well as waste incinerators, power plants and similar installations emit heavy metals. Toxic organic compounds are released by plastics and chemicals factories, dry cleaning establishments, waste treatment plants and incinerators, and automobiles. Radioactive gases and particles as well as toxic fibres are often released from building materials where they either occur naturally or were added for insulation purposes.

It was recently reported that around 1.1 million tonnes of toxic trace pollutants are currently released from the United States into the atmosphere each year.

Table 1. HEALTH EFFECTS OF SELECTED TOXIC TRACE AIR POLLUTANTS, Organic compounds

Pollutant	Major health effects
Acryronitrile ($CH_2=CH-C=N$)	Dermatitis; haematological changes; headaches; irritation of eyes, nose and throat; lung cancer
Benzene (C_6H_6)	Leukemia; neurotoxic symptoms; bone marrow injury incl. anaemia, chromosome aberrations
Carbon disulfide (CS_2)	Neurologic and psychiatric symptoms, incl. irritability and anger; gastro-intestinal troubles; sexual interferences
1,2 Dichloroethane ($C_2H_2Cl_2$)	Damage to lungs, liver and kidneys; heart rhythm disturbances; effects on central nervous systems, incl. dizziness; animal mutagen and carcinogen
Formaldehyde (HC HO)	Chromosome aberrations; irritation of eyes, nose and throat; dermatitis; respiratory tract infections in children
Methylene chloride (CH_2Cl_2)	Nervous system disturbances
Polychlorinated bi-phenyls (PCB) (coplanar)	Spontaneous abortions; congenital birth defects; bioaccumulation in food chains
Polychlorinated dibenzo-dioxins and -furans	Birth defects; skin disorders; liver damage; suppression of the immune system
Polycyclic Organic Matter (POM) [incl. benzo(a)pyrene (BaP)]	Respiratory tract and lung cancers; skin cancers
Styrene ($C_6H_5-CH=CH_2$)	Central nervous system depression; respiratory tract irritations; chromosome aberrations; cancers in the lymphatic and haematopoietic tissues
Tetrachloroethylene (C_2Cl_4)	Kidney and genital cancers; lymphosarcoma; lung, cervical and skin cancers; liver dysfunction; effects on central nervous system
Toluene ($C_6H_5-CH_3$)	Dysfunction of the central nervous system; eye irritation
Trichloroethylene (C_2HCl_3)	Impairment of psychomotoric functions; skin and eye irritation; injury to liver and kidneys; urinary tract tumors and lymphomas
Vinyl chloride ($CH_2=CHCl$)	Painful vasospastic disorders of the hands; dizziness and loss of consciousness; increased risk of malformations, particularly of the central nervous systems; severe liver disease; liver cancer; cancers of the brain and central nervous system; malignancies of the lymphatic and haematopoietic system

Source: OECD

Over 100 000 tonnes of these emissions are cancer-causing compounds including, for example, more than 10 000 tonnes of benzene, which is known to cause leukemia. This is about 5 per cent of the tonnage of current US SO_2 emissions. Unlike sulphur, however, most of these substances are not assimilated in the environment, and they are toxic at much lower exposure levels. A survey of the 320 most abundant chemicals emitted in the air in the United States found that 60 are carcinogenic, which may imply that no "safe" exposure level exists.

The US estimate is based on reports from about 15 000 manufacturers, and does not include emissions from automobiles, dry cleaning establishments, and hazardous waste facilities. If these were included, emissions in the United States might be triple the current estimate of 1.1 million tonnes. In the United States, the chemical industry is expected to grow faster than any other industry, and that growth is likely to increase the range and quantity of toxic substances released into the environment.

Risk of human exposure to toxic trace pollutants

It is much more difficult to estimate the exposure of a population to toxic trace pollutants than to the traditional air pollutants, because the former are not routinely monitored in most countries; it is even more difficult to assess the health risk. To date, negative health effects have been observed only at occupational levels, which are higher than those normally found in the ambient or indoor air. For most of these pollutants, data regarding their effects on humans are not available, but are deduced from animal studies. In addition,

HER MAJESTY'S INSPECTORATE OF POLLUTION

Her Majesty's Inspectorate of Pollution (HMIP), responsible for the inspection and enforcement of pollution regulations in England and Wales, was formed in 1987 and is part of the Department of the Environment. It brought together three existing inspectorates: the Industrial Air Pollution Inspectorate; the Radiochemical Inspectorate; and the Hazardous Waste Inspectorate; and took on a new role in the control of water pollution.

On its formation, HMIP was given the following aims and objectives:

- To exercise efficiently and effectively statutory powers for controlling radioactive substances, emissions to air from scheduled processes and water authority discharges to water;
- To monitor the efficiency and effectiveness with which water and waste disposal authorities exercise their powers of control and to secure improvements where appropriate;
- To ensure the development of economically sound technical practices for disposing of waste in the most environmentally acceptable way;
- To help develop feasible methods of applying a cross-media approach to pollution control;
- To develop plans for implementing the Government's strategy for radioactive waste management.

An Integrated Approach to Pollution Management

The creation of HMIP laid the foundation for a more integrated approach to pollution control. This is in recognition that environmental pollution can be transferred between media and that it makes little sense to look at single aspects of control in isolation. Also, the integration of the former inspectorates into a single agency would provide value-added benefits from improved administrative co-ordination. But it was clear from the outset that effective implementation of a cross-media approach would depend on the introduction of new legislation to establish a different format for the control of discharges from industrial processes.

Implementing Cross-media Pollution Control

Proposals for integrated pollution control legislation would make HMIP the statutory pollution control agency for those industrial processes that discharge significant quantities of harmful non-radioactive wastes.

Processes giving rise to harmful wastes would be "scheduled" under the new legislation. Operators of such processes would require an authorisation from HMIP which would specify the use of the best available technology not entailing excessive cost to prevent the emission or discharge of pollutants. In addition, the overall pattern of wastes discharged from a facility operating a scheduled process would be considered by HMIP in order to render any emissions that could not be prevented, harmless and inoffensive to people and the environment as a whole.

Regarding water pollution, the newly created National Rivers Authority is responsible for authorising discharges from sewage works. HMIP's role here will concentrate, through integrated pollution control legislation, on regulation of the most dangerous substances whose discharge to sewer and controlled water needs to be minimised because of their particular noxious effects.

On waste disposal, new legislation will create Waste Regulatory Authorities responsible for licensing and inspection of private and public waste disposal sites. HMIP will be required to formally audit and report on the performance of these Authorities, and to provide advice and guidance. HMIP inspectors will continue to be responsible for authorisation, registration and inspection of premises to hold and dispose of radioactive waste.

Organisation of Her Majesty's Inspectorate of Pollution

To implement its responsibilities, the inspectorate has been organised on a regional basis. Within the regional structure, field inspectors will operate in multi-disciplinary teams responsible for all aspects of HMIP's work in their area, and trained to consider pollution control in respect of all media. HMIP's present manpower complement is 250. There are currently more than 200 staff in post of which over 100 are professionals.

Contribution from the United Kingdom

it may not be sufficient to know the health risk associated with one of these toxic pollutants since they can be additive, cumulative, and possibly synergistic.

Although a few of the toxic trace pollutants present an ambient air problem in the outdoors, many of them constitute a greater risk to people indoors (at home, in vehicles, in the office and other working places) where concentrations are much higher because of the lack of ventilation, etc. This is of particular importance insofar as most people spend about 90 per cent of their time indoors. A US study of comparative risk placed such indoor air pollution among the top environmental problems facing the nation.

These pollutants come, for instance, from tobacco smoke, building materials, furnishings, space heaters, gas ranges, wood preservatives, cleaning agents, glues, and other solvents. Harmful trace pollutants of concern in the outdoor air are mainly benzene from traffic and gasoline vapours, polycyclic organic compounds from wood and other incomplete combustion processes, and tetrachloroethylene from industrial solvent use, as in automobile coating or dry cleaning operations.

Whereas the exposure to toxic trace pollutants in the ambient outdoor air depends primarily on the amounts emitted, proximity to sources and prevailing weather conditions, the exposure levels inside buildings depend mainly on the different materials used and on the ventilation of the building. Related to this problem was the interest shown in the 1970s and 1980s for building more energy-efficient houses. This often resulted in air-tight and poorly ventilated houses that now show the "sick building syndrome", where people complain of eye, nose, and throat irritations, fatigue, headaches, nausea, irritability, and forgetfulness.

Although these irritations are unpleasant, they may still be considered relatively minor. On the other hand, many of the toxic trace pollutants are known to cause chronic, irreversible effects that may ultimately lead to premature death. For example, it has been estimated that in the United States 500 to 5 000 non-smokers die each year of lung cancer because they were exposed to *tobacco smoke*. Furthermore, indoor *radon* – a radioactive gas naturally occurring in many rocks and soils and thus in building materials – is possibly the leading cause of lung cancer among non-smokers, and may be responsible for as many as 5 000 to 20 000 lung cancer deaths per year in the United States. Both risks present indoor pollution problems.

A rough US estimate of the lifetime risk of developing lung cancer from environmental exposure to *asbestos* indoors and outdoors ranges from 3 per million for female non-smokers to 64 per million for male smokers. Asbestos also causes mesothelioma, a rare cancer of the lining of the chest and abdominal cavities; its lifetime risk has been estimated to amount to 9 per million. Some of the risks from predominantly outdoor exposure to toxic trace pollutants have also been quantified. For example, in Norway the number of *benzene*-induced leukemia deaths each year has been estimated to be about 2 per million. The above are just a few examples of the better-known risks from exposure to individual toxic trace pollutants. In their daily lives, however, people are exposed at home, at work or school, in vehicles, and outdoors to a complex mixture of pollutants from a large variety of sources.

Recent legislation and regulations to limit exposure to toxic air pollutants, and future outlook

By now several OECD countries have passed legislation to limit the emission into ambient air from specific sources of individual trace air pollutants whose

Table 2. HEALTH EFFECTS OF SELECTED TOXIC TRACE AIR POLLUTANTS, Metals

Pollutant	Major health effects
Arsenic (As)	Lung cancer; dermatological disorders, incl. ulcerative dermatitis; haematological effects, incl. anaemia
Beryllium (Be)	Dermatitis; ulcers; inflammation of mucous membranes
Cadmium (Cd)	Acute and chronic respiratory disease; renal dysfunction; animal carcinogen
Chromium (Cr)	Lung cancer; gastro-intestinal cancers; dermatitis
Lead (Pb)	Interference with bloodforming processes; liver and kidney damage; neurological effects
Mercury (Hg)	Effects on nervous system, incl. deficits in short-term memory, disturbance of sensory and co-ordination functions; kidney failure
Nickel (Ni)	Respiratory illnesses, incl. asthma; impairment of respiratory defence system; birth defects and malformations; nasal and lung cancers
Thallium (Tl)	Bioaccumulation; toxic to plants and animals
Vanadium (V)	Respiratory irritation; asthma; nervous disturbances; changes in the blood formula

Source: OECD

Harmful substances that have been measured inside homes and office buildings include radon, asbestos, mercury, and an array of organic compounds such as formaldehyde, chloroform, and perchloroethylene.

AIR POLLUTION AND ART IN ITALY

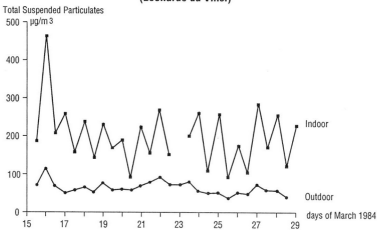

FRESCO OF THE LAST SUPPER
(Leonardo da Vinci)

The many paintings, sculptures, and ruins found in Italian cities and in the countryside are part of mankind's cultural heritage. Although many important works of art have survived for centuries, these are now threatened by high levels of air pollution, particularly in cities and in buildings.

Outdoor Air Pollution and Monuments

The damage to stone monuments from polluted air is mainly due to sulphur dioxide. This pollutant reacts with the main component of the stone, calcium carbonate, to form calcium sulphate (gypsum) which, in turn, can be washed out by rain. The result is an alteration and weakening of the stone crystal structure.

A field study conducted in the centre of Rome investigated the effects of atmospheric pollution on the Marcus Aurelius marble column. Findings show a close correlation between the hourly concentrations of sulphur dioxide and domestic heating in the cold season. The lower concentrations of sulphur dioxide measured in the summer months result from road traffic and industrial activities. In the air samples obtained near the column, gypsum is by far the most prevalent substance, an indication of a slow but continuous process of degradation of the monument.

Indoor Pollution and Art

To protect indoor art from the harmful effects of air pollution, care needs to be exercised in the control of air quality in such buildings as museums, galleries, churches and palaces. These have not been designed to provide the optimum climatic and environmental conditions required to effectively preserve their works of art.

The extent of damage caused by a given pollutant is determined not only by its concentration inside the building, but also by the mechanisms by which the pollutant is transported from outside and deposited on the indoor surfaces. An example of this is the fresco of The Last Supper, by Leonardo da Vinci, in the Refectory of the monastery of Santa Maria delle Grazie in Milan. It has been observed that the indoor air conditions, the thermohygrometric conditions and the flow of visitors can result in concentrations of suspended particles near the painting being up to five times greater than those outside. The damage caused by these particles is partly due to the acidic substances they contain in winter and partly due to deposition on the painting's surface, which gradually darkens.

A study in March 1984 on indoor and outdoor concentrations of total suspended particles identified greater dust levels inside the Refectory. The study allowed the causes of indoor air pollution to be well identified and an action plan to be formulated. The Central Institute for Restoration is currently carrying out this plan.

Contribution from Italy

toxicity has been positively proven, such as asbestos, vinyl chloride, benzene, polychlorinated dibenzo-dioxins and -furans, as well as some heavy metals. Other countries, such as western Germany and Switzerland, have taken a preventive approach by also requiring control of potentially toxic pollutants with the best available control technology. A multitude of these pollutants, however, still remain uncontrolled in spite of the fact that many countries have some regulations about the quality of indoor air.

To assess the full impact of toxic air pollutants on human health, personal monitors which reflect the actual exposure situation indoors and outdoors should be used, in addition to ambient and indoor air monitors. This is, however, a rather expensive way, presents methodological problems, and still leaves some gaps when estimating total population exposures.

Given the enormous number of toxic compounds emitted into the air, it does not seem efficient to try to regulate them on a substance-by-substance basis. An alternative route to reducing human exposure is to strictly enforce and possibly tighten existing VOC and PM emission standards and invest in improved process and combustion technologies. In this way a large part of the emissions of organic pollutants and toxic metals and fibres would be controlled.

2. LARGE-SCALE AIR POLLUTION

Besides global atmospheric pollution problems, such as global warming and the destruction of the protective stratospheric ozone layer (see Chapter on Global Atmospheric Issues), the most pressing large-scale air pollution problems are currently:

- The acidification of the environment in various parts of the world through the deposition of sulphur and nitrogen compounds;
- Damage to ecosystems such as lakes, forests, and cropland caused by acid deposition and large-scale photochemical smog, among other possible factors.

In contrast to the local and urban pollution problems, these large-scale ones are international by nature and can be controlled only partly by national measures.

By the early 1970s, scientists in Europe had realised that sulphur pollution travelled long distances through the atmosphere and contributed to lake acidification and the associated decline in fish populations at remote sites in Scandinavia. Since then, it has become a well-established fact that many air pollutants travel long distances, cross national boundaries, and can have negative impacts on the environment far away from sources.

In 1981 German scientists reported damage to national forests and attributed this to large-scale air pollution. Two possible adverse influences were thought to be soil acidification resulting from continental-scale transport of sulphur and nitrogen, and regional-scale ozone formation in the lower troposphere.

Acid deposition of sulphates and nitrates

Acidification of the environment became a major concern in most OECD countries in the late 1970s and early 1980s, although the Pacific OECD countries, including Japan, have not so far found any evidence of large-scale damage from acid rain. Large parts of eastern China, on the other hand, have already been affected by acid deposition.

Aquatic ecosystems are highly vulnerable to acid deposition. Since the 1950s, fish populations have declined and species have disappeared in certain areas of the United States, Canada and Sweden. The speed of lake acidification has accelerated over time, especially in the last few decades. Measured in terms of "potential of hydrogen" (pH), which rates pure water as 7.0 and acid solutions as anything less than that, more than half the lakes in Europe and North America with a pH of under 5.0 are fishless, compared to one in seven of those with a pH of over 5.0.

The impact of acidity depends on the system's buffering capacity. If the soil in the watershed contains limestone or other substances that neutralise acidity, lakes acidify less rapidly. In addition to acidity, dissolved aluminium released from sediments can also be toxic to fish and other aquatic organisms.

Acidification affects the land as well as lakes and groundwater. Large areas of forest soils have increased in acidity by factors of five to ten over the past 20 to 50 years. Acidity in the soil can increase the amount of aluminium, which kills fine roots, or it may cause a deficiency of magnesium.

Sulphur is the major component of increased acidification of the environment. Atmospheric sulphur is not usually absorbed by vegetation but travels through to the soil in the form of sulphate. Nitrogen, which is used as a fertilizer, can also be a pollutant in excessive quantities. Emissions of sulphur and nitrogen may return to earth dry (in the form of gases and particles), wet (in rain and snow) or as condensation (as fog and cloud droplets). Acid compounds can fall to earth a short distance from the source or thousands of kilometres away. The further the distance travelled, the more wet deposition tends to dominate the deposition process. In North America it is estimated that almost 40 per cent of sulphur deposition in the northeast originates in the mid-west.

Photochemical smog pollution by ozone and NOx

Cases of urban-scale photochemical smog have been observed for several decades in large cities throughout the world. But it is only since the early 1980s that evidence has been produced to show that ozone and its precursors can also be transported and accumulate over large areas ranging from several hundred to several thousand square kilometres. Large-scale ozone pollution has mostly been observed in North America and Europe, especially in the summer, but attention is increasingly focused on the rise in long-term ozone levels and background concentrations in the free troposphere. The ecological consequences of high ozone levels include damage to all types of vegetation, including agricultural crops where significant economic losses may be incurred. In California, it is estimated that ozone causes annual losses of up to 20 per cent of important crops like cotton and grapes.

Current levels of ozone in Europe and North America frequently exceed WHO ceilings for both short- and long-term ozone concentrations by a wide margin on a large scale.[1] In addition, ozone levels in the free troposphere are thought to have doubled during this century. Both NOx and VOC contribute to the generation of ozone; NOx levels in many parts of the world fall into the range where a reduction might lead to a commensurate decrease in ozone concentrations. A reduction in NOx and VOC levels, through stringent emission controls of all motor vehicles, would not only curtail the incidence of summer-time smog but also bring down long-term levels of photo-oxidants in general.

Deposition of heavy metals

Whereas at least seven metals are essential for all forms of life and others are needed by certain organisms, there are some "heavy" metals, such as arsenic (As), cadmium (Cd), mercury (Hg) and lead (Pb) that are probably of no biological importance and are often highly toxic at low concentrations. In fact, most metals in concentrations above natural conditions are toxic to life but heavy metals are of particular concern in the natural environment because they have long survival times and some of their derivatives accumulate in the food chain.

The deposition of heavy metals changes the bio-chemistry and biology of soils, and their build-up in aquatic and terrestrial eco-systems inhibits the vitality of plants and animals. Metals enter the food chain through fish and cows' milk and can cause serious health problems.

In heavily industrialised areas, the principal sources of metal emissions are smelters, power plants, waste incinerators and traffic. In rural areas, heavy metals originate from both local natural souces and distant anthropogenic ones. Despite their name, "heavy" metals can remain in the atmosphere for one to 10 days and be transported over distances of up to 2 000 kilometres. To reduce the long-range transport of heavy metals, lower and strictly enforced emission levels need to be established for particulate matter given off by coal and waste combustion facilities and metal smelting plants.

International policies for combating transboundary air pollution – initiatives and achievements

The knowledge that environmental problems in one country can be caused by emissions from another has given risen to intensive international negotiations in recent years. Co-operative international and bi-lateral programmes have been implemented since the early 1970s, leading to some important agreements in the mid-1980s.

The European Community issued a series of directives in the 1970s, setting ambient air quality standards for SO_2, NO_2, particulate matter and lead, emission limits for automobiles and large combustion installations, and ceilings for the lead and sulphur contents of fuels. In 1980 the United States and Canada also signed a Memorandum of intent to assess the impact of the long-range transport of air pollution in North America.

To tackle air pollution problems in both Europe and North America, 35 countries signed the United Nations Economic Commission for Europe Convention on Long-Range Transboundary Air Pollution, which came into force in 1983. The ECE subsequently published a Protocol in 1984 providing for SO_2 emissions to be reduced by 30 per cent from 1980 levels. The Protocol took effect in 1987 after being ratified by 18 countries, which are implementing a variety of policies to meet the stated goal. Japan has already demonstrated that sulphur emissions can be cut by as much as 90 per cent from their uncontrolled levels. A NOx agreement was subsequently signed in 1988 providing for NOx emissions to be held at their 1987 level up to 1994. At the same time, 12 western European countries committed themselves to a reduction of 30 per cent by 1998. (See Chapter on International Responses)

3. CONCLUSIONS

Progress

Over the last two decades, control stategies and technologies have been developed in OECD countries for reducing the emissions and concentrations of traditional air pollutants (SO_2, NOx, CO, PM, VOC, O_3). They include:

- Restriction of the use of highly polluting fuels and limits on the sulphur, lead and benzene contents of fuels;
- Flue gas treatment after combustion from stationary sources, especially from power plants as well as certain large industries;
- Emission controls on motor vehicles.

Such control strategies and technical progress have been combined to substantially reduce air pollutant emissions in many countries, against a backdrop of growth and structural change in economies and energy demands. This applies particularly to sulphur oxides, particulates and lead emissions. As a result, some progress can be reported mostly at the local and urban level in heavily industrialised and populated areas:

- Urban *sulphur dioxide concentrations* have decreased on average by between 30 and 75 per cent in OECD countries;
- Urban *particulate matter concentrations* have declined in OECD countries, from average concentrations of between 50 and 100 $\mu g/m^3$ in the early 1970s, to levels now ranging between 20 and 60 $\mu g/m^3$;
- Urban *lead concentrations* have decreased significantly; in North America, on average, by as much as 85 per cent, and in large European cities by about 50 per cent.

However, since some of the problems in one country may be caused by emissions from another and cannot be alleviated by national measures alone, substantial international negotiation has taken place over the past decade. In the 1980s a number of international agreements for reducing air pollution at the regional and continental levels were signed.

Remaining and emerging problems

In spite of the above successes, urban *pollution* continues to be a problem because:

- *VOC and NOx emissions* have generally increased compared with the early 1970s; the resulting *photochemical smog pollution* often exceeds recommended standards. The main reason is that motor vehicle fleets and kilometres travelled have increased in many countries at a much faster rate than the implementation of emission controls;

- *Ambient air quality standards* and guidelines by the WHO for NO_2 and O_3 *are still exceeded* in many OECD countries;
- The air quality in some *cities* and densely populated regions, especially in the south of Europe, is still deteriorating. The main reasons are that pollution control regulations are not strong enough, or not vigorously enough enforced, and that energy and transport policies do not emphasize energy savings and substitutions capable of offsetting the effects of economic growth.

Further, *large-scale and international air pollution* problems remain:

- Over the past two decades, air quality has become a concern at *rural and remote sites* in many parts of the OECD region as a result of long-range transport of air pollutants;
- These increased levels of large-scale air pollution have exerted greater *stress on forests and other natural ecosystems*, soil, inland waters and crops.

Lastly, newly emerging problems also add to the challenges of providing for cleaner air:

- More and more *toxic pollutants* (e.g. cadmium, benzene, radon, asbestos) are being released into the atmosphere. Even though they are emitted in smaller quantities than traditional air pollutants, they may have equal or greater impacts on the natural environment and human health; many of them are carcinogenic or cause other long-term irreversible health effects. The combined intake of several of these toxic trace pollutants, not only from air but also through food and drinking water, may exert an even greater effect than that of any of them taken singly;
- Available evidence shows that *indoor air* may be of considerably lower quality in many instances than outdoor air, and that people may be exposed to much higher levels of traditional and toxic trace air pollutants than was originally believed, since they spend about 90 per cent of their time in buildings or vehicles.

Air management

In order to deal with these local and international problems, and notwithstanding the global atmospheric pollution problems reviewed separately, better management of air resources is needed. Aims include:

- Better enforcement of existing national regulations and policies, and rigorous implementation of international agreements;

CONTROLLING AIR POLLUTION IN OSAKA (JAPAN)

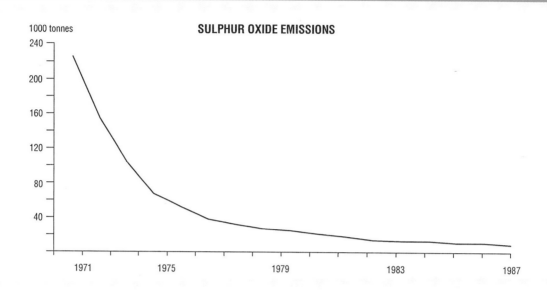

SULPHUR OXIDE EMISSIONS

1000 tonnes

A History of Air Pollution Control

Osaka prefecture has a population of 8.7 million people yet it covers only 0.5 per cent of Japan's territory. As Osaka has a long history of industrialisation, it is one of the first prefectures to have taken measures aimed at controlling air pollution.

First, in 1877, Osaka established an all-prefectural Directive concerning the control of air pollution from blacksmith shops, metalcasting factories and public baths. In 1897, in a revision to this directive, the word "pollution" was introduced into Japan for the first time.

In the late 1960s, intense industrial growth made air and water pollution worse. In response, authorities established the Osaka Prefectural Environmental Pollution Control Ordinance in 1971, coinciding with the creation of the Japanese Environment Agency. In 1973 a local environmental control programme was enacted. This program focused on the purifying ability of the environment since one of its important themes was the concept of environmental capacity. For example, as a measure against air pollution from sulphur dioxide, emission standards were formulated which considered the height of emission sources and the sulphur content of fuels used. Fuel use was reduced, as were sulphur dioxide emissions, which decreased by about 96 per cent from 1971 to 1987.

Wide-Ranging Environmental Protection Measures

A more comprehensive approach to air pollution control was adopted in Osaka in 1982. Specific features of this approach included defining permissible pollutant emissions by area and by source, controlling emissions from motor vehicles and encouraging more effective use of resources.

In 1984, Osaka established a comprehensive environmental impact assessment code for large-scale enterprise development. This is aimed at preventing environmental pollution and is likely to have a great effect on the environment. Examples of projects which have been reviewed and screened from an environmental viewpoint include a fossil fuel power station, a waste disposal facility and Kansai international airport.

Environmental monitoring is carried out in Osaka by means of telemeters monitoring pollutant emissions from factories and stations sampling ambient environmental quality. Also, under construction are an environmental monitoring system that uses remote-sensing by earth-observing satellites, and an environmental information system to forecast environmental impact of pollution.

Beyond Osaka - Towards Global Environmental Protection

The new comprehensive environmental control programme, begun in 1990, seeks to promote co-operation on environment issues and advocates life-styles and city development patterns which are environment-friendly. Building on previous measures, new steps will be taken which will make Osaka a city which contributes to the resolution of global as well as local environmental problems.

Contribution from Japan

FORECASTING EMISSIONS TO AIR IN NORWAY

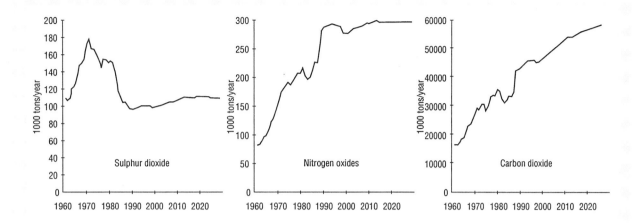

HISTORIC AND PROJECTED EMISSIONS

Forecasts of pollutant emissions to air are made on a routine basis in Norway and concern sulphur dioxide, nitrogen oxides, carbon monoxide, carbon dioxide, volatile organic compounds, lead and particulates. These estimates of future emissions are based on model calculations of expected economic growth in Norway, performed on a disaggregated sectoral level and with due attention paid to both implemented and planned governmental action against air pollution. Currently, the possibility of including the greenhouse gases methane, nitrous oxide and chlorofluorocarbons in the forecasting procedure is under study.

Emission Forecasts by Pollutant to 2025

Yearly emissions of sulphur dioxide are expected to remain approximately stable for the forecasting period. Emissions of nitrogen oxides are expected to grow in the period to the year 2000, but to stabilize thereafter. This is in large part due to the introduction, in 1989, of new regulations concerning exhaust gases from automobiles which, however, will only take full effect after the year 2000. Carbon dioxide emissions are expected to grow at almost the historic rate of growth, unless effective control policies against the use of fossil fuels can be implemented.

Factors Influencing Emission Levels

The main factors influencing the calculated levels of future emissions are:

- Overall economic growth, determined to a large extent by future growth in the labour force and sectoral technological changes. The world market price of oil is also of importance since income from oil and gas production in the North Sea contributes substantially to the total national income;
- Structural changes in the economy due to differentiation in growth rates among economic sectors;

- Growth in exports since the exporting industries are among the most polluting sectors in Norway;
- Price of oil products relative to the price of electricity and other commodities. The exogenously determined price of crude oil influences both demand for oil and gasoline and the general activity level in the economy;
- Growth and structure of private consumption in general and growth in private transport, in particular;
- Planned environmental control policies.

A Valuable Tool in Environmental Policy Design

The model calculations of future emissions are used as a basis for the design, analysis and assessment of possible future environmental protection policies, in terms of both environmental and economic impacts. Thus, presently proposed abatement strategies for reducing emissions of sulphur dioxide and nitrogen oxides are based on forecasts made along the lines described above.

In addition to assessing the potential costs to society associated with the implementation of various emission control policies -- such as regulations or environmentally-motivated taxes -- the model framework has recently been extended to include some estimates of potential economic benefits from an improvement in environmental quality. These cover reduction in damage from acidification of soil and water, reduced material corrosion, improvements in health and reductions in noise levels due to a possible reduction in road traffic. Several studies indicate that benefits from such environmental control policies as taxation on use of fossil fuels compensate to a large extent for the estimated loss in Gross Domestic Product.

Contribution from Norway

- More efforts concerning indoor pollution problems and issues relating to total human exposure to pollution;
- Better knowledge of toxic pollutants, monitoring of indoor pollution and of relatively new pollutants, and more thorough understanding of actual human exposure to a mix of pollutants and the consequences of such exposure;
- Better integration of air, water, soil and waste management in a cross-media perspective;
- Continued innovation and investment in respect of clean technologies, product substitution and pollution abatement techniques;
- Incentives to decrease the use of private automobiles, in order to reduce emissions from one of the major man-made sources of atmospheric pollution;
- Better integration of air quality concerns in the sectoral policies (energy, transport, industry) affecting the air resource, with emphasis on the principle of pollution prevention and energy savings;
- More rigorous efforts to conserve energy in order to avert air pollution problems and potential global climatic changes.

NOTE AND REFERENCES

1. WHO ozone guidelines (1987):
   - in order to protect public health:
     1-hour O_3 average of 150-200 $\mu g/m^3$;
     8-hour O_3 average of 100-120 $\mu g/m^3$.
   - in order to protect vegetation:
     1-hour O_3 average of 200 $\mu g/m^3$;
     24-hour O_3 average of 65 $\mu g/m^3$;
     growing-season (May through September; 9 h-17 h) O_3 average of 60 $\mu g/m^3$.

OECD (1979), *Photochemical Oxidants and Their Precursors in the Atmosphere – Effects, Formation, Transport and Abatement*, Paris.

OECD (1983), *Control Technology for Nitrogen Oxide Emissions from Stationary Sources*, Paris.

OECD (1983), *Polycyclic Aromatic Compounds in the Air – Report of an Experts Meeting*, Paris.

OECD (1984), *Emission Standards for Major Air Pollutants from Energy Facilities in OECD Member Countries*, Paris.

OECD (1984), *Environment and Economics*, Background papers, Volume II, Paris.

OECD (1985), *Control of Toxic Substances in the Atmosphere – Benzene*, Paris.

OECD (1985), *Development of Photochemical Oxidant Control Strategies Within an Urban Airshed*, Paris.

Chapter 3

INLAND WATERS

Fresh water resources are of major environmental and biological importance because water is a basic life support system for man and ecosystems. They are also of key importance for agriculture, industry, hydro-electricity production, and navigation. The public is concerned with flooding, droughts and pollution of surface waters, and demands clean water, and water-related recreation and tourism. Rivers, lakes and aquifers are often shared by different countries and/or affected by pollution emitted in other countries. The provision of drinking water and the construction of dams or water treatment plants further imply international trade and aid. But rivers still receive and take to the sea significant treated and untreated loads of sewage, wastes and soiled storm waters. Sustainable development of the inland water resource is thus an essential goal to be achieved through wise and efficient management.

1. DEVELOPMENT OF WATER RESOURCES

Water quantity: use and trends

Information available for the 1970s suggests that during that period about 830 km³/year of fresh water was withdrawn by OECD countries from the surface and ground waters for subsequent use. Comparable estimates for the 1980s suggest that there has been a 10 per cent increase to over 900 km³. Throughout the period approximately 20 per cent of the total withdrawal was from ground water. When ground water is available it is often preferred as a source of drinking water.

The rate of per capita water withdrawal varies greatly across OECD countries. The United States population draws nearly 2 000 m³ per person annually from ground and surface water sources while the Swiss draw under 150 m³ per person. Throughout the 1970s and 1980s some OECD countries such as Belgium, Japan, Norway, Sweden, the United Kingdom, and the United States stabilised their per capita consumption. However, other countries such as Canada, New Zealand, France, western Germany, Portugal, and Spain experienced increases of 30 per cent or more. (Figure 12)

Because the water use profiles of OECD Member countries depend largely on climatic conditions and the needs of their agricultural and industrial communities, they vary widely. In the Nordic OECD countries, surface water is abundant; there are no massive water redistribution programmes; and hydroelectricity is an important source of energy. This contrasts with the more arid OECD countries such as Spain, Turkey, southern Australia, and the western United States, where water supply problems can be severe. Public works projects involving dams, weirs, and channels have been set up to divert and use water supplies for agriculture, hydroelectricity, public water supply, navigation, and controlled waste transport and disposal.

Ground water was once viewed as an abundant and pristine source of water and its use developed rapidly as technology permitted access to deeper aquifers. However, it has been demonstrated in several urban areas including Houston, Osaka, Tokyo, and Venice that massive groundwater withdrawal can lead to surface subsidence and necessitate costly remedial engineering.

Agricultural irrigation, electrical cooling and industrial processing represent the largest portion of the total amount of fresh water withdrawn for human uses. Regardless of the use, fresh water is often unavailable for re-use because of discharge into coastal waters or loss as water vapour. The larger the volume of use, the less renewable the resource is likely to be; hence it is

Figure 12. **WATER WITHDRAWAL**

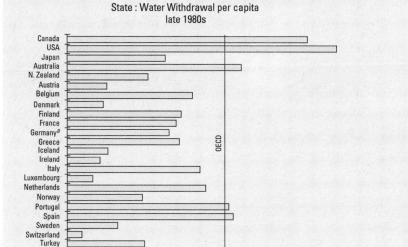

State : Water Withdrawal per capita
late 1980s

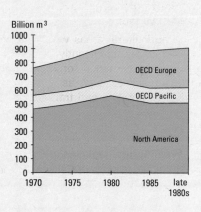

Trends: Total Water Withdrawal
1970 - late 1980s

Note: a) Includes western Germany only.

	Total Water Withdrawal million m³	Water Withdrawal by Major Uses *a*, late 1980s			
		Public Water Supply %	Irrigation %	Industry No Cooling %	Electrical Cooling %
Canada	43 888	11.3	7.1	9.1	55.6
USA *c*	467 000	10.8	40.5	7.4	38.8
Japan *b*	84 831	16.1	66.8	15.7	1.0
Finland	4 000	10.6	0.5	37.5	3.5
France *c*	43 273	13.7	9.7	10.4	51.9
Germany *d*	44 390	11.1	0.5	5.0	67.6
Italy *b*	56 200	14.2	57.3	14.2	12.5
Spain	45 845	11.6	65.5	22.9	..
Sweden	2 996	32.4	3.1	40.2	0.3
Turkey	29 600	12.8	79.1	9.8	..
UK *c,e*	13 221	48.6	0.3	10.8	18.8

Notes: a) The four sectors do not necessarily add up to 100%, since "other agricultural uses than irrigation", "industrial cooling", and "other uses" are not covered in this table.
b) 1980.
c) Industry includes industrial cooling.
d) Includes western Germany only.
e) Irrigation: total agricultural water withdrawal.

Source: OECD

among large-volume users that the largest opportunity for making gains towards use reduction and decreased loss of fresh water is to be found. (Figure 12)

Industrial water use has declined steadily in many OECD countries, including Japan, the United Kingdom, and the United States, as recycling programmes and technologies have made the use of water more efficient. Regulations that mandate removal of harmful contaminants prior to discharge have made in-plant recycling a cost-effective tool.

In agricultural areas where seasonal evaporation and other losses significantly exceed precipitation, there are sustained demands for fresh water. Conventional irrigation practices such as ditch inundation result in massive evaporative and transpiration losses of water, over-saturated soils, poor soil oxygenation, and salty residues. However, innovative agricultural irrigation practices have been developed over the last two decades to improve efficiency and reduce adverse side effects. Countries such as Canada, France, Portugal, and the United Kingdom are using more cost effective methods, such as spraying, that decrease water loss and, when properly managed, minimise the harmful side effects mentioned above.

Floods and droughts

A primary objective of all countries is to manage their water supply effectively. The focus is on short- and long-term planning to ensure that during normal conditions there is sufficient water to satisfy ecological, commercial, agricultural, and domestic needs. Often, however, the extremes of climate cause floods and droughts, impose hardship on people and create severe economic and public health consequences. A variety of new technology has been responsible for significant advances towards limiting the impact of flooding and drought.

Floods can ruin crops, contaminate water supplies, and destroy communities and their inhabitants. (Table 3) But floods also provide benefits; many

Table 3. MAJOR FLOODS AND RELATED LOSSES, OECD countries, 1975-1990

Date		Country	Type	Extent of damage		
				Number of deaths	Monetary damage	
					Million US$[a]	Type
1975	June	Japan	Landslide, flooding	> 30	..	—
1977	July	USA	Flooding	51	200.0	Property
	September	USA	Flooding	25	50.0	Property
	November	USA	Flooding	..	32.0	Insured
	..	USA	Dam	37	..	—
1978	May	Germany	Flooding	..	349.3	Total
	October	New Zealand	Flooding	..	25.9	Insured
1979	November	Greece, Yugoslavia	Flooding	22	..	..
1980	February	USA	Landslide, flooding	36	500.0	Property
1981	March	Yugoslavia	Heavy rain	70	..	..
	August	Australia	Flooding	..	229.9	Agriculture
	December	France	Flooding	..	165.6	Total
1982	January	USA	Landslide, flooding	..	39.9	Insured
	January	United Kingdom	Storm	..	174.8	Insured
	January	France	Storm	..	152.2	Total
	March	USA	Tornado	8	40.0	Total
	December	USA	Tornado	20	47.0	Insured
	December	USA	Storm	..	200.0	Total
1983	January	USA	Tornado	11	25.0	Insured
	Feb.-March	USA	Storm	..	66.0	Insured
	April-May	France	Storm	..	598.9	Total
	August	Spain	Heavy weather	42	223.0	Total
	October	USA	Flooding	10	100.0	Property
	November	Portugal	Flooding	12	..	..
	December	USA	Tornado	..	18.0	Insured

Table 3. **MAJOR FLOODS AND RELATED LOSSES, OECD countries, 1975-1990** *(Cont'd)*

Date		Country	Type	Extent of damage		
				Number of deaths	Monetary damage	
					Million US$[a]	Type
1984	January	New Zealand	Storm	. .	21.9	Insured
	April	USA	Tornado	. .	68.0	Insured
	May	USA	Tornado	. .	98.0	Insured
	May-June	USA	Heavy rain	> 10	93.6	Insured
	June	USA	Tornado	. .	277.0	Insured
	October	USA	Tornado	. .	75.0	Insured
	November	Australia	Landslide, flooding	15	. .	. .
1985	April	USA	Tornado	. .	55.0	Insured
	May	USA	Tornado	. .	79.8	Insured
	July	Italy	Dam	> 200	. .	. .
	November	USA	Heavy weather	> 42	. .	. .
1986	February	USA	Landslide, flooding	13	124.5	Insured
	March	New Zealand	Flooding	1	19.8	Insured
	May	USA	Tornado	. .	55.0	Insured
	June	Switzerland	Storm	. .	23.3	Insured
	September	USA	Flooding	6	25.0	Insured
	September	USA	Hail	. .	45.0	Insured
	October	USA	Flooding	. .	76.0	Insured
	October	USA	Flooding	. .	21.0	Insured
1987	Feb.-March	USA	Tornado	7	36.5	Insured
	July	Switzerland	Storm	2	34.7	Insured
	July	Canada	Flooding	1	174.0	Total
	July	Italy	Flooding	24	625.7	Insured
	August	USA	Storm	. .	40.0	Insured
	August	USA	Storm	. .	150.0	Insured
	August	USA	Storm	. .	35.0	Insured
	August	Japan	Flooding	24	123.4	Insured
	October	USA	Storm	. .	20.0	Insured
	November	USA	Storm	. .	63.0	Insured
1988	March	USA	Storm	. .	100.0	Insured
	April	USA	Storm	. .	60.0	Insured
	May	USA	Storm	. .	20.0	Insured
	October	France	Flooding	9	500.0	. .
1989	April	USA	Storm	. .	95.0	Insured
	April	Australia	Tornado	10	94.3	Insured
	April	USA	Storm	. .	95.0	Insured
	May	USA	Storm	> 21	380.0	Insured
	May	USA	Storm	2	120.0	Insured
	May	USA	Storm	. .	100.0	Insured
	June	USA	Storm	5	115.0	Insured
	July	USA	Storm	. .	92.0	Insured
	November	USA	Heavy weather	> 27	225.0	Insured
1990	January	United Kingdom	Storm	. .	540.0	Insured
	February	United Kingdom, Germany, France	Storm	. .	730.0	. .

Note: a/ Current value of currency and current exchange rates. Damages expressed in US$ refer to total damages (total), insured damages (insured), or property damages (property).
Sources: OECD, SIGMA, UNDRO

of the richest agricultural areas in the world owe their productivity to nutrient-laden, river-borne sediments deposited by seasonal overbank flooding. The tools used to control the effect of floods include advance warning networks that can predict an imminent rise in water levels and notify communities; systems of dams, channels and levees for containment; and development restrictions to ensure that building is limited or modified in floodplains. These options can entail sizable expenditures that must be weighed against the costs associated with floods, whose size and severity normally cannot be predicted.

Flood control cannot be developed without considering the indirect consequences of waterway modification. Dams are costly and, although they offer multiple uses (recreation, water supply, hydroelectricity and flood control), they can also create the need for effective watershed management. Levees are an alternative to development restrictions. However, levees not only prevent overbank flooding and ultimately foster agricultural enterprises that require nutrient supplements but also contribute to deterioration in water quality, restrict sediment input in subsiding wetlands systems,

and can lead to impoverished quality of riparian ecosystems. Effective dam safety legislation should be enforced to reduce environmental damage caused by failures.

Droughts also have devastating impacts that can leave localities without a domestic water supply and reduce agricultural production. Substantial technical developments in the last two decades have helped reduce the impact of drought conditions. First, a wide range of recycling and efficient-use technologies has been developed for industrial and agricultural application. Desalinisation plants applying advanced methods such as reverse osmosis have been used, for example, in the United States and Japan for conversion of saline ground water and sea water into drinking and irrigation water. Finally, deep ground water resources such as those in southern Australia have been developed. Large regional-scale water distribution networks route water into arid areas. Artificial recharge of aquifers is being used successfully in some areas, particularly in the Nordic countries. Wider application of these methods is still being studied, particularly in the Nordic and Northern European OECD countries.

2. QUALITY OF WATER RESOURCES

The ultimate water resource management objective is to conserve, improve and then maintain the quality of inland water bodies, so that fresh water resources will attain a level of quality that is appropriate for their use.

Domestic discharges

Domestic discharges, which often contain oxygen-consuming materials as well as nutrients, have created water quality problems for many years. Eutrophication is the term applied when water bodies are overenriched with nutrients. Nutrients may contribute to excessive growth of algae, microorganisms, small planktonic and benthic animals. As these organisms grow and die, their remains must be assimilated by the system as a whole. Oxygen-consuming decay commences and may reach the point where oxygen is consumed at a rate that cannot be met by natural processes. Anoxia – the absence of dissolved oxygen – develops in the fresh-water system and often kills fish and causes odour. In addition, the accumulation of organic material can foster the growth of pathogenic microorganisms.

Control of domestic discharges has long been recognised as a primary tool in the management of inland fresh water systems. As a result, in OECD countries the percentage of populations served by domestic waste-water treatment increased from 33 per cent in 1970 to 60 per cent in the late 1980s. There is, however, a wide

variation among countries (Figure 13 and Table 4). In the late 1970s and early 1980s existing plants were substantially improved, to provide more advanced treatment. Primary treatment, normally designed to remove suspended material, was often improved to secondary treatment designed to remove oxygen-consuming materials and, less frequently, nutrients through biological and chemical treatment. Countries such as Austria, Denmark, western Germany, Luxembourg, and Sweden have enhanced their primary treatment facilities with secondary treatment technology. As a result the percentage of their population served by primary treatment only has declined, while the percentage served by secondary treatment has risen. Canada, Norway, Portugal and Spain are building both primary and secondary treatment plants, with advanced "tertiary" treatment occasionally added. However, 330 million people in OECD countries are still not served by waste-water treatment plants.

In a number of OECD countries, progress in programmes to construct treatment plants receives considerable public attention and is identified with progress in water pollution control. This is only partly the case, however; once constructed, treatment plants must be properly operated and maintained. Otherwise, the benefits produced do not match the investments made. Various types of problems occur. The untreated waste-water may have such properties that the purification

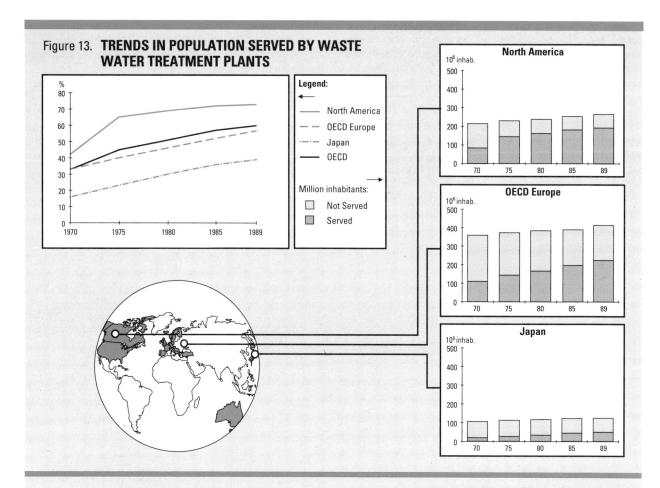

Figure 13. **TRENDS IN POPULATION SERVED BY WASTE WATER TREATMENT PLANTS**

	Total Population Served				Population Served by Type of Treatment (late 1980s) % of total population			
	1970	1980	1985	late 1980s	Primary Treatment	Secondary Treatment	Tertiary Treatment	Total
Canada	..	56	57	66	13	53	-	66
USA	42	70	74	..	15	59	-	74
Japan	16	30	36	39	..	..	..	39
N. Zealand	52	59	88	..	8	79	1	88
Austria	17	33	65	72	5	60	7	72
Denmark	54	80	91	98	8	78	12	98
Finland	27	65	72	75	-	10	65	75
France	19	43	50	52	..	..	..	52
Germany *a*	62	82	88	90	2	13	75	90
Italy	14	30	..	60	..	..	..	60
Luxembourg	28	81	83	..	14	69	-	83
Netherlands	..	72	85	89	7	47	35	89
Norway	21	34	43	43	6	25	12	43
Spain	..	18	29	48	6	41	1	48
Sweden	63	82	94	95	1	10	84	95
Switzerland	35	70	83	90	-	90	-	90
UK	..	82	83	84	6	53	25	84
North America	42	69	72	73	..	..	..	73
OECD Europe	33	46	52	57	..	..	..	57
OECD	33	51	57	60	..	..	..	60

Note: a) Includes western Germany only.

Source: OECD

process is greatly hindered; this can happen if the waste water is too diluted or too toxic, owing to the uncontrolled admission of industrial effluents to the sewage network. Treatment plants may be too complicated or sophisticated. This leads to large operating and maintenance costs which include a high consumption of energy and chemicals, or it may make excessive demands in terms of manpower. More broadly, inadequate maintenance or inappropriate operation will accentuate shortcomings or cause further ones; then even the best treatment plant will eventually break down.

Table 4. TRENDS IN PUBLIC WATER POLLUTION EXPENDITURES

	In % of total public pollution control expenditures			Per capita expenditures for water pollution control[a]		
	Mid 1970s	1980	Mid 1980s	Mid 1970s	1980	Mid 1980s
Canada	30	25	27	37	33	31
USA	75	74	73	53	57	54
Japan	59	68	49	54	98	60
Denmark	..	64	58	..	78	66
France	75	68	62	40	47	44
Germany[b]	..	69	64	..	85	71
Netherlands	..	48	51	..	44	59
Norway	..	88	54	..	93	48
Sweden	..	64	48	..	76	52
UK	54	..	61	41	..	39

Notes: a) In US$ per capita, at 1980 prices and exchange rates.
 b) Includes Western Germany only.
Source: OECD

One particular problem in the operation of sewage treatment plants is sludge disposal. Sewage sludge is produced in almost all purification processes. Sludge is frequently disposed of on land after dehydration, by using it as fertilizer for agricultural purposes or by processing it into compost or other useful products. In a number of OECD countries, however, the use of these methods of disposal is limited. Concentrations of toxic substances, particularly heavy metals, in the sludge may restrict its use for growing agricultural commodities for livestock feed or direct human consumption. Incineration or land disposal of the sludge may then be the only means of handling. Incineration is quite costly and the air emissions in turn can cause concern, while land disposal consumes large amounts of valuable landfill and potential farm land. Standard sewerage and waste treatment is ill-adapted to scattered habitat conditions. Significant progress is still required to control pollution from dispersed housing. (See Chapter on Land)

Industrial discharges

Although numerous industrial sectors in many OECD countries have decreased their consumption of raw water (e.g. iron and steel, agro-industry), the trends in the volume of contaminants they discharge are not well known. Industry is highly varied in the degree and nature of contamination problems. Some industrial plants, such as pulp and paper mills, produce organochlorine and oxidisable materials. Further, industry may produce contaminants that can have chronic or acute toxic effects even in small concentrations. These contaminants include a wide variety of metals and synthetic organic compounds. Certainly, efforts to concentrate pollutants by decreasing flow volumes and recycling process waters to stimulate and reduce consumption have had a positive influence on industrial wastewater discharges. However, as studies of acid and toxic precipitation have shown, industrial discharges can enter the water cycle in ways other than through effluent discharges.

Management of industrial discharges has often taken the form of requirements, guidelines, or permit systems that allocate to each discharger on a water body an allowable volume of pollution. Treatment systems are designed so that a sufficient amount of material is removed to meet the allocations. The relationship between industrial dischargers and municipal treatment works must be closely managed. Programmes that allow industrial dischargers to connect with domestic sewers can create problems because industrial discharges can contain a wide range of toxic compounds. If industrial wastes are allowed to discharge in an uncontrolled manner to municipal sewers, the waste will ultimately stress and possibly completely destroy the microbial-based systems used to treat domestic wastes. Then neither the industrial nor the municipal waste is effectively treated.

It has also become clear that simply limiting the amount of dissolved or suspended material discharged in industrial waste waters is not sufficient, because wastewater treatment produces, as a by-product, sludges of concentrated and often toxic contaminants. If these sludges are not disposed of properly, they can leach into the ground water or be absorbed into the food chain.

Diffuse discharges

A substantial portion of the pollutant loading can be attributed to diffuse sources. Examples of non-point sources include land run-off from cities and agricultural areas; infiltration from the surface into vulnerable aquifers — seepages from underground and surface mining operations — and wet and dry deposition into lakes and streams. The pathways of such discharges are difficult to control, and their management is fundamentally different from that of "point" sources of pollution.

It is difficult to monitor and assess the contribution of diffuse sources of contamination for two reasons: non-point sources of pollution often influence large areas and the bulk of the input often happens during brief storms. Agriculture has a special responsibility because of diffuse pollution from large-scale animal breeding and from intensive use of agro-chemicals such as fertilizers and pesticides.

Management initiatives have involved the routing of sewer and storm water overflows into treatment systems; however, this can greatly diminish treatment effectiveness. Farmers can be encouraged through information, pricing and regulatory instruments to use conservation practices: to restrict plantings and tillage in sensitive areas; to use natural vegetative filters to remove sediments from runoff waters; and to refrain from over-applying nutrients and pesticides.

State of surface waters

These domestic, industrial and diffuse discharges continue to place intense pressure on surface waters in OECD countries. The physical, chemical and biological parameters used to characterise water quality should ideally be evaluated in terms of water aptitude to sustain specific, desired water uses. In practice, the level of surface water pollution can be assessed with reference to three sets of criteria: those that influence the stream's oxygen regime (which permits fish and other aquatic life to survive); those that cause algal growth (eutrophication) in rivers, whether otherwise clean or not; and potentially toxic or dangerous substances, which often are referred to as "micropollutants".

The *oxygen regime* in OECD rivers has generally improved, but much remains to be done. The annual mean concentrations of biological oxygen-demanding substances at mouth or downstream frontier of rivers give a kind of summary balance of oxygen-demanding pollution minus depollution efforts in the upstream river basin (Figure 14). An improvement can be identified for many rivers, and this is confirmed by measures of dissolved oxygen. This largely reflects progress with wastewater treatment (Figure 13). National inventories of water quality supplement this summary view. For instance, in the Netherlands, from 1969 to 1988, river pollution by oxygen-consuming substances was reduced from the equivalent of the sewage of 40 million people to that of 6 million. In England and Wales, over 80 per cent of sewage receives secondary (biological, 80/90 per cent efficiency) treatment; river quality, which improved in the past, now stays constant at a generally acceptable level. In the United States, some overall improvement measured on NASQUAN stations reflects the efforts to reduce oxygen-demanding wastes from industries and municipal facilities. However, despite these improvements, many regional or local problems remain; in southwest France, for example, small streams must cope with excessive industrial effluents. In Italy, the unsatisfactory operation of existing sewage treatment systems, and heavy discharges from animal husbandry, create serious problems: the Po is reported to receive oxygen-consuming pollution equivalent to the sewage of 138 million people. In Japan, many sites still exist where the pollution level remains high; treatment capacity is relatively low and must follow urban development. Some pristine areas are also endangered by increased tourism.

The *algal growth* in surface waters is becoming a major problem in Member countries. The annual mean concentration of nitrates at mouth or downstream frontier of rivers is usually increasing, mainly as a reflection of pollution from agricultural origins such as animal manure and excess fertilisers (Figure 14). This general trend is confirmed by national inventories. In the Netherlands, many of the waters which are vulnerable to eutrophication show high content levels of nitrates, phosphorus and chlorophyl: this particularly affects the major lake districts in Friesland and Zuid-Holland. The flows of the rivers Meuse and Loire, in Belgium and France, are cut by dams and reservoirs; their quality can be two classes of quality lower than expected because of algal growth. In the United States, non-point sources of pollution account for over 80 per cent of the nitrogen and phosphorus reaching surface waters; nitrogen concentrations have increased in a large majority of stations. The Po river receives 250 000 tonnes per year of nitrogen, 60 per cent resulting from agricultural and zootechnical practice. In the United Kingdom, for nine out of 25 rivers sampled, mean nitrate concentrations in the period 1981-1985 were found to be higher than in any previous period, primarily in arable areas such as East Anglia. However, a few cases of improvement can be reported for phosphorus pollution. In Canada, phosphorus has decreased in the Great Lakes area, due to 20 years of joint efforts with the United States; the nitrate situation is not so clear, as fertilizers are now used on almost three times the previous farmland area. In Sweden, where the sewage treatment of phosphorus is high, some similar progress in phosphorus concentrations is reported in many rivers over the period 1971-1985. None of the same rivers experienced decreased nitrate levels.

As regards *metals and toxic substances*, some progress can be reported in the case of lead: concentrations near mouths of rivers in Canada, Japan, Belgium, western Germany and the United Kingdom are decreasing over the period 1970-1985; while the US network of monitoring stations reported very few increases and many decreases in lead concentrations over a similar period. Trends in other metals and toxic substances are less encouraging, despite efforts to reduce discharges. Although some localised decreases of substances can be reported, no general progress in concentrations appears to have taken place on available evidence; such substances often are persistent, accumulate into bottom sediments and can be released over long periods of time once initially deposited. A rapid 50 per cent reduction of remaining discharges of toxic substances into the Rhine water basin is the main objective

Figure 14. **WATER QUALITY OF SELECTED RIVERS, 1970, 1975, 1980, late 1980s**

Biological Oxygen Demand (BOD)

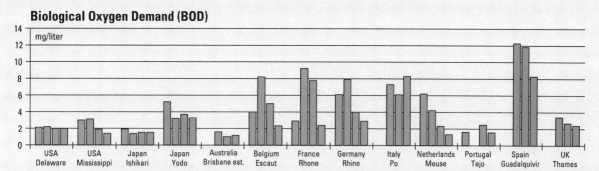

Nitrate Concentration

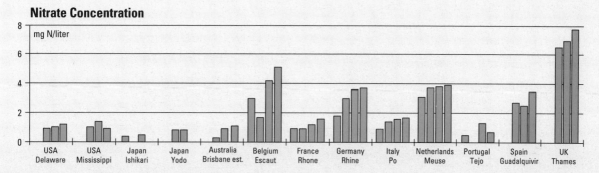

Note: Measured at mouth or downstream frontier of rivers.

		Biological Oxygen Demand (BOD) (mg/liter)			Nitrate (mgN/liter)		
		1970	Late 1980s	Average last 3 years available	1970	Late 1980s	Average last 3 years available
USA	Delaware	2.1	2.0	2.1	..	1.20	1.12
	Mississippi	3.0	1.4	1.5	..	0.90	1.10
Japan	Ishikari	1.9	1.5	1.3	0.36	..	..
	Yodo	5.2	3.3	3.5	..	..	..
Australia	Brisbane est.	..	1.2	..	..	1.05	..
Belgium	Escaut-Doel	4.0	2.3	2.7	3.00	5.06	4.98
Denmark	Gudenaa	..	3.5	3.0	..	1.25	1.39
Finland	Tornionjoki	3.0	2.6	2.8	..	0.47	..
France	Loire	6.7	6.4	6.9	1.58	2.53	2.56
	Rhone	2.9	2.4	4.4	0.88	1.38	1.82
Germany	Rhine	6.1	2.9	3.1	1.82	3.70	3.77
	Donau	4.8	2.5	2.5	0.20	0.50	1.53
Italy	Po	..	8.3	7.2	0.95	1.68	2.34
Netherlands	Meuse	6.2	1.3	1.5	3.07	3.86	4.08
	Ijssel-Kampen	5.7	..	..	2.76	4.33	..
Norway	Skienselva	..	..	..	..	0.20	0.25
Portugal	Tejo	1.6	1.5	1.7	0.52	0.67	0.97
Spain	Guadalquivir	..	8.3	9.2	..	3.47	3.34
Switzerland	Rhine	..	..	..	..	1.76	1.70
Turkey	Porsuk	..	1.2	1.4	..	1.28	1.36
UK	Thames	..	2.4	2.5	..	7.67	7.07
	Mersey	..	5.9	5.1	..	2.86	2.82
Yugoslavia	Dunau	4.3	3.5	4.1	..	2.42	2.21

Source: OECD

GROUNDWATER CONTAMINATION AND MANAGEMENT IN PRINCE EDWARD ISLAND (CANADA)

Prince Edward Island, Canada's smallest province, is located in the Gulf of St. Lawrence off the country's Atlantic coast. Surface water resources are limited and the productive aquifer underlying the province provides the only natural water storage reservoir. Since the province's 125 000 residents depend on groundwater for practically all of their water needs, it is imperative that this vital but vulnerable resource be properly managed and protected from contamination.

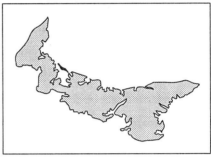

Groundwater Contamination

The principal threats to groundwater result from the main socio-economic activities in the province:

- Agriculture and food processing: of all Canadian provinces, Prince Edward Island has the highest percentage of land devoted to agriculture and grows 23 per cent of the country's potatoes; pesticides and nitrates are the main concerns;
- Transport: contamination by roadsalt and by leaks or spills from underground tanks storing fuels used for transport purposes;
- Residential facilities: leaking septic systems, leaks and spills from home heating-fuel tanks, and saltwater intrusion into groundwater caused by residential (cottage) development along the seaside.

Recent monitoring of groundwater has identified contaminants in several wells in Prince Edward Island. In agricultural regions nitrate concentrations as high as 22 milligrams per litre (mg/l) have been found in observation wells in potato fields. About 2 per cent of all sampled well water contained nitrate levels above 10 mg/l, the value of the Canadian drinking water guideline. A number of agricultural pesticides have also been detected. Aldicarb, a chemical until recently widely used on potatoes, has been found in concentrations up to 16.4 micrograms per litre in observation wells in potato fields, a level distinctly above the drinking water guideline of 9 micrograms per litre. Traces of other pesticides such as metribuzin, phorate, disulfoton, and atrazine were also found in some private and municipal wells.

Between 1977 and 1987, 330 spills from petroleum storage tanks were reported; 102 of these resulted in wellwater contamination. Similarly, the provincial Department of the Environment investigates between 10 and 20 reports of bacterial contamination from sewage systems annually. The likelihood of contamination increases when the wells or the sewage disposal systems have been poorly constructed or when the density of sewage disposal systems is high, a situation more common in cottage areas. On average about four cases of well contamination from road salt are reported every year. Leaching from salt storage piles and heavy salt application on roads are the principal causes of this form of contamination.

An Integrated Strategy for Groundwater Protection

The discovery of contaminants in groundwater has heightened concern about the quality of the resource. Provincial and local authorities have responded with a comprehensive approach to groundwater management which treats groundwater protection as part and parcel of an overall strategy to manage water resources and the pressures imposed on them.

Environmental impact assessment is a key instrument of a preventive approach to groundwater protection. Proponents of development projects are required by law to obtain written approval from the Environment Department prior to proceeding with a project. The Department will determine if an assessment is warranted and can, ultimately, deny permission to proceed or impose specific mitigation procedures. Land-use planning is another component of the strategy. Provisions of the provincial Planning Act require development permits for all construction. Sewage facilities, petroleum storage tanks and all other facilities that pose a threat to groundwater may be diverted away from areas which have been identified as particularly sensitive to contamination. Storage of hazardous wastes, including materials such as dry cleaning solvents, is prohibited on the province's territory.

Other preventive measures include restrictions placed on some agricultural chemicals - use of the pesticide aldicarb was banned in 1989 - and public information and education programmes are provided on request by the Environment Department.

Enhanced monitoring of groundwater quality is expected to facilitate evaluation of the adequacy of these measures and provide early warning of any new contamination problems.

Contribution from Canada

of the Rhine Action Programme. In 1985, France, western Germany, Luxembourg, the Netherlands and Switzerland still discharged 56 tonnes of chloronitrobenzene, 24 tonnes of cadmium, 500 tonnes of copper and 37 tonnes of chloroanilines. The Rhine carried up to 40 kg per day of the pesticide atrazine in 1989. In Sweden, the discharges of toxic metals were reduced from 1 300 tonnes to 55 tonnes per year between 1972 and 1985; 40 tonnes per year of chrome were still being discharged, however. In Italy, much chrome is found in rivers downstream of tanneries. The rivers flowing into the North Sea from western Germany, the Netherlands or the United Kingdom carry several thousand tonnes of heavy metals and arsenic into it yearly; however, it is reported that the stream concentrations are not generally such as to hinder water uses or harm aquatic life. In 1985, French discharges have come down from 86 to 44 national toxicity units. In the United States, 160 000 industrial and commercial facilities discharge wastes containing hazardous constituents into publicly owned treatment facilities. In Japan, very significant progress has been made in fighting toxic pollution: the number of "bad" samples came down from 564 out of 89 074 (0.63 per cent) in 1971 to 32 out of 142 796 (0.03 per cent) in 1987.

The impact of *accidental pollution* on clean rivers has put water management in the news. Also, in several Member countries a succession of rather dry years has caused an increase in the effects of pollution during low-flow periods. This has been reflected in improved public consciousness of the value of water quality.

Primary concerns in *lake ecosystems* are increasing bottom water anoxia and acidification. Lacustrine eutrophication and seasonal warming and mixing contribute to oxygen deficits. Low oxygen levels encourage less diverse and less productive bottom communities. Fish populations experience increased stress, decreased food supply, behavioural changes, and poorer reproduction. Similarly, some lake ecosystems have been restructured and in some cases decimated by acidification. In some OECD countries, such as Sweden, 16 000 lakes have been acidified to the extent that sensitive organisms have disappeared; expensive liming programs are regularly employed, based on the degree of acidification. An emerging problem is so-called "toxic rain" and the related deposition of toxic substances on land and aquatic ecosystems.

State of ground water

At the beginning of the 1970s it was widely assumed that ground water in many areas offered a sustainable and pristine supply of fresh water. Thinking has changed over the last 20 years. Uncontrolled releases to underground waters caused by activities such as agriculture, timber production, waste disposal, domestic sewage treatment, and industrial storage and waste containment have in numerous cases caused both localised and widespread deterioration of ground water quality.

Deep sources of ground water are often protected by overlying impermeable layers. Sometimes the deep aquifers are not potable because of a high level of dissolved salts. However, when deep aquifers are usable, they can be overexploited; in some circumstances they are at risk of being contaminated. Where the water table is near the surface, ground water is the least expensive to access, but is often directly subject to and affected by these perturbations.

Ground water can be highly vulnerable and negatively affected when located in areas where agriculture is practised. Fertilizers and pesticides, common to commercial agriculture, are applied in large quantities, sometimes in such a way that they affect ground waters. Many countries, in particular the United States, Denmark, France and the Netherlands, have now documented widespread and substantial increases in ground water nitrate concentrations. Ground water contamination by pesticides is also of concern, particularly because the mobility of modern, less permanent herbicides has considerably increased. For example, on Long Island, in the eastern United States, there is widespread and significant contamination of ground water by a herbicide that was applied to golf courses. In addition, withdrawal of large amounts of water for irrigation can alter subsurface water flows and cause the introduction of saline water into freshwater aquifers. (See Chapter on Agriculture)

Inappropriate disposal of wastes, both hazardous and domestic, has repeatedly been found responsible for the deterioration of local ground water supplies. Wastes have been disposed of in areas where surface sediments are permeable and interconnected with aquifers. Disposal in waste piles and landfills without modern containment and engineering has resulted in ground water plumes of organic substances and metal contamination. Volatile organic compounds such as trichloroethylene and chloroform are particularly mobile and have caused substantial concern in many countries, notably the United States, Japan, western Germany, and Italy. (See Chapter on Solid Waste)

Failures of industrial storage devices have been responsible for contaminating drinking water supplies. One reason is that storage tanks, particularly those used for petroleum products and for storage of automobile, aviation, farm, and industrial applications, are often old and below ground. These tanks cannot be visually inspected and often are not checked routinely for small changes in inventory status. The result is that leakage problems are not identified early, when they are small.

REDUCING LEAD IN DRINKING WATER (UNITED STATES)

Lead: A Multi-media Pollutant

Lead is a metal with many commercial applications. It is used for the conveyance of water, and also in gasoline, paint, automobile batteries, glass and crystal, pencils, plastic pipes, pesticides, newsprint, and cable sheathing, and as a fruit growth regulator.

Lead contamination of the environment is a serious problem in both developed and developing countries and is of particular concern to human health. Exposure to high levels of lead can damage the brain, kidneys, nervous system and the blood-forming process. Children and fetuses are most susceptible to lead's health effects.

Efforts in the United States over the past 10 to 15 years to reduce exposure to lead from all sources have been quite successful. Restrictions on lead in gasoline and the virtual phase-out of lead-soldered food cans have reduced average blood lead levels in children by approximately two-thirds in that time period.

Reducing lead in drinking water is a current focus for the United States Environmental Protection Agency (EPA) control efforts, coinciding with evidence that lead's adverse health effects occur at lower exposure levels than previously thought -- indeed, at levels previously considered "safe".

How Lead Contaminates Drinking Water

Lead most often contaminates drinking water after the water has left the water treatment plant. It results from the corrosive action of the water upon the materials of the plumbing system. In the United States, the lead solder which is used to join copper pipes in household plumbing is probably the single greatest contributor to lead contamination of drinking water, but lead pipes and many brass and bronze fixtures also contribute to the problem. Consequently, lead levels are generally much higher at residential taps than in the water distribution system.

Reducing Exposure to Lead in Drinking Water

Because lead occurs primarily as a by-product of corrosion, the preferred method of treatment is to make the drinking water less corrosive. This generally involves reducing its acidity or adding bicarbonate or chemical corrosion inhibitors.

Many other actions are under way to reduce exposure to lead in drinking water. In 1986 materials containing lead were banned from use in public water supplies and in residences connected to them. More recently, the Lead

ANNUAL COSTS AND BENEFITS

Estimated population at risk

42 million persons

Estimated annual benefits

Children's health benefits	$ 200 million
Adult health service	300 million
Benefits of avoided corrosion damage	500 million
Total annual benefits	$ 1.0 billion

Estimated annual costs

Annual capital & operating costs	$ 250 million

Contamination Control Act was passed to address lead contamination of school drinking water and, in particular, the risks associated with water coolers that may contain lead. In addition, in 1988 EPA proposed that the current limit of 50 parts per billion (ppb) for lead in drinking water be reduced to 5 ppb for lead in water leaving the treatment plant, and to 10 ppb for tap water.

Costs and Benefits of Reducing Lead in Drinking Water

In 1986, EPA estimated the total annual economic and health benefits of reducing lead in drinking water to be about US $1 billion. Of this total, US $500 million can be economised simply by making water less corrosive and thus less damaging to the United States water supply systems.

The corresponding annual capital and operating costs of the control programme were estimated at about US $250 million. Thus the benefits of reducing lead in drinking water are four times greater than the costs.

Contribution from the United States

3. DRINKING WATER

Sources and structure of distribution systems

The sources of drinking water vary widely between OECD countries. In the past and notably in the early 1970s there was a preference for acquiring most domestic-use water from below-ground sources. However, Canada, Japan, Norway, Spain, Sweden and the United Kingdom obtain a substantial proportion of their domestic-use water from surface water supplies. Ground waters are in limited supply and overexploitation has resulted in permanent loss of aquifer capacity in some areas. Supply management strategies that utilise ground water as a source to mix with surface waters offer one means of sustaining the ground water supply.

In many OECD countries community water systems are not large; they serve small rural communities and distribute ground water that requires limited or no treatment. The suppliers are often private enterprises, but may also be publicly operated. Often only a small percentage of the total population is served by large treatment works; these are normally in large urban areas, are publicly operated or regulated, and their volume requirements demand the use of surface waters.

Water suppliers that rely on surface water must confront large capital, operating, and maintenance expenditures. First, advanced treatment devices must be installed and operated for producing and delivering safe water. Then monitoring of the source waters must ensure that there is no significant contamination problem. Ageing water system distribution infrastructures in older metropolitan areas pose health problems because of the presence of older leaded piping and reduced flow areas which promote the growth of microbial contaminant. Older systems also lose efficiency because of leakage from their piping systems. This inefficiency and the cost of rebuilding pose major funding problems for many cities.

It is clear that such costs have to be reflected in water pricing and water-facility financing mechanisms. (See Chapter on Economic Responses)

Contaminants

The most obvious drinking water problems are the easiest to control. Poor taste, odour, colour, suspended materials, and bacterial and viral contamination were often responsible for the permanent or temporary quarantine of entire drinking water systems. Many OECD countries have demonstrated that successful implementation of proper controls can reduce these problems so that they become of limited concern.

Metals, nutrients and synthetic organic compounds in raw waters continue to pose a subtle and substantial threat. Contaminants found in drinking water as a result of low quality raw waters include impure treatment reagents — by-products formed during purification using chlorine, chlorine dioxide, and water softeners — and asbestos, metals, and organics from piping. These contaminants are not visually apparent to the consumer, but can have long-term chronic health implications.

4. WATER MANAGEMENT

Integration of water quality and water quantity management

Water quality management frequently emphasizes the purification of wastewater discharges and of raw water prior to use; less attention is given to other methods of improving water quality. Water quantity management by such means as damming, transport or withdrawal of surface waters is sometimes applied without considering the effects these measures have on the quality of water. There is, however, a strong relationship between water quality and water quantity management. The use of ground waters and surface waters depends not only on the quantity of water but also on its quality. Measures to ensure water availability should therefore take into account both the quality and the quantity of the water. This applies, for example, to the construction of drinking water reservoirs or irrigation systems and also to the artificial infiltration of surface waters into ground waters to replenish supplies. Moreover, the dilution and mixing of water resources can have considerable consequences on water quality.

How can quantity determine or modify quality? For instance, artificial increases or reductions in water flows caused by canalisation or damming will affect the concentrations of pollutants and therefore limit downstream uses. The damming of semi-stagnant waters may increase the chances that symptoms of eutrophication will appear in those waters. The withdrawal of fresh ground water may lead to the infiltration of neighbouring saline waters. The quantitative relationship between water quality and quantity must be thoroughly evaluated prior to a management decision. In the Netherlands, for instance, fresh water is not let into polder regions when its quality is below a certain level.

RESTORING THE MERSEY BASIN (ENGLAND)

The Basin of the Industrial Revolution

The Mersey river system was the natural resource which enabled the Industrial Revolution to take place. The Basin can be sub-divided geographically into three distinct sections: the estuary, the mid and southern catchment and the upper catchment areas. Because of its history of industrialisation and low investment in pollution control, the basin has long suffered from water quality degradation.

Severe Water Pollution

In the estuary, most of the 320 kilometres of rivers are in the "poor" or "bad" categories of water quality. This is due to a combination of three factors: a very high pollutant load, an exceptionally inadequate inheritance of sewerage, sewage disposal and treatment systems, and the configuration of the estuary with its wide, shallow basin leading to a narrow outlet, which restricts water renewal. Marked improvements in water quality will be achieved when the 56 million ECU Sandon Dock sewage treatment plant is completed.

In the mid and southern catchment region, water quality is especially affected downstream from the town of Warrington. Typical problems are structurally unsound sewers and flooding and pollution of watercourses - all concentrated in a relatively small area.

In the upper catchment region is found the greatest concentration of problems in the entire Mersey Basin. The Greater Manchester area is particularly affected, due to woefully inadequate investment in the past. Much of the sewerage system was constructed in the last century when the towns developed from villages. As the towns grew rapidly, the sewerage systems were extended piecemeal with crude overflows to water courses. The result today is large stretches of polluted rivers.

Addressing the Challenge of Renewal

Due to the extent of the pollution, regeneration of the Mersey Basin is a great challenge. It is being addressed through the Mersey Basin Campaign, an integrated programme which aims to improve water quality and to develop the land alongside. The Campaign has both short-term and long-term goals. In the short term (by 1995), it aims to prevent further deterioration in river water quality and to reduce and, as far as possible, eliminate any pollution of the rivers that constitutes a gross nuisance. In the long term (by the year 2010), the Campaign aims to restore the worst parts of the river system to "Fair" condition, and to put some of the existing "Fair" waters into the "Good" classification.

These goals are to be achieved through a massive programme to renew and improve sewers and to upgrade sewage treatment works. Already, a programme calling for 505 new sewerage and sewage treatment projects and begun in 1984, costing 560 million ECU, is well advanced. On the landward side imaginative schemes for waterside development are being implemented with waterfronts as focal points.

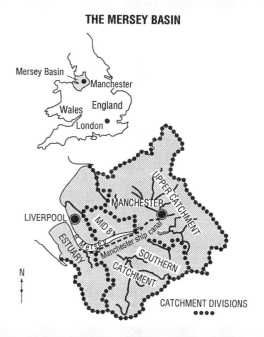

THE MERSEY BASIN

CATCHMENT DIVISIONS

Encouraging Multi-Sectoral Participation

Consultation and participation are important features of the Mersey Basin Campaign. While the responsibility for large scale initiatives rests with North West Water Ltd., water quality standards are being set and monitored by the National Rivers Authority, established in September 1989. Participation by individuals, voluntary groups and private sector bodies is being actively encouraged. For example, a Voluntary Sector Network has been created to co-ordinate the many activities of voluntary bodies throughout the Mersey Basin participating in the Campaign.

Substantial private sector investment has already been attracted to fund outstanding examples of waterside regeneration such as Salford Quays in Manchester and the Albert Dock in Liverpool. The Campaign organisation, which consists of over 30 local authorities and 3 Urban Development Corporations, is promoting furthur private investment to develop the many opportunities which exist throughout the Basin.

The European Community (EC) is also involved. The Mersey Basin programme became one of the earliest of the EC's European Regional Development Fund programmes for the period 1984-1987, with grant aid of 92.3 million ECU to assist water quality and land-based projects. A second-phase Mersey Basin programme has now been approved for further financing by European Community grants.

Contribution from the United Kingdom

POLLUTION AND RECLAMATION OF LAKE ORTA

Lake Orta is the seventh largest in volume of the Italian lakes, with a water mass of 1300 million m^3, a surface area of 18.2 km^2 and a maximum depth of 143 metres. It is situated south of the north-western Alps in an area of great natural beauty, and should be a valuable reserve of freshwater with biological characteristics similar to those of other Italian sub-alpine lakes.

The Pollution of Lake Orta

In 1926, waste water heavily contaminated with copper and ammonium sulphate began to be discharged into the lake from a factory (Bemberg) producing artificial silk. Pollution eventually reached a level which rendered Lake Orta un-inhabitable for most forms of aquatic life: in a few years the zooplankton disappeared completely, while fish populations were drastically reduced.

The situation deteriorated even further during the following decades when additional pollution sources began discharging into the lake, particularly factories involved in cleaning and chrome-plating taps and bathroom accessories.

In 1958 the Bemberg factory installed a recovery plant which resulted in its copper load to the lake being significantly reduced. In the meantime, however, the factory continued to discharge ammonium sulphate, while the bathroom accessory factories on the western shore generated a sharp increase in the loads of copper, zinc and chrome reaching the lake. During this period, ammonium and nitrate continued to accumulate in the lake and the acidity of the water was becoming progressively higher.

Recovery Interventions

In the early 1980s, the Bemberg factory installed a treatment plant which reduced by over 99 per cent the amount of ammonium reaching the lake; it declined from a maximum of 3000 tonnes per year to about 27 tonnes per year. During the same period there was also a partial treatment of the waters coming from the urban and industrial areas in the south-western part of the watershed.

These measures led to a significant decrease in loadings to the lake of ammonium and copper, but the situation remained extremely serious due to the acidity of the water (for the last ten years the pH has ranged between 4.0 and 4.5) and because the lake's content of ammonium and toxic metals was still too high.

Furthermore, it was possible, on the basis of a predictive model, to estimate that a complete and successful recovery would take a very long time: a minimum of 15 to 20 years in the absence of any pollution.

Restoring pH Balance Through Liming

The authorities concerned put forward a "Plan for a Direct Recovery Operation" to be performed through liming. This is being done by spreading over the surface of the lake a semi-liquid suspension of calcium carbonate in successive

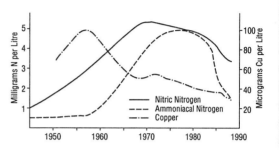

TRENDS IN CONTAMINANT CONCENTRATION

lots, up to a total input of about 23,000 tonnes. The lime used is of natural origin, free from clays, and has a very low metal content.

The operation, begun in May 1989, involves the entire volume of the lake, with an addition of calcium carbonate equal to 18 grams per cubic metre. In this way the definitive recovery process will be set in motion, with the gradual achievement of the following benefits:

-   The water will be neutralized and the alkaline reserve reconstituted; there will be an immediate effect as regards bathing, which, forbidden since 1986, will be allowed again;

-   The nitrification rate of ammoniacal nitrogen will increase, leading to its complete removal and thus eliminating the primary cause of acidification in the lake;

-   Heavy metals in the lake will undergo a partial but significant decrease in their solubility, with a subsequent sharp decline in their toxicity, particularly for copper and aluminum;

-   A richer and more balanced biological community will be reconstituted, leading to the normal development, reproduction and survival of the fish population in a restored environment.

Lake Orta's recovery will restore important ecological, aesthetic and economic benefits to the region. The curative measures taken to address pollution in the lake will also act as preventive measures for the future.

Contribution from Italy

Interaction among inland waters, oceans, land and air

Water resources can be divided into ground, inland surface, near coastal, open ocean, and atmospheric waters. In the past these resources have been managed separately. The need to manage all water resources collectively is becoming increasingly apparent.

Ground waters and surface waters may influence each other: surface waters may infiltrate through the soil and recharge ground waters, while ground waters may eventually discharge as springs and seeps to surface waters. These exchanges may occur naturally. They may also be induced by human intervention, for instance by artificial replenishing of ground water supplies, by construction of drainage systems or by surface water withdrawal. The ecological function of the soil in general may also be affected; areas of particular ecological value, such as freshwater wetlands, are frequently damaged by careless ground water or surface water management.

Similarly, the relationship between inland waters and the marine environment is important. Much of the surface water eventually reaches the sea, leading to an accumulation of pollutants attached to silt and clay particles. In estuaries, which are frequently of great biological importance, this may have unfavourable consequences even in the short term. Long-term effects may also be expected in coastal waters and the sea. Sludge deposited in brackish waters causes a specific pollution problem: when this sludge and other contaminated spoil has to be dredged for navigational purposes, safe disposal is often difficult.

Finally, atmospheric influences on surface and even ground waters can be substantial. However, the relationship between air and water is often ignored in the management of the water cycle. Air emissions are scrubbed by treatment devices to some degree; the resulting waste water is only partly treated to remove contaminants and then discharged. Acid and toxic rain may also lead to the acidification and pollution of lakes and ground water.

Integration of environmental concerns into economic sectors

It is often better technically and economically to prevent water pollution rather than curb pollution in treatment plants. This means that production processes in sectors such as agriculture, industry and energy have to be designed to minimise pollution. This can be accomplished in several ways: by using fewer or even different inputs; by minimising the loss of raw materials in producing the end product; and by ensuring that pollutants in the wastewater flow are concentrated as much as possible. Treatment may then be relatively easy. The pace of progress made in this area in OECD countries in recent years has been determined by the capacity of investment.

Industry and agriculture in many OECD countries have started more extensive application of ingenious approaches for preventing the introduction of contaminants into waste streams. Initiatives have involved searching for alternative agricultural practices that eliminate or reduce the need for fertilizers and pesticides, new raw materials that serve the same purpose, and processes that generate less noxious byproducts.

Appropriate pricing is a key tool for water management. Among existing water rate structures in use in Member countries, some lead to economy, some to waste. In general, however, water is still an underpriced natural resource. Accurate pricing could make a major contribution to achieving environmentally sound water use.

5. CONCLUSIONS

Several of the biggest environmental water problems already identified in 1970 in OECD countries were mastered during the last two decades. However, new problems have cropped up and the equipment resulting from early investments is aging rapidly. While most environmental expenditure is concentrated on water, the situation is not improving as fast as was hoped. A more integrated approach to water management is required.

Progress

During the 1970s and 1980s the OECD countries continued to invest in water projects, and to develop legislation and institutions for the improved management of water systems. As a result, a number of problems were overcome:

- The percentage of population served by wastewater treatment has increased widely, and localised progress has been made in the treatment of permanent industrial effluents; consequently the pollution of waterways and lakes by organic substances has been reduced;

- Significant pathogenic microbial contamination of drinking water supplies has been virtually eliminated.

Remaining problems

- The *risks* relating to floods, droughts and accidental pollution remain a threat to the sustainable development of economic activities such as agriculture, and to the continuity of water provision to households;
- *Primary treatment of wastewater* has yet to be provided to 330 million people in OECD countries, particularly in southern Europe, and in Japan;
- *Pollution of ground waters*; once perceived as invulnerable to contamination, and a precious reserve of clean water, ground waters have deteriorated because of local and diffuse pollution sources, such as urban runoff, the nitrogenous fertilizers and pesticides used in agriculture, and seepages from abandoned, contaminated industrial sites;
- Nitrate pollution of *waterways* is increasing; river sediments have accumulated a backlog of pollution by heavy metals and synthetic organic compounds;
- *Lake* eutrophication and associated oxygen deficits as well as lake acidification from atmospheric deposition lead to adverse ecological consequences;
- *Drinking water* delivered at the tap may suffer from the introduction of contaminants in the course of treatment of low-quality raw waters and in the course of its distribution;
- Deteriorating *infrastructures* and inadequate secondary containment make industrial accidents more and more likely and hence more and more of a major threat to inland waters.

Water management

Because of these problems, better management of water resources is needed; it will require time, determination and money. Aims include:

- Stricter enforcement of existing regulations;
- Continued investment in the management of the quantity and quality of the resource, and in the replacement or renovation of deteriorating infrastructures and obsolete processes and equipment;
- Adequate pricing of water resources, reflecting the "polluter pays principle" and concern with long-term sustainable development of the resource;
- Management of natural waters (rivers, lakes) as ecosystems, with ecosystemic objectives and constraints incorporated in strategies;
- Closer integration of air, water, soil and coastal area management in a cross-media perspective, with reference, for instance, to acidification of water bodies and sludge disposal;
- Closer integration of water-related concerns in the sectoral policies (agriculture, energy, industry) affecting water resources, with emphasis on the principles of multiple use and prevention;
- Fuller knowledge of diffuse and local pollution effects and of drinking-water quality at the tap, as well as better monitoring of water reserves, and water resource accounts.

REFERENCES

OECD (1977), *Water Management Policies and Instruments*, Paris.

OECD (1980), *Water Management in Industrialised River Basins*, Paris.

OECD (1982), *Eutrophication of Waters: Monitoring Assessment and Control*, Paris.

OECD (1983), *Control Policies for Specific Water Pollutants*, Paris.

OECD (1985), *Management of Water Projects. Decision-Making and Investment Appraisal*, Paris.

OECD (1986), *Water Pollution from Fertilizers and Pesticides*, Paris.

OECD (1987), *Pricing of Water Services*, Paris.

OECD (1989), *Renewable Natural Resources. Economic Incentives for Improved Management*, Paris.

OECD (1989), *Water Resources Management. Integrated Policies*, Paris.

Chapter 4

MARINE ENVIRONMENT

The marine environment is an essential part of the global biosphere. The oceans cover almost three-fourths of the earth's surface, contain over 90 per cent of the world's water resources, and are home to many forms of life.

Primary productivity in the seas is significant: oceanic production of plant material is roughly equal to the annual growth of land plants, providing an important link in the nitrogen, oxygen, hydrogen and carbon cycles. The constant interaction between the atmosphere and the marine environment influences complex patterns of global weather, which in turn influence the hydrological cycle. The oceans' role as a global regulator is particularly evident in their capacity to absorb carbon dioxide, a factor important in establishing global temperatures.

The many features and resources of the seas have been extensively used and exploited by humans. The sheer vastness of the seas has encouraged their use for waste disposal. The aesthetic beauty of the marine environment supports a large tourism industry and many recreational activities in coastal areas. Resources such as fisheries have been exploited for centuries, providing food and economic benefits to many. The marine environment is also used extensively for the transport of goods, and as a source of non-renewable resources like petroleum and minerals.

Many of these uses are in potential conflict. Thus, how the oceans are used, and by whom, are questions of increasing importance. The oceans have almost always played a strategic role in defining relationships among nations, and new and complex issues continue to emerge. For example, fishing and navigational rights, environmental accidents, coastal pollution and waste transport at sea rank high on both national and international agendas.

This chapter reviews these issues by focusing on the relationship between human activities and the state of the marine environment. Individual sections review pressures on the marine environment, the state of the marine environment in five regional areas, and the sustainable use of living marine resources: fisheries and aquaculture.

1. PRESSURES ON THE MARINE ENVIRONMENT

Many natural factors – for example, nutrient upwelling and subsequent biological productivity – influence conditions in the oceans. In addition, the marine environment is exposed to numerous anthropogenic pressures from diverse human activities. These pressures may result in adverse changes to marine ecosystems and their resources, often having consequences for human health and economic development. (Table 5)

Waste inputs to the oceans

For many wastes the oceans are the ultimate sink. These wastes can reach the seas through various channels. Some materials are discharged directly or are transported from distant regions by rivers and the atmosphere. Overall, land-based sources are responsible for the bulk of the wastes entering the oceans, chiefly in the form of sewage, industrial discharges, and agricultural runoff. Other sources include ocean dumping, offshore energy production, and ocean shipping.

Many wastes originating from land-based sources are deposited in the coastal zone, often in or near sensitive and productive marine areas. Rivers, for example, funnel pollutants from distant sources upstream and deposit them in productive estuaries.

Table 5. PRESSURES ON THE MARINE ENVIRONMENT

Pressure	Substance or activity involved	Major anthropogenic sources	Potential effects
Waste inputs to the oceans	Nutrients	Sewage; agriculture; aquaculture; industry	Eutrophisation
	Pathogens	Sewage; agriculture	Disease and infection; shellfish contamination
	Oil	Industry; sewage; shipping; automobiles; urban runoff	Oiling of birds and animals; seafood tainting; beach contamination
	Synthetic organic compounds	Industry; sewage; agriculture; forestry	Metabolic dysfunction
	Radioactive wastes	Nuclear weapon tests, nuclear fuel reprocessing; ocean dumping nuclear generating station accidents	Metabolic dysfunction
	Trace metals	Industry; sewage; ocean dumping; automobiles	Metabolic dysfunction
	Plastics and debris	Litter; shipping wastes; lost fishing gear	Entanglement of wild life; digestive interference
	Solid waste (organic and inorganic)	Sewage; ocean dumping; industry	Reduced oxygen; habitat smothering
Environmental restructuring	Coastal development	Dredging; industrial, residential and tourism development	Aesthetic and habitat loss; coastal erosion
Resource exploitation	Fish and shellfish harvesting	Harvesting activities	Stock depletion; ecosystem changes
	Petroleum development	Drilling; accidents	Oil and chemical contamination
	Mineral development	Dredging; tailings disposal; extraction	Decreased water quality; coastal erosion
Atmospheric change impacts	Carbon dioxide, CFC's, other "greenhouse" gases	Energy production; transportation; agriculture; industry	Sea level rise, coastal flooding, wetland loss, damage to infrastructure, habitat alteration, decreased oceanic productivity

Source: OECD

Thus a distinction must be made between the coastal zone, a sensitive and heavily stressed region receiving concentrated waste inputs, and the open ocean, a vast area receiving fewer wastes from more diffuse sources.

For many substances, gaps in the information base are such that it is difficult to determine accurately whether their disposal to the marine environment is decreasing, and if so, by what amount. Progress has been achieved through national and international action in regulating inputs of some substances, chiefly those originating from point sources. In contrast, waste inputs from diffuse sources remain largely unregulated. Use of the seas for waste disposal is in potential conflict with other activities such as fishing, tourism and recreation.

The status of selected substances of concern is discussed below.

Nutrients

Rising levels of nutrients have become a serious concern in the coastal regions of some OECD countries. Elevated levels of nutrients, particularly nitrogen and phosphorus compounds, can enhance productivity, potentially resulting in eutrophic conditions. Excessive growth of phytoplankton may result and subsequent decomposition of organic material can create anoxic conditions, causing the deaths of many marine species. Furthermore, some phytoplankton species produce toxins which contaminate shellfish, making them unsuitable for human consumption, while others may damage the gills of fish, a problem of particular concern for aquaculture.

The major anthropogenic sources of nutrients are sewage wastes, agricultural runoff, some industrial effluents, aquaculture operations, and the atmosphere. The importance of coastal land-based sources and inputs from rivers is reflected in many coastal areas and enclosed seas. For example, in areas of the Baltic Sea, increased levels of nutrients have been measured since 1980, and large phytoplankton blooms have occurred. Similarly, off the Dutch coast, nitrogen in seawater increased by a factor of four between 1930 and 1980. In Japan's Inland Sea, serious problems are caused by elevated levels of nutrients; aquaculture there is affected through the impact of phytoplankton toxins.

Sewage

Sewage accounts for much of the volume of wastes discharged into the world's coastal waters. Disposed of mainly through municipal wastewater systems, sewage consists largely of organic matter and nutrients, and may also contain pathogens, trace metals, and other chemicals. The problems associated with sewage wastes are largely a function of the rate and volume of discharge, the extent of treatment applied, and the characteristics of the receiving environment.

In marine ecosystems, sewage wastes may interfere with phytoplankton productivity, and the bacterial degradation of sewage can lower dissolved oxygen. Increased sedimentation resulting from the discharges may also alter the benthic environment.

Pathogens in sewage pose a threat to human health and economic activity. Consumption of contaminated seafoods (e.g. shellfish) may lead to gastro-intestinal disorders, while bathing in pathogen-contaminated waters can cause infections. For these reasons, public health authorities regularly close shellfish harvesting and bathing areas which exceed a "tolerable" level of contamination; as a result, economic opportunities are lost in the coastal areas concerned.

Many of the problems associated with sewage releases to the marine environment can be controlled through proper siting of outfalls (into well-flushed areas), and sewage treatment. Secondary treatment can reduce bacterial levels, while tertiary treatment is effective in reducing nutrient content. The overall trend of the past 20 years in OECD countries has been towards increased levels of sewage treatment (marine and freshwater discharges combined), although there are important differences among countries. However, continued closures of shellfish growing areas and of bathing waters in many areas suggest that sewage wastes continue to affect the quality of coastal waters.

Oil

Oil pollution of the seas is one of the most visible and widely publicised forms of marine pollution. The total input of oil to the world's oceans is difficult to determine precisely. Most estimates cite a volume of between 3 and 4 million tonnes per year; about half is of continental and half of marine origin. Industrial discharges, sewage disposal, river runoff, and non-accidental maritime transport are the major sources. Atmospheric fallout from incomplete fuel combustion and shipping accidents are quantitatively less important sources.

Massive accidental spills can be lethal to many forms of marine life, including seabirds and marine mammals. More chronic forms of oil pollution in estuaries or near oil rigs can affect benthic populations, other resident biota, and critical habitats such as spawning grounds. In areas of significant oil production or tanker traffic the accumulation of tarballs on beaches is a persistent problem. Many of these problems have an economic dimension, ranging from losses of economically valuable marine species and decreased revenues from tourism to high after-spill clean-up costs.

Some progress has been achieved in controlling oil pollution. A reduction in the volume of oil carried at sea and international and regional co-operation to control tanker traffic and accidental spills have been reflected in a decreased rate of tanker accidents. (Figure 15 and Table 6) Operational shipping discharges have also been reduced, due in part to the MARPOL convention, which requires the fitting of oil-water separators on some vessels, and which has designated special areas (e.g. the Baltic and Mediterranean Seas) where oil discharges from shipping are prohibited. However, oil continues to cause ecological and economic damage, largely a result of the many low-volume but ongoing releases from land-based sources and ocean shipping.

Synthetic organic compounds

Many synthetic organic compounds are characterised by extreme stability and persistence, toxicity, and/or lipid solubility; these characteristics allow them to accumulate in the fatty tissues of aquatic organisms. Atmospheric transport has facilitated global distribution of even the less volatile members of this class of compounds.

Figure 15. **OIL POLLUTION OF THE SEAS**

ORIGIN OF OIL POLLUTION

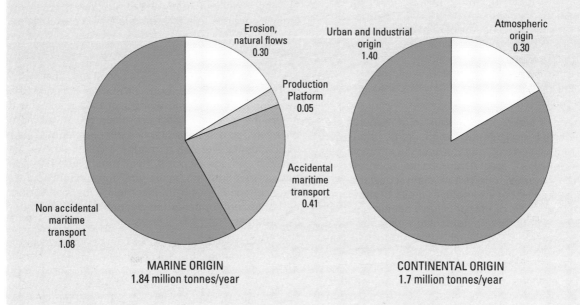

Erosion,
natural flows
0.30

Production
Platform
0.05

Accidental
maritime
transport
0.41

Non accidental
maritime
transport
1.08

MARINE ORIGIN
1.84 million tonnes/year

Urban and Industrial
origin
1.40

Atmospheric
origin
0.30

CONTINENTAL ORIGIN
1.7 million tonnes/year

Source: US National Academy of Sciences

ACCIDENTAL OIL SPILLS over 700 tonnes, 1974-1988

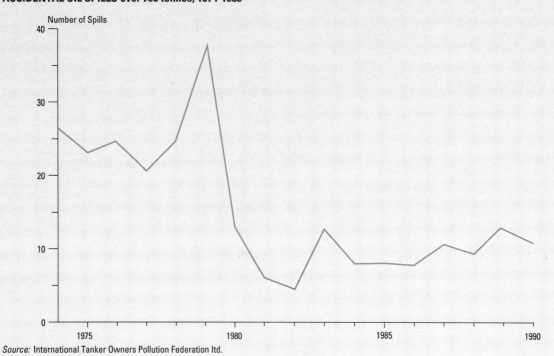

Number of Spills

Source: International Tanker Owners Pollution Federation ltd.

Table 6. SELECTED ACCIDENTAL OIL SPILLS, World[a]

	Date	Name of ship	Flag	Country affected	Quantity spilled (tonnes)
1967	March	Torrey Canyon	Liberia	United Kingdom, France	121.2
1968	June	World Glory	Liberia	South Africa	45.0
	November	Spyros Lemos	Liberia	Spain	20.0
1969	November	Keo	Liberia	USA	25.0
	November	Paocean	Liberia	Bahrain	30.0
1970	February	Arrow	Liberia	Canada	12.0
	March	Ennerdale	United Kingdom	Seychelles	49.0
	December	Chrissi	Panama	USA	31.0
1971	January	Oregon Standard	USA	USA	7.7
	February	Wafra	Liberia	South Africa	63.2
	March	Texas Oklahoma	USA	USA	35.0
	November	Juliana	Liberia	Japan	4.0
1972	January	Golden Drake	Liberia	Azores	31.7
	April	Giuseppe Giulietti	Italy	Spain	26.0
	June	Trader	Greece	Greece	35.0
	July	Tamano	Norway	USA (Maine)	3.6
	December	Sea Star	South Korea	Gulf of Oman	120.3
1973	March	Zoe Colocoltroni	Greece	USA, Puerto Rico	8.0
	June	Napier	Liberia	Chile	36.0
1974	June	Imperial Sarnia	Canada	Canada-USA	6.0
	August	Metula	Dutch Antilles	Chile	53.5
	—	Yugo Maru 10	Japan	Japan	50.0
1975	January	Showa Maru	Japan	Singapore	3.8
	January	British Ambassador	United Kingdom	Japan (Pacific)	45.0
	January	Jakob Maersk	Denmark	Portugal	84.0
	January	Corinthos/E.M. Queeny	USA-Liberia	USA (Delaware)	40.0
	April	Spartan Lady	Liberia	USA	25.0
	April	Shell Barge No. 2	USA	USA	..
	—	Epic Colocoltroni	Greece	St. Dominique	57.0
	—	Mitsu Maru 3	Japan	Japan	5.0
1976	February	Saint Peter	Liberia	Colombia	33.0
	May	Urquiola	Spain	Spain	101.0
	June	Nepco 140	USA	USA, Canada	1.2
	July	Cretan Star	Cyprus	Indian Ocean	28.6
	October	Boehlen	German Democratic Republic	France	11.0
	December	Argo Merchant	Liberia	USA (Massachusetts)	28.0
1977	January	Irenes Challenge	Liberia	Pacific	34.0
	January	Borag	Liberia	East China	4.0
	February	Hawaiian Patriot	Liberia	Honolulu (Pacific)	99.0
	May	Caribbean Sea	Panama	Nicaragua	30.0
	December	Venoil/Venpet	Liberia	South Africa	26.0
	December	Grand Zenith	Panama	USA (Massachusetts)	29.0
1978	March	Amoco Cadiz	Liberia	France	228.0
	May	Eleni V	Greece	United Kingdom	3.0
	July	Cabo Tamar	Chile	Chile	60.0
	October	Christos Bitas	Greece	United Kingdom	5.0
	December	Esso Bernica	United Kingdom	United Kingdom (Shetlands)	1.1
	December	Andros Patria	Greece	Spain	47.0

Table 6. SELECTED ACCIDENTAL OIL SPILLS, World[a] (Cont'd)

	Date	Name of ship	Flag	Country affected	Quantity spilled (tonnes)
1979	January	Betelgeuse	France	Ireland	27.0
	February	Antonio Gramsci	USSR	Sweden, Finland, USSR	6.0
	March	Messlaniki Frontis	Liberia	Greece	6.0
	March	Kurdistan	United Kingdom	Canada	7.0
	April	Gino	Liberia	France	42.0
	June	Aviles	Liberia	Arabian Sea	25.0
	July	Atlantic Express	Greece	Tobago	276.0
	August	Ionnis Angelicoussis	Greece	Angola	30.0
	September	Chevron Hawaii	USA	USA	2.0
	November	Burmah Agate	Liberia	USA (Texas)	40.0
	November	Independenta	Romania	Turkey	94.6
1980	January	Princess Anne Marie	Greece	Cuba	6.0
	February	Irenes Serenade	Greece	Greece	102.0
	March	Tanio	Madagascar	France, United Kingdom	13.5
	December	Juan A. Lavalleja	Uruguay	Algeria	40.0
1981	January	Jose Marti	USSR	Sweden	6.0
	March	Ondina	Dubai	Germany	5.0
	July	Cavo Cambanos	Greece	France	18.0
	November	Globe Assimi	Gibraltar	USSR	16.0
1983	August	Castello de Belver	Spain	South Africa	255.5
	September	Sivand	Iran	United Kingdom	6.0
	November	Feoso Ambassador	China	China	4.0
1984	January	Assimi	. .	Oman	51.4
	December	Pericles GC	. .	Qatar	46.6
1985	February	Neptunia	Liberia	Iran	60.0
b	December	Nova	Liberia	Iran	71.1
1989	March	Exxon Valdez	USA	USA, Alaska	35.0
	December	Kharg 5	. .	Morocco	. .

Notes: a) Inclusion criteria: over 25 000 tonnes of oil spilled by tankers or over $5 million of indemnity.
b) 1986-1988: no major oil spills over 25 000 tonnes.
Sources: OECD, IMO, IOPC-Fund, ACOPS, IFP, TAC

The compounds of greatest prevalence and concern are DDT and PCBs, but other substances, including the biocides chlordane, toxaphene, lindane, dieldrin, and organotin compounds (particularly tributyltin or TBT), are also present in the marine environment. These enter the oceans through rivers, runoff from agricultural land, atmospheric deposition, municipal and industrial discharges and, in the case of TBT, through deliberate use in anti-fouling paints.

Beginning with their concentration in planktonic organisms, some synthetic organic compounds concentrate readily in fish, marine mammals, and birds. Potential sub-lethal effects include retardation of growth, decreased reproductive success, and impairment of natural resistance to stress and disease.

Many of these effects have been identified in marine biota. The first indication of DDT toxicity to the marine ecosystem was noted in the 1960s, when a serious decline in the brown pelican population of Anacapa Island in the United States was linked with a high DDT content in the birds' fish diet. Later, in the 1970s, high levels of DDT and PCBs were identified as the cause of southern California sea-lion abortions and premature births. Similarly, in the Baltic Sea area, PCBs were implicated in declining populations of seals in the 1970s and early 1980s; in the same period DDT affected

76

the reproductive capacity of the sea eagle. More recently, other synthetic compounds, such as dioxins, have been detected in marine organisms. In Canada, shellfisheries have been closed in the vicinity of pulp mill outfalls as a result of dioxin contamination.

Some progress has been achieved in controlling the use of some synthetic organic compounds. The production and use of the more persistent and/or toxic substances (e.g. DDT, PCBs, TBT) has been banned or curtailed in many OECD countries, and encouraging signs, such as the recovery of certain wild life populations (e.g. the brown pelican), have been noted. However, levels of many of these substances remain high in marine wild life and coastal sediments, and they continue to be used in other regions of the world. Furthermore, since a number of new chemicals are introduced each year, careful attention is required to ensure that the problems of the recent past are not repeated.

Metals

Metals occur naturally in the marine environment, and are widely distributed in both dissolved and sedimentary forms. Some are essential to marine life while others may be toxic to numerous organisms. Metal toxicity is very complex and dependent on factors such as chemical form, concentration, temperature and salinity, as well as the life stage, adaptability and species of organism affected. Rivers, coastal discharges, and the atmosphere are the principal modes of entry for metals to the marine environment, with anthropogenic inputs occurring primarily as components of industrial and municipal wastes.

Trace metals can affect organisms through acute or chronic toxicity. Marine organisms vary widely in their bioaccumulative capacity for metals. Phytoplankton and bivalve molluscs readily accumulate metals while crustaceans and fish are generally able to regulate essential elements such as zinc and copper but tend to accumulate non-essential metals such as mercury, cadmium, and lead. Since metals are usually introduced into the ocean as components of other wastes, it has been difficult to attribute noticeable negative effects in the marine environment solely to excessive metal inputs. Much of the concern about the effects of trace metals is caused by their potential impact on human health. In this regard the metals of greatest concern are cadmium, mercury, and lead.

Mercury, in methylmercury form, poses the most serious risk, followed by lead and cadmium. Ingestion of sufficient quantities can cause severe neurological effects. The case of mercury in Minimata Bay, Japan, in the 1950s generated effects – and related compensatory payments – which continue today. Partly as a result of this disaster, many countries have established environmental objectives for mercury in the marine environment, and have moved to restrict discharges from industrial operations. Thus, concern over the presence of toxic forms of metals in the seas has

decreased, although in contaminated areas in estuaries and near industrial sources, levels in sediments are often high compared to background levels.

Radionuclides

Anthropogenically produced radionuclides have been present in the world's oceans since the 1940s. The largest source has been the atmospheric testing of nuclear weapons. Since the 1940s as well, the United States, some West European countries and Japan have engaged in the ocean dumping of some radioactive wastes. To date, a total of approximately 60 000 TBq[1] of radioactive waste has been dumped into the world's oceans. In comparison, atmospheric testing of nuclear weapons has introduced 200 000 000 TBq of radioactive waste into the world environment as a whole.

The input of artificial radionuclides must be viewed in conjunction with the radioactivity which occurs naturally in the oceans. Over geological time the oceans have been exposed to low-level radiation from the natural radioactive material present in seawater, and from radionuclides originating in the atmosphere. In total this has amounted to some 20 billion TBq, a level much greater than the input of radionuclides originating from human activities. However, although the anthropogenic input of radionuclides represents only a small fraction of the natural radioactivity present in the marine environment, too little is known to accurately assess potential long-term ecological effects.

Over the last two decades the disposal of radioactive wastes has come under international regulation which aims to limit disposal quantities and ocean dump sites. Since 1972, with the formulation of the London Dumping Convention, dumping of high-level radioactive waste has been prohibited. Intermediate and low-level wastes continued to be dumped until 1983, when a moratorium on ocean dumping of such waste was established. In 1985 the moratorium was extended indefinitely, pending the outcome of numerous environmental and socio-economic studies. Progress has also been achieved in regulating and reducing operational discharges of radionuclides from industrial installations.

Persistent litter and debris

Although a marine debris problem has been recognised since the 1970s, concern about this form of marine pollution has grown only recently. Plastic, due to its persistence, widespread use and detrimental effects, is the chief substance responsible for the problem.

The development and use of plastics has grown to encompass a wide range of everyday and specialised products. Many of these products end up in landfills or are incinerated, but unknown quantities end up in the oceans. Although the problem has not yet been adequately documented from a global perspective, shipping, rivers, municipal drainage systems, and

CONTROLLING TBT ANTIFOULING PAINTS

Recognition of an Environmental Problem

In recent years, tributyltin (TBT) compounds have been used increasingly in antifouling paints. However, research carried out during the 1980s showed that the toxic effects of TBT were not confined to the surface of a boat's hull.

The first evidence of environmental damage came from observations in France and the United Kingdom of growth abnormalities in a type of cultivated oyster (*Crassotrea gigas*). TBT appeared to affect the calcification mechanism in shell formation. Shells became thickened and deformed, and when cut through showed, in extreme cases, numerous chambers filled with a jelly-like substance. Shell thickening and "chambering" could be so extreme, and the meat yield so reduced, that the shellfish became unmarketable. In some areas oyster reproduction was heavily affected and it was not possible to maintain viable populations. Field observations and laboratory tests in France showed that these effects were related to the presence of marinas and the use of TBT paints. Further laboratory tests in the United Kingdom demonstrated the specific role of dissolved or particulate TBT.

Meanwhile, a wide range of marine organisms were being studied, particularly in the United States and the United Kingdom, to determine what levels of TBT affected reproduction, mortality, growth and other characteristics. In many places concentrations found in coastal waters exceeded those producing toxic effects in the laboratory. TBT clearly had the potential to cause severe damage to marine life.

Action Taken and Evidence of Recovery

Small boats have been identified as the main contributors to high TBT concentrations in inshore waters. This is because they occur in high densities, for long periods, at moorings in enclosed or shallow waters having limited exchange.

In France, the use of TBT-based paints on small boats was banned in 1982. Following this, monitoring of oysters from Arcachon Bay showed rapid recovery. The percentage of oysters with both shells chambered dropped dramatically in 1983 and has remained low. However, the incidence of less severe deformities fell initially but rose again in 1986. This could reflect illegal use of TBT-based paints and indicates the importance of proper enforcement of regulations.

In the United Kingdom, monitoring of TBT started in 1982. Progressive restrictions were applied to the tin content of paints sold in 1986 and 1987 and a guidance note was published on how to clean and repaint boats safely. Despite these actions, however, a review of the scientific evidence in 1987 indicated that a ban was necessary and justified. From July 1987 TBT-based products for use on boats less than 25 metres long or on mariculture equipment have been prohibited. All new antifoulants must be registered and approved before they can be marketed and used. Environmental concentrations continue to fall but there is still some way to go before the most sensitive marine species will be protected.

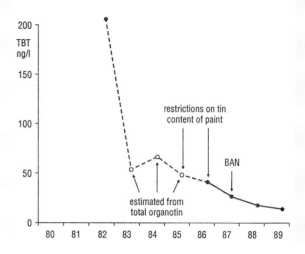

TBT CONCENTRATIONS IN RIVER CROUCH (U.K.)
(Apr-Sept mean values)

In the European Community, legislation in the member states is to be harmonized as a result of a Directive agreed on in 1989. In the United States, the use of organotins on small boats was banned in 1988 and several other countries are evaluating the evidence or taking action.

Remaining Issues

The importance of other TBT sources, such as large ships and drydock facilities, remains to be determined precisely. At present, large vessels, because they operate in deeper waters with greater capacity for dilution and dispersal of TBT, are thought to make only minor contributions under normal operating conditions, but further research is being carried out to clarify their significance as other sources fade away. The United States already sets an upper limit to the TBT release rates of antifouling paints approved for use on large vessels, and the need for wider controls on the types of paints used is being considered by the International Maritime Organization.

Shipyard operations can release large amounts of TBT into marine waters. The United Kingdom recently adopted a statutory "environmental quality standard" of 2 parts per trillion which will lead to a tightening of controls on releases from dry docks. Codes of practice are also being developed for more acceptable means of cleaning and repainting boats.

Contribution from the United Kingdom

beachgoers are believed to be the major sources. Fishing gear, packaging materials, convenience items and raw plastics account for the bulk of plastic materials entering the oceans.

The environmental effects associated with plastics in the oceans are: death and injury to marine fish and wild life either through entanglement or ingestion, and littering of beaches. In the North Pacific, for example, some 30 000 northern fur seals are estimated to be dying annually as a result of entanglement in lost or discarded fishing gear. Off the Norwegian coast between 50 000 and 60 000 animals are known to have been caught in fishing gear in 1987, although the actual figure may have been much higher. In other areas, other species, such as sea turtles, have reportedly been killed by plastics. Plastic litter has been reported from beaches throughout the world, including remote beaches in the Arctic and South Pacific. Organised beach clean-ups regularly remove tonnes of debris from beaches. For example, a national beach clean-up in the United States in 1988 removed some 907 tonnes of debris from 5 600 km of shoreline. Of this, 62 per cent was plastic.

Although more study is needed to quantify the magnitude and ecological significance of marine debris, action to resolve the problem is beginning in some countries. In the United States, for example, 11 of 23 coastal states have banned the use of non-degradable beverage rings. In Australia's exclusive economic zone the use of pelagic driftnets exceeding 2.4 km in length has been prohibited. In many countries beach clean-ups are held, although this cannot be considered a permanent solution. At the international level, Annex V of the International Convention for the Prevention of Pollution from Ships, which deals with the disposal of trash from ships, came into force in December 1988. However, additional measures are needed, such as more public education and a means of minimising damage from drifting plastic items.

Environmental restructuring

Environmental restructuring refers to the physical alteration of the environment. Pressures arise from construction, landscape modification, and dredging activities, as well as from the alteration of natural river flows. Without proper safeguards, these activities can disrupt or destroy sensitive and valued resources such as coastal wetlands, beaches, coral reefs, and wild life habitat. The aesthetic impacts may also be significant.

One broad indication of restructuring pressure is the growth of human populations in coastal zones. In the Mediterranean region, for example, large seasonal increases in populations exert significant pressures on coastal resources. In the United States, where more than half the population already live within 80 km of the coast, coastal populations are rising in absolute terms and will continue to grow in the years ahead. In these and other coastal regions of OECD countries

restructuring pressures have already resulted in significant changes to coastal landscapes (e.g. wetland losses) and conflicts among competing land users.

Resource exploitation

Humans derive significant benefits from the many resources of the seas. However, the exploitation of these resources may exert pressure on the marine environment. The extraction of non-renewable resources such as oil and minerals can lead to pollution and decreased water quality. In the North Sea, for example, inputs of hydrocarbons from drilling form a significant part of the total input. Since the mid-1970s, in response to a rise in oil prices, oil exploration and/or production in some OECD regions has expanded considerably, particularly in such areas as the North American Arctic and the North Sea. Ocean mining of solid mineral deposits remains relatively low-scale, although a potential for growth exists and will require the use of careful operational procedures.

Renewable resources such as fish stocks and shellfish are heavily exploited. Stock depletion occurs when the rate of harvesting exceeds the regenerative capacity of the resource, a situation which has occurred with some fisheries. In addition, overfishing can complicate fisheries management by altering ecological balances among species. (See section 3, below)

Atmospheric change

The effects of atmospheric change will be felt in the world's oceans and coastal regions, but these must be discussed in tentative terms since much remains uncertain regarding their nature and magnitude. These impacts will result from two separate but related phenomena: climate warming and stratospheric ozone depletion. Climate warming is expected to result in a rise in sea-levels, particularly because of thermal expansion of seawater and melting of polar icecaps. During the past 100 years the global sea level is believed to have risen some 10 centimetres. Predictions of average sea-level rise over the next century vary around an estimated 65 cm above present levels.

Damage to stratospheric ozone will result in increased amounts of ultraviolet (UV) radiation reaching the earth's surface. A range of potential impacts is possible. New thermal and hydrological regimes and increases in UV radiation may have adverse effects on such marine organisms as phytoplankton and zooplankton. These organisms are important base components of marine food chains, and support commercially important fisheries. Hence, for fisheries these pressures could potentially be more disruptive than existing pressures from pollution and harvesting. Similarly, other marine organisms will come under stress as they are forced to adapt to changes compressed from tens of thousands of years into a much shorter period. Coastal wetlands, already under significant restructuring pressure, may be lost or undergo substantial change due

MONITORING OF COASTAL BATHING WATER

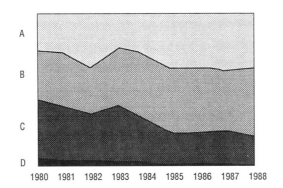

A - Very good quality water

B - Good quality water

C - Temporarily polluted water

D - Polluted water

1980 1981 1982 1983 1984 1985 1986 1987 1988

Regular Monitoring since 1972

In France, beaches are subjected to intensive use, especially for tourism and recreational purposes during the summer months. The Ministries of Health and the Environment are both responsible for monitoring bathing-water quality. A European Communities Council Directive adopted on 8th December 1975 lays down quality standards for bathing water.

In France, some 20 000 tests are carried out each year between 1st June and 30th September. In 1989, about 1 716 coastal points, beaches and bathing areas were kept under surveillance, with measurements taken on average once a week, in 625 communes throughout the 27 coastal departments.

Local and Public Information

Samples are analysed locally in authorised laboratories and the results, together with comments on ambient conditions and an interpretation of the findings, are sent by the departmental Ministry of Health office to the mayors of the communes concerned.

Mayors must ensure that the public is kept informed by displaying the results at beaches and town halls. Information can also be obtained by telephone from the local health authorities or via the French videotex system (Minitel).

When analysis reveals that bathing water has reached or exceeded pollution limits, additional samples are taken and a more stringent survey is carried out, often with new types of parameters.

If bathing water is shown to be polluted, the mayor must close the beach or bathing area concerned. The prefect of the department may take action in the place of the mayor if he considers it appropriate. Meanwhile, monitoring continues so that the ban can be lifted when conditions return to normal.

National and Public Information

At the close of the season, each departmental health service issues a report on the local situation. This will contain all the results and relevant comments, drawing attention to pollution and contamination sources if known. The report is then sent to the departmental Health Council for consideration along with sanitation proposals and discharge permit applications submitted by firms or local authorities. It also helps in setting priorities for general sanitation plans and providing local authorities with guidance on restoring contaminated spots.

A press conference attended by Health and Environment Ministers is organised every year at the start of the holiday period. The results of the previous year's bathing season are presented in full. Documents are subsequently published, including diagrams and a colour map in three languages; over the past few years, these have greatly contributed to the coverage of findings in the local, national and international media, including the main television channels, and to public access to the information provided by the national bathing-water monitoring network.

A Policy Tool

Such information can influence not only user choice of bathing areas and holidays in general but also local and national government investment in bathing-water pollution control.

Contribution from France

to rising sea levels. Rising sea levels could also threaten coastal infrastructure (e.g. dams, port facilities) as the frequency and intensity of flooding increases. The economic cost of reinforcing and protecting these structures may prove extremely high.

Conversely, the oceans may play a pivotal role in moderating climate change through absorption of carbon dioxide and diffusion of heat into the ocean depths. (See Chapter on Global Atmospheric Issues)

2. THE STATE OF THE MARINE ENVIRONMENT

The results of human activities can now be seen in virtually all oceanic waters. Traces of artificial substances are detectable in the open ocean, while oil slicks and litter are found along many sea transport routes. Nonetheless, concern about the state of the marine environment continues to focus largely on the world's coastal and nearshore areas. This concern is growing for several reasons, the most important of which is that coastal zones are where human settlement and use are most concentrated. As a result, coastal regions bear the brunt of pressures from human activities, a reflection of the importance of land-based pollution sources. Furthermore, coastal environments are often complex and sensitive to pollution because of slow water renewal and generally limited depth. Finally, they are productive areas characterised by a diversity of flora and fauna which is often specific to them. It is in these regions that the most detrimental ecological effects have been observed.

The data and information required to identify changes in the state of the marine environment and determine their significance remain incomplete for many regions. For example, comprehensive estimates of inputs of critical substances to the marine environment are unavailable for many countries and regions, and data on the distribution of marine contaminants are often difficult to compare. Progress has been made in this area, particularly through the work of regional organisations (e.g. International Council for the Exploration of the Sea [ICES], Paris Commission, Helsinki Commission) but more efforts to develop a consistent database are required. Nevertheless, it can generally be observed that many coastal regions are suffering from a slow but continuous degradation in marine environmental quality. In many areas contaminant levels remain high and adverse effects are occurring over larger areas. Increasingly, use conflicts are occurring in coastal zones and potential uses such as shellfish harvesting and recreation are being foreclosed.

The state of the marine environment is reviewed here in five regional areas: the North, Baltic, and Mediterranean Seas, and the coastal areas of Japan and North America.

The North Sea

Located on the continental shelf of northwestern Europe, the North Sea is a heavily used and exploited sea. The Straits of Dover, which provide the Sea's southern connection to the Atlantic, are among the world's most heavily utilised shipping lanes. Gas and oil reserves in the central and northern regions of the Sea are extensively exploited, and in several areas sand and gravel deposits are dredged for the construction industry. These and other coastal activities are in potential conflict with the sea's role as Europe's most important and productive fishing area.

State of the North Sea

Contaminant inputs from diverse sources such as large rivers, direct industrial and municipal discharges, runoff from farmland, waste dumping and incineration, and the atmosphere represent the greatest threat to the health of the North Sea. Rivers, particularly those draining agricultural and industrial areas in central and western Europe, contribute about two-thirds of the nitrogen and three-quarters of the phosphorus entering the North Sea from land-based sources. In fact, recent estimates indicate that rivers now introduce four times as much nitrogen and seven times as much phosphorus as would be introduced without them.

As regards concentrations of contaminants, monitoring information is available for nutrients, petroleum hydrocarbons, trace metals, and some synthetic compounds. In the case of nutrients, water column levels in the coastal belt from the Netherlands to the north of Denmark have generally doubled. For petroleum hydrocarbons, concentrations in the open sea are relatively low but increase in the vicinity of oil platforms and estuaries such as those of the Thames, Elbe, and Rhine rivers. Synthetic compounds such as pesticides have been detected in several locations. Generally, the Belgian coast and the Oslofjord are identified as being more contaminated with PCBs, and the German Bight, Oslofjord and the Humber estuary with organochlorine pesticides. While concentrations of contaminants in the North Sea such as DDT and PCBs were declining, there are relatively high concentrations of chlorinated hydrocarbons in the coastal area, especially in estuaries.

The most disturbing ecological effects appear linked to high nutrient levels. Over the past few decades, marked changes in plankton communities have been observed, particularly along the southern continental coast but also in Swedish and Norwegian waters. In recent years a succession of spectacular algal blooms has occurred, many with adverse ecological

TOXIC ALGAE BLOOMS IN THE NORTH SEA

Rising Concern about Algae Blooms

Mass occurrences or "blooms" of planktonic algae (microscopic single-cell organisms) in the sea are known to occur worldwide, but are usually restricted to coastal waters. Some bloom-forming species are toxic and may cause mass mortality to fish and other aquatic species, or toxicity in mussels, thus making them unsafe for human beings to eat. Since these blooms frequently cause discolouration of seawater, they are often referred to as "red tides".

In the North Sea Basin (including the Skagerrak and Kattegat, and numerous fjords) blooms of specific non-toxic species of algae have been known to occur for a long time. However, there is strong evidence that blooms of toxic species occurred with increasing frequency in the 1970s and 1980s.

Early Signs of Trouble

A massive bloom of the species *Chrysochromulina polylepis* occurred in the spring of 1988. The first sign that something was wrong appeared on 9th May when aberrant behaviour in cultivated rainbow trout was observed in the Gullmar fjord on Sweden's west coast. Two days later most of the trout were dead, and aberrant behaviour was being reported from several sites along the Swedish coast from Gothenburg to the southern tip of Norway. For the next six days many of the cultivated fish in the area of the bloom died, and the first reports of mortality in wild fish populations arrived.

On 17th May the wind direction shifted and the surface layer of the bloom drifted off the southern coast of Norway, much to the relief of aquaculture businesses. This relief was shortlived, however: five days later the wind direction shifted again and the algae-bearing layer of water drifted towards the west coast of Norway. Again, mortality of fish was reported, but fortunately, researchers had by now begun to monitor the drift of the algal layer and were thus in a position to give proper warning of its movement.

Effects of the *Chrysochromulina* Bloom

Altogether, the *Chrysochromulina polylepis* bloom spread across the Kattegat and Skagerrak and much of the Belt Seas area, and along the Norwegian coast north to Haugesund. Mass mortality of fish occurred in fish farms from Gothenburg to Stavanger. In Norway about 440 tonnes of cultivated salmon and rainbow trout were lost, with a value of about 2.5 million ECU. These losses would have been at least ten times greater if the owners of aquaculture businesses had not received early warning and towed their net cages away from the affected area.

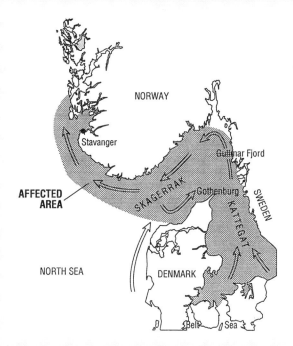

The cost of this salvage operation has been estimated at about 5 million ECU. Equally dramatic was the mortality of wild stocks of fish and bottom fauna along the Skagerrak coast.

Determining Causative Factors

Several factors are likely to have been responsible for the *Chrysochromulina polylepis* bloom: the direction and strength of sea currents - which may have caused upwelling of enriched deep waters - and possibly the magnitude of land runoff at the time of the bloom. These factors are important influences on the rate of nutrient supply, a critical factor which can initiate an algae bloom. In the affected area, however, only anthropogenic supplies of nitrogen nutrients - for instance, from agriculture and from fuel combustion - can explain the distribution of nutrients present when the bloom occurred.

Thus the increasing frequency of algae blooms in parts of the North Sea over the past 15 years appears to indicate that the affected areas are becoming progressively enriched by nutrients from anthropogenic sources. It is therefore to be expected that, unless inputs of nutrients are reduced, algae blooms will continue to occur at least at the present rate.

Contribution from Norway

and economic effects. One of the most extensive of these occurred in May 1988 when the flagellate *Chryso-chromulina polylepis* and other algal species multiplied in large quantities off the Skagerrak coasts of Sweden and Norway, causing losses of salmon on fish farms and other forms of ecological damage.

Despite some reductions, the presence of certain metals and synthetic organic compounds still causes concern; in the past, PCBs have been identified as affecting reproductive success in marine mammals and seabirds.

In the summer of 1988, a disease epidemic among North Sea and Baltic Sea seal populations resulted in the deaths of some 18 000 animals. Although a contagious viral infection was identified as the likely cause, the significance of environmental factors such as pollution remains unclear.

Marine quality prospects

Progress has been made in reducing inputs of metals and organic materials from both rivers and direct discharges, and also in reducing oil inputs from refineries and reception facilities. But continued high inputs and levels of nutrients and their associated impacts constitute a major remaining problem.

Coastal states have been meeting at the North Sea Ministerial Conference to establish priorities and determine suitable pollution control strategies. In this way specific reduction targets for nutrients and other selected substances have been established. Meeting these targets and assessing their adequacy are important challenges facing all countries in the region. Co-ordinated action among the coastal states is facilitated through the actions of the Paris and Oslo Commissions, and the ICES, including the North Sea Task Force.

The Baltic Sea

The Baltic Sea is a shallow, semi-enclosed sea which can be further sub-divided into several distinct regions; among these are the Baltic Proper, the Gulf of Finland, the Bothnian Sea and Bay, and the Gulf of Riga. It is one of the largest brackish water bodies in the world, and supports a diversity of flora and fauna which consist of adaptations from both saltwater and freshwater species. Exchange between the Baltic and the open ocean occurs indirectly via the Danish Straits which connect it to the North Sea. Total renewal of Baltic Sea water is estimated to occur over a 20-25 year period, and strong stratification inhibits vertical mixing, so that deep waters have high nutrient but low oxygen levels. These characteristics combine to make the Baltic especially sensitive to stresses arising from human activities occurring within its drainage basin.

State of the Baltic Sea

Human activities in the region relevant to the state of the Baltic Sea include agriculture, fishing, sand and gravel extraction, sea transport, and industrial and energy production. The cumulative effects of industrial and municipal discharges, and inputs of harmful substances from rivers and other sources have resulted in profound changes in the ecology of the Baltic Sea.

The major concern at present is the trend towards increasing nutrient concentrations, contributing to more frequent oxygen depletion and the occurrence of hydrogen sulphide in deep areas of the Baltic proper. In addition, exceptionally strong algae blooms have recently occurred in areas such as the Kattegat and the Gulf of Finland, causing depletion of oxygen in deep waters and mortality of benthic fauna. Agricultural runoff and rivers are the principal nutrient sources, and their contributions have grown, while some success has been achieved in controlling nutrient inputs from municipalities and industry.

Synthetic organic chemicals such as DDT and PCBs are important contaminants in the Baltic. Sources include airborne fallout, industrial and municipal incineration, and discharges from pulp and paper mills. Generally, levels of these substances have declined since the mid-1970s, although studies in the mid-1980s showed relative increases of substances similar to PCBs in some areas. Continued reproductive problems in Baltic seals and white-tailed eagles may be due to contamination by PCBs.

Inland municipal and industrial releases carried by rivers and those produced by coastal installations are the primary anthropogenic sources of trace metals to the Baltic, although some metals enter via atmospheric deposition. Generally, metal concentrations in offshore waters are relatively low, but higher levels are to be found in coastal sediments. For example, in certain coastal areas of the Gulf of Bothnia elevated levels of zinc, copper, cadmium, and mercury are believed responsible for skeletal deformities observed in some fish populations.

Marine quality prospects

Through the work of coastal states, co-ordinated by the Helsinki Commission, inputs to the Baltic sea of many substances except nutrients have been reduced. Present concerns, in order of importance, focus on nutrients, synthetic compounds (e.g. organochlorine pesticides), trace metals, and oil. Further input reduction targets for many of these substances have been established by the Helsinki Commission. Achieving these goals will require effective national actions by all coastal states, implemented within the Helsinki Convention framework.

The Mediterranean Sea

The Mediterranean Sea is one of the world's most developed regional seas, and its shore is one of the world's most heavily populated. It is a deep, virtually tideless sea, completely surrounded by land except for a narrow passage to the North Atlantic through the Strait of Gibraltar, another by way of the Bosporus to the Black Sea, and a man-made link to the Red Sea through the Suez Canal. The Mediterranean's water

THE VENICE LAGOON

Venice is not only a cultural and tourist centre but also a major economic hub for northern Italy. The concentration of activity in the area, especially heavy industry in Porto Marghera, puts constant pressure on the lagoon ecosystem.

State of the Environment

Efforts were made during the 1970s and 80s to combat growing pollution. There was a substantial reduction in air pollution and a marked fall in concentrations of ammonia, bacteria, heavy metals and some organic pollutants in the lagoon waters.

Much still remains to be done, however. Current environmental conditions in the lagoon are characterised by:

- Growing salinization, resulting in particular in the depletion of typical lagoon wildlife and fish species.
- A very high concentration of nutrients, leading to extensive eutrophication.

The two main causes are:

- Substances originating outside the lagoon, produced by human activities throughout the catchment area as a whole (domestic and industrial pollution, urban and agricultural pollution from non-point sources); and
- Substances originating within the lagoon mainly in the form of sediments containing industrial, urban and agricultural pollutants which have accumulated over the years.

Other kinds of pressure affect the entire catchment area, such as toxic industrial waste, often in uncontrolled dump sites; cooling water from power stations; and risk of accidents related to the storage, production and transport of hazardous substances.

Venice also has to face sea level rise because of land subsidence and as a possible consequence of climate change. To combat this phenomenon, the Italian state has prepared a first action plan to protect the city from high waters through a system of mobile gates. These mobile gates make it possible to isolate the lagoon from the sea and to preserve the hydrodynamic and ecological balance of the lagoon. This action plan is financed by the State and was started in 1983.

Plan of Action Against Pollution

More recently, the Ministry of the Environment and the Veneto regional authorities initiated a plan to reduce pollution and reinstate the lagoon ecosystem. The aim is to make a concerted effort for the whole of the lagoon catchment area, covering 185 000 hectares and containing parts of three provinces (Venice, Padua and Treviso) and around one hundred local districts.

In order to take action as rapidly as possible, guidelines and steps to be taken have been determined without reference to competent national, regional or local authorities, whose interests are often conflicting.

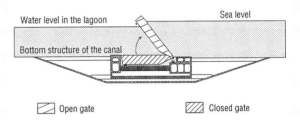

SECTION OF A MOBILE BARRIER

Water level in the lagoon   Sea level

Bottom structure of the canal

▱ Open gate   ▨ Closed gate

The plan is in two phases, lasting from 1992 to 1998. It identifies ten measures to be planned and paid for by local authorities in the catchment area and alongside the lagoon. The measures are as follows:

- Treatment of household and industrial effluent;
- Prevention and treatment of urban pollution from non-point sources;
- Prevention and treatment of agricultural pollution;
- Changes in irrigation systems (less water);
- Treatment and regulation of lagoon water-courses;
- Urban and industrial waste management;
- Safety measures for industry and movements of industrial products within the lagoon;
- Maintenance and restoration of the lagoon environment;
- Creation of a Venice Lagoon Park;
- Establishment of an information system on the environment of the lagoon catchment area.

To ensure that the plan is correctly implemented and followed through, provision is made for the creation of a standing committee whose main function will be scientific and technical co-ordination between the authorities concerned. The committee's first tasks will be to draw up a detailed programme of operations and establish an information system on the lagoon and its catchment area.

An "integrated" plan of this type requires the co-operation of all concerned, as well as efforts by industrial, urban and agricultural interests. By restoring the lagoon ecosystem, it aims to ensure the sustainable development of the economy and the tourist industry in the Venice area.

Contribution from Italy

renewal rate is slow: complete renewal requires a period of 70 years. These characteristics, combined with high coastal populations in some states, make the Mediterranean extremely vulnerable to pollution.

State of the Mediterranean Sea

Important pressures on the Mediterranean Sea include restructuring pressure and pollution resulting from sewage disposal, nutrients, oil, metals, and synthetic organic compounds. Land-based pollution sources are especially significant, being responsible for approximately 85 per cent of the Mediterranean's pollution burden. For example, high coastal populations and an influx of some 100 million tourists each summer add to already high sewage discharges. Tourism and other socio-economic activities have also spurred coastal development, causing extensive physical restructuring of shorelines. Large rivers such as the Ebro, Po, and Rhone, all of which drain heavily industrialised areas, are also important sources of contaminants. These pressures are strongest along the northern coast, particularly along the shores of France, Italy, and Spain. (See Chapter on Socio-Demographic Changes)

Sea transport is also significant, since approximately one-quarter of world tanker traffic occurs in the Mediterranean. Some port facilities receiving oily wastes from tankers remain inadequate to handle discharges of oily water from bilges and ballast tanks. Chronic low-level oil pollution is therefore far more critical than contamination arising from accidental discharges or spills.

The effects of these pressures are to be seen in many coastal areas. In parts of the upper Adriatic Sea along the Italian coast, algae blooms have intensified in recent years, posing a threat to recreational users of the sea as well as affecting marine organisms. Eutrophic-like conditions also occur in other, usually poorly flushed or semi-enclosed areas (e.g. Tunis lagoon, Elefsis bay, etc.) where sewage discharges and/or rivers carry large quantities of nutrients into the sea.

Many confined coastal areas adjacent to large urban centres exhibit signs of contaminant accumulation and changes in benthic community structure. Also impacted in these (and other) areas are Mediterranean seagrass meadows, which have also been affected by trawling activities.

The Mediterranean provides a good example of the effects associated with the introduction of exotic species and the alteration of natural river flows (restructuring). The construction of the Suez Canal introduced Red Sea species which have affected commercial fish catches, while the damming of the Nile at Aswan has drastically reduced sediment input and consequently the productivity of living resources in the Nile delta and nearby areas.

Because the region is used so intensively for recreation and tourism, concern for human health is especially high, focusing largely on the bacteriological quality of seawater and the contamination of shellfish. Although progress in improving sewage treatment has been made, large quantities of inadequately processed waste continue to be discharged into the sea. As a result, public health problems from the consumption of contaminated shellfish occur regularly, as do infections of the ear, eye, skin, and upper respiratory tract in bathers in certain areas.

Marine quality prospects

The Mediterranean is the focus of an extensive study within the UNEP Regional Seas Programme intended to illustrate the future environmental consequences of decisions taken (or not taken) now to manage environmental pressures. The projections indicate an increase in many of the pressures currently affecting the Mediterranean; the increase would occur largely as a result of increasing coastal populations, and associated socio-economic activities. Scenarios developed for the year 2025 indicate that the state of the environment in the region is likely to deteriorate considerably, and that policies more vigorous than those currently in place must be decided upon and implemented now if such a scenario is to be avoided.

Japan's marine environment

Since Japan is a country completely surrounded by the sea, its coastal areas are used intensively for fishing, aquaculture, and living space. Major urban and industrial areas are most prevalent along the Pacific coast, the western coast being less developed. In Japan's coastal and offshore waters the Kuroshio, a warm current from the south, mingles with the Oyashio, a cold current from the north, forming one of the world's most valuable fishing areas.

State of Japan's marine environment

Pressures on this environment result largely from intense coastal land-use, industrial operations and shipping traffic. Restructuring pressures have been especially strong, claiming some 28 000 hectares of tidal flats between 1945 and 1978 (33 per cent of the 1945 total), and reclaiming by 1985 some 170 000 hectares of land area from the sea. Waste inputs have created marine pollution problems, with nutrients, oil, synthetic organic compounds and trace metals being important marine contaminants. Generally speaking, aquatic pollution peaked during the 1960s and 1970s and has since been declining, although important concerns remain.

Problems associated with high nutrient levels have plagued Japan's coastal waters since the 1970s. Widespread phytoplankton blooms have been documented in numerous areas. In the Seto Inland Sea, for example, over 100 red tides (the excessive growth of certain phytoplankton) occur annually. These also occur frequently in other heavily industrialised coastal areas such as Tokyo, Ise, and Osaka Bay. Nutrient inputs from municipal and industrial discharges, agricultural runoff, and aquaculture are believed responsible.

Japan's reliance on oil imports results in heavy tanker traffic in coastal waters, making oil pollution a constant threat. It has been reported that the Kuroshio is extensively polluted with floating tar; tanker discharges along sea routes towards the industrial zones near Tokyo and Osaka are likely sources. In contrast, oil pollution in the Okhotsk Sea as well as the seas west of Japan is considered negligible.

Marine contamination from metals has, in the past, had a critical impact on human health. One of the most widely discussed examples of metal contamination is Japan's experience with Minimata disease, which resulted from the long-term ingestion of fish and shellfish contaminated with mercury compounds. These incidents occurred in the 1950s but continue to have repercussions even today in the form of continued health effects and compensation costs. An array of toxic chemicals (metals, synthetic organic compounds) has had biological effects on aquatic organisms, in addition to human health effects. Skeletal anomalies and neoplasms are some of the more frequently observed disorders, and have been identified in many fish species inhabiting coastal and estuarine waters.

Marine quality prospects in Japan's marine environment

Japan's primary concerns regarding its marine environment will be likely to continue to focus on coastal land-use allocation, effects associated with high nutrient levels, and concern for human health. Progress has been made in rationalising coastal land-use and reducing pollutant inputs. Human poisoning from consumption of seafood has declined in the past two decades, and a decline in the numbers of red tides recorded annually has been noted, although these continue to occur at a high rate. Nonetheless, the intensity of human activities in coastal areas will require careful planning and marine management.

North America's marine environment

North America's coastlines (Canada and United States) extend from the Arctic to the sub-tropics, incorporating wide physical and ecological diversity. Waste inputs from diverse sources and environmental restructuring activities are important pressures in many marine areas.

Marine pollution stems primarily from land-based sources, generally following the pattern of coastal settlement and industrialisation, with contaminant levels frequently elevated in estuarine environments. For instance, in the United States, non-point pollution sources (such as agricultural and urban runoff) are believed to be responsible for almost 50 per cent of all contaminants present in coastal waters, with industrial and municipal discharges being the largest point sources. Restructuring pressures are strongest in the United States, due to the large and growing coastal populations. Wetland losses, for example, have averaged 8 000 hectares annually over the past 25 years.

The Atlantic Coast

Much of the eastern US coastline is densely populated and heavily industrialised. In contrast, the Canadian coastline is more sparsely populated, with a clustered distribution of urban centres amid numerous coastal settlements.

Generally speaking, an array of contaminants, including synthetic organic chemicals, trace metals, and assorted litter, can be found in zones along the east coast. Findings from the US Musselwatch programme (which monitors contaminant accumulations in bivalves) indicate high contaminant levels near many urban and industrial sites. For example, the highest PAH levels are recorded in the Hudson-Raritan estuary and Boston Harbor. Elevated PAH levels are also found in Long Island Sound and the New York Bight. Generally, PCB and pesticide levels follow a distribution pattern similar to that of PAHs. Canadian studies have similarly identified contaminants in harbours, bays, and estuaries near population centres. For example, the St. Lawrence estuary, which drains the most industrialised area of Canada, has been shown to be extensively contaminated with numerous organic and inorganic compounds. Using seabirds as indicators of contaminant concentrations, the greatest contamination is found in the St. Lawrence estuary, followed (in order) by the Gulf of St. Lawrence, Bay of Fundy, and Newfoundland.

Many and diverse ecological effects have been identified, although direct cause-effect relationships are often unclear. For example, fin erosion and lesions have been detected in Boston Harbor winter flounder, and seasonally low oxygen levels occur regularly in (among other regions) Chesapeake Bay and the New York Bight.

Shellfish harvest closures are a continuing problem in many areas of the Atlantic coast, due largely to fecal contamination from sewage waste, but also to chemical contamination and naturally occurring toxins. In Atlantic Canada, approximately 146 000 hectares of potential shellfish harvesting areas were closed in 1988 due to fecal pollution, with a slow but steady trend towards increasing closures. Similar closures affect many regions in the USA, and the problem is increasing rapidly in the southeast coastal area.

The Gulf of Mexico

The Gulf of Mexico is a resource-rich and heavily used region. Fish and shellfish harvests total some 1.13 billion kg annually. Offshore oil and gas production is substantial, as is the shipping tonnage passing through Gulf ports. Furthermore, the many estuaries,

CONTAMINANTS IN THE ARCTIC OCEAN

A Sensitive Ecosystem

The Arctic Ocean is relatively small and almost completely encircled by the landmasses of North America, Eurasia and Greenland. Its waters extend well into the many inlets, passages and bays of surrounding states, and the sea ice which is present over much of the area reflects incoming solar radiation and restricts primary productivity. Biological diversity is quite limited, and it has been suggested that the Arctic's short, simple trophic network may be particularly vulnerable to pollutant stress. Other characteristics, such as the climate extremes and slow biomass turnover, also contribute to the Arctic's vulnerability.

Pollution from Distant Sources

Compared to contaminated marine ecosystems in other regions of the world, the Arctic Ocean remains relatively pristine. However, monitoring programmes and related scientific studies indicate that human activities have affected the quality of the arctic marine environment.

Traces of toxic chemicals occur in the Arctic Ocean: industrial chemicals, such as PCBs and lead; and agricultural pesticides such as DDT, chlordane, lindane and toxaphene. These contaminants have been found in Arctic air, surface seawater, suspended sediments, fish, marine mammals, seabirds and terrestrial mammals. Their presence in marine mammals such as seals and polar bears shows that they are fully distributed throughout the marine food web. The potential effects on humans (consumption of fish and other "country foods" is high among northern residents), indeed, on all species at higher trophic levels, is a concern.

Exact sources of many arctic contaminants are unknown but are global in nature. Recent research in Canada has demonstrated that long-range transport via the atmosphere has introduced measureable quantities of organic contaminants derived from distant agricultural and industrial sources. Other important contaminant pathways to the Arctic include ocean currents and large rivers. In contrast, sources of metals such as mercury and cadmium are believed to be local.

Indicator species such as polar bears, seals and seabirds are useful for determining trends in the presence and geographic distribution of organic contaminants in arctic marine ecosystems. In the Canadian Arctic, studies have suggested that temporal trends of PCB and DDT contaminants in seals and seabirds are downwards or static between the early 1970s and the present. In polar bears the data are more difficult to interpret. Levels of organochlorine contaminants measured in 1983 were double the levels measured in 1969; however, other factors than a general increase in marine contamination (such as age of bears at the time of sampling) may account for the perceived increases. Concerning metals, high levels of cadmium and mercury have been measured in arctic marine mammals, but their sources are mainly natural and local. However, lead detected in the arctic marine environment originates mainly from distant

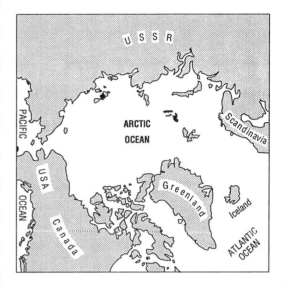

industrial sources. This is reflected in Greenland's glacial ice deposits and in mussels, which show higher levels now than in pre-industrial times.

International Co-operative Research and Action

Research on pollution in the Arctic Ocean has expanded significantly in the last few decades. Several countries bordering the ocean have established local environmental monitoring programmes and pollution prevention zones. These have increased understanding of the state of the Arctic Ocean and have facilitated more effective management of human activities in the region.

More recent actions to protect the arctic environment are increasingly being coordinated among arctic states. Bi-lateral co-operation has led to the development of several agreements between Canada, the Soviet Union, the United States, Denmark and other northern nations. A 1989 initiative by Finland on protection of the arctic environment has brought the eight circumpolar nations together to explore ways of co-operating on legal, scientific and operational issues related to, among other things, arctic pollution, scientific research and monitoring, and protection of arctic fauna and flora.

These actions are essential. Due to the importance of distant contaminant sources, resolving contamination problems in the arctic marine environment will require that measures to control pollution be taken in industrialised countries further south.

Contribution from Canada

wetlands and barrier islands in the region provide important wildlife habitat, including that of most migratory waterfowl traversing the USA. In the decade spanning 1970 to 1980 human population on the Gulf coast increased by 30 per cent, and serious conflicts are now emerging among users and coastal resources.

Nutrients pose a threat to many estuaries in the region. These are becoming enriched with nitrogen and phosphorus, originating mainly from rivers and upstream sources such as agriculture. Consequently, in many estuaries algae blooms and oxygen depletion are recurring problems.

Environmental restructuring pressures are very strong in the Gulf. The demand for coastline residential development has led to the drainage and infilling of many coastal wetlands and the subsequent loss of important habitats. This problem is most pronounced in Louisiana, where up to 80 per cent of annual coastal wetland losses in the United States now occur. In recent years the rate of annual wetland loss has increased substantially, from 4 100 hectares in 1971 to roughly 15 500 hectares in 1989.

The warm temperatures and low water renewal rates present in many areas provide ideal conditions for the growth of pathogens originating from sewage wastes. As a result, in 1987 so many shellfish were found to be pathogen-contaminated that 648 000 hectares of shellfish growing areas along the Gulf coast were closed, a situation resulting in substantial economic losses.

Chemical and petrochemical industries account for roughly 48 per cent of the total point source wastewater discharge to the Gulf. Furthermore, the extraction and transport of oil introduces significant amounts of petroleum hydrocarbons and associated contaminants into the marine environment of the region.

The Pacific Coast

Pressures on North America's Pacific coast vary regionally. The Alaskan and Northern Canadian coasts are sparsely populated and relatively pristine; oil shipping constitutes the major threat to the quality of the marine environment. In the more densely populated southern regions, the most significant pollution problems result from the disposal of municipal and industrial wastes.

Industrial discharges along the west coast originate primarily from forest-product industries, metal processing plants, mining operations, smelters, and food processing plants. Coastal waters, bottom sediments, and marine organisms near these areas are often contaminated with metals, synthetic chemical compounds, or organic debris. For example, in the USA the highest concentrations of PAHs in bivalves have been found in Elliot Bay, Washington State, and elevated levels have been detected in San Diego and San Francisco Bays. The general distribution of PCBs follows a pattern similar to that of PAHs. In Canada, concerns focus primarily on discharges from pulp and paper mills and runoff from wood product industries. Organic wastes from pulp mills cause oxygen depletion while solid wood wastes tend to smother benthic habitat. The production of dioxin contaminants from pulp mill processes, and their presence in marine organisms such as shellfish, has recently been discovered.

At highly contaminated sites, diseases and related effects in marine organisms are frequently observed. For example, non-cancerous lesions of the type known to be caused by PAHs have been identified in the livers of English sole from Vancouver harbour. In the USA, tumours have been identified in mussels from six west coast locations, most frequently in the Puget Sound, Commencement Bay, Elliot Bay and Sinclair Inlet areas.

Pollution from sewage wastes also affects areas along the west coast. In British Columbia, approximately 70 500 hectares of bivalve shellfish harvesting beds were closed by 1988 for reasons of bacterial contamination. This number continues to increase slowly every year, although the increase is partially due to sampling being conducted over larger areas. In 1988 and 1989, a further 67 500 hectares were closed because of dioxine contamination affecting mainly crustaceans, some bivalves and shellfish harvesting.

Because the Pacific coast is an important shipping route for the transport of oil between production fields in Alaska and consumers in the lower USA, oil spills are a constant risk. Two recent accidents – the massive spill of the Exxon Valdez in Alaska and the smaller Netussca spill off Vancouver Island and the State of Washington – caused significant ecological and economic damage and brought renewed calls for more effective measures to counteract such events.

Marine quality prospects

Progress made in protecting North America's marine environment has been largely associated with the control of point source pollution discharges and the regulation of coastal land use through instruments such as zoning. However, this progress has to some extent been counterbalanced by increasing pressures due to intensifying coastal populations and land uses.

As pressures grow, so will the need for additional protective and preventive measures. In particular, these must be targeted at non-point pollution sources (e.g. agricultural runoff), certain types of industrial operations, and sewage discharges as well as specific pollutants such as dioxins and TBT. Recent marine management efforts are adopting a more integrated area-wide approach, as exemplified by estuary and coastal zone management programmes being implemented in the USA and, to a lesser extent, in Canada. The rigorous implementation of these measures is essential for ensuring the long-term vitality of North America's coastal waters.

INTEGRATED COASTAL ZONE MANAGEMENT IN TASMANIA (AUSTRALIA)

The island of Tasmania is Australia's southernmost state. For centuries, the many resources of its rich and varied coastal zone provided abundant food for early aboriginal inhabitants. Today, the coastal zone supports an expanding aquaculture industry, is the site of numerous industrial operations and a place of recreation and relaxation for both tourists and local residents.

Conflicting Coastal Uses

Many of the uses made of Tasmania's coastal zone are in potential conflict with one another, and the finite nature of the coast is increasingly being realised. Sharing the coast with a multiplicity of uses is now a matter of necessity, yet many conflicting uses still require resolution. These include:

- Aquaculture vs. activities which contribute to coastal pollution. Aquaculture has recently been undergoing rapid expansion in many coastal areas of Tasmania and is now a multi-million dollar industry. Yet in some areas the growth of this industry is limited by pollution. In the Derwent River estuary, for example, discharges of industrial and sewage effluent have caused the contamination of shellfish with bacteria and heavy metals (such as mercury and cadmium), and have prevented aquaculture farms from being established. Similar cases exist near many other effluent disposal locations;
- Aquaculture vs. tourism and recreation. The recent advent of fish farming in traditional recreational areas in southern Tasmania has created much potential for conflict. The successful farming of fish such as young salmon relies strongly on favourable farm site characteristics such as sheltered and unpolluted bays. Many of these characteristics directly overlap with those of preferred recreational areas or cottage sites, and many aquaculture leases are now in close proximity to long-established holiday settlements;
- Coastal development vs. preservation of marshlands and wetlands. Salt marshes are important in both marine and terrestrial food chains and for fish nurseries. Salt marsh, however, is poorly protected in Tasmania. Of the State's estimated 3,300 hectares of salt marsh, fewer than 100 hectares are secure within State reserves. Factors such as cattle grazing, off-road vehicles, landfill and dams are having a deleterious effect, especially with regard to exotic species invasion, water quality and fish nurseries. Coastal wetlands, among the world's most productive natural systems, face similar pressures from development.

Implementing Coastal Zone Management in Tasmania

The problems and conflicts which have arisen in Tasmania's coastal zone have all too often resulted from a lack of knowledge and foresight: buildings unwisely located on frontal dunes, inadequate control of pollution discharges in aquaculture zones, interference with water flows in wetlands and saltmarshes. These have been compounded by a lack of governmental policy with regard to the

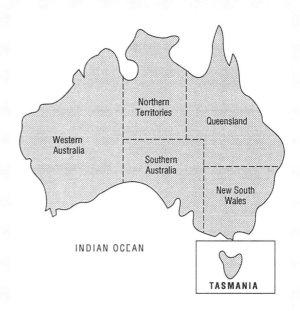

protection of the coastal zone, a lack of clear principles for coastal management, and a lack of official focus for information, research and other aspects related to coastal areas.

The purpose of Tasmania's coastal zone management initiative is to be embodied in the Coastal Management Plan, seeking to achieve a balance between the protection of environmental quality and provision for the social and economic needs of individual communities. Each specific targeted area has its specific plan which will contain the following components:

- Description of the significance of the area;
- Profile of the area's ecosystem, including critical parameters for the sustainable development of its resources;
- Existing use, development and capability of the area;
- Current problems and issues;
- Identification of opportunities to enhance the area;
- Future land and water use, and an environmental management strategy including goals, policies, objectives and performance standards;
- An implementation strategy, including organisation of administration, monitoring and feedback.

These plans make possible integrated planning for development of an area's potential, as well as an integrated approach to the resolution of existing conflicts.

Contribution from Australia

3. SUSTAINABLE USE OF LIVING MARINE RESOURCES: FISHERIES AND AQUACULTURE

The living organisms of the oceans provide food for humans (between 10 and 20 per cent of world protein intake) and sustain economic activity in many nations and coastal regions. Being renewable resources, fisheries and aquaculture can provide benefits to humans indefinitely, provided they are properly managed on a sustainable basis.

Fisheries

In 1988, global fishery harvests amounted to some 85 million tonnes (92 million tonnes if aquaculture is included), 15 million tonnes below the Food and Agriculture Organisation's (FAO) estimated maximum global sustainable yield of 100 million tonnes. The overall global trend has been towards increased landings of fish, a 44 per cent increase over the 1970s and 1980s. Assuming these trends continue, the FAO figure is expected to be exceeded before the turn of the century. Although global harvests are presently below sustainable yield estimates, many of the more valuable fish stocks are overfished, and the steady trend towards increased global harvests is achieved partly through exploitation of new and/or less valuable species.

OECD countries play an important role in world fisheries. (Figure 16) In 1988 total OECD landings amounted to approximately 31 million tonnes. Within the OECD area, Japan is the largest fishing nation by volume, accounting for about 14 per cent of the world total. Second in importance is the USA (6.7 per cent), followed by Denmark (2.3 per cent), Norway (2.2 per cent), Iceland (2.1 per cent), Canada (1.8 per cent), and Spain (1.7 per cent).

Fishery productivity is greatly influenced by both natural and human factors. Since ocean currents and upwellings transport nutrients which contribute to biological productivity, they influence the location and productivity of fisheries. In addition, human activities such as waste disposal and harvesting also have a significant impact.

Waste materials released into estuaries and coastal zones can have damaging effects on coastal fisheries. Morphological changes, skin ulcerations and other diseases are some of the frequently observed effects, although on a broad scale the relationship between coastal pollution and fishery productivity remains unclear.

Despite the problems of coastal pollution, the most significant pressure affecting fisheries results from harvesting. Overfishing has in the past depleted major fishing resources such as those of the Alaskan king crab in the 1980s and of Peruvian anchovies in the 1970s. It continues to be a problem: landings from the Mediterranean, the Black Sea and the northwest Pacific regions are reported to exceed those regions' estimated sustainable yields, while the northeast and northwest Atlantic regions are near their estimated sustainable yields.

The risks of overexploitation have increased, because of the growing world need for protein and the improvements in harvesting technology (larger and/or more efficient fishing fleets). The economic importance of fisheries, coupled with the prospect of increased harvesting pressures, clearly point to the need for sound management. Progress has been made: generally speaking, since the early 1970s the growth in landings has been slower and the management of stocks stricter than in the prior period. Also, the definition of Exclusive Economic Zones (EEZ) and the establishment of regional fisheries organisations have encouraged national action and international co-operation to further fisheries management. However, the science of stock assessment and fisheries management in general remains imperfect and continuing disputes among nations over fishing rights, and over the ways in which quotas are determined and allocated, threaten the sustainable development of the resource.

Aquaculture

The worldwide commercial rearing of marine species is a relatively new development in the production of food for humans. Total world production from aquaculture is now between 12-14 million tonnes annually. That represents 14-16 per cent of world fish landings, but aquaculture products generally have a high value and comprise about one-third (US $12 billion) of total production value.

In the OECD, aquaculture, as an expanding industry, plays an increasingly important economic role in many coastal regions. The largest producers by volume are Japan, the United States, Spain, and France. (Table 7) The largest producers in terms of value are Japan, the United States, Norway, France, Italy, Australia and the United Kingdom. In the late 1980s total production value for all OECD countries amounted to about US $7.0 billion.

As a coastal industry, cultivation in saltwater (mariculture) is both a source and a victim of marine pollution. As a source, mariculture releases uneaten food and feces into surrounding waters, thus contributing nutrients which may cause local eutrophication problems. Feces may also impact the benthic zone through sedimentation. Other topics of concern are the use of antibiotics fed to fish, the potential spread of disease to wild stock, and use of antifoulants on the facilities.

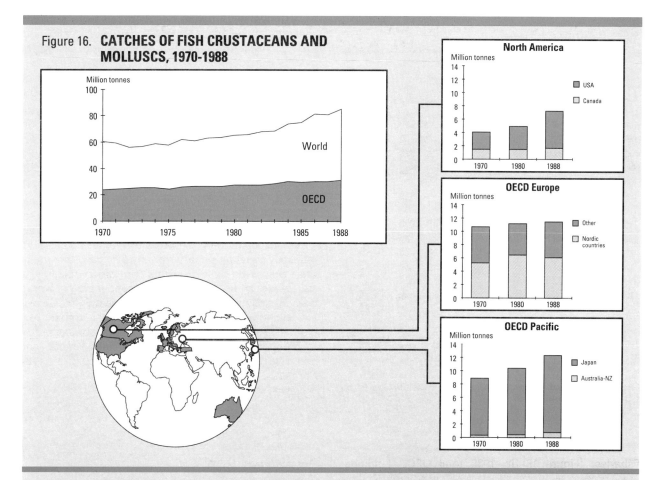

Figure 16. **CATCHES OF FISH CRUSTACEANS AND MOLLUSCS, 1970-1988**

	1970		1980		1988	
	1000 tonnes	% of World	1000 tonnes	% of World	1000 tonnes	% of World
By major fishing areas:						
North Atlantic	14 741	24.9	14 725	22.9	13 553	16.0
Central Atlantic	5 038	8.5	6 879	10.7	7 463	8.8
Southern Atlantic	3 583	6.1	3 822	5.9	5 128	6.0
Indian Ocean	2 423	4.1	4 278	6.6	5 596	6.6
Northern Pacific	14 733	24.9	20 725	32.2	30 041	35.4
Central Pacific	4 724	8.0	6 634	10.3	8 530	10.0
Southern Pacific	13 931	23.5	7 358	11.4	14 637	17.2
World Total	59 173	100.0	64 420	100.0	84 949	100.0
By selected countries:						
Canada	1 295	2.2	1 293	2.0	1 545	1.8
USA	2 729	4.6	3 565	5.5	5 656	6.7
Japan	8 658	14.6	10 213	15.9	11 700	13.8
Denmark	1 217	2.1	2 010	3.1	1 948	2.3
France	761	1.3	761	1.2	855	1.0
Germany *a*	598	1.0	289	0.4	184	0.2
Iceland	733	1.2	1 514	2.4	1 759	2.1
Italy	378	0.6	4 672	7.3	501	0.6
Norway	2 906	4.9	2 409	3.7	1 826	2.1
Spain	1 517	2.6	1 282	2.0	1 400	1.7
UK	1 077	1.8	831	1.3	921	1.1
OECD Total	23 529	39.8	26 616	41.3	31 080	36.6

Note: a) Includes western Germany only.

Source: FAO

Table 7. AQUACULTURE

| | Aquaculture production | | | Fisheries production Total (mill. US$)[b] | Aquaculture vs. fisheries (%) |
	Fish (tonnes)	Molluscs (tonnes)	Value (mill. US$)		
Canada	3 100	8 600	23	930	2
USA	224 100	57 700	496	2 760	18
Japan	291 600	892 600	3 620	17 220	21
Australia	1 200	8 400	..	400	..
New Zealand	500	15 000	13	..	..
Denmark	27 400	..	75	440	17
Finland	10 100	..	45	40	116
France	38 500	173 300	404	980	41
Germany[a]	20 200	21 000	55	120	45
Greece	4 600	2 300	19	360	5
Ireland	1 800	11 000	11	80	13
Italy	33 000	87 900	128	1 300	10
Netherlands	700	102 000	51	360	14
Norway	50 000	200	233	670	35
Portugal	2 800	8 200	..	320	..
Spain	16 900	250 400	60	1 550	3
Sweden	4 000	300	13	100	14
UK	21 200	4 100	92	530	17

Notes: Aquaculture refers to farming of fish, molluscs, crustaceans and algae both in inland and in marine waters.

    a) Includes western Germany only.

    b) Includes fish for reduction, but excludes aquaculture. However, production of fisheries includes aquaculture for France and Japan.

Source: OECD

Conversely, marine pollution can have a significant impact on aquaculture. Poor water quality and toxic phytoplankton blooms can preclude, disrupt or destroy aquaculture operations. A striking example is the toxic algae bloom which occurred in the North Sea off Norway in the spring of 1988. Losses to salmon and trout farms in the south of the country totalled some 480 metric tonnes, but the physical relocation of growing pens to unaffected areas averted even larger losses.

Another related issue is that of coastal land use. As a competitor for coastal land, the industry's rapid expansion in some areas has led to conflicts. Aquaculture sites may block or restrict public access to important recreational areas, inhibit residential development, or impact on wildlife habitat.

The continued expansion of the aquaculture industry depends on a number of factors, the major ones being the cost of production, the availability of suitable locations (given the unprecedented growth of human coastal populations), technology, resources, and the influence and effectiveness of government regulations. Aquaculture's dependence on fishmeal puts it in competition with other commercial markets, and could become a limiting factor of aquaculture development.

4. CONCLUSIONS

Over the past 20 years, much has been achieved in advancing knowledge about and protection of the marine environment. Scientific understanding of basic oceanographic properties and processes and of factors which affect productivity in the oceans has increased. This improved knowledge base has stimulated the development of an ocean management regime operating at the international, regional and national levels. Activities such as fishing, ocean dumping, shipping, and use of specific substances have all come under increased regulation.

Despite some limited progress in the past two decades, *most problems remain*:

- Levels of *some synthetic organic compounds* have decreased in many heavily contaminated areas of OECD countries, largely due to restrictions placed on their manufacture, use, and release into the environment. However, their persistence in coastal sediments and bioaccumulation in the fatty tissues of marine wildlife remain important concerns;

- Levels of *trace metals* such as mercury, cadmium and lead, some of which have been the cause of severe human health problems, have also declined, although in many areas levels in sediments remain high in the vicinity of important point sources;

- *Oil inputs* to the oceans have decreased, due in part to a decreased frequency of large shipping accidents and spills. However, oil pollution from continental origin (from rivers, coastal activities and atmospheric origin) as well as from routine maritime transport persists; its effects on beaches and various forms of marine life continue;

- To some degree the uncontrolled *harvesting of world fisheries* has been reduced. However, disagreements persist among fishing nations regarding sustainable harvesting levels and overfishing remains a problem for some species and in some regions;

- *Surveillance and knowledge* of the state of the marine environment has improved, and monitoring activities have expanded into new areas. Nonetheless, important gaps remain regarding the scale of pollutant inputs from many sources, their distribution and concentration in the environment, and the magnitude and significance of the resulting effects.

At the same time, a number of new *concerns have emerged*:

- In some coastal regions *nutrient* levels have increased, as have the duration, frequency and intensity of algal blooms. In some parts of the North and Adriatic Seas, for example, these now occur over larger areas, causing significant ecological and economic losses. The control of diffuse nutrient sources such as agricultural runoff remains largely unresolved;

- The accumulation of *polluting substances in marine organisms* is another important concern. In the Arctic, for example, this involves the long-range transport and bioaccumulation of synthetic organic compounds in marine mammals. In other marine areas the accumulation of pathogens, largely as a result of sewage waste disposal, has contaminated numerous shell fisheries;

- The accumulation of *plastic debris*, including discarded fishing gear, in the marine environment causes adverse effects on marine wild life and coastal areas such as beaches;

- The *restructuring and development of shorelines*, marshes and other coastal areas continues virtually unabated. In the process important wild life habitats and other ecologically valuable areas are being lost, often irreversibly. The coasts of southern Europe and the southern USA are particularly affected;

- Finally, and in relation to the analysis developed in the Global Atmospheric Issues chapter, concern has emerged regarding the possible *impact of atmospheric changes on sea-levels and oceanic productivity*.

Degradation of the marine environment such as depletion of fish stocks, forced closures of shellfish beds, and fouling of beaches from oil residues and debris represents a significant economic cost to the economies of many coastal areas. In fact, the degradation of the quality of the marine environment threatens the sustainable development of fishing resources, aquaculture and coastal tourism activities in a number of these coastal areas. Furthermore, the prospect of possible sea level rise relating to global atmospheric issues threatens the development of coastal areas where a high proportion of population and capital is concentrated. The effective and efficient implementation and enforcement of measures adopted at local, national and international levels, as well as new preventive and protective measures, will be indispensable to ensure the sustainable development of marine and coastal resources and areas.

NOTE AND REFERENCES

1. Terabecquerel (TBq) = 10^{12} Bq = 27 Curies. One Bq (Becquerel) arises from one nuclear disintegration per second.

OECD (1985), *The State of the Environment*, Paris.

OECD (1985), *Problems of Trade in Fishery Products*, Paris.

OECD (1987), *Review of Fisheries in OECD Member Countries*, Paris.

OECD (1989), *Aquaculture: An Emerging New Industry*, Paris.

OECD (1989), *Aquaculture: Review of Recent Evidence*, Paris.

OECD (1989), *OECD Compendium of Environmental Data 1989*, Paris.

Chapter 5

LAND

Throughout the history of man, the value of land as a resource has played a critical role in his survival. Its importance may be expressed from three general viewpoints: social, economic and natural.

From a social viewpoint, land acquires value through ownership and through cultural and traditional heritage. Local, regional, state or provincial and national governments bear the responsibilities of stewardship of public land(s). The land in public ownership takes a number of forms: municipalities, large national tracts for parks, preserves, forests, rangeland, offshore land, deserts, and rights to the living and non-living resources therein. Degrees of access to public land vary from prohibited (e.g. wilderness areas) to limited (e.g. forests) and unlimited (e.g. urban parks). Private ownership of land may range from small plots on which homes are built to large tracts of open land – forests, rangeland, and so on. Less tangible but no less important are the cultural, historical heritage and traditional values of land, including passing of family land down from one generation to the next.

The economic value of land may range from survival-level benefit to financial gain on a very high level. It is derived from agricultural and forestry activities, mineral extraction and activities linked to the built environment. Agriculture, together with manufacturing and transport, often forms the backbone of a country's economy and is of particular importance because of its increasing significance in international trade. Sylviculture, also an economic mainstay in some countries, has export/import significance and, along with agriculture, is particularly susceptible to certain transboundary environmental effects. Onshore mineral extraction, processing and transport are of significant economic value and at times there can also be important environmental costs. The built environment gives land economic value expressed mainly in terms of revenue to government from real estate taxes, revenue to the private sector from real estate sales, commercial profit, and capital assets for private and public institutions.

A more abstract but no less important economic aspect of land is its aesthetic value – scenic vistas of mountains, lakes, undisturbed countryside. The natural value of land benefits man and other living things both directly and indirectly, through exploitation and protection by man and through natural functions. Local, regional and national parks are often designed and managed for multiple use by man as well as for plants and animals. Man's uses include such activities as camping, hiking, boating and riding. Plants and animals are generally protected from hunting and collecting, but may be widely observed. Wilderness areas are set aside as natural enclaves untouched by man's presence and activities. These areas are designed and managed to preserve wildlife and, in many cases, consist of the last remaining ecosystems and species that have otherwise disappeared. The diverse functional services of natural areas range from flood control, waste treatment and nutritional nurseries for larval species of wetlands to the contribution of atmospheric oxygen by trees, from the hydrologic recharge properties of undisturbed forest floors to the decomposition and recycling of minerals and nutrients by soil organisms. OECD countries' total percentage of arable and cropland, permanent grassland and forest and other wooded land can be compared to the worldwide percentage. (Figure 17)

1. SOILS

Natural roles

In mountainous, rocky or arctic regions, the soil depth is only a few centimetres, whereas in fertile forests or prairies it may be a metre or two. Yet nearly all the terrestrial life of the planet depends on this small veneer. The basic natural roles of soils include life support, cycling of elements and stabilisation.

Life support soil systems are found both on and under the surface. The topsoil contains the predominantly organic portions: nutrients and moisture to support surface-dwelling plants and animals through litter,

Figure 17. **STATE OF LAND USE, 1988**

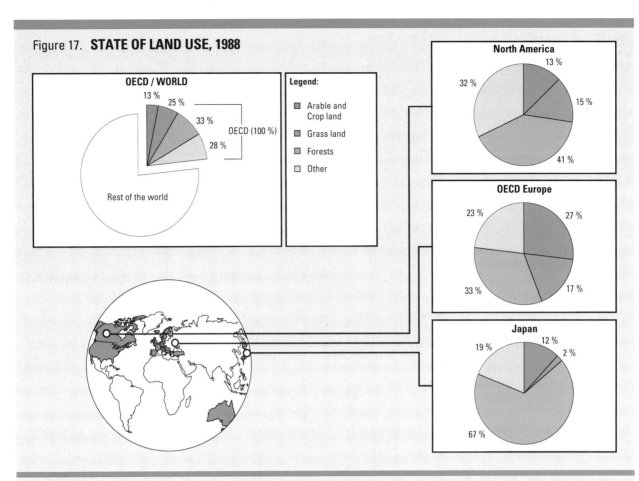

	State 1988				Changes 1970 - 1988 (%)		
	Land Area 1000 km²	of which: Agricultural Land		Forests and Woodland %	Agricultural Land		Forests and Woodland
		Arable and Cropland %	Meadows and Pastures %		Arable and Cropland	Meadows and Pastures	
Canada	9 215	5	4	49	10	44	2
USA	9 167	21	26	32	-1	-1	-3
Japan	377	12	2	67	-15	122	0
Finland	305	8	0	77	-8	-21	0
France	550	36	21	28	8	-16	8
Germany *a*	244	31	18	30	-1	-19	3
Italy	294	41	17	23	-15	-5	10
Netherlands	34	27	32	9	6	-18	1
Norway	307	3	0	27	6	-15	6
Portugal	92	39	6	34	-6	0	11
Spain	499	41	20	31	-4	-12	9
Sweden	403	7	1	70	-4	-21	1
Turkey	770	36	11	26	1	-17	0
UK	242	29	48	10	-3	-1	25
North America	18 382	13	15	41	1	3	0
OECD Europe	4 239	27	17	33	-2	-10	4
OECD	30 883	13	25	33	2	-3	1
World	130 693	11	25	31	4	1	-3

Note: a) Includes western Germany only.

Source: OECD, FAO

leaf mould and humus; habitat for near surface dwellers, decomposer organisms, worms and insect larvae that form part of the ecosystem. Within the sub-soil are found the predominantly inorganic portions of leached soil and mineral soil. The latter is formed from the bits and pieces of rocks and minerals chipped away from the earth's crust. The rocks and minerals contain chemicals for plant nutrition and determine the acidity of the soil. A little known fact is that the amount of total organic material within the soil is many times greater than that found on the surface. For example, one kg of rich soil in central and northern Europe contains up to a trillion bacteria, a trillion fungi, and a billion algae, as well as thousands of different worms, insects, and mites.

The cycling of elements by the soil involves minerals, nutrients and water. Minerals from plant and animal decomposition are held in the soil by humus and made available for plant uptake. Soil is a good habitat for decomposers, which recycle inorganic and organic chemicals such as nitrogen, phosphorus and carbon. Soil with stable vegetation and a topsoil layer becomes a good route for water to percolate into groundwater or deeper into aquifers, an important step in the hydrologic cycle. Soil types tend to govern the chemical composition of groundwater. Soil bacteria have been useful in treating wastes from septic systems.

Soils and vegetation have mutually benefiting roles: stable soil allows vegetative growth which, in turn, holds the soil together to allow more growth. The stable characteristics of soils also play a major role in man's activities, particularly in excavations and the building of large structures.

Soil loss and degradation

In most systems, the rate of soil production is equal to or greater than the rate of removal, so soil depth and fertility increase with time. *Soil erosion* by wind and water is a natural process, but can be magnified by man's activities to the extent where it exceeds the rate of new soil formation, as it now does on 35 per cent of the world's cropland. Industrialised countries can compensate with increased fertilization, but in Third World countries soil loss is reducing land productivity. In the 1980s erosion in the United States averaged about 10.5 tonnes per hectare per year, and about 44 per cent of cropland there is now losing soil faster than it is being formed. The Darling Downs in Australia, where average wheat production per hectare is five times the national average, are losing four to eight millimetres of topsoil to erosion each year and in 30 to 50 years would will be exhausted without the active soil conservation programme now under way. One of the most significant impacts of soil loss, chiefly through erosion but also through other degradation, is a reduction in the soil's ability to sustain development. As erosion diminishes the productive ability of the soil, input costs for fertilizers, pesticides and irrigation rise and

offset profits until it is no longer cost-effective to farm the land.

Growing pressure has been put on arid lands by the demands from increasing populations for jobs, food or water. If fields are not irrigated, there is a constant threat of drought that will destroy crops and leave the soil bare and vulnerable to erosion. If the disruption is severe enough, grasses and shrubs cannot re-establish themselves, and without plants rainfall is not retained. When soil quality and moisture content decline, a productive semi-arid region can be converted into a desert, a process known as *desertification*. Desertification may also occur from over-grazing. Where rainfall is low and evaporation is high, the risk of desertification is great. OECD countries such as Australia, Canada, Spain, Turkey and the United States are affected by this phenomenon. The potential effect of climate change on desertification in OECD countries should be considered.

The amount of land irrigated is quite significant in a number of OECD countries, but some irrigation is unsustainable because of *salinisation* and *waterlogging* effects. In arid and semi-arid regions high evaporation rates leave salts from irrigation water in fields. Over time this saline accumulation may cause damage to the plants and leave the soil unproductive. A typical irrigation application rate is 10 000 m^3 per ha. per year, which adds two to five tonnes of salt to the soil annually per ha. In the mid-1980s in the USA, 5.2 million hectares of irrigated land were damaged by salinisation, representing 27 per cent of the gross irrigated area. Another effect of unsustainable irrigation is waterlogging. Bad drainage causes seepage from unlined canals and over-watering of fields raises the underlying groundwater. As the groundwater rises, the plants' roots become waterlogged, eliminating oxygen and thus interfering with plant growth. In arid and semi-arid regions waterlogging may be accompanied by salinisation as the sun evaporates the water near the surface, creating a salt buildup.

Soil degradation from *pollution* occurs as air emissions settle out on land and as larger amounts of hazardous materials, as well as conventional waste, are disposed of both on and within the soil. (See Chapters on Air and Solid Waste) In the soil these compounds impair the growth of wild and cultivated plants and have a negative effect on soil bacteria. Unless the soil is rich in neutralising limestone, the acidic precipitation runs off into lakes and rivers where further damage is done. Soils may also become contaminated by the dumping of hazardous materials and from polluted river bottom sediment. Reclamation may involve removal of the soil and dumping elsewhere, processing the soil material and replacement or isolation *in situ* to prevent the pollutant from spreading.

Intensive agriculture which relies on multicropping, addition of chemicals and irrigation may degrade the soil. (See Chapter on Agriculture). Each crop requires

SOIL EROSION AND MANAGEMENT: THE PORTUGUESE CASE

A Natural Process of Transformation

A primary concern for natural-resources managers is ensuring soil preservation in temperate regions. The natural processes of degradation result in organic material loss upon which soil fertility depends.

Climate variability and environmental diversity affect the natural processes of soil degradation. Soil degradation is more significant when the rains are irregular and fall over a short period of time, as is the case in Mediterranean regions.

In Portugal, the natural degradation processes are varied due to the country's diverse environmental characteristics. Portugal is situated on an ancient plateau, the "Meseta". The plateau has hills in the south-central regions (the peneplains of Alentejo and Beira), a Primary Era granite intrusion in the northwest, limestone hills along the western and southern coasts, fluvial and coastal sedimentation (Tejo and Sado) and igneous bedrock (Lisboa and Monchique) from volcanic activity during the Tertiary Era. In addition, the alluvial plains are characterized by sedimentary deposits due to sea level oscillations of the Quaternary Era.

Human Activities and Soil Degradation

Human activities affect soil conditions as well. The soil is particularly vulnerable to human activities with the presence of agents such as dryness, temperature change and wind during periods of little rain. For example, cattle raising in the pastures of SE Alentejo, typified by a scattered vegetative covering, is barely sustainable and thus quite vulnerable to increases in soil degradation processes.

Overuse of the soil caused by human activities can increase the rate of soil degradation. The degradation mechanisms, erosion and sedimentation, can be linked to factors such as deforestation and the alteration of inland water discharge by dam construction. These human activities contribute to the depletion of soil productivity.

Of all human activities, agricultural production has had the greatest impact on soil degradation. Traditionally, farming practices had been well-balanced with soil sustainability. Overuse and the application of new technologies pose a threat to this balance.

This threat is particularly relevant in Portugal, whose arable soils represent only 12 per cent of the entire country. Portugal's soil generally is not very thick, fertile or stable. The soil is highly vulnerable to the Mediterranean climatic conditions and type of farming methods, as illustrated in the Alentejo cornfields. Moreover, 23 per cent of the land used for farming is characterised by unsuitable soils.

Vast areas of land have been exposed to erosion processes as land is taken out of cultivation or subjected to new competitive farming. At times, the improved competitive farming is inappropriate to the regional environmental characteristics.

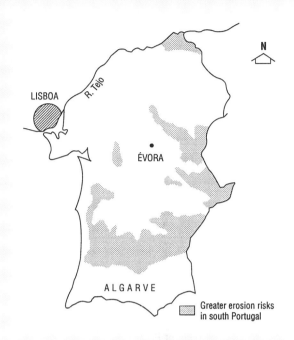

Greater erosion risks in south Portugal

A Framework for Action

The combination of Portugal's climatic variability, environmental diversity, and historical human activity has resulted in a mosaic of different soil conditions. Laws for soil conservation, forestry (as a means of protecting soils) and natural resources have existed in Portugal since the mid-1970s. Such policies, however, were not sufficient for a number of regions around the country due to a lack of information and sufficient regulations to enforce soil conservation methods.

In 1989, Portugal amended an earlier law by enacting the National Agrarian Reserve. This law focuses on conserving the high quality soils.

Other laws, recognising forest as an economic resource and a natural means of soil protection, regulate the harvesting, uprooting and replanting of trees. These legislative initiatives make forest land-use changes more difficult, thus protecting the typically unstable soil.

Finally, two laws, the National Ecological Reserve of 1990 and the Protected Areas Regulation, are designed to protect natural resources. These laws recognise the soil as a basic life resource and encourage its use in ways that are sustainable.

In conclusion, despite some lack of information and regulation in areas of great natural diversity, as is found in the northern part of the country, Portugal has in place the legislative framework necessary to implement effective soil management for a variety of environmental conditions.

Contribution from Portugal

ACIDIFICATION OF SOIL AND WATER IN SWEDEN

Despite recent emission reductions in many countries, several hundred million tonnes of sulphur and nitrogen compounds are still released into the air every year from the world's urban and industrial areas. In the atmosphere, a considerable part of these compounds are transformed into strongly acidifying substances such as sulphuric acid and nitric acid. Sooner or later these substances reach the ground. In heavily industrialised areas, such as Europe, the acidic fallout may be ten times greater now than in the pre-industrial period.

Acidification of Terrestrial and Aquatic Ecosystems

In some parts of the world, notably Canada and northern Europe, the prevailing types of primeval rock afford little protection against acidic fallout. In most parts of Sweden for instance, the supply of acids to the soil has exceeded its neutralizing capacity for several decades. Comparisons of recent soil data from southern Sweden with measurements made in the same places up to 60 years ago reveal three- to thirtyfold increases in the acidity of the soil. In those parts of Sweden where the acid deposition is strongest, this effect now extends several metres below the soil surface.

Soil acidification may be an important factor, although probably not the only one, behind the forest damage observed in many parts of Europe during the 1980s. Since this acidification has caused a strong depletion of magnesium and similar mineral nutrients in the soil, it may in the long run endanger productivity even in apparently undamaged forests. The aquatic environment is also affected. Of Sweden's more than 80 000 lakes, about 16 000 had become so acidic by the late 1970s that the ability of sensitive plant and animal species to survive there was affected. In about 4 000 of these lakes the pH value was so low that only the very hardiest species remained; many lakes were entirely devoid of fish. Acidification has also disturbed animal and plant life along 100 000 km of rivers and streams, one-third of the total extent of Swedish watercourses.

Comprehensive estimates regarding the economic costs of acidification are not available in Sweden, but several specific studies have been made. For example, the value of depleted fish and crayfish stocks in Swedish lakes and watercourses is believed well above 12.3 million ECU annually. Even higher losses may be incurred through the degradation of historic buildings and cultural objects and the possible effects on forest productivity.

Liming: A Temporary Solution

To help remedy this situation, a liming programme has been in operation in Sweden since the early 1980s. Today, almost 200 000 tonnes of finely ground limestone are applied to acidic lakes and streams each year. The annual cost now amounts to more than 12.3 million ECU, most of which is covered by government subsidies. This programme is the largest of its kind in the world, but not the only one. Operational liming on a smaller scale is performed in Norway, and liming experiments have been carried out in Canada, the United Kingdom and the United States.

CHANGE IN FOREST SOIL ACIDITY

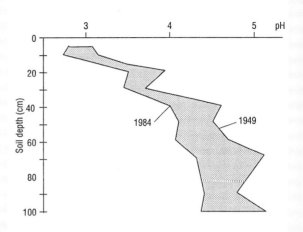

To date, almost 6 000 Swedish lakes covering more than 75 per cent of the total acidified lake area in the country have been limed, as well as streams with a total length of several tens of thousands of kilometres. In most of these waters the original diversity of their flora and fauna has been restored as a result.

However, the effects of liming do not last very long. If lake liming is not repeated at intervals of a few years the lakes in question will soon be acidified again. Moreover, lake liming does not stop the gradual acidification of the soil. Liming soils as well would be a vastly greater and more expensive undertaking than the present lake treatment. Therefore liming can only be seen as a temporary and very incomplete solution to the acidification problem.

Reducing Acidic Deposition: A More Permanent Remedy

Soil acidification will be reduced and lakes recover without human intervention only when the acid deposition falls below a critical value, which is primarily determined by inherent characteristics of the soil. For most soils in Sweden the critical load of sulphur amounts to 3 to 8 kilograms per hectare per year.

In southern Sweden the present sulphur deposition is 15 to 25 kilograms per hectare per year. Not until the load has decreased to one-third or one-fourth of this level can acidification problems be permanently solved in affected areas. Since acidic pollutants can be transported across large distances, such a decrease will be possible only if sulphur emissions to air are reduced very sharply in most parts of Europe.

Contribution from Sweden

two to three ploughings, but the advantages of ploughing are offset by the negative factors of water loss through drying and subsequent erosion by wind and water before the establishment of vegetative cover. Multicropping also increases the rate at which soil nutrients are removed, thus exhausting the soil more rapidly. Fertilizers, when applied in large amounts, tend ultimately to enter water systems: excessive nitrogen percolates down into the groundwater while phosphorus tends to attach to soil particles and, through erosion, enters surface waters as a conventional pollutant from non-point-source discharges. Pesticides (insecticides, herbicides, and fungicides) are heavily used to minimise crop losses and, like fertilizers, tend to find their way eventually into waterways. Frequent and/or heavy application of water to crops, particularly in semi-arid regions, can create highly saline soil, already described. Compactions of soil from the agricultural use of heavy machinery is another concern. In Japan an inventory of agricultural soil polluted since the start of the 1970s revealed that a decade and a half later a total of 7 050 ha. were contaminated with levels of cadmium, copper and arsenic that were higher than allowable standards. Remediation has involved soil removal, soil replacement and water source conversion. In recent years, recycled organic substances have been increasingly used in farmland.

Interdependencies with other media

One of the principal impacts of air pollution has been the change in temperate forests due to acid precipitation. By the mid-1980s about 14 per cent of all the forests in Europe were seriously damaged. In Germany the Black Forest and the Sieberg Forest suffered damage to trees, particularly on the tops of hills and mountains where the pH of fog is even lower than that of acid rain or snow. In southern California at that time, a fog with a pH of 1.7 was recorded. Serious trans-boundary issues have arisen because of economic damage to soils and vegetation and attendant changes in land use due to acid precipitation. Losses in the agriculture, sylviculture and recreation industries, for example, run into billions of dollars. Air pollution damage to plants excluding that caused by acid rain is also significant; it is estimated to total $1 to 2 billion in the United States. Serious impacts also arise from the influence of soil management upon other media – water in particular. (See Chapter on Air)

Additions of sediment and other conventional pollutants plus toxic materials occur principally during rainfall and snow-melt when land surfaces are "washed" and residuals flow with the water into streams and lakes. Heavy additions of nitrogen and phosphorus to coastal waters have forced the Danish government to take measures to decrease nitrogen input by 50 per cent and phosphorus input by 80 per cent by 1993 in an effort to reduce eutrophication. Examples of these non-point-source discharges include sediment, oils, greases and other organic wastes from urban land use (suburban discharges are similar, with additions from gardening – pesticides and fertilizers); sediment, fertilizers and pesticides from cropland; and sediments from forest and grasslands.

The use of land for disposal of solid wastes can have a significant impact on the air as a result of the release of gases and toxics, on groundwater from contaminants leaching out of the landfill, and on land use around the landfill site. Most existing disposal sites of municipal waste are close to saturation, and in the surrounding countryside communities resist their relocation. (See Chapter on Solid Waste)

The use of groundwater at a sustained rate greater than the rate of recharge can cause land subsidence. In Japan since 1970, the pumping out of groundwater for use in agriculture (3.4 per cent), industry (29 per cent), drinking water (28 per cent) and construction (10 per cent) has caused land subsidence of at least 2 cm in 60 areas of 36 prefectures.

2. LAND USE

Land is a factor input to most human or natural activities, since all activities need space on which to locate or develop. Land is therefore an environmental resource that has to be shared among these activities, and conflicts may arise among them. Land cover refers to major patterns of cover containing major ecosystems. Many changes in land use are naturally reflected in changes in land cover.

Land use and land cover patterns

Broad cover patterns of arable and cropland, permanent grassland, and forest and other wooded land accounted for 72 per cent of total OECD land area in the late 1980s.

Since 1970, there has been a 1 per cent increase in cropland in North America due primarily to a significant increase in Canada, and a 16 per cent increase in Australia-New Zealand as a whole, notwithstanding a sharp drop in New Zealand itself, but declines in Japan and Europe, with notable exceptions in France, the Netherlands, Norway and Switzerland. On balance, there has been an overall increase of 2 per cent in arable and cropland in OECD countries over the past two decades. (See Chapter on Agriculture)

Figure 18. **MAJOR PROJECTED AREAS, 1950-1989**

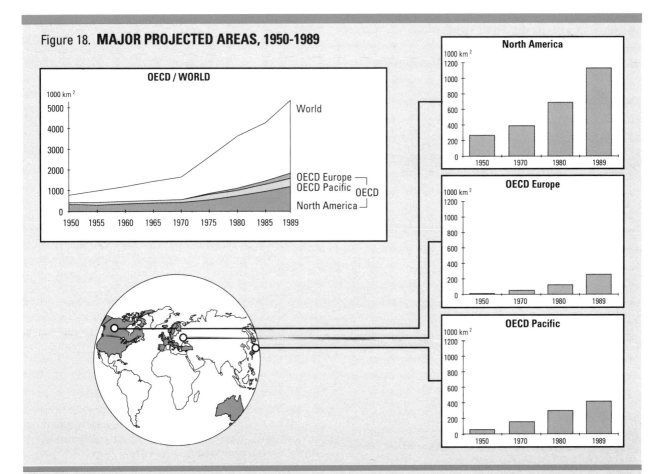

	1950 Sites		1970 Sites		1980 Sites		1985 Sites		1989 Sites		1989
	Number	1000 km²	Number	1000 km²	Number	1000 km²	Number	1000 km²	Number	1000 km²	% of land area
Canada	29	118.6	48	148.2	71	214.6	78	229.5	311	338.9	3.7
USA	105	147.7	168	234.5	223	473.9	251	649.5	396	790.4	8.6
Japan	16	17.4	29	19.7	47	21.3	50	22.0	61	24.0	6.4
France	4	0.6	7	4.7	56	12.8	37	16.5	73	45.0	8.2
Germany *a*	4	0.3	11	1.3	13	2.9	45	5.3	86	27.6	11.3
Italy	4	2.6	7	3.0	25	4.1	34	5.2	100	12.7	4.3
Netherlands	12	0.5	25	0.9	30	1.1	50	1.6	47	1.5	4.4
Portugal	-	-	1	0.7	7	2.5	12	3.8	27	6.2	6.7
Spain	2	0.3	26	9.2	52	16.8	56	17.0	110	25.6	5.1
Sweden	8	2.7	29	5.0	51	10.6	77	15.9	68	17.1	4.2
Turkey	-	-	7	0.5	12	2.3	15	2.9	15	2.5	0.3
UK	1	0.0	36	13.0	48	13.2	57	15.5	84	25.7	10.6
North America	134	266.3	216	382.7	294	688.5	329	879.0	707	1 129.2	6.1
OECD Pacific	119	54.4	305	153.8	469	298.2	778	404.0	808	417.1	5.0
OECD Europe *b*	53	9.1	214	49.8	412	121.0	595	154.5	1008	254.4	6.0
OECD *b*	306	329.8	735	586.3	1 175	1 107.7	1 702	1 437.4	2 523	1 800.7	5.8
World	582	729.2	1 512	1 597.1	2 564	3 566.2	3 514	4 237.7	5 289	5 290.8	4.0

Notes: -- Protected areas refer to IUCN management categories I-V. National classifications may differ.

     a) Includes western Germany only.

     b) Excluding Greenland which has 2 protected areas of a total size of 710 500 km².

Source: OECD, IUCN, WRI

Grassland has expanded by 3 per cent in North America, due primarily to a significant increase in Canada. In Japan it still accounted for only 1.7 per cent of the total land area in the late 1980s. In Europe, there was an overall decline of 10 per cent. Altogether, there has been a 3 per cent decrease in the grassland area of OECD countries since 1970. (See Chapter on Agriculture)

The area of forest and other wooded land has remained stable in North America. In Japan, there was virtually no change, while in Europe there was an increase of 4 per cent. The total wooded area of OECD countries has thus increased slightly since 1970. (See Chapter on Forest)

Protected Areas

Protected areas include scientific reserves, national parks, natural monuments, nature reserves and protected landscapes. These areas are subjected to the effects of air pollution, mainly acid rain, but also to the impacts of any operation nearby – agriculture, power plants and human activity within and near the protected areas (such as use of off-road vehicles, camping, hiking and boating). Protected areas, however, are increasing both in number and area. (Figure 18) Between 1950 and 1989 in OECD countries the number of protected sites increased from 306 to 2 523 and the areas protected from 329 751 km^2 to 2 511 239 km^2, including two areas in Greenland totalling 710 500 km^2.

Pressures come from two basic sources:

– Any increased intensity of use. United States national and state parks are an example: in 1955 they received 250 million visits, but in the 1980s the number had risen to almost 1 000 million. Even the most careful hikers and campers have an impact, no matter how slight; thus the popularity of the parks is becoming their downfall. Increased visiting has resulted in the construction of more roads, service stations, picnic grounds, hotels and restaurants. Today, traffic jams are common in the most popular parks and waiting lists for accommodation are the norm. This has resulted in a use conflict between those who espouse a multi-use policy and those who promote conservation of natural ecosystems;

– Commercial use of protected areas. In the case of parkland, there is the development of service facilities to accommodate increased numbers of visitors. In the case of forestland there is the pressure from the timber industry to increase the amount of leased land for harvesting and to increase road construction for accessing new areas. In both of these examples there is, on the one hand, resistance from conservationists and, on the other, the need for the government to counter shrinking

budgets for managing protected areas with other revenue sources.

Critical areas

As more land is used for housing, for commercial and industrial development and for transport, and as people have more leisure time and own more vehicles, critical land areas suffer the consequences. Two of them are reviewed here: congested areas such as coastal regions, with attendant shifts in land use and impacts; and wetlands, with their permanent losses.

Coastal and shore areas, environmentally unique and thus particularly exposed to disruption, are vulnerable to this congestion phenomenon. There are high densities of population, for example, on the Mediterranean coast, the North Sea coast, and the Pacific coast of Japan. In the United States over 50 per cent of the population, 40 per cent of manufacturing plants and 65 per cent of electrical power generators are located within 80 km of the oceans or Great Lakes. The waterways provide a resource for many uses – international transportation, cooling water, mining, manufacturing, waste discharges, food and recreation. These uses cannot all be accommodated simultaneously and conflict is inevitable.

One of the serious global impacts of a possible warming of the earth's atmosphere is a forecasted rise in sea level and the ensuing social, economic and environmental impacts this would have in coastal areas. Although the accuracy of global models is debated, it appears that warming could raise the sea level 20 centimetres by the year 2030 and 65 centimetres by the end of the next century. (See Chapter on Global Atmospheric Issues). A rise of this magnitude would inundate deltas, coral atoll islands and other coastal lowlands, erode beaches, exacerbate coastal flooding and threaten water quality in estuaries and aquifers. Although many countries have ground high enough to permit gradual adaptation, substantial investments in infrastructure and losses of important ecosystems would be incurred. Between 50 and 80 per cent of coastal wetlands could be lost. Protecting the entire East Coast of the United States is estimated to cost more than $300 billion by 2100.

Wetland resources have declined over the years. In the United States the original wetland area totalled between 500 000 km^2 and 1 000 000 km^2, excluding Alaska, but by 1950 one-third of the original wetlands had been destroyed and by 1985 one half had disappeared. Natural use of wetlands for the regulation and control of water (flood control, water purification) and for the maintenance of crucial wildlife habitat (larvae and juvenile stages, birds, fish, reptiles, amphibians, plants) has been converted to land use for factories, power stations, housing developments, shopping malls, croplands, golf courses, city dumps and sewage treatment plants. A major cause of loss of wetlands has

LOUISIANA'S VANISHING COASTAL WETLANDS

A Unique Resource under Pressure

The coastal region of Louisiana, in the southern United States, covers about 3.1 million hectares of a broad, flat coastal plain that rims the north-central Gulf of Mexico. Approximately 1.7 million hectares of coastal wetlands, about 41 per cent of the United States total, are located in this region. Unfortunately, these wetlands are rapidly deteriorating and converting to open water. Over 40 per cent of the wetlands in Louisiana's Barataria Bay were lost between 1945 and 1985, and these rates are typical of the Mississippi River's deltaic plain. In the remaining marsh, the rate of loss is increasing steadily.

The economic and cultural consequences of this land loss are severe. The value of the land already lost is conservatively estimated at US $3 billion. The state's fishing industry, currently valued at US $680 million, could face devastating losses since estuarine marshes serve as nursery grounds for 98 per cent of the commercially significant fish in the region. Another cause of concern is the loss of storm buffering capacity provided by wetlands, particularly since Louisiana's cities, including New Orleans, lie squarely in the North American hurricane belt. The state's fur industry, worth some US $25 million annually (40 per cent of the United States total), is also threatened as the marshes provide habitat to many fur-bearing mammals. As land loss continues, the prospects of the region's French-speaking "Cajuns", whose traditions and way of life evolved along the bayous and wetlands of southern Louisiana, also diminish.

Factors Influencing Wetland Formation and Loss

Coastal wetlands in Louisiana evolved on sediments deposited by the Mississippi River. Over the past 10,000 years the river's main channel has moved at least six times, discharging sediments first at one location, then moving several hundred kilometres to another. At each location a growing river-mouth delta formed, then eventually stagnated and retreated as the river lost most of its flow to a lesser distributary with a more direct connection to the Gulf. The natural cycle of this delta-switching process has historically created and sustained Louisiana's vast wetland resource.

Human activities have significantly influenced this pattern of wetland formation over the last century. Virtually the entire length of the Mississippi River is lined with levees that prevent overbank flooding, effectively starving adjacent wetlands of sediments. Since these levees, along with control structures, prevent smaller rivers from capturing the Mississippi's flow, these rivers cannot form new channels to the sea and contribute to large-scale active delta-building. The historic cycle has therefore been broken. New wetlands are no longer extensively formed to compensate for land loss in the old deltas.

Other pressures on Louisiana's wetlands include the thousands of kilometres of dredged canals that criss-cross the marshes, and a projected sea-level rise due to global warming. Canals often accelerate inland intrusion of salt water from the Gulf of Mexico, with devastating results on

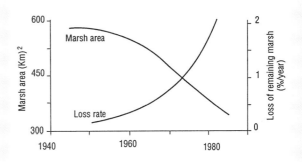

AREA AND RATE OF WETLAND LOSS

wetland plants adapted to a freshwater environment. Rising sea levels threaten to destroy existing wetlands, or force their retreat into areas less amenable to the creation of new wetlands.

The Challenge of Managing Wetlands

There is no simple, easy or complete solution to Louisiana's wetland loss problem. The best long-term solution is to put the Mississippi River back to work building land. This will require major changes in the management of the river. Already a small portion of the river's flow is being diverted over deteriorating wetlands, but much more is needed to slow the land loss significantly. Bolder alternatives include constructing a separate navigation channel to New Orleans for ocean-going ships, freeing the river to flood marshes below the city, or allowing the river's main channel to divert into its major distributary, thus stimulating growth of a major new delta. Additional needs are to stabilize the barrier islands, and fill in canals to reduce saltwater intrusion and restore natural marsh flooding.

Developing and implementing a wetland management strategy is an important challenge for Louisiana. This strategy must find a balance among the many conflicting uses of the region's resources, and exist within the limits placed on it by the geological processes influencing coastal submergence and subsidence, sea-level rise, and a finite sediment source. Only then will the important ecological, economic and cultural benefits provided by Louisiana's wetlands be secured.

Contribution from the United States

been and continues to be drainage for new agricultural land. In France, about 10 000 ha. are drained every year.

In wetlands and other natural areas which are subjected to such pressures, the result is an inability to maintain the ecosystem and a consequent loss of its products and services, which has broad social, economic and ecological implications.

Mining and extraction impacts

While the amount of surface area involved in mining is small compared to other land uses, the impacts can be significant. Firstly, extraction impacts are generated from both shaft mining and strip mining. In the latter case the entire land surface is removed (stripped) and processed until all of the cost-effective ore is extracted. It is also in strip mining that the greatest amount of "tailings" or residual rock is generated after the mineral content has been removed. This material is prone to erosion and to leaching into natural systems. Secondly, processing ores such as hematite and magnetite (iron), bauxite (aluminium), Cu_2S (copper), and galena (lead), chemical production of the element from the ore by smelters releases sulphites into the air which contribute to acid precipitation. After shaft mines cease to be exploited, water with acidic waste often drains out for years, affecting nearby streams and the associated plant and animal life.

As prices of minerals and fuels become higher, issues over priority land use become sharper. This is particularly true in the exploitation of fuel reserves – e.g. vast coal seams under fertile wheat fields of Montana and the Dakotas in the USA and Saskatchewan in Canada, or oil and gas reserves adjacent to the US-Canadian Glacier National Park and under the Arctic National Wildlife Refuge in northern Alaska. Which resource takes precedence? Perhaps one of the most serious concerns regarding fuel resource extraction is the impact, particularly on wild life habitat, from leaks and spills of petroleum, much of which is extracted on land but transported by pipeline and/or ship.

3. LAND USE AND NATURAL DISASTERS

Land resources are related to natural disasters in two ways. Firstly, some disasters have a geological, land-based origin, such as volcanic eruptions, earthquakes and landslides. Secondly, in many cases damages due to natural disasters, whether of a geological or a meteorological origin, are directly linked to population and properties located in exposed areas: the role of land use policies is thus very important. (Table 8)

Earthquakes

An earthquake is a sudden release of energy accumulated in rocks through the action of global tectonic processes – the major movements of the plates that form the earth's crust. Earthquakes occur mainly along these plate boundaries. Most of the seismicity of the earth, that is the energy released through tectonic movements, is concentrated in two of these boundaries: about 75 per cent on the Circum Pacific Belt and more than 20 per cent on the African Asian Belt. The USA, Canada, Japan and New Zealand, located along the Circum Pacific, and Italy, Greece and Turkey, located along the African-Asian Belt, are the OECD countries most exposed to earthquakes.

The total seismicity of the earth seems to remain approximately constant at the world level, but the detailed distribution over time, the locations and strengths of the earthquakes and the related damage show great variations. The example of Italy is particularly characteristic: four disasters occurred in the 25 years between 1905 and 1930, with a total of 120 000 victims. After 1930 there were no major earthquakes until the disasters of Friuli and Naples in 1976 and 1980, respectively.

The average annual number of earthquake victims globally has been estimated to be about 35 000 since the beginning of the twentieth century and about 42 000 for the 1970-1979 period. The total for the OECD countries is a relatively small yet significant proportion of these figures.

The cost of property damage due to earthquakes is more difficult to calculate accurately but available evidence shows that property damage is increasing. The growth of population and capital stock in exposed areas has contributed greatly to this mounting cost of disasters.

In view of current scientific knowledge and the pattern of urban development in earthquake-prone areas, priority has to be given to the prevention of damage through careful land use management and building regulations rather than through earthquake prediction, although isolated but famous examples have shown that prediction can be successful. Disaster mitigation should receive proper attention through appropriate emergency plans, sanitary action and careful reconstruction once the earthquake has occurred.

Volcanic eruptions

Volcanic eruptions consist of the ejection of molten rock and/or the release of gas or particulates through craters or fissures in the surface of the earth. They can occur either on land or on the seabed; in the

Table 8. MAJOR NATURAL DISASTERS OF GEOLOGIC ORIGIN, OECD countries, 1975-1989

	Date	Country	Type of disaster	Number of deaths
1975	August	Japan	Landslide, flood	> 30
	September	Turkey	Earthquake	> 2 300
1976	April	Italy	Earthquake	> 1 000
	June	Japan	Landslide	35
	November	Turkey	Earthquake	5 300
1977	November	Greece, Turkey	Earthquake	> 50
1978	January	Japan	Earthquake	25
	June	Japan	Earthquake	21
	June	Greece	Earthquake	47
1979	April	Yugoslavia	Earthquake	100
	June	Yugoslavia	Earthquake	200
1980	January	Portugal (Azores)	Earthquake	60
	February	USA	Landslide, flood	36
	March	Turkey	Landslide	> 60
	May	USA	Volcanic eruption	62
	July	Greece	Earthquake	—
	August	Japan	Landslide	20
	November	Italy	Earthquake	3 000
1981	February/March	Greece	Earthquake	20
	December	Portugal	Landslide	26
1982	December	Italy	Landslide	—
1983	May	Japan	Tidal wave	100
	July	Japan	Landslide	> 70
	October	Turkey	Earth tremors	1 330
1984	April	Italy	Earthquake	. .
	September	Japan	Earthquake	> 20
1985	July	Japan	Landslide	26
1986	September	Greece	Earthquake	> 20
1987	March	New Zealand	Earthquake	. .
	July	France	Tidal wave	23
	July	Italy	Landslide	44
	August	Japan	Landslide	24
	October	USA	Earthquake	7
1988	June	Turkey	Landslide	> 63
1989	October	USA	Earthquake	> 63
	December	Australia	Earthquake	> 10

Sources: OECD, SIGMA, UNDRO

latter case they are responsible for tsunamis, which are major waves hitting and often flooding coasts. Most recent volcanic eruptions occurred close to plate boundaries, a location similar to those of earthquakes.

Volcanic eruptions may cause extensive destruction; however, over a very long time they have generated soil that is fertile after weathering. The major damages related to volcanic eruptions are deaths, destruction of houses and public assets and damage to forests or crops and rivers. Secondary effects such as climatic changes have been observed. Records at the global level since the beginning of the century amount to 128 000 deaths over 75 years, or an average of 1 700 deaths per year. Only a small percentage of these deaths relates to OECD countries, in which the latest major event was the Mount St. Helens eruption in the USA in 1980, which killed 62 people. No significant trends can be shown over the longterm.

In contrast to earthquakes, scientific knowledge of the history of a volcano as well as on-site monitoring of current activity allow a much better assessment of the risk to which populations and properties are exposed. Scientists and public authorities are then in a position to better evaluate the safety levels to be achieved and to better implement preventive policies and issue warnings in order to reduce future damages.

Landslides

Landslides most often occur when heavy precipitation has saturated the soil on a steep hillside or mountain side and the additional weight of the water brings down the soil and rocks and all vegetation in their path. In urban and suburban regions of known landslide activity, such as southern California, where blocked highways and houses sliding into canyons are an annual occurrence, building permits and insurance are being designed to prevent development. In forested, natural regions, where timber harvesting on topsoil-thin mountainsides has left exposed areas, landslides may occur during heavy rainfall or snowmelt, leaving even larger areas of unprotected and unstable soil which can, in turn, lead to erosion until ultimately land is no longer productive.

Climatic and meteorological disasters

The impacts are direct: loss of life and property from wind and precipitation in rain storms, tornadoes, hurricanes, snow storms and hail storms, all of which are discrete events. Indirect loss of life and property emanate from longer-term phenomena such as drought. Some impacts, such as floodings from storms or prolonged heavy rainfall, are events in themselves and entail considerable loss.

The growth of population and property assets in risk-prone areas is a clear trend in all OECD countries concerned. The number of people at risk from tropical cyclones in the USA has increased because of the shift in population to the Gulf of Mexico and the south Atlantic coast. In many OECD countries, increasing numbers of people and property assets are located in flood-exposed valleys. (See Chapter on Inland Waters). Trends concerning damage related to meteorological or climatic accidents are similar to those observed for other natural disasters: while deaths seem to decrease, economic property damages are increasing.

Prolonged periods of heat and of little or no precipitation may create a drought which can have particularly significant economic effects on agriculture, water-borne transport and water supplies for industry and municipalities. If prolonged, the drought can have a more lasting effect on land use by causing a serious loss of top soil by wind, thus precluding establishment of vegetation and creating a permanent change in land use. An example of the long-term effect is the US Dust Bowl of the 1930s, and examples of what just a two-year drought can do are the economic losses in US agriculture and river transport in 1987 and 1988.

Most loss of life from major natural disasters of climatic or meteorological origin between 1975 and the late 1980s was caused by severe wind storms such as hurricanes or cyclones, and cold weather storms in North America, Europe and Japan. A 1987 heat wave in Greece, Italy and Yugoslavia also took 750 lives. In the case of major floods and related losses for OECD countries during the same period, the most frequent causes in descending order were prolonged rainfall, particular storms, two landslides, heavy rain, dam failure and hail.

Land use and the management of natural disasters

Property damages related to natural disasters are high and seem to be growing. Although deaths and casualties are also high, trends show a decrease in deaths related to natural disasters; in Japan, for instance, annually recorded deaths decreased by a factor of 10 between the 1950s and 1980s. The number of deaths associated with natural disasters is generally much lower than that associated with other types of disasters; in Japan, for instance, on average four times fewer people died from natural hazards than from road accidents.

There is no scientific evidence to show that most natural disasters will be either more or less frequent in the future than they have been in the past, whether of geological, climatic or meteorological origin. Nevertheless, the populations and capital assets at risk from natural disasters and therefore the potential damages associated with them have greatly increased and will certainly increase in the future.

Careful land-use planning can help to reduce the risks associated with some types of disasters. But these must be supplemented by specific preventive policies for building technologies and better forecasts of disasters whenever possible. Mitigation policies also need to be strengthened, bearing in mind that legislation, planning and management activities relating to natural disasters involve difficult problems of decision making amidst scientific, economic, social and political uncertainties.

THE LANDSLIDE OF VALTELLINA (ITALY)

Early Signs of the Landslide

From 17 to 19 July 1987, heavy precipitation fell on the valley of Valtellina in northern Italy, while an unusual heat wave caused snow and glaciers to melt.

Erosion occurred throughout the area as a result of the exceptional rainfall and large volume of water. In particular, on 18 July a small landslide of around 200 000 cubic metres of moraine deposits fell from Val Pola into the bottomland of the river Adda. The earthflow blocked the main road and invaded the river bed, causing its waters to overflow into the village of Sant'Antonio Morignone. This event was seen as a warning signal by the authorities, who promptly evacuated the inhabitants from the area at risk. It also altered the precarious equilibrium of the Mount Zandila slope.

The Valtellina Landslide

On 28 July 1987, at 7 a.m., a landslide of around 30 million cubic metres fell from the eastern slope of Mount Zandila in the Val Pola region. The magnitude of the landslide was such that it reached the river Adda valley (Valtellina) in 23 seconds at a velocity of 200 kilometres per hour. The nearby stations of the National Geophysics Institute recorded the event as being equivalent to an earthquake of 5 to 7 on the Mercalli scale.

The landslide material hit several small villages (Presure, Morignano, Sant'Antonio Morignano, Alquilone, among others), surged 250 metres up the opposite slope and fell back down, submerging the valley for about 2.5 kilometres. Some 40 million cubic metres of displaced material raised the Adda valley floor by about 50 metres, and a lake of about 3.5 kilometres in length and 18 million cubic metres in volume was formed.

The landslide caused 27 deaths, destroyed human settlements and cut off the only highway linking the valley from the rest of Italy so that for a long time afterward, road traffic had to be diverted through Switzerland. Damages were estimated at around ECU 2.6 billion.

The immediate risk of flooding, due to the collapse of the landslide material upstream from the newly-formed lake, was averted by building an artificial drain to regulate the water discharge. The cost of the repair work was estimated at about ECU 1.3 billion.

Underlying Geological Causes

Several features of this region make it highly prone to events such as landslides. During the glaciations of the Quarternary period, the rocks found in the region underwent alternate periods of relaxation and compression, making them vulnerable to the action of erosive agents such as water. Also, over the course of time, the river Adda has etched out its bed in a valley characterised by

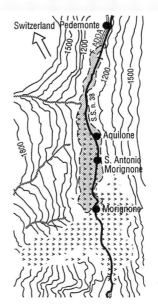

⌑⌑⌑ Zone of accumulation of fallen material   ▨ Newly created lake

increasingly steep slopes. These characteristics, and others such as the faults found in the region, undoubtedly facilitated the catastrophic events of July 1987.

Providing Early Warning of Landslides

Although the causes of such phenomena as earthquakes and landslides are essentially natural, the magnitude of their effects are often a result of human factors such as the siting of dwellings and transportation networks. These effects can be minimised through proper land-use planning and through measures which provide early warning of geological phenomena.

Steps to enhance early-warning detection of landslides and related events have been taken in the Valtellina region. A monitoring network using instruments such as piezometers, inclinometers, strain guages and geophones has been installed in this area to follow progression of these phenomena. A co-ordination centre set up by the regional government of Lombardy elaborates the data collected by the instruments and these are transmitted in real time.

The monitoring system has already proven effective as an early-warning system, having forecast the mass movements which caused landslides totalling around 200 000 cubic metres.

Contribution from Italy

RADON IN HOUSES IN THE UNITED KINGDOM

HOW RADON GETS IN

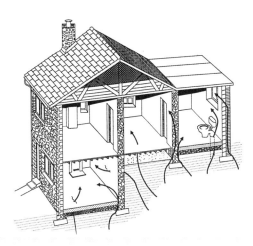

A "Hidden" Source of Radiation

Radon is a natural source of radiation which produces almost half of the total radiation received by humans in the United Kingdom. Radon gas, produced by the breakdown of the uranium which is present in minute quantities in all soils and rocks, can mix with air in the soil and seep out of the ground. In open air it is normally diluted to low levels, but higher levels can collect in enclosed spaces such as houses.

Radon levels are higher in some parts of the United Kingdom than in others because the uranium content of rocks and soils varies from place to place, and some rocks and soils allow air to move more freely than others. Radon itself breaks down to form radioactive particles called radon daughters. Some of these may be breathed in and deposited on the lungs where radiation from them can damage lung tissue and increase the risk of lung cancer.

Determining Exposure to Radon

The National Radiation Protection Board, which advises the government on radiation matters, recommended in January 1990 that exposure to radon daughters in the home be limited to an average concentration of 200 Bq/m3.

Surveys have been conducted to determine the extent of household exposure to natural radiation: a representative national survey and selective surveys of regions where high radon concentrations were expected.

The first regional surveys were conducted on the assumption that higher radon levels were likely in areas having particular geological characteristics. Hence, these surveys were made in Cornwall, Devon, the central uplands of England and parts of Scotland. Subsequent surveys have been commissioned by the government to identify more precisely the extent of the problem.

On the basis of these surveys, it is estimated that about 75 000 houses in the United Kingdom may have average radon concentrations exceeding the action level of 200 Bq/m3. The problem is concentrated in particular areas of the country, both in the number of houses and in the degree to which they are affected. In Devon and Cornwall, in about 12 per cent of the housing stock, or 60 000 homes, radon levels may be above this level. In three other English counties -- Somerset, Northamptonshire and Derbyshire -- 1-2 per cent of housing, or perhaps 10 000 houses may have radon at or above the action level.

Measures to Reduce Household Radon

The most effective way to reduce radon concentrations in existing dwellings is to reduce the radon influx by making the floor a better barrier or by diverting radon to the open air. The Building Research Establishment in the United Kingdom is currently carrying out research into remedial and preventive measures.

It is estimated that at present several thousand dwellings in which doses to occupants may exceed the action level of 200 Bq/m3 are built each year. For these dwellings, it is likely that appropriate modifications to conventional building practices will suffice to prevent elevated concentrations. About 2 000 homes have been or are being built following interim guidance issued by the government in June 1988. At present all new houses in the parts of Devon and Cornwall which are particularly at risk are built according to this guidance.

Contribution from the United Kingdom

4. CONCLUSIONS

Over the past two decades, the following progress and remaining problems can be identified in OECD countries.

Soil degradation is, or ought to be, giving rise to great concern in most OECD countries because of several developments:

- Although not a serious concern in all OECD Member countries, *erosion* is a significant, growing problem in many OECD countries, such as Australia, Spain and the United States;

- While *desertification* can be a natural phenomenon in arid and semi-arid regions, it is also being exacerbated by bad soil management, and OECD countries such as Canada, Spain and Turkey are affected;

- Soil degradation also occurs through other human activities, in the form of *salinisation* and *waterlogging* from poor irrigation techniques and land *subsidence* from heavy withdrawals of groundwater;

- Soil degradation and attendant loss of productivity from *pollution* is a continuing, serious and costly problem affecting all OECD countries, some more heavily than others. It includes the following impacts: acid deposition, a transboundary problem, affecting crops and other landcover vegetation; disposal of inadequately treated sewage sludge contaminating soils and vegetation; disposal of hazardous wastes with toxic impacts on soils and associated living material; disposal by landfill of solid wastes affecting soil productivity and other media, such as groundwater; intensive agricultural use of chemicals possibly contaminating both soil and products.

Concerning land use:

- There has been an increase in *protected areas*, such as parks and refuges, throughout OECD countries;

- The major *uses of land* have changed little in total aggregated area, but there have been shifts in some sub-sectors e.g. losses in agricultural land, encroachment of infrastructure and land set-asides;

- Critical areas such as *wetlands* remain threatened by recreational and agricultural development and by industrial, domestic and agricultural water demands;

- Competition for land use is becoming more intense, particularly in coastal areas and valleys;

- *Mining* leaves behind problems of land restoration, disposal of tailings and acid mine drainage;

- Finally, land use is a major determinant of the level of risk associated with *natural disasters*. While prevention and mitigation policies have helped to bring about a significant drop in the death tolls of natural disasters, the accumulation of capital assets in disaster-prone areas has led and will lead to an increase in the damage caused by natural disasters.

Chapter 6

FOREST

The word forest is ambiguous since it refers to a set of often greatly differing plant formations that may be considered from two quite separate viewpoints:

- First, a forest is a part of a complex ecosystem with a tree cover varying in density;
- Second, a forest is an area producing various natural resources, including wood, that are exploited by man for economic purposes.

Forests are difficult to manage because these two viewpoints must be simultaneously taken into account to ensure sustained development.

Forests as ecosystems

All the major types of forest exist in OECD countries:

- Boreal forests;
- Temperate forests;
- Mediterranean forests;
- Dry tropical forests;
- Moist tropical forests;
- Mountain forests.

The areas of these different types of forests vary greatly according to the geographical position of the countries concerned. Tropical forests are much less extensive in OECD countries than the other types.

These different forests form complex and diversified ecosystems in which numerous factors interact: climatic factors (temperatures, precipitation volume and distribution, winds); geological and pedological factors (nature of parent rock, soil composition and depth); topographical factors (altitude, slope, exposure); and biotic factors (type of wild life). All these factors influence the nature and structure of the forest cover. Conversely, the forest cover influences the microclimate, soil characteristics and plant and animal life.

Tree growth and regeneration periods (decades) and the even longer periods of soil evolution (centuries) mean that forest ecosystems change very slowly. The forests now existing in the OECD countries in the northern hemisphere have gradually appeared since the end of the würmian glacial episode, about 10 000 years ago.

When a forest has been destroyed by natural causes (such as landslides, volcanic eruptions, fires, storms, floods, extreme cold) or by man (clearing, over-felling – often termed "mining" – and destructive pollution), its regeneration cycle takes decades and sometimes even centuries: pioneer species appear first, then post-pioneer species and, finally, protected by the latter, climax species.

Owing to the timespans involved, any study of the use of forest resources must take the very long term into account.

Different methods of forest exploitation

Without man's intervention, most of the land in OECD countries would now be covered by forests, with the exception of regions where it is too cold (polar regions and very high mountains) or too dry (grasslands, steppes and deserts).

Action by man has in fact left its mark for thousands of years and, combined with natural factors, has contributed greatly to establishing the forests' evolutionary process. Mankind's impact on forests has constantly increased over the centuries. It goes back furthest in the countries with an ancient rural civilisation (Europe, Japan), and is more recent in the "new" countries (North America, Oceania). Practically no virgin forests unaffected by man's presence exist today in Europe's temperate or Mediterranean regions. On the other hand, in the same regions, the forest is spontaneously reappearing in formerly cultivated or grazed areas that were abandoned as the rural population moved out and agriculture declined, especially in mountain regions with a harsh climate.

There are four main stages in the way human societies use forest resources, depending on the amount of timber removed and the type of forestry operations:

- *Gathering*: this is the spontaneous form of resource utilisation by both primitive and advanced societies when the resource exceeds needs. The term "gathering" is appropriate as long as the removal rate is less than the renewal rate. If the latter rate is exceeded, there is a risk of depletion;
- *Non-renewal exploitation*: this situation arises when resource regeneration no longer offsets timber removals. If it persists, the resource may disappear, at least locally. In response to this risk, management rules are frequently imposed, often by government, in order to ensure resource renewal;
- *Classical "rational replacement" exploitation*: its purpose is to ensure regular use of the resource in a way compatible with its regeneration. Forest management methods have been developed in Western Europe since the eighteenth century. Initially they were mainly based on natural regeneration processes. Intensive cultivation techniques were then gradually introduced;
- *Intensive tree growing*: when cultivation techniques are used intensively (planting of selected varieties or selected clones, substantial use of fertilizers, herbicides and pesticides, mechanised planting and harvesting operations), tree growing increasingly resembles crop farming. This type of cultivation is particularly suitable for fast-growing species (eucalyptus, poplars, some softwood trees, etc.).

Economic uses of forests

The products which forests can provide are potentially numerous and have varied greatly with different civilisations and periods of history. They include:

- Animals living in forests, which are hunted for their meat or fur;
- Forest plants, which are gathered as food or for their medicinal properties;
- Fruit and nuts (for example, for centuries man's staple food in certain Mediterranean regions was the chestnut);
- Food for domestic animals (cattle, sheep, goats, pigs), such as undergrowth plants, acorns, beechnuts and branches cut from trees;
- Wood, which can be used in quite different ways.

These further include:

- Uses in which wood merely serves as a source of carbon, mainly for combustion (up to the start of the industrial age wood was the main source of energy; in some regions of Africa and South Asia, it still accounts for over half the energy consumed); wood is also used for carbonisation and distillation;
- Uses based on the wood's fibrous microstructure after mechanical pulping or chemical processing, mainly for paper and paperboard manufacturing, as well as the different compression or glueing techniques providing reconstituted wood;
- Uses based on the wood's macrostructure and its mechanical resistance properties: posts, mine timber, sleepers, shuttering, box making, cooperage, carpentry, joinery, turnery, cabinet making, etc.

Traditional rural societies used wooded areas extensively for supplies of firewood, food for themselves and their animals, and materials for crafts and building.

Many of these uses have disappeared in modern industrial societies. On the other hand, the demand for sawlogs and especially for pulpwood has increased considerably. One characteristic of industrial demand is the requirement for large quantities of products that do not vary in quality and are obtainable at the most competitive prices possible. This demand is therefore quite different from that concerning traditional uses where the aim was to exploit all the resources, often at the cost of very hard work.

This change in demand has basic effects on forestry management: in rural societies, the economically most advantageous forests were those which provided a range of resources and were located near the consumption points, as the transport costs for heavy goods were very high. But in industrial economies, the most advantageous forests are those providing vast areas of the same kinds of wood that can be exploited mechanically.

Hence the emphasis in the modern economy is on forests that are mainly man-made and planted to provide the types of product demanded, and on the northern softwood forests, which are generally extremely homogeneous over vast areas.

On the other hand, forests in the Mediterranean regions (very heterogeneous and often slow growing), mountain forests (heterogeneous and difficult to exploit) and forests divided into small lots are at a disadvantage. Many of them are hardly exploited since the costs of wood harvesting and transport are at least as great as the value of the products obtained.

Among the forests managed in a classical ("rational") way, only those which have been developed for the production of top quality wood (hardwood or softwood logs with very good technical properties) are still economically very valuable.

The exploitation of the tropical forests outside the OECD area, which nonetheless provide heavy export flows to Member countries, seems profitable in the short term, for in the vast majority of cases it does not entail the renewal of the resource base, which keeps costs low.

FOREST MANAGEMENT IN PORTUGAL

Evolution of the Portuguese Forest

Portugal's forests are, above all, a product of civilisation, and are in constant interaction with natural conditions, soil and climate. They have long had to contend with deforestation, spurred on by such activities as agriculture, mineral exploration in previous historical periods, and harvesting of trees for shipbuilding during the age of navigation and discovery some five centuries ago. More recently, factors such as land-use in relation to the growth of urban areas have influenced the evolution of Portugal's forests.

Concern about the state of the country's forests became more widespread and institutionalised in the nineteenth century, and, as a result, pressures on forests were increasingly managed and therefore reduced. It is during this period, however, that Portugal's forests began to be transformed on a large scale. They were expanded in the first half of the nineteenth century, when many exotic, non-traditional tree species were introduced.

Today, the few remaining examples of primaeval forest, composed largely of the northern oaks (*Quercus robus* and *Quercus petraea*), cork oak (*Quercus suber*) and ilex (*Quercus elix*), illustrate the extent of the transition which Portugal's forests, a blend of Atlantic and Mediterranean species, have undergone.

Portugal's Forest Today

The tree species which has come to dominate the Portuguese forest is the sea pine (*Pinus pinaster*), which now covers about 40 per cent of the country's total forested area. This species was first introduced in the fourteenth century, but expanded most rapidly in the nineteenth century as it proved well adapted to the different soils and many of the climatic regimes found in Portugal. The rapid growth rate of this species compared to that of traditional species found in Portugal has also facilitated its widespread distribution.

These characteristics of the sea pine encouraged its use for soil protection measures such as dune stabilisation (especially in the 1930s and 1940s) and as a means of combatting soil erosion by water, particularly in steep and sloping areas.

Cork oak is the next most prevalent tree species, covering approximately 22 per cent of total forested area but concentrated more strongly in the region south of the Tagus and in the western part of Alentejo. Ilex, which covers 15 per cent of the forested area, is found mainly in arid areas of the southern interior. A variety of other tree species, both coniferous and deciduous, complete the Portuguese forest mosaic.

More recently, the eucalyptus tree (particularly *E. Globulus*), which has proven well adapted to the prevailing soil and climatic conditions of Portugal, has steadily transformed the diversity of the country's forests and is now, in terms of forested area, the third most prevalent species. The expansion of eucalyptus has been especially strong since 1960, going from 100 000 hectares then to

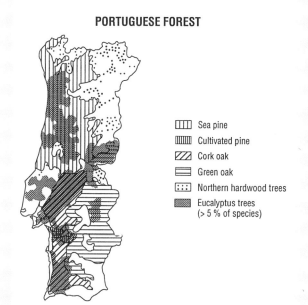

PORTUGUESE FOREST

Sea pine
Cultivated pine
Cork oak
Green oak
Northern hardwood trees
Eucalyptus trees
(> 5 % of species)

400 000 hectares in 1985, and has occurred at the expense of sea pine and oak.

Several factors have contributed to the spread of eucalyptus: they include the decline of resinous tree species due to forest fires and the dieback of very old oak. More important, however, has been the popularity of eucalyptus among private forest lot owners, who hold approximately 85 per cent of Portugal's forests. Eucalyptus is often grown in intensive monoculture stands and sold as raw material for the country's expanding pulp and paper industry.

Resolving Multiple-use Conflicts

The rapid spread of Eucalyptus trees has raised public concern regarding the make-up, nature and uses made of Portugal's forests. In response, the government of Portugal has elaborated a Forestry Action Programme and drawn up regulations aimed at improving forest management. The objectives of this new policy are:

- To re-afforest large uncultivated areas with indigenous tree species, using financial support from the European Community;
- To reduce the disorderly expansion of intensive plantations of fast-growing tree species;
- To prohibit the systematic replacement of traditional tree species by other, more lucrative species through regulation of reforestation in areas affected by forest fires;
- To give specific protection to the traditional oak species.

Contribution from Portugal

Social role of forests

Like their economic uses, the social uses of forests are numerous. They are available for recreational activities such as walking, hunting, the gathering of products, and nature studies, as well as for various sports such as hiking, cross-country running, riding, climbing, and so on. They are a greatly appreciated scenic setting for a permanent or holiday home and, in certain regions, are often a basic tourist attraction.

In addition to these "objective" uses, the forest has a very strong emotional and symbolic connotation in a great many cultures. The forest is seen as a special place lying outside the everyday social ambit. The root of the word forest in both English and French is thus the Latin "for-", meaning something that is foreign or external. In the symbolism of these cultures, the forest is perceived as a permanent rather than a temporary feature, and sacred as opposed to profane.

This relationship with the forest has persisted in modern societies: the forest is seen by town-dwellers, for instance, as something natural in contrast to the artificiality of everyday urban and industrial life. The current longing for nature is very closely associated with forests. This very emotional relationship may explain why people react so sharply when forests seem to be in danger, especially if the danger is caused by something artificial like pollution or building sites.

The forest's social role thus far exceeds its directly observable recreational uses, for attachment to forests is part of the overall feeling for nature which is now becoming more pronounced in developed countries. It is all the more difficult to take this role into account since it goes beyond rational considerations, such as economic uses, to symbolic and emotional aspects.

1. FOREST RESOURCES IN OECD COUNTRIES

Wooded areas

In the last 20 years the wooded areas of most OECD countries have remained stable or increased. Their 10.2 million km² account for 25 per cent of wooded areas worldwide and 33 per cent of the total land area of OECD countries. (Figure 19) Overall, total wooded areas in OECD countries present some increase. Wooded area is stable or increasing in OECD countries, with only very few countries showing a decrease. The total figures, however, may conceal differing trends: in some cases, forests with a high economic or scenic value may be disappearing although this is statistically masked by the development of artificial forests.

The wooded area is decreasing somewhat in North America, while it is expanding in Europe. In all European countries it is stable or increasing; those where it is expanding the most in absolute terms are France, Italy, and Spain. It is significant that these three countries have a high proportion of mountain and Mediterranean forests. The increase in wooded areas is due to reforestation policies and spontaneous forest growth in marginal areas where crop and stock farming has been abandoned. After these three countries come Austria, Canada, western Germany, Ireland, New Zealand, Norway, Portugal, Sweden, Switzerland, and the United Kingdom. In some of these countries which were sparsely wooded, the increase in relative terms has been considerable (Ireland 38 per cent, United Kingdom 26 per cent) and is the result of an active reforestation policy. In Japan, the wooded areas which cover 67 per cent of the country have remained stable, but there has been a net decrease in the proportion of natural forest.

Growing stock and annual increment

Growing stock in the dense productive forests of OECD countries amounted to about 63 000 million m³ in the late 1980s, or about 20 per cent of the world total, but commercially exploitable growing stock in OECD countries represents approximately 35 per cent of the world total.

Both the volume of growing stock and its annual increment in the forests now being exploited commercially have risen considerably over the past 20 years in the United States, OECD Europe and Japan. (Table 9) During that same period, total growing stock in natural forests has declined in Australia and New Zealand, but that decline has been offset to some extent by an increase in planted growing stock. The volume of growing stock in Australia and New Zealand should rise in the future, and the annual increment should be up considerably in Europe.

There are, nevertheless, big differences in the density of the growing stock (expressed in m³/ha) and in the annual increment among the various OECD countries: average growing stock in Switzerland is 364 m³/ha as against 58 m³/ha in Turkey. A number of

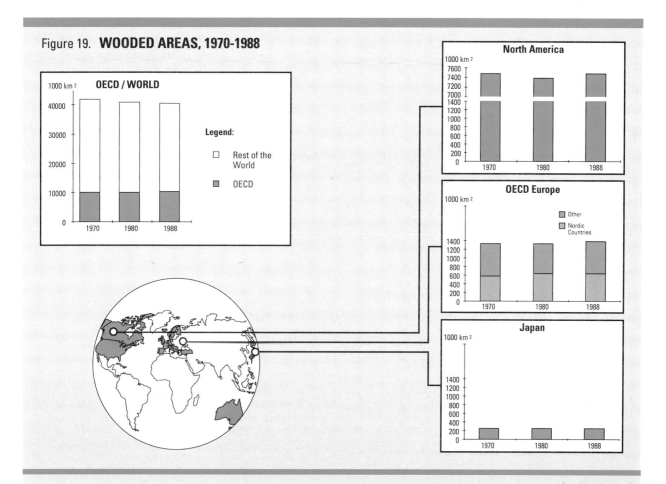

Figure 19. **WOODED AREAS, 1970-1988**

	Area of Forests and Other Wooded Land			Percent of Total Land Area	
	1970 1000 km²	1988 1000 km²	1970-1988 % change	1970 %	1988 %
Canada	4 431	4 500	1.6	48	49
USA	3 050	2 946	-3.4	33	32
Japan	253	253	0.1	67	67
Finland	234	234	-0.1	77	77
France	140	152	8.2	26	28
Germany a	72	74	2.7	29	30
Italy	62	68	9.5	21	23
Norway	79	83	5.6	26	27
Portugal	28	31	10.9	30	34
Spain	144	157	8.9	29	31
Sweden	276	280	1.4	67	70
UK	19	24	25.5	8	10
North America	7 480	7 446	-0.5	41	41
OECD Europe	1 347	1 398	3.8	32	33
of which: - Nordic Countries	595	603	1.4	51	52
- Other	752	795	5.7	24	26
OECD	10 089	10 229	1.4	33	33
World	41 907	40 490	-3.4	32	31

Note: a) Includes western Germany only.

Source: OECD, FAO

Table 9. COMMERCIAL FORESTS: GROWING STOCK AND EFFICIENCY IN USAGE OF TIMBER RESOURCES

	Growing stock m³/ha 1980-85 average	Annual net increment m³/ha/year 1980-85 average	Efficiency in usage: annual growth/ total harvest 1950s		1970s	1980-85
Canada	74	2	. .	. .	2.1
USA	109	4	1.7	1.8	1.7
Japan	106	3	. .	. .	1.9
Australia	64	1	. .	. .	2.6
New Zealand	151	15	. .	. .	1.2
Austria	274	6	0.7	1.2	1.3
Belgium	148	8	0.9	0.8	1.6
Denmark	141	8	1.1	0.9	1.3
Finland	86	3	1.1	1.0	1.2
France	120	4	0.9	1.3	1.6
Germany[a]	224	6	0.7	1.0	1.0
Greece	73	2	1.0	1.1	1.4
Ireland	102	7	1.5	4.5	3.2
Italy	154	3	1.0	1.2	1.3
Luxembourg	249	4	0.8	1.6	1.5
Netherlands	103	4	0.8	1.0	1.1
Norway	83	3	1.2	1.6	1.6
Portugal	90	4	1.0	1.1	1.1
Spain	68	4	. .	1.5	2.1
Sweden	101	3	1.3	1.0	1.4
Switzerland	364	6	1.1	1.1	1.1
Turkey	58	3	. .	1.0	1.0
United Kingdom	108	6	0.7	1.5	2.3
Yugoslavia	138	4	0.4	0.9	1.4
North America	89	3	. .	. .	2.0
OECD Europe	114	4	. .	. .	1.4
OECD	93	3	. .	. .	1.9

Note: a) Includes western Germany only.
Sources: OECD, IIASA

countries in central Europe have annual increments of about 7 m³/ha, but in Greece and Canada the figure is 1.8 m³/ha and 1.7 m³/ha. These differences are due to the influence of ecological conditions. (Table 9)

Efficient use of forest resources

Efficiency in the use of forest resources can be judged initially by examining the ratio between annual increment and annual harvests: when greater than one it shows that these resources have not been over-utilised; when less than one, it indicates that they have been over-utilised and that the sustained development of the resource is in danger if the trend persists. Most forest resources in Europe were over-utilised immediately after the Second World War. But since the 1970s it may be said that OECD countries' forest resources have been managed with a view to sustained development, since the ratio of annual increment to annual harvest exceeds one on the basis of the results for the 1980-1985 period. It must be stressed, however, that the ratio used provides no information about the breakdown of the harvest among different categories of forest. In some cases economically accessible forests are over-exploited, while inaccessible ones remain unexploited. However, efficiency in the use of forest resources might be defined as encompassing other ecological and social functions of forest resources.

2. DEMAND FOR FOREST PRODUCTS

The demand for wood raw materials depends on the demand for finished forest products. Demand for finished products itself depends on a number of factors; some apply to a particular finished product, while others are of a general kind such as population, economic development and prices. Using these factors, it is possible to model future demand for finished products.

Demand for industrial roundwood

The paper pulp industry ranks second as a consumer of forest products after those using sawnwood and wood-based panels. The demand for paper pulp itself depends on demand for paper and paperboard, which is expected to rise sharply. (Figure 20) Three new trends will affect the future consumption of wood fibres in pulp and paper production. First, greater use will be made of recycled fibres, because they cost only about 40 to 50 per cent of the price of bleached softwood fibres: indeed the recycling process makes it possible to reduce waste paper to stock, and it is now technically feasible to use recycled fibres in most existing grades of paper.

Figure 20. DEMAND FOR SELECTED FOREST PRODUCTS, 1985-2010

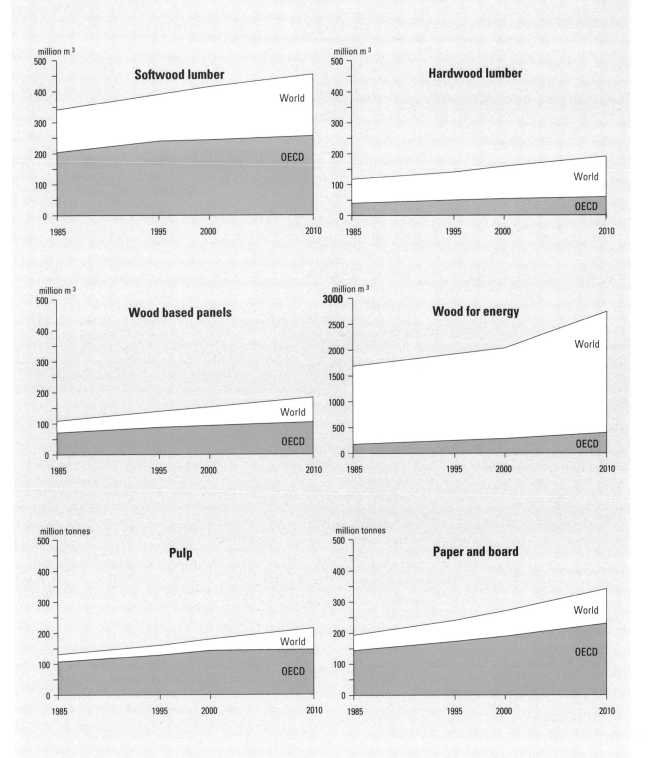

Source: OECD, IIASA

The second trend will be the increasing use of fillers and coatings. It is now feasible to manufacture on a commercial scale printing and writing paper with a virgin fibre content of less than 50 per cent; it is estimated that by the year 2010 the consumption of these fillers and coatings will exceed the consumption of the virgin pulps available on the market. The third trend in the paper industry will be the use of more and more varied species of trees (especially hardwoods) and high-yield pulp technologies, such as CTMP (chemi-thermo-mechanical pulping). To sum up, there will be fewer virgin fibres, more recycled fibres, more fillers and coatings, more high yield pulp, fewer softwood fibres and more hardwood fibres.

Supply of industrial roundwood

It has also been possible to estimate the future supply of industrial roundwood. (Table 10) In 1985 OECD countries accounted for over half the world stock of industrial roundwood. By 2010, it is estimated that the OECD's share of that stock will decline slightly.

Industrial roundwood balances

Excluding from these balances wood used as an energy source, which is a particularly important use in developing countries, we can compare demand for industrial roundwood with an estimate for its supply. The estimate is not given as a forecast but simply as a possible scenario based on certain assumptions concerning consumption and production. In this scenario, the main trends are the following. (Table 10)

In all OECD regions, production will rise steadily over the period, assuming improved management based on the principle of sustained growth. In these same regions, consumption will also increase but much less quickly after the 1990s. NorthAmerica will maintain its surplus, while the deficit of European and Pacific OECD countries will remain. The production surplus of non-OECD countries will decrease, falling sharply after the 1990s because of internal consumption. At a world level this scenario shows a deficit of about 110 million m³ in 2010. In reality, however, production and consumption will have to be balanced.

All in all, foreseeable demand pressure calls for *more careful management of world forest resources* so that demand can be met without endangering the resource base:

- As a result of the demand for wood and wood products, prices will probably be on an uptrend in the long term;
- This uptrend in prices will slow down the rise in consumption and encourage certain technological changes (e.g. the recycling of waste paper, reconstituted wood products, etc.);

Table 10. INDUSTRIAL ROUNDWOOD BALANCES, 1985-2010

Million m³ roundwood equivalent

		1985	2010
North America	Demand	503	651
	Supply	521	673
	Balance	18	22
OECD Europe	Demand	296	425
	Supply	219	263
	Balance	-77	-162
Japan	Demand	96	110
	Supply	36	49
	Balance	-60	-61
OECD	Demand	917	1 218
	Supply	799	1 045
	Balance	-118	-173
Non OECD	Demand	561	1 017
	Supply	679	1 078
	Balance	118	61
World	Demand	1 478	2 235
	Supply	1 478	2 123
	Balance	0	-112

Sources: OECD, IIASA

- Greater demand will justify the replacement of overfelling practices by forestry management intended to achieve a sustained yield. Such a change is particularly desirable in the case of forests that can supply sawnwood and veneers with good technical properties;
- Higher demand will also justify the development of fast-growing plantations to supply the industries producing paper pulp and reconstituted wood panels;
- To make up for a deficit which is expected to rise by about 5 million m³ a year, intensive management techniques must be used for about half a million hectares more per year. At a world level, that is not unrealistic;
- It must be realised, however, that some intensive forestry techniques can have detrimental effects on the environment as reviewed in the next section.

3. ENVIRONMENTAL EFFECTS OF FORESTRY MANAGEMENT

This section reviews the environmental effects of the main categories of forest resources exploitation defined in the introduction.

Effects on the climate and atmosphere

There is much sound scientific evidence attesting to the considerable impact of forests on the microclimate. When it is dense enough, the forest cover has many effects: it intercepts a large part of the radiation from the sun; it modifies the landscape's reflectivity; it reduces the volume of rain reaching the ground; and it greatly reduces wind speed at ground level. The microclimate under the tree cover is thus quite different from that in a clearing: the light is less intense, the air is less mobile, relative humidity is higher, and temperature differences are less marked. A special kind of wild life develops in this forest environment, and the soil's pedogenetic processes are also greatly influenced.

It is more difficult to assess accurately the effects of forests on the regional climate and the global climate. It seems certain, however, that deforestation on a very large scale can lead to highly detrimental climatic changes resulting in a decrease in precipitation volume and an increase in temperature differences.

Forests help to clean the atmosphere by acting as a pollutant filter. A forest's leaf area is five to 15 times greater than the forest's ground area, so trees can trap the solid matter and aerosols suspended in the atmosphere and absorb certain chemical compounds causing pollution. In excess of certain tolerance levels, however, trees are affected by physiological troubles which slow down growth and may gradually kill them. Forests' anti-pollutant role is limited by those levels, therefore.

Photosynthesis in trees produces oxygen. The production of a tonne of dry plant matter consumes about 1.5 tonnes of carbon dioxide and supplies slightly more than a tonne of oxygen. A healthy temperate forest usually produces between 10 and 20 tonnes of dry matter per hectare per year. A forest in difficult conditions (high mountains, dry boreal, Mediterranean or tropical region) produces less; a moist tropical forest or a mainly artificial forest may produce more. It must not be forgotten, however, that oxygen is consumed by the respiration of living plants and by the decomposition of plants or parts of dead plants. A forest that is not exploited and is in a state of ecological equilibrium has an even oxygen balance, i.e. oxygen consumption cancels out its production.

Net production of oxygen occurs only if a forest is in a growth phase and is accumulating standing wood, or if the forest is exploited. Even so, the wood sooner or later consumes the oxygen it has helped to produce, as in the case of firewood when it is burnt, and paper, paperboard and wooden objects when they are eliminated as waste.

In terms of global environmental equilibria, forests can stock carbon dioxide only if their total biomass increases, in which case they can store several hundred tonnes of carbon dioxide per hectare. On the other hand, deforestation over very large areas releases this stock. Besides this release of CO_2 there are other effects of very extensive deforestation, such as the modification of the world's radiation balance and disruptions in the movements of air masses and in the water cycle. Above certain limits, these effects may be extremely harmful to the way in which the biosphere works.

From the viewpoint of climatic and atmospheric effects, the different forms of forest management have much the same impact, with the exception of non-renewable exploitation which, if it concerns very large areas, may prove extremely detrimental, particularly in tropical regions.

Effects on the soil

The forest cover greatly influences the formation and evolution of the soil: roots contribute to deeper soil at the expense of parent rock and will draw off deep-lying inorganic substances which are returned to the surface as the leaves fall. The falling leaves also supply the surface layers with organic substances. The microclimatic conditions prevailing under the trees in a forest environment encourage the development of ground microflora and microfauna, which decompose the organic substances in the litter and incorporate them in the soil.

Most of the cultivated soils in OECD countries today (with the exception of grassland soil) were formed under forests: agriculture has therefore benefited from the forest pedogenesis of these soils by using their fertility.

In regions with a fragile soil, the forest often plays a vital protection role. This is particularly the case of soil that is sensitive to wind erosion (presence of dunes) or to rainwater erosion (erodable soil in mountain regions). In many OECD countries very large reforestation programmes are being carried out to control erosion.

Forests also contribute to protection against natural hazards in mountain areas such as avalanches, falling stones and floods. Reforestation is an integral part of the programmes to control these hazards.

Classical ("rational") forest management methods have the same advantages as natural forests with regard to soil effects. On the other hand, mismanagement and especially non-renewable exploitation may have very detrimental effects if they destroy the forest cover protecting a fragile soil. These effects vary with the situation. For example, the soil may be destroyed by erosion on steep slopes or on unstable

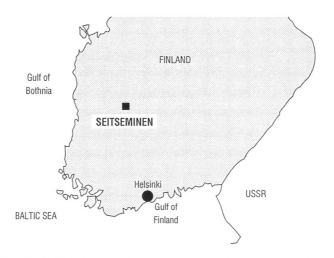

Seitseminen National Park, like all Finnish national parks, is a nature reserve which is to be kept in its natural state. It was established in 1982 as a result of the second programme for the creation of national parks launched in 1976. The park has an area of 41 km^2 and is under the administration of the National Board of Forestry.

Protecting the Primaeval Forest

The primaeval forests in the vicinity of Multiharju Ridge and Lake Pitkajarvi, the sand esters, kettle holes and delta formations of Seitsemisharju and Hirviharju Ridges, the many lakes and pools, the small peat bogs and the upper reaches of Seitsemisjoki Brook all together make this area particularly varied and interesting. Furthermore, Seitseminen National Park accurately represents the nature of southern and middle Finland as it includes a good selection of forests, peatlands and small bodies of water.

Seitseminen includes areas which were long used for forestry purposes before the park's creation: those forestry practices have now ceased, allowing flora and fauna to return gradually to a natural state. No other human activities (such as farming) or settlements (apart from facilities for scientists and visitors) are found within the park boundaries. The park therefore preserves a unique ecosystem of special value to Finland.

A Habitat for Wild Life

The forests harbour a fauna typical of primaeval forests and peatland, including such species as the pygmy owl (*Glaucidium passerinum*), the Ural owl (*Strix uralensis*), the goshawk (*Accipiter gentilis*), the black woodpecker (*Dryocopus martius*), the rustic bunting (*Emberiza rustica*), the capercaillie (*Tetrao urogollus*), the tree-toed woodpecker (*Piciodes tridactylus*), the red-breasted flycatcher (*Ficedula parva*), the marten (*Martes martes*) and the flying squirrel (*Pteromys volans*). The willow grouse (*Lagopus lagopus*), the crane (*Grus grus*), the whooper swan (*Cygnus cygnus*) and the golden plover (*Charadrius apricarius*) dwell in the wetlands of the park.

A Living Laboratory

As human populations and economic activities expand, ecosystems everywhere are coming under increasing pressure. Their preservation is an investment in the future, since unique ecosystems are essential for educational purposes as well as for an array of scientific studies which help us understand environmental change and its significance.

National parks like Seitseminen are essential biological laboratories, and their creation is an important instrument of preservation.

Contribution from Finland

ground; the ground may become waterlogged (in poorly drained sectors when the felling of trees that acted as a "pump" raises the water level); the soil may lose some vital trace elements and nutrients from clearfelling practices; the soil may be impoverished by over-rapid mineralisation of organic matter, a risk which is especially high in tropical forests where the soil may soon deteriorate if it is suddenly exposed to light.

The possible impact on soil must be carefully taken into account, particularly in any intensive and highly artificial type of forestry. The wrong choice of reforestation species or of cultivation techniques may result in soil degradation. For instance, the soil may be acidified by the litter of certain species, or mineral salts may be removed by felling at over-short intervals. In many cases, however, there are solutions for intensifying forestry without degrading the soil.

Effects on water

Forests have various and often marked effects on water. Their effect on total annual precipitation is not marked in the case of small stands. But there is an undeniable effect in the case of vast forest regions, since extensive deforestation contributes to a drier climate in the regions concerned.

Whatever the size of a catchment area, a forest has a major effect on water flow characteristics. Branches and leaves intercept a part of the precipitation and attenuate the effect of water dropping onto the ground; the roots improve water infiltration into the soil; the litter creates a "sponge" effect by storing a large volume of water. With the same rainfall, the runoff under a forest is less than on grassland and much less than on bare ground; it may even be zero in the case of a moderate rainfall. It follows that the concentration times in wooded catchment areas are considerably longer and that the flood levels of the streams flowing from these areas are much lower. Conversely, the improved infiltration of water into the forest soil helps to replenish the ground water, so the dry-weather flows are boosted. By reducing flood flows and boosting dry-weather flows, forests play a very important part in regulating water flow characteristics.

When a substantial proportion of precipitation is in the form of snow, forests also have another type of regulatory effect: a varying amount of snow slides along the branches and piles up on the ground. In the spring, this mass of snow receives much less light than if it were spread in the open air, so it melts more slowly. Forests thus lengthen the thaw period since more water from the snow seeps into the soil and the flood waters due to thawing are lower, as they are spread over a longer period.

The quality of the water provided by a forest catchment area is generally excellent: since erosion in the area is usually low or nil, the water from it contains very little suspended solid matter. However, water with a low pH may come from forests which themselves have

a litter with a very acidic humus and poor decomposition characteristics.

With the same level of annual precipitation, the volume of water from a wooded catchment area is generally lower than from a bare or grass-covered area, for forests evaporate and transpire more. However, any disadvantages of this greater water consumption by trees are usually very largely offset by the benefits provided by forests, i.e. regulation of stream flow characteristics and the very marked reduction in sediment content.

Efficient replacement exploitation has the same advantages as a natural forest as regards its effects on water. Intensive artificialisation techniques may involve some risks, however, especially with regard to water quality, as demonstrated by the sediment load following intensive groundworks, water acidification due to forest humus acidification after reforesting with an acidifying species, and fertilizer, pesticide and herbicide residues following intensive treatment. However, if artificial growing techniques are well selected and well understood, these risks can be reduced considerably.

Conversely, non-renewal exploitation or deforestation can quickly have very detrimental effects on water, even in quite small catchment areas, by reducing the concentration time in these areas and causing erosion and flood risks which increase with the fragility of the soil. Very negative effects on water quality may also occur when deforestation results in the rapid destruction of the forest humus and the organic and mineral products from its decomposition are swept away in the runoff water.

In order to improve water management in catchment areas many countries have carried out very extensive reforestation programmes with the aim of reducing runoff, regulating flow characteristics and reducing the volume of sediments deposited in reservoirs and artificial lakes.

Effects on the diversity of wild life

Natural forests are seldom homogeneous. They include a variable number of species (tropical forests have a much wider range of species than temperate forests; the forests of North America and Japan have a wider range than those in Europe) in every stage of development, including young, adult and dying trees. They thus provide a large number of varied ecological niches sheltering plants and animals of all sizes and forming complex ecosystems as a result of their interaction.

As long as gathering and hunting remain relatively limited and dispersed, they do not endanger the diversity of the genetic heritage of the flora or fauna. However, excessive gathering or hunting may eliminate certain species from some regions.

Replacement exploitation generally involves operations concentrating on one or two species of tree

NEW ZEALAND'S POLICY ON INDIGENOUS FORESTS

Valuable But Depleted Forests

New Zealand's heritage of indigenous forests has been severely depleted. Originally, over 80 per cent of New Zealand's land area was covered in indigenous forest. Now only one-third of that area remains. Much of the loss has occurred in the last 150 years as settlers have cleared and burned forests to make way for agricultural production.

These indigenous forests are significant for a number of reasons:

- They are part of the nation's heritage;
- They maintain the integrity of ecological systems, help soil stabilisation and flood control;
- Their scenic value is a major attraction to tourists;
- They absorb carbon dioxide, thereby doing their share to mitigate the "greenhouse effect."

Policy Objectives and Implementation

By far the largest share of the remaining indigenous forests is held publicly by the Crown, while one-sixth is held privately. Of the Crown estate of indigenous forests, only 150 000 hectares, some 3 per cent, are available for timber production. There are covenants that require long-term sustained yield management of all indigenous production forests on Crown land.

The objective of the policy is to maintain or enhance, in perpetuity, the current area of indigenous forest, either by protection, sustained yield management or reafforestation of indigenous species. The policy is based on the following set of principles:

- Recognise the rights and responsibilities of private landowners;
- Recognise the rights and obligations of the government to maintain wildlife habitat and to reflect international agreements entered into by the government;
- Recognise the rights and obligations of Maori landowners and of the government under the Treaty of Waitangi;
- Be efficient, cost-effective, and equitable.

Where maintenance of ecological, historical, cultural, or recreational values of indigenous forest is clearly of paramount importance, these forests will be permanently protected. All other indigenous forests must also be protected unless sustainable management is a viable option. "Sustainable management" is the management of a forest in a way that maintains its ability to continue to provide products and natural amenities in perpetuity, while retaining or enhancing the forest's natural ecological processes and genetic diversity for the benefit of both present and future generations. This policy will apply to forest which does not warrant full protection.

Encouragement to protect indigenous forests will be given to landowners through private trusts or directly by the Government via the Department of Conservation. The

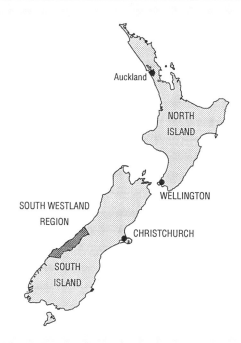

policy also includes a new proposal which is similar to a trust fund and whose purpose is to assist the protection of Maori-owned land covered in indigenous forests.

Protecting South Westland's Forests

An example of how this policy works may be found in South Westland: 311 000 hectares of former state forest were identified for protection in 1989. These areas have been placed under the Department of Conservation and are being submitted to UNESCO for nomination as a South Westland World Heritage Area.

The protection of this entire region creates an opportunity for increased tourism, based on its unique natural, cultural and scenic features. Furthermore, other activities, such as the harvesting of sphagnum moss, animal grazing and other forms of land use are encouraged or reviewed from a sustainable use viewpoint. The overall policy does much to meet the concerns expressed by the local people about the need to maintain employment and community viability. It clearly reflects a determination to preserve the indigenous forests while encouraging economic initiatives which do not conflict with that goal.

Contribution from New Zealand

with a high production value for the region concerned. They also lead to the disappearance of very old or dying trees. In many cases (even-aged forests, coppices), all the trees are much the same age. In such forests, therefore, the ecosystems are simplified compared with natural forests, and there are fewer niches, so the wild life is likely to be less abundant and varied.

Non-renewal exploitation leading to the complete disappearance of a wooded area radically affects forest ecosystems, thereby eliminating the flora and fauna dependent on them. This wild life is replaced by species found in more exposed environments. However, when mining leads to the disappearance of only part of the forest, it may result in a pattern of open and closed spaces providing a greater range of wild life than a forest with a completely closed canopy.

The more intensive artificial cultivation is, the more it contributes to simplified ecosystems. The detrimental effects of artificial cultivation on soil and water can be reduced by using appropriate techniques. On the other hand, artificial cultivation inevitably greatly reduces the diversity of flora and fauna, whatever the techniques used, for it is precisely intended to produce a simplified ecosystem in which a single plant species is encouraged at the expense of others that might compete with it, parasitize it or consume it.

Effects on social uses

Natural forests usually provide beautiful scenery, but they are not very suitable for recreational activities as they are mostly very difficult to penetrate. Their symbolic value is very high, for as ecosystems unchanged by man, they represent the natural as opposed to the artificial. The scarcity of really virgin forests in OECD countries and particularly in Europe adds further to this symbolic value.

Forests that are exploited by gathering usually retain their scenic and symbolic value, unless the gathering of certain produce becomes too intensive and over-emphasizes the presence of man. They are considerably more valuable for recreational activities than virgin forests as they are easier to penetrate. In addition, both gathering and hunting are becoming a recreational activity in developed societies.

Classically ("rationally") managed forests mostly retain a high scenic value and are suitable for recreational activities. In OECD countries some forest management programmes are even increasingly intended mainly for the public and for recreational activities in forests near major urban centres: amenities such as car parks, footpaths, bridle paths, cycle tracks, picnic areas, playgrounds, botanical walks, nature information boards, and so on have been provided. Production in such forests is generally a secondary factor. Whatever the management objective, classically managed forests retain much of their symbolic value, but to a lesser extent than natural forests, for man's action leaves its mark. Conflicts may arise when this action is perceived as too intrusive (cutting over large areas, planting of trees different from those growing spontaneously, and so on).

Non-renewal exploitation usually spoils the scenery, which takes time to recover, and leaves an area not very suitable for recreation. It is in direct conflict with the forest's symbolic value, for it is assimilated with the destruction of nature.

Intensive artificial cultivation usually creates very uniform scenery, made up of very large areas of trees of the same age and kind that are exploited at relatively short intervals. Their scenery is less appreciated than in the case of natural or traditionally managed forests. Neither are these monotonous forests very suitable for recreation. Since man's action is quite apparent, their symbolic significance is reversed: they become the outward sign of the intention to domesticate nature for utilitarian purposes. This explains the hostile reactions from those in the community who closely identify forests with nature.

Conclusions

The various methods of forest management have different effects on the environment. Non-renewal exploitation has mainly negative, if not extremely negative, effects on the air, climate, soil, water, the diversity of flora and fauna, scenery, recreational activities and the symbolic value of forests. On the other hand, replacement exploitation with little use of artificial techniques makes it possible to retain most of the forest's assets in the interests of the environment. However, the artificial techniques required for intensive tree growing are a threat to a number of these assets. By choosing the most appropriate techniques and using them very skilfully, it is often possible to prevent the risks of negative effects which artificial processes may have on the soil and water. But there is scarcely any way of preventing artificial processes from greatly reducing the diversity of the flora and fauna, the scenic value of forests, their suitability for recreational activities and their value as a symbol of nature.

Classical replacement exploitation methods maintained a balance between forests' protective functions, their productive role and their social uses. The use of artificial techniques for intensive production tends to destroy this balance since certain forests are earmarked for intensive production at the expense of their other uses. At the same time, the trend in demand is such that the exploitation of many forests subject to difficult physical or climatic conditions is increasingly less profitable. These forests are tending therefore to lose their production role. These two tendencies, which have the same cause, namely an industrial demand for large quantities of homogeneous products at competitive prices, may gradually lead to some specialisation of forest resources:

- Resources cultivated in a very artificial way for the intensive production of wood are bound to develop increasingly, particularly in the private forest sector;

- Traditional forest management reconciling production, protection and social uses is perfectly suitable for the production of high-quality wood requiring long rotations;
- Forest management programmes with the special objectives of giving protection (erodable areas) or providing recreational facilities for the public (sectors receiving a great many visitors) are still perfectly justified; but they concern relatively limited areas;
- In many regions, a growing proportion of forests is in an intermediate position: as a result of production conditions, they are exploited at a loss, they play their protective role spontaneously and they attract relatively few visitors. Forests of this kind require extensive sylviculture operations to keep their ecosystems balanced at the least cost.

4. EXTERNAL PRESSURES ON THE FOREST RESOURCES OF OECD COUNTRIES

Forest resources in OECD countries are at present threatened by a number of external factors.

Atmospheric pollution

From the very beginning of the industrial age, damage was observed in the forests situated near industrial plants. In the 1960s the first warnings of potential extensive damage were heard. Then at the beginning of the 1980s great concern was expressed publicly concerning the decline of forests, which was blamed on air pollution in Europe and in a part of North America. Industrial pollutants directly attack trees near emission sources, or are carried by winds and spread over vast areas before falling with the rain onto the leaves of trees and penetrating the soil. Nitrogen compounds may act as fertilizers. Most atmospheric pollutants, however, may well weaken and destroy the assimilation capacity of needles and leaves. Pollutants may also accumulate in the soil and increase its acidity. It is generally acknowledged that pollutants and an increase in acidity speed up leaching of nutrients from low-base capacity soils and therefore cause a substantial decrease in the soils' fertility. (See Chapter on Air)

This has led to the creation of an international co-operative programme to evaluate and monitor the effects of air pollution on forests in Europe, – a programme conducted by the United Nations Economic Commission for Europe (UNECE) with the support of the United Nations Environment Programme – and to bilateral work by Canada and the United States. The decline is measured in terms of foliage density and the yellowing of needles and leaves. Since many other factors can lead to defoliation – planting of softwood outside its natural growing areas, very dense stems that are too old, periods of drought, damage caused by insects and fungal diseases – it is not possible to draw final and incontrovertible conclusions on the causes of the observed symptoms. Research shows, however, that air pollution plays a major role in the decline of certain forests, since in many cases neither the existence nor the extent of this decline can be explained without taking into account the influence of air pollution.

The UNECE Timber Committee has endeavoured to express the decline in European forests affected by defoliation in terms of volume: in Europe as a whole (excluding the European USSR), the total standing volume of trees affected in one way or another by air pollution is the equivalent of about 14 average annual harvests in the region. The International Institute for Applied Systems Analysis (IIASA) has carried out an in-depth study on the future of forest resources in Europe. It concludes that the potential harvest on a sustainable basis in the next 100 years would be about 535 million m^3/year in the absence of emissions and 450 million m^3/year with the emissions between 1985 and 2000, as compared with the present harvest of about 425 million m^3/year. The potential thus exists for an additional harvest of about 110 million m^3/year in the next 100 years in the absence of emissions and for only 25 million m^3/year with the emissions for the period 1985-2000.

No quantitative forecasts concerning the effects of this type of pollution on forests are available for the other OECD regions. It is generally considered in Japan that atmospheric pollution has had no significant effects on the volume of the country's forest resources. The threat to forests from air pollution in the various OECD regions can be expressed in qualitative terms, however. Atmospheric pollution is already or could become a serious threat to forests in all OECD regions.

Climate change and the greenhouse effect

It is acknowledged that the increase in the carbon dioxide content of the air is largely caused by the burning of fossil fuels for man's activities and the oxidation of the plant biomass, which is mainly due to felling and to the destruction of forest organic resources. The effects of carbon dioxide concentrations in the atmosphere could be attenuated by the reconstitution of forest resources. (See Chapter on Air)

None of the global circulation models are at present able to forecast changes in the frequency of extreme climatic events, which are of vital importance

DECLINE IN CANADA'S SUGAR MAPLE STANDS

An Economic and Cultural Resource

Maple sugaring is the production of syrup and sugar from the sap of sugar maple (*Acer saccharum*) trees. This species, like several other species of the genus *Acer*, contains sap which has a much higher than usual sugar content. The process of "sugaring off" involves the collection of the sap from the trees as it begins to rise in the early spring and then boiling it to remove water and thicken it into a sweet syrup. Further boiling will convert it into sugar. About 40 litres of sap are needed to produce one litre of syrup.

Maple sugaring is a centuries-old tradition in eastern North America. The early European settlers arriving in the new world were fascinated by this process, which they learned from the native inhabitants. Making syrup and sugar was very important to these settlers as they seldom had access to the expensive imported cane sugar. Over the years this process has developed into a cottage industry throughout the range of the sugar maple in Canada and the northeastern United States. For many, maple sugaring has come to signal the advent of spring, and it also provides a welcome income in rural parts of the country. In 1988 the Canadian maple syrup industry produced some 13.8 million litres of maple syrup for sale around the world, valued at US$ 77.5 million.

THE RANGE OF SUGAR MAPLE

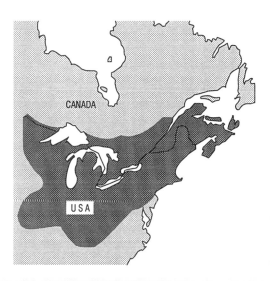

Decline and Dieback in Sugar Maple Stands

Scientists have long known that natural declines occur in many species, including ash, yellow birch and red spruce. However, since the early 1980s concern has mounted regarding the health of maple stands over much of the species' range. A full inventory of damage has yet to be completed, but in the province of Quebec surveys have shown that although only 1 per cent of maple forests have canopy loss in excess of 25 per cent, 49 per cent of the stands have canopy losses ranging between 11 and 25 per cent.

The phenomenon of maple dieback or, as it is usually called, decline, is first noticed as a progressive dying of branch tips, and premature yellowing and fall of leaves. This becomes more severe and may lead to death of trees. Affected trees may be rendered more susceptible to natural stress factors such as insects, diseases, or unusual but normal climatic events such as drought. It is therefore difficult for scientists to determine the precise cause of decline and subsequent death of trees. This is even more complicated when declines occur over large areas.

Recently, both scientists and the landowners of maple forests have expressed an additional concern: the potential link between tree health and airborne pollutants, acid rain and other toxic chemicals. Air pollution should be considered an additional stress factor and, although no direct cause-and-effect relationship can be shown, there is much concern that this added stress will cause widespread damage in maple stands. The maple stands now affected by decline are in areas where acid deposition is highest in Canada. However, the perceived damage to maple stands has not yet resulted in a loss of syrup production.

Searching for Solutions

What is being done and what can be done in the future? Research on the maple decline phenomenon began in 1986 and is investigating the contribution of climate, insects and diseases, air pollution (including acid rain) and soil nutrition to the survival and growth of sugar maple. Since then, the governments of Canada and the United States have published a manual on sugarbush management techniques. It is hoped that, through the use of effective forest management, stress on the sugar bushes can be relieved and that this will lead to the recovery of damaged trees.

In Canada, the Federal and Quebec governments are co-operating on a program of fertilization of maple stands. This is designed to relieve some of the symptoms of decline and will help replenish soil nutrients which are deficient. However, the underlying causes of decline are complicated and fertilization may be only a temporary solution. If the results of scientific investigation indicate that the damage is initiated or aggravated by the presence of air pollution, then reduction of that pollution and its effects on the forests will be necessary in order to solve the problem.

Contribution from Canada

in assessing the impact of climate changes on forests. If an increase in temperature of between 1.5 and 4.5 °C occurs at the same time as significant changes in precipitation characteristics between now and the year 2050, scientists agree that the impact on forest resources and the forest industry will be extremely pronounced, with:

- Changes to the geographical boundaries of forests;
- Changes in mortality and regeneration rates;
- Changes in forest species;
- Genetic changes;
- Changes in growth rates;
- Changes in wood quality;
- A decrease in forest areas as a result of dieback, invasion by insects, cryptogenic diseases, and damage due to windthrow and floods;
- Changes in transport conditions.

Forest fires

Forest fires have immediate, very serious consequences: burnt wood loses some or all of its commercial value, the scenic value and recreational possibilities of the forest are greatly reduced and serious erosion risks may appear if violent storms occur soon after a fire and if the soil is fragile. All these kinds of damage are obviously compounded by the costs of fire protection and fire-fighting.

However, the problem of forest fires must not be exaggerated, since fire has always been an element in many forest ecosystems, at least in those in a climate with periods of drought when the undergrowth litter becomes inflammable. Fires have always had natural causes (mainly lightning). They sometimes covered vast areas (millions of hectares), but they were very infrequent, and the ecosystem usually had time to regenerate between two fires. A distinction must be made between forest fires and controlled burning, deliberately carried out for a sylvicultural purpose; if it is done with sufficient care, such burning does not have harmful consequences.

The seriousness of the problem is due to the fact that natural causes have been compounded by man's action, i.e. negligence, accidents, reckless burning as an agricultural or grazing practice, and arson. In densely populated regions, such causes are now very largely preponderant compared with natural causes: for example, in certain Mediterranean regions, the latter account for only about 2 to 5 per cent of outbreaks but in Canada they account for 36 per cent.

It is essential, therefore, to take energetic steps against this marked increase in fires caused by man. If fires occur too frequently, there is not enough time between them for the forest ecosystem to be reconstituted, and irreversible damage occurs with the erosion of the soil, the disappearance of many wild life species and greater risks of flooding and drought.

It would be unrealistic to think of completely eliminating forest fires. The objective of prevention and control policies is to ensure that fires do not threaten life and property, and occur seldom enough for forests to have time to regenerate afterwards.

Plant diseases

The damage to forests through diseases caused by micro-organisms and fungi, or parasites, lepidoptera, coleoptera and other invertebrates, is less spectacular than that due to fires and atmospheric pollution. However, it may result in considerable economic losses especially in the case of forests grown artificially. The latter are particularly sensitive as they consist of trees belonging to a single species and have a small number of origins or clones selected for their productive qualities. The risk may be reduced by selecting species and origins well adjusted to the ecological characteristics of the rewooded area. On the other hand, a poor choice often causes a high risk of contagious plant diseases.

Natural forests and forests with limited artificial characteristics, which generally consist of more or less varied species from a suitable local source, are less sensitive to most plant health risks. Diseases in epidemic proportions may attack certain species, however, and even threaten their survival: a particularly serious case is that of Dutch elm disease, which is caused by a fungus, *Ceratocystis ulmi*. The most dangerous occurrence in this connection is the transfer of a disease or a parasite between two continents, for instance between Europe and North America. This type of transfer explains certain catastrophic epidemics. When an epidemic has taken hold, the treatment is always very costly and often inefficient. The best policy is very careful prevention and action at a very early stage to prevent an epidemic from starting.

Changes in land use

Much of the land now used for farming in OECD countries has been obtained by clearing forests. In some countries (Australia, Canada, the United States), natural grassland ecosystems have also been converted into agricultural land. But in other OECD countries, virtually all crop or grazing areas were once forests which were often cleared in ancient times going back to the neolithic age.

The balance between cleared and forest areas has varied in the course of time with the fluctuations in population. For example, large areas of land were cleared in Mediterranean and Atlantic Europe during the period of Roman prosperity. After the barbarian invasions and during the early Middle Ages, much land was abandoned and taken over by the forests again, as a result of demographic and economic decline. Clearing was actively resumed in the eleventh and twelfth centuries. Land was again abandoned and the forests spread after the Great Plague in the middle of the fourteenth century and during the troubles at the end of the

Middle Ages. Clearing started again during the classical and modern periods. The total forest area decreased to an absolute minimum in the first half of the nineteenth century in France and at a later date in the other countries of Mediterranean and Atlantic Europe. The decrease in forest areas was halted thanks to action by the forestry departments set up by governments and to the withdrawal of the least productive land from crop farming.

Today the forest area is stable or rising in almost all OECD countries, as the result of a balance between the loss and the creation of wooded areas.

Some of the losses are caused by clearing for agricultural purposes, which is still the practice in certain sectors, but concerns relatively limited areas. The others are due to increasing urban and industrial development with the creation of housing, industrial and office areas, facilities used intensively for recreational purposes, transport infrastructure (roads, railways, canals, airports, energy supplies), dams, and so on. Such development generally occurs at the expense of agricultural rather than forest land.

In many cases, new forests are located on land vacated by farmers, often because it is marginal. They may be created in two ways: reforestation by growing artificial stands, or the spontaneous evolution of the natural environment, with natural regeneration taking place more or less rapidly on fallow land abandoned by farmers. The distribution between these two processes varies with the region: where the forest potential is good, afforestation predominates and produces stands which are expected to have a high commercial value. In regions where the forest potential is limited (Mediterranean mountains, for example), natural forests have a more important place; their commercial value is low but their environmental value is considerable.

Overall, the balance in changing land uses is to the advantage of forests. In some areas this does not prevent valuable forests from being threatened by extinction, especially as a result of urban development and the infrastructure required by it. The defence and conservation of these forests are thus justified by their environmental and social values.

5. CONSEQUENCES FOR THE REST OF THE WORLD

The consumption, output and trade of forestry products in OECD Member countries also have effects on the rest of the world.

Trade in forest products

OECD countries account for 73 per cent of world imports of forest products. An analysis of the volume of trade shows that OECD countries import forest products mainly from developed countries (70 per cent of wood-based panels, 80 per cent of wood raw material and 90 per cent or more of sawnwood, pulp, paper and paperboard); OECD imports from developing countries are limited in terms of volume and value. These imports are mainly from Asia but those from Latin America are increasing.

The pattern of world trade is marked by its internationalisation and the growing importance of imports by the developing countries. Trade flows from North America have grown, especially towards Japan and developing countries, and declined towards Europe. Trade flows within Europe have expanded.

Developing countries, however, depend to a large extent on their imports from the OECD area, which have increased appreciably in the past 20 years; but trade among developing countries has also grown. As a rule, the higher the value added of a forest product, the more it is exported by the OECD area to developing countries. The ratio of annual exports to imports (expressed in value) between OECD and the developing regions is thus 2:1.

Trade between the OECD and Eastern Europe plus the USSR has been quite limited in the past. In the 1980s the main direction of this trade was from Eastern Europe and the USSR to the OECD area; the main products in this trade were wood raw material, sawnwood and wood-based panels.

The OECD countries with a high net export balance are Canada, Finland and Sweden; those with a high import balance are western Germany, Italy, Japan, the United Kingdom, the United States, and, to a lesser extent, France and the Netherlands. (Figure 21)

Tropical deforestation

Tropical deforestation is one of the major challenges to the entire international community. In-depth studies are now being conducted in an attempt to identify the main causes of tropical deforestation, since 25 to 30 different factors contribute to various deforestation processes. These factors include the exploitation of tropical industrial roundwood.

Pressure on tropical forests will continue because of rising consumption in OECD Member countries, but also because of very rapidly expanding demand in tropical countries themselves.

The most recent forecasts point to a much greater decrease in the tropical forest area (30 to 35 per cent before 2035) than the FAO estimated at the start of the 1980s (16 to 18 per cent). Such a deforestation rate will not only affect the environment of the tropical countries concerned but will also be instrumental in reducing the

Figure 21. TRADE IN FOREST INDUSTRY PRODUCTS, 1988

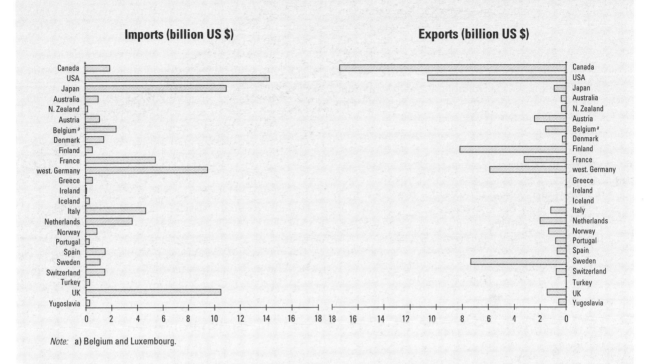

Imports (billion US $) **Exports (billion US $)**

Canada, USA, Japan, Australia, N. Zealand, Austria, Belgium ª, Denmark, Finland, France, west. Germany, Greece, Ireland, Iceland, Italy, Netherlands, Norway, Portugal, Spain, Sweden, Switzerland, Turkey, UK, Yugoslavia

Note: a) Belgium and Luxembourg.

Directions of trade

Share of world trade (%) from: to :	Developed countries				Developing countries
	North America	Western Europe	Northern Europe	Eastern Europe	
Developed countries					
North America	17%	—	1%	—	1%
Western Europe	7%	12%	20%	3%	2%
Eastern Europe	—	1%	2%	—	—
Japan	7%	—	—	—	3%
Developing countries	6%	2%	3%	1%	6%

Notes: Arrows ( ) show 1970-1988 trends; — indicates shares smaller than 1%.

Source: OECD, FAO, IIASA

world's genetic resources, increasing CO_2 concentration and accentuating the process of climate change.

Sustainable development in different regions

Only a very small proportion of tropical forests is actively managed at present – about 1 per cent of Africa's and South America's dense forests and 11 per cent of Asian forests. In developing countries, international trade accounts for about only 3 to 18 per cent of the harvest, while the remainder is used on the spot as firewood or for other purposes.

OECD countries have a direct influence on the sustained development of tropical broadleaved resources. Multinational companies also participate actively in cutting and processing tropical broadleaved trees in developing regions. In Africa, European and North American organisations hold or control most of the operating permits. In Asia, many Japanese and a number of North American companies hold the permits. In Latin America exploitation is mainly in the hands of national companies and the number of North American companies is very small.

It must be stressed that, even when logging in tropical regions does not really result in deforestation, it may have extremely negative effects on the environment both within and outside the logging site.

OECD countries owe it to themselves, therefore, to encourage the use of forestry and commercial policies that will correct and prevent too uneven an international distribution of industrial wood resources as well as the decline in tropical forest resources.

6. CONCLUSIONS

Forests in the OECD area account for 25 per cent of the world's wooded area and 33 per cent of the total land area of OECD countries. In volume terms, growing stock in OECD countries is about 20 per cent of the world total but 35 per cent of the world's commercially exploitable forests. The state of forest resources in the OECD area is by and large fairly satisfactory. OECD countries are aware, and often have been aware for a long time, of the need to manage their forests with a view to sustainable production. They have taken measures suited to that goal – in some cases, for centuries; in other cases, more recently. These include legislation regulating the various uses of the forest, development of the techniques of sylviculture and forest management, creation of forestry agencies in charge of monitoring the application of this legislation and the implementation of these techniques. As a result of such policies, the forest resources of the OECD as a whole are actually increasing. In the past 20 years, the surface covered by forest has been stable or increasing in almost all countries. Both the stock of timber and the average annual growth also increased during those years. The foreseeable trend for the years to come is that there will be further increase unless pollution or climate changes occur on such a large scale as to upset the ecological equilibrium of forest ecosystems.

From an environmental standpoint, most of the forests in OECD countries have a relatively high ecological stability compared with other regions of the world. In the 1980s, however, a very strong consciousness developed in OECD countries as to the necessary conditions for the ecological protection of forests. A number of problems have appeared which call for greater alertness in the years to come:

– The pressure from demand for industrial roundwoods will probably be stronger and stronger; this will lead to developing artificialisation techniques (severe selection of sources or clones, mechanised operations, use of fertilizers and pesticides) in order to make the most productive forests more productive still. This will mean an evolution comparable to the one that has occurred in agricultural production. If this intensification is carried out by means of suitable techniques, the impacts on land and water resources should remain limited. Negative impacts, on the other hand, will occur with regard to flora and fauna as well as landscape and uses of the forest other than wood production. But in forests where growing or operating conditions are difficult (Mediterranean forests, forests situated on steep slopes), the use of relatively costly artificialisation techniques will probably be scarcely profitable. Management of these forests could become more extensive and their value as relatively natural spaces could increase;

– Replacement exploitation policies with a view to sustained yield are not yet fully effective in all countries. Implementation of measures to efface the consequences of non-renewal exploitation must be completed, and the conditions needed for a sustainable development of forest resources must be created;

– Various types of "attack" on forests can occur: pollutants, forest fires, invasions by harmful insects or epidemics of cryptogamous diseases. There are also pressures from demand to clear land for urban, industrial, commercial or leisure development or for transport infrastructure. In order to keep the impact of such attacks to a minimum, extreme vigilance and suitable legislative and technical measures will be indispensable;

— Factors which will act in favour of forestry include the abandonment of land which, for agricultural purposes, was marginal, thus making spontaneous or artificial reforestation feasible, and the need for access to nature which is more and more vigorously expressed by urban populations;

— Regional and global atmospheric problems (long-distance pollution, the greenhouse effect, and so on) are likely to have impacts which are not well understood as yet but may be extensive. (See Chapters on Air and on Global Atmospheric Issues) If such impacts do occur, then the validity of the conclusions just outlined will become questionable.

In many countries outside the OECD, and particularly in tropical countries, the current state of forest resources is a cause for real concern. In a number of those countries, the area and quality of forest resources are declining rapidly. Estimates vary somewhat from one author to another; the most pessimistic estimates, often based on field studies or on the interpretation of satellite images, are extremely alarming. Among the numerous causes is the harvesting of valuable woods from wet tropical forests and the export of part of the wood thus harvested to OECD countries. Other causes include clearing land for agricultural purposes, over-harvesting firewood, and over-grazing.

This massive deforestation has very grave consequences for the countries concerned: erosion, disturbance of water regimes, disappearance of biotopes and species, wasting of economic resources, destruction of traditional lifestyles. It also has consequences on a worldwide scale: decline of the global forest resource

potential at a time when world demand is expected to increase (some forecasts give a total deficit of 110 million m^3 of industrial roundwood by the year 2010). Above all, this deforestation will contribute to aggravate global climatic problems, since tropical forests play a vital role in biosphere mechanisms both as a stock of carbon (which their destruction would release into the atmosphere in the form of CO_2, thus intensifying the greenhouse effect) and as a regulator of the planet's radiative and water balance. Disappearance of tropical forests could modify the ground's reflective function and hence its thermic balance, as well as the evapotranspiration of entire regions and thus the pluviometric regime of very extensive zones.

These national and global consequences, the economic and ecological interdependencies and their potential gravity justify the concern to maintain the tropical forest area. That goal can be pursued in two ways: by protecting existing valuable tropical forests and by developing highly productive artificial plantations in all regions of the globe with real forestry potential. Such plantations would make it possible to meet the foreseeable worldwide demand for wood. Once the demand was met in this way, pressure on the protected forests would diminish, making conservation easier to ensure. The sustainability of forest resources could be achieved on a worldwide scale and on an equitable basis for the partners concerned. Thus, the major challenge as regards forest resources in the years to come is to extend the principles of forest management with a view to achieving sustainable development throughout the planet. These principles have been applied in OECD countries' forests for a long time, varying from one country to another, and have made it possible for the resource base to increase overall in those regions. OECD countries have a major share of the responsibility for the future of the world's forest resources, since they are the major consumers and importers of wood.

Chapter 7

WILD LIFE

Wild life encompasses all non-human organisms and the ecosystems of which they are a part. These organisms range from mammals, birds and trees to the microscopic life that underpins all living systems.

Human society is dependent on wild life for material needs, for its role in maintaining life-support systems, and for quality of life. It is an essential physical and psychological part of our existence. Wild life has economic and political significance far beyond its use as a natural resource. This chapter examines the status of wild life in OECD countries and discusses problems already being addressed and those that remain and are emerging, as well as new opportunities in the 1990s.

1. USES AND VALUE OF WILD LIFE

Wild life supports human culture in myriad ways. These range from its functions in the ecosystems that man depends on and the materials he needs, to contributions to his emotional and spiritual quality of life. All of these values have economic and political dimensions, and all relate to the important issue of biological diversity.

Biological diversity

Biological diversity refers to the variety of life at all levels: genetic factors, species and their component populations, ecosystems, and the natural processes that maintain life in all these forms. If any part of this diversity is lost, the options for evolution and for human use of these resources are diminished. Continued loss will impair the proper functioning of the earth's natural systems, to the detriment of all life.

Biological diversity is being rapidly lost through extinction of species and populations, and human alteration of ecosystems, in all parts of the world, especially in the tropics. Global interdependence, both environmental and economic, makes loss of biodiversity anywhere in the world a matter of concern for everyone.

Environmental value

As the living component of the earth's ecosystems, wild life helps to regulate the cycles of energy, water, oxygen, nutrients and other basic elements. Loss of plants or animals can disrupt that function. The threat of global climate change, triggered by increasing amounts of carbon dioxide and other "greenhouse" gases in the atmosphere, has brought to public attention the role of forests in regulating CO_2. Growing forests absorb more CO_2 than they release, whereas forest clearing and burning does the opposite – hence the widespread calls for more tree planting and less destruction of the world's forests. (See Chapter on Forest)

Vegetation in all forms moderates temperature extremes, reduces soil erosion, protects watersheds, filters particles from air and sediment from water. Aquatic plants have been used to reduce the acidity of mine drainage.

Plants and animals have evolved together, in a system of checks and balances. Human-caused loss of any part of this system may result in rapid increase or disappearance of other parts, producing an imbalance (such as insect outbreaks) that is often harmful to human interests.

Economic value

Wild life affects economies in ways both obvious and subtle. Recent studies have documented the monetary value of wild life in wood products, fishing, other food, medicine, industrial products, trapping and collecting, and recreational pursuits. Trade in timber products, for instance, amounts to US$40 billion a year, and fishery products to US$12 billion a year. The value

USING SEED BANKS TO CONSERVE BIODIVERSITY: THE UNITED STATES EXAMPLE

In recent decades, as a result of human activities, biological systems everywhere have come under increasing pressure. Through the conversion of natural ecosystems to human-modified landscapes, the earth's biological diversity is being reduced at a rate that may increase over the next several decades. In the United States, seed banks are seen as an important instrument for the preservation of biological diversity.

Maintaining Biological Diversity with Seed Banks

Seed banks and clonal repositories store and preserve plant genetic material offsite, i.e. away from the places it is found naturally. The technologies used in seed banks are designed to preserve an adequate amount of germplasm, sustain its viability and preserve its original genetic constitution. In the United States and in other countries, the status of seed bank initiatives generally may be summarised as follows:

- Seed storage techniques are being used to conserve the genetic diversity of cereals, legumes and many other crop species. Priorities for collecting and maintaining germplasm of major crop plants are internationally co-ordinated, but are not well organised for minor crops or for wild plants which are endangered or which have economic potential;
- New technologies can increase the success of maintaining diversity offsite, but there is a lack of fundamental research. Pending major breakthroughs in biotechnologies which might eventually lead to fundamental changes in how biological diversity is maintained in seed banks, existing technologies, such as cryogenic storage of germplasm, should be improved.

Seed Banks in the United States

In the United States the most significant seed preservation programme is the National Plant Germplasm System, a seed bank network under the jurisdiction of the Department of Agriculture and involving state institutions, private industry and individuals. The mission of this system is to acquire, maintain, evaluate and make accessible as wide a range of genetic diversity as possible in the form of seed and clonal materials to crop breeders and plant scientists. Among the facilities maintained through the programme:

- The National Seed Storage Laboratory, which is the principal storage facility for agricultural crop seeds in the United States;
- The Plant Genetics and Germplasm Institute, which includes the Plant Introduction Office, the Plant Molecular Genetics Laboratory, the Germplasm Resources Information Network and the National Small Grains Collection;
- Germplasm collections, such as the Regional Plant Introduction Stations for maintaining major crops and the newly established clonal repositories.

MAINTENANCE PROCESS OF A PLANT SEED BANK

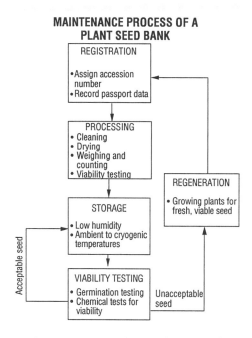

Private individuals and voluntary organisations are preserving a significant amount of agricultural crop diversity not found in government collections. For example, the Seed Savers Exchange helps preserve heirloom vegetable varieties and other vegetable seeds not readily available.

No federal equivalent exists for wild plant species. The most significant offsite programs for wild germplasm are financed and managed in the private sector. An example, based at the Arnold Arboretum in Boston, is the Centre for Plant Conservation, which consists of regional botanic gardens and arboreta.

International Efforts

Internationally, there are roughly 2 million accessions of plant germplasm in seed banks. The International Board for Plant Genetic Resources co-ordinates a global network of gene banks to provide plant breeders with the genetic resources necessary to develop better crops. Begun in 1974, it now involves 106 countries and gene banks now number more than 100, 40 of which have agreed to long-term maintenance of genetic resources.

Contribution from the United States

of prescription drugs with plant-derived ingredients was estimated at US$8 billion for 1980 in the United States and about US$40 billion for all OECD countries.

Between 1976 and 1980, the United States produced and imported on average each year US$87 million worth of food products from wild sources. These included such native items as maple syrup, pecans, blueberries and wild rice, and foreign ones such as Brazil nuts and oregano. United States trade in industrial products from wild species, such as rattan, cork and gum arabic, amounted to US$142 million.

Wild life-based recreation and tourism is also a big industry. Surveys in the United States in 1975 and 1980 showed that Americans spend about US$30 billion a year on fishing, hunting and non-consumptive activities such as feeding wild birds and photographing wild flowers. Similar surveys in Canada gave a total of US$4.2 billion. Tourists from OECD countries provide a large part of the foreign currency receipts of a number of African countries with a particularly rich wild life endowment.

Commercial breeding of wild species is growing. Finland now has over 3 000 fur farms with close to 3 million minks and polecats and 2 million blue foxes and doglike racoons. Finland is the world's second largest exporter of mink pelts. (See Chapter on Agriculture) Aquaculture has developed considerably in countries such as France, Japan or Norway. (See Chapter on Marine Environment) Alligator farming and commercial growing of the medicinal plant ginseng in the United States are relatively new activities.

Other economic benefits from wild species are more difficult to quantify but are perhaps equally or more important. The genetic resources in wild species are the foundation of continued viability of the world's major food crops. Through cross-breeding, the wild relatives of maize, wheat and other crops improve the resistance of these crops to diseases and pests, and yield other benefits. Many wild species of plants and animals could be domesticated to provide food and other needs.

Pollination of plants of economic value is a vital service performed by insects and bats. Bees, wasps, flies, beetles and other insects pollinate many fruit, vegetable, forage and other crops. In the southwestern United States, bats pollinate such crops as avocados, bananas, cashews, figs and agave.

Algae, common to both fresh and salt water, supply extracts of commercial importance in ice cream and other products. Some larger algae are dried and consumed directly. Bacteria, besides playing key roles in nutrient cycling, offer many possibilities for human use. Genetically engineered bacteria can be sprayed on caterpillars infesting trees and on oil spills to degrade the crude oil. Potential applications include crop protection (control of the corn ear worm in France and crown gall in Australia), extraction of elements from ores (leaching of uranium in Canada), industrial fermentations and production of chemicals.

Still more hidden and diffuse are economic contributions related to the quality of life. People in urban areas are willing to pay more to live, work, and play where the setting is more natural.

Cultural value

Wild life, whether perceived as individual plants and animals or viewed collectively as "nature", is important to people simply because it comprises other forms of life that share the same planet. Man is attracted by wild life. This is demonstrated not only by the extent of wild life-based recreation, but also by the popularity of books and television programmes on wild life, growing concern for the ethical treatment of animals, and the growth and political impact of conservation organisations. Wild life is more than a resource; it is a part of the human psyche.

2. CONDITIONS AND TRENDS

The status of wild life can be measured directly or in terms of habitat available, the primary limiting factor. Direct measurement of wild life populations is difficult, especially for the smaller, more reclusive organisms. Habitat measurement is easier. Both approaches are used here. The extent of protected areas and changes in land use are used as indicators of habitat available for wild life.

Wild life populations

Estimates of the number of species on earth range from 5 million to more than 30 million. The majority are in the poorly-known tropics, and are invertebrates. Only about 1.7 million species have been identified, however. Of these, about 1 million are found in the temperate zone, which has received the most study. OECD countries together probably have appreciably fewer than 1 million species.

Obviously, it is impossible to keep track of the global populations of several hundred thousand species. Data are best for economically important species, such as those hunted or fished, and easily observed groups, such as birds. One approach is to focus on species that are thought to be threatened with extinction. It should be kept in mind that the data reflect

Figure 22. **STATE OF WILD LIFE, Late 1980s**

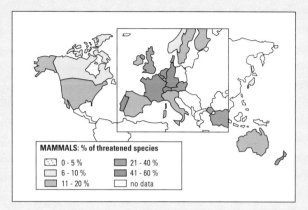

MAMMALS: % of threatened species

- 0 - 5 %
- 6 - 10 %
- 11 - 20 %
- 21 - 40 %
- 41 - 60 %
- no data

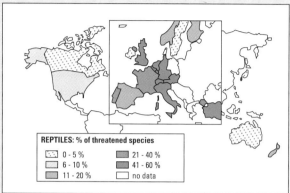

REPTILES: % of threatened species

- 0 - 5 %
- 6 - 10 %
- 11 - 20 %
- 21 - 40 %
- 41 - 60 %
- no data

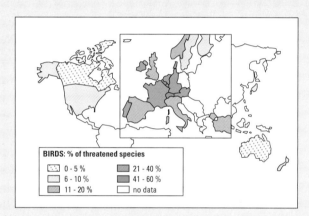

BIRDS: % of threatened species

- 0 - 5 %
- 6 - 10 %
- 11 - 20 %
- 21 - 40 %
- 41 - 60 %
- no data

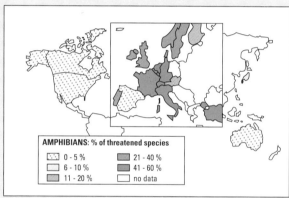

AMPHIBIANS: % of threatened species

- 0 - 5 %
- 6 - 10 %
- 11 - 20 %
- 21 - 40 %
- 41 - 60 %
- no data

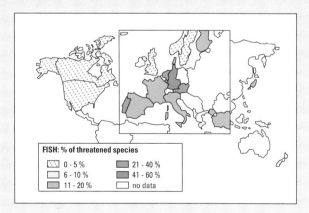

FISH: % of threatened species

- 0 - 5 %
- 6 - 10 %
- 11 - 20 %
- 21 - 40 %
- 41 - 60 %
- no data

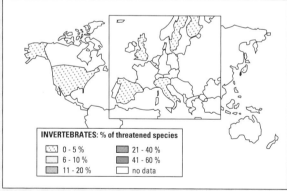

INVERTEBRATES: % of threatened species

- 0 - 5 %
- 6 - 10 %
- 11 - 20 %
- 21 - 40 %
- 41 - 60 %
- no data

Note: Information on Germany refers to western Germany only.
Source: OECD

not only the actual status of populations but also the state of knowledge about them. Differing definitions of "threatened" may also affect the numbers. (Figure 22)

As regards mammals, Australia, Canada, Japan and the United States have the largest number of species, probably because of large territorial extent and/or variety of habitat. France, western Germany, Luxembourg, the Netherlands, Portugal and Switzerland all report over 40 per cent of their mammal species threatened. Many marine mammals in particular are threatened, principally from overharvesting in the past for oil, meat or pelts. A moratorium on commercial harvesting of all 12 species of great whales, ranging from the gigantic blue whale to the much smaller minke, has been in force since 1987. Numbers of most of these species are low, and some species, such as the very scarce blue whale, may not recover. Careful monitoring has revealed only about 250 North Atlantic right whales. The populations of minke and grey whales, on the other hand, are thought to be increasing.

The widespread decline of large carnivores is exemplified in long-term statistics from Norway, where the kill of certain species has been recorded since 1846. The yearly average populations for the 1846-49 and 1980-86 periods are: bear, 270 and two; wolves, 235 and zero; wolverines, 74 and four; lynxes, 119 and 28. The trend was steadily downward over that whole period.

Concerning birds, France, western Germany, the Netherlands, Portugal and Switzerland all report more than 30 per cent of their species threatened. Countries with low population densities, such as Australia, Canada and Finland, report less than 10 per cent as threatened. An exception to the pattern is Japan, which has the second highest population density of all OECD countries but reports only 8.1 per cent of its bird species as threatened.

One of the most extensive monitoring programmes for birds is the North American Breeding Bird Survey. Since 1966 it has annually deployed hundreds of birdwatchers to sample bird populations along 2 000 routes in the United States and Canada. One study using these data examined 62 migrant species in the eastern United States and Canada. It found that during 1966-78 more of these species increased than decreased. But during 1978-87, 20 showed significant decreases and only four had significant increases. Deforestation of the tropical wintering grounds, along with heavy use of pesticides on South American plantations, were thought to be the main factors responsible for the decreases. Fragmentation of forests in North American breeding grounds may also be a factor.

Duck populations in North America have been on a downtrend for several decades, largely because of loss of wetlands. The breeding populations of 10 common species decreased from 42.9 million in 1955 to 26.5 million in 1989. Pintails, mallards and blue-winged teal showed the largest numerical drops, while gadwalls and green-winged teal showed modest increases.

Concerning fish, Austria, western Germany and Luxembourg report 36 to 70 per cent of their species threatened. Most other countries with data reported less than 15 per cent threatened, perhaps partly because of incomplete information. Water pollution and acid deposition, as regards freshwater species, and overharvesting and destruction of coastal wetlands, as regards marine species, are among the most common causes.

Concerning reptiles, amphibians and invertebrates, most of the European OECD countries have few reptile and amphibian species, and many of these are considered threatened; drainage or acidification of breeding pools are probably important factors in amphibian declines. Data on invertebrates are scarce; western Germany presents the gloomiest picture, with 10 600 of its 40 000 known species of invertebrates threatened.

Concerning plants, Belgium, western Germany, and Switzerland report about one-quarter of their vascular plant species as threatened, other countries less.

Protected areas

Many species of plants and animals cannot adapt to human-modified landscapes, often because they require a specialised natural habitat or because, in the case of many large predators, their way of life conflicts with man's. For such species, protected areas are essential. A total of 2 599 sites had been established by 1989; while all OECD countries had designated some sites, the percentage of national land area protected ranges from 0.3 to 25.1 and seems to bear little relationship to the size or population density of a country. Austria, western Germany, Luxembourg, New Zealand, Norway and the United Kingdom are all above the 10 per cent level often cited as a minimum goal. (See Chapter on Land)

There were 115 biosphere reserves in 19 OECD countries in 1989. A biosphere reserve is intended to combine preservation of nature in a core area with experimental research in a buffer zone to study methods for achieving a form of development that conserves resources and biological diversity. Many OECD biosphere reserves also fall under one of the first five categories of protected area identified by the International Union for the Conservation of Nature and Natural Resources (IUCN), such as national parks, and are included in the total of 2 599 sites.

Considerable progress has been made in the last few years in designation of Wetlands of International Importance under the Wetlands Convention signed at Ramsar, Iran, in 1971. Signatories imposed obligations upon themselves to protect and use wetlands wisely. By 1985, 20 OECD countries had designated 234 sites totalling 13 790 200 hectares. By 1989, 23 countries had designated 316 sites totalling 19 635 100 hectares.

JAPAN'S "GREEN CENSUS"

NUMBER OF OBSERVED BIRDS

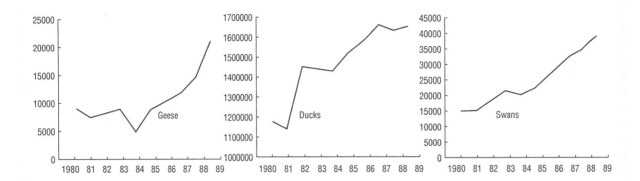

Information for Environmental Management

Japan's archipelago stretches from the sub-arctic to sub-tropical zones and includes a wide variety of ecosystems, fauna and flora. Many of these ecosystems are coming under increasing pressure from human activities such as intensifying land use and industrialisation.

To better understand how the environment responds to these pressures, national surveys on the state of the natural environment, popularly known as the "Green Census," are carried out every five years. The Green Census identifies conditions and trends in diverse types of fauna and flora, surface water resources, coastal areas and other aspects of the natural environment. The results of the Green Census provide information essential to the elaboration of nature conservation plans and are also used to assess the environmental impacts of proposed development projects.

Extensive Public Participation

The first national survey on the natural environment was carried out in 1973, the second in 1978/79 and the third in the period spanning 1983 to 1987. A fourth survey is presently underway.

As the Green Census has evolved, public participation in the survey has grown. On the third survey, the distribution of 70 species of popular and familiar plants and animals was identified in co-operation with the widespread participation of volunteers. Surveyed species were chosen on the basis of two criteria: they would indicate the present state of wild life in Japan, and were well-known to the Japanese people. After receiving the survey manual, data cards and maps, volunteers recorded on their cards where they sighted the plants and animals. About 100,000 people participated in the survey and completed 1.9 million data entries on approximately 280,000 cards. Involving members of the public in the Green Census helps improve awareness about the state of the environment and is especially popular with students. This approach is being used in the fourth Green Census survey.

The results of the Green Census are available to the public. A comprehensive report is published which details the findings of each survey; maps showing wild life and plant distribution and reports on each survey genre are also publicly accessible.

Surveying Wild Bird Populations

Wild birds are among the many types of fauna and flora surveyed in the Green Census. In addition, various species of geese and ducks have been surveyed since 1970 and their populations continue to be monitored. The nationwide survey, carried out around 15th January of each year, examines the locations and geographical conditions of the birds' principal wintering areas. Bird species and the number of specimens at all locations are also determined.

The latest results of the wild bird surveys, released in January 1989, revealed that the following populations (approximate figures) had been observed in Japan: towards 40 000 birds of the swan family, 21 000 birds of the goose family, and 1.651 million birds of the duck family. The overall trend of the past ten years has been towards increasing populations in all three families of birds, although trends vary among specific species.

Contribution from Japan

Although the total wetland area of OECD countries is still declining, a strong effort is being made to save wetlands of special importance for wild life and other purposes.

Land use trends and wild life

Most OECD countries have designated less than 10 per cent of their land as protected areas, which means that most wild life lives on land that is used for other purposes and may be greatly altered from its natural condition. Wild life diversity is generally lowest in urban areas and highest in forest and wetland areas, with intermediate diversity in suburban, cropland, and pasture areas.

Increases or decreases in cropland, permanent pasture and forest and woodland usually will mean increases or decreases in species able to live in those environments, although much depends on the type and condition of cropland, pasture or forest. "Other land" consists of uncultivated land, grassland not used for pasture, built-on areas, wetlands, wasteland and roads. Obviously, the implications for wild life of an increase or decrease in "other land" depends on which of the constituent types are changing in area. Built-on areas and roads have increased and wetlands have declined; both trends have negative implications for wild life. Between 1950 and the late 1980s, Sweden lost 9 per cent of its wetlands, the United States 12 per cent, Finland 24 per cent, the Netherlands 55 per cent, and western Germany 63 per cent. (See Chapter on Land)

The forest area in western Europe has increased since the second half of the nineteenth century, and this trend continues. The acreage of forest in most European OECD countries has remained stable or increased since 1950; in Great Britain it nearly doubled between 1950 and 1988. Outside Europe, the trend is mixed. This general increase has particularly benefited forest wild life where the expanded forest is natural. However, much of the forest increase since 1950 has been in plantations, primarily coniferous, which are planted in rows and cleared of underbrush and dead wood. Such forests are relatively poor in wild life, but they do take some logging pressure off natural forests. (See Chapter on Forest)

In the majority of OECD countries, mainly European, cropland and, even more so, permanent pasture have shrunk in area. The land these categories have lost is turned over primarily to urbanisation and forestry. On balance, the land use changes in most OECD countries must be considered detrimental to wild life.

3. THE IMPACT OF HUMAN ACTIVITIES

Wild life is subject to both natural and human influences. It has evolved under and adapted to the natural processes. In many cases it has not been able to adapt to human activities and has suffered extinction or losses.

Habitat modification

The implications for wild life of land conversion from one use to another are discussed above. Management practices within a given type of land use may have consequences almost as great.

Many developments in agriculture since 1960 have been unfavourable to wild life. Enlargement of fields and "clean" farming have eliminated many hedgerows, fencerows and odd corners that were useful to wild life. Expanded irrigation, drainage of wetlands and increased use of fertilizers and pesticides have also impaired farmland as habitat for wild life. OECD-wide, the irrigated area has increased 22 per cent since 1970. This average figure conceals broad variations among countries. The withdrawal of surface water for irrigation makes it unavailable for instream users, such as fish and invertebrates. If flows are reduced enough to dry up large portions of a river and associated wetlands, waterfowl are affected as well. Irrigation also affects the quality of water returned to the stream. It is often highly saline and high in dissolved solids, leached fertilizer, and toxics from pesticides. Fertilizers in runoff contribute to eutrophication and lowered oxygen levels, a condition that can be fatal to fish and invertebrates. Pesticides become concentrated on stream and lake bottoms, where they leach slowly into the water and enter the food chain, becoming more concentrated at each higher level. Corrective efforts have begun in some countries. They include the use of less harmful pesticides (synthetic pyrethrins and carbamates) and organic cultivation techniques. Unique habitat has also been lost through agricultural practice; examples are the heaths, fens and bogs of Denmark, which have been overgrazed, overgrown or drained. Many species in Denmark, particularly birds, have suffered: the black grouse, which numbered 2 400 in 1943, had declined to fewer than 40 by 1980. (See Chapter on Agriculture)

Some forest management practices are inimical to wild life. The relative biotic poverty of monocultural forest plantations was referred to above, as was the effect of forest fragmentation on birds. Forest fragmentation reduces not only the total amount of forest habitat but also the size of forest patches. Birds that breed in forest interiors require certain minimum sizes of forest, and reduction in the area of an individual forest will make it unsuitable for some species.

CAUSES OF PLANT SPECIES DECLINE IN GERMANY

RESPONSIBLE FACTORS

Number of species affected by :

- 305 Change of land use
- 284 Abandonment of land use
- 255 Destroying of special site
- 247 Filling, development
- 201 Dehydration
- 176 Soil eutrophication
- 163 Mining and excavation
- 123 Mechanical interference
- 115 Interference such as weeding, clearing, fire
- 103 Collecting
- 68 Changes and maintenance of waterways
- 59 Soil levelling
- 43 Introduction of exotic species
- 38 Air and soil pollution
- 36 Eutrophication of water bodies
- 35 Water pollution
- 27 Creation of artificial waters
- 26 Use of herbicides, seed purification
- 22 Urbanisation of villages
- 8 Discontinuation of certain field crops

Total number of affected species : 711

RESPONSIBLE SECTORS

Number of species affected by :

- 513 Agriculture
- 338 Forestry and hunting
- 161 Tourism and leisure
- 158 Raw material extraction
- 155 Trade, housing and industry
- 112 Water management
- 79 Fish rearing
- 71 Traffic and transport
- 71 Waste and sewage disposal
- 53 Military activity
- 40 Science, education and culture
- 8 Food and pharmaceutical industries

Total number of affected species : 711

Numerous Endangered and Extinct Species

In Germany, 727 of the approximately 2 700 native species of ferns and flowering plants are either endangered or have become extinct. For 711 of these species it has been possible to identify the nature and source of the threat which caused or contributed to their decline. Many have been affected by several factors which, in combination, pose an even greater threat to their survival.

Factors Causing Plant Species Decline

At the top of the list of causes of decline is the destruction of habitats through the conversion of land from extensive to intensive cultivation. Scattered meadows, sheep pastures or oligotrophic grasslands have been converted to intensively used arable and grass land with fewer species.

Almost as widespread are the effects caused by interference with habitats. With increasing intensification of agricultural practices, field and vineyard terraces, hedgerows, stone fences, embankments, ponds, wide forest borders and the like are disappearing. Almost all forms of plant life are affected by this; for instance, moist meadows suffer severely.

The destruction of habitats as a result of landfill, tipping or levelling of land - often undertaken in conjunction with the construction of housing estates, industrial plants and streets - has a similar effect to that of quarrying and excavation, particularly on dry grasslands communities,

moors and moist meadows and their species. Drainage is similarly one of the most common causes of this impact on habitat sites. It mainly affects plants in semi-wet and wet biotypes, especially in moors, marshes and wet forests.

The direct impacts on plant populations have less far-reaching effects for the species than the change and destruction of habitats. The most important instances are walking, waves from motorboats, mechanical weeding in waters, use of herbicides, fire, clearing and finally, the collection of attractive species.

Sectors Causing Plant Species Decline

The main sector responsible for the endangering of species is agriculture, particularly where measures have been introduced to improve the structure and location of farmland. This has been identified as the source of threat to 513 species, 72 per cent of species on the Red List of threatened and endangered species.

Other sectors responsible for plant species decline are forestry and hunting (338 species) - particularly through re-afforestation of dry grasslands and heaths and the conversion of deciduous forests into coniferous forests -, tourism, leisure and sport (161 species), extraction of raw materials and small-scale open-cast mining - above all gravel quarrying (158 species) - commercial activity, housing and industry (155 species) and water management (112 species).

Contribution from Germany

Likewise, many wild life species require old-growth forests. But these are also the stands that yield the greatest volume of timber and therefore are most valuable for logging. It is not surprising that management of old-growth forests has become a conservation issue, particularly in Finland, New Zealand and the United States. In the US Pacific Northwest states, the conflict has focused on the northern spotted owl, which needs old growth for breeding and was recently declared a threatened species. This implies protection of its habitat, which might mean fewer jobs and less profit for timber companies. How to balance competing uses of forests, including protection of wild life habitat, is a worldwide problem. (See Chapter on Forest)

Most modifications of aquatic habitat have involved either additions to water, structural changes to the water course or removal of the habitat. Habitat removal is normally accomplished through dredging, filling and draining. An example of a preventive approach to loss of coastal habitat, taken up by many countries, comes from France, where in recognition of the threat of urban development to coastal areas, the Conservancy of the Coastal Zone and Lake Shores was created in 1975. This agency, responsible for the purchase of property and, together with local authorities, for the protection and management of natural areas, has acquired 225 properties covering 28 556 hectares and 380 kilometres of shoreline.

Excessive and illegal exploitation

In most cases, harvest levels of game and commercial species in OECD countries have been regulated in a way that maintains adequate populations. Exceptions include whales and some marine fish species. Most exploitation problems now involve illegal taking and trade, which are often linked.

Certain marine fishing grounds or species are or have been overexploited. (See Chapter on Marine Environment) The whale situation is under continuous study. Although there is a moratorium on commercial taking of great whales, Iceland, Japan and Norway still legally take small numbers for scientific purposes, and are pressing for resumption of commercial capture of minke whales, which are still numerous. More scientific information on whale population trends and dynamics is needed for future management of great whales. The same can also be said for small cetaceans, which are harvested by many countries. Large numbers of dolphins are also inadvertently captured in commercial fishing nets.

Poaching of wild life probably continues to occur in all countries. The illegal killing of elephants and rhinoceroses for their ivory and horns has been most publicised, but many other species are targets. Deer, elk and black bears have been poached in some US national parks for years, and some of this poaching is now conducted to obtain animal parts for sale to Asian markets. Rare cactuses are poached from desert areas

of the United States and Mexico for sale in the live plant trade.

OECD countries figure more prominently as markets than as sources of illegal wild life trade. The World Wildlife Find estimates the minimum value of world trade in wild life and wild life products at US$5 billion annually, of which about one-third is estimated to be illegal. The trade in elephant ivory is valued at US$200 million annually, a lynx coat can fetch US$100 000, a single macaw or cockatoo can bring over US$10 000 and rhinoceros horn is literally worth more than its weight in gold. The principal international measure for controlling wild life trade is the Convention on International Trade in Endangered Species (CITES). (See below, and Chapter on International Responses)

Pollution and climate change

All of the chemicals and solid wastes released into the environment affect wild life to varying degrees. These substances and their impacts range from the obvious harm done by oil spills to the subtle and pervasive effects of pesticides. The threat of global warming, largely a by-product of the use of fossil fuels, hangs over wild life as much as over human life. (See Chapter on Global Atmospheric Issues)

Oil spills, such as that of the Amoco Cadiz on the Brittany Coast of France in 1978 and the Exxon Valdez in Prince William Sound, Alaska, in 1989, have taken a heavy toll of wild life. Overall, the Alaskan spill caused a projected commercial loss of more than $100 million. (See Chapter on the Marine Environment)

Pesticides continue to threaten wild life, even the persistent ones like DDT, the use of which has been largely banned in OECD countries although it is still freely traded elsewhere. In Canada in 1984, levels of DDT and deldrin in puffin eggs were still one-third to one-half of the levels recorded in 1972. DDT levels in smelt in Lake Ontario dropped by two-thirds or more from 1972 to 1974 but as of 1982 had not declined further.

The effects in receiving waters of conventional and toxic pollutants include eutrophication caused by nutrients, lowered oxygen caused by heavy organic waste loading, and direct damage and long-term damage from low pH, metals and synthetic chemical waste. These effects may eliminate aquatic species and cause others to be more susceptible to disease and predation. (See Chapters on Inland Waters and on Marine Environment) The immediate cause of the die-off of over 11 000 harbour, grey and common seals in the North Sea region in 1988 apparently was a virus, but scientists suspect that exposure to pollution could have lowered the animals' resistance by affecting their immune systems.

Air pollution effects on wild life have been most apparent in aquatic species and certain tree species. Acidic deposition has led to disruption of life cycles and loss of whole populations of fish in the waters of southern and western Sweden. In southern Norway, lakes with a total surface area of 13 000 square kilometres support no fish, and stocks have been depleted over an additional 20 000 square kilometres. Scientists have observed a worldwide decline in amphibians that may be due in part to acidification of breeding pools. Coniferous trees are also especially vulnerable to air pollution. By the mid-1980s, forest die-back attributable partly to air pollution had affected forests throughout Europe. Air pollution is one suspected cause of the recent die-off of spruce trees in the Appalachian Mountains of the eastern United States, and high ozone levels have killed pines in the Santa Monica Mountains of California. (See Chapter on Air)

Global warming, if it occurs as presently predicted, can be expected to have a major, widespread impact on wild life. Many or most species of plants and animals would have to migrate to higher latitudes or altitudes to remain in compatible temperate zones. Such migration, however, would be difficult because of the rapid rate of warming and the natural and human barriers. Population and species extinctions are likely. The degree of warming and thus its effects are forecast to be lowest in the tropics and highest towards the poles. Sea level rise due to expansion of the warming water and melting of glaciers and sea ice would destroy large areas of coastal wetlands. Other results of warming, such as changes in patterns of precipitation, fire, floods and hurricanes, would also strain the ability of species to adapt.

Species introduction

Many plants and animals have been introduced by accident or intentionally from indigenous to new habitats, ecosystems and biomes. Grasses and vines have been introduced to stabilise soil. Aquatic plants have been introduced to waterways. Animals have also been introduced, largely for economic reasons, often to control pests or predators. While sometimes beneficial, moving an organism into an area where it is not native is more likely to be unsuccessful or damaging to the ecosystem it enters.

For example, several hundred years ago domestic cats were introduced into New Zealand. Many of the cats, however, established wild or feral populations. Predation by these feral cats has caused extinction of at least five species of birds found only in New Zealand.

A parasitic fungus inadvertently imported into the United States in the early twentieth century killed most American chestnut trees, an extremely valuable component of that country's eastern forests. Even when they do not cause extinction, invading species can cause economic problems. Parasitic mites that attack honey bee drone larvae have spread throughout the world, from the Soviet Union in 1965, to Eastern Europe in the 1970s, to western Europe in the 1980s and the United States towards the end of the 1980s. Accidental spread of organisms from one part of the world to another is likely to remain a problem as global travel and commerce increase.

4. PROTECTION AND MANAGEMENT

Two main themes are apparent in wild life conservation today. One is the importance of integrating conservation with development. The other is the need for international co-operation, spurred by increasing global communications and the transboundary nature of many resources.

Integration of conservation and development

Conservation and development depend on each other in a number of ways. Development needs the resources supplied by conservation. And conservation of wild life increasingly must be carried out in conjunction with economic activities since there are limits to the amount of land that can be dedicated solely to the preservation of nature.

One type of economic development that is benefiting wild species is the commercial raising of some of them. This helps to take the pressure off wild populations. Fur and alligator farms have already been mentioned. Aquaculture of marine and freshwater species is growing rapidly. Salmon are in serious decline in some parts of the world; in Spain, however, where the transition to aquaculture of salmon has occurred, the 1986 catch in continental waters was 11 000 tonnes and the harvest in aquaculture was 14 000 tonnes. The differences in Norway are even more striking: more than 49 000 tonnes of salmon and trout in 1986 from aquaculture, while only 2 052 tonnes were taken from rivers and the sea. This trend continues in Norway: 1988 aquaculture production of salmonids was 87 600 tonnes and the projection for 1989 was 110 000 to 120 000 tonnes.

Numerous examples exist of successful integration of wild life conservation and development at various geographic scales. In Turkey, where planned resort development on the Aegean coast threatened one of the few remaining nesting beaches of the endangered loggerhead sea turtle, a compromise was worked out which protected the nesting beaches by reducing the scale of tourist facilities at this location and instituting a public education programme. This may actually increase tourism in this area because of people's desire to see the turtles.

THE NORTH AMERICAN WATERFOWL MANAGEMENT PLAN

Waterfowl and Wetlands in Trouble

Over the last ten years, concern has arisen regarding the destruction of wetland habitat and corresponding declines in waterfowl and other wildlife in Canada and the United States. The decline in waterfowl populations is symptomatic of a larger-scale land-use problem which not only affects all wetland species, but also threatens the sustainability of agriculture and outdoor recreation and tourism.

Loss of habitat is the most serious threat facing North America's waterfowl. Hundreds of thousands of hectares of wetlands are destroyed every year by urban and industrial development, and by agricultural practices. In addition to wetlands, remnant tracts of native grasslands - the most important nesting habitat of prairie ducks - are being lost at a fast rate. In the last decade, one-third of the remaining grasslands in the north-central United States have been converted to cropland. In Canada, only about 12 per cent of the original natural prairie grasslands remain. Habitat loss is also a concern in areas used by waterfowl for rest-stops during migration and for wintering.

To reverse the declining numbers of waterfowl populations and their habitats, it became clear that both countries needed to take new and innovative initiatives concerning nesting, staging and wintering habitats throughout North America.

Specific Restoration Targets and Objectives

The United States and Canada have joined forces to reverse the decline in wetland habitat and certain populations of ducks and geese. In 1986, the North American Waterfowl Management Plan (NAWMP) was signed by the Canadian Minister of the Environment and the United States Secretary of the Interior. Mexico has since agreed to participate. Provisions have been made for the expenditure of US $1.5 billion over a 15-year period.

The Plan establishes specific objectives for the restoration of waterfowl and wetland habitats. It recognises that conservation of waterfowl and its habitat requires long-term planning and co-ordination of management activities across borders, co-operation and financial contributions from users of the resource and scientific research in support of conservation measures. The specific goal for the year 2000 is to have restored waterfowl populations to the level of the 1970s by securing millions of hectares of key habitat in Canada and the United States. This means achieving and maintaining a breeding population of 62 million ducks capable of producing an autumn flight of 100 million birds.

Implementation Through Partnerships

Partnerships are a key strategy for ensuring implementation of the Plan. Implementation activities are

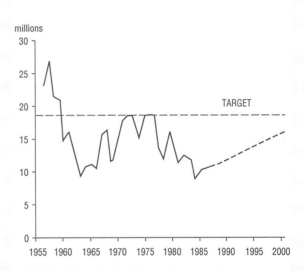

DUCK SPRING POPULATIONS

co-ordinated by a committee made up of 6 United States and 6 Canadian members. Provincial, territorial and state governments are involved in Plan implementation, as are federal departments and major non-governmental organisations such as Ducks Unlimited, Wildlife Habitat Canada, the Nature Conservancy and the National Fish and Wildlife Foundation. Local non-government organisations commit time and labour as well as funds.

Particularly in the prairie states and provinces, the support of the agricultural community is essential to achieving the Plan's objectives. Land management practices which benefit both wild life and agriculture, such as wetland retention, flood reduction and practices which minimize soil erosion, are encouraged.

Economic Benefits Will Be Realised

In addition to the obvious environmental benefits, important economic benefits will be realised from the Plan. For example, the value of economic activities associated with waterfowl in Canada (for example, hunting and birdwatching) is about US $1 billion and some 40,000 jobs a year in goods and services. In addition, new jobs will be created in tourism and recreation, and with most of the projected US $1.5 billion being spent on local, on-the-ground projects, there will be many local economic benefits.

Contribution from Canada and the United States

The province of Quebec, Canada, has developed a system of "zones of controlled exploitation" in which a piece of land is owned by the province (crown land) and the fishing and hunting rights, as well as access rights, on that land are managed by a local group for the benefit of the public. Self-interest dictates that the local group protects the resource. Quebec has 110 salmon rivers: 10 are in such zones, 33 are in crown reserves, managed by the provincial government, 30 are leased by private outfitters on crown land, and 37 have free access.

In the United States, the 1990 Farm Bill continues and strengthens conservation measures begun with the 1985 Farm Bill. Farmers are compensated for taking erodable and other fragile or marginal land out of production and restoring trees or other natural vegetation on it. Compensation is also paid for planting windbreaks and restoring wetlands. "Swampbuster" penalties are included to discourage drainage of wetlands. These measures provide additional wild life habitat at the same time as they reduce soil erosion and protect water quality.

International co-operation

International trade in wild life products, common fishing grounds in the oceans of the world, long-distance movement of air and water and the attendant pollution, the international migrations of many species, and other large-scale phenomena make it imperative to achieve better co-operation among nations in the use of wild life resources. This is not to say that much has not already been accomplished. Between 1933 and 1980, 13 multilateral conventions related to "flora and fauna" were signed and ratified by at least four OECD countries. They cover topics ranging from whaling and fishing to wetlands, polar bears, and migrating species. The CITES Convention (see Section 3) is the principal international measure for controlling wild life trade. Regional agreements are also important, such as the North American Waterfowl Development Plan approved by Canada, the United States and Mexico.

At present, 103 countries, covering 90 per cent of the earth's land surface and including 21 OECD mem-

bers, have signed the CITES. Appendix I of the CITES lists some 2 000 plant and animal species currently considered endangered and which may be traded only for scientific purposes. Appendix II lists more than 45 000 species that could become endangered by trade; commercial trade in these is allowed, but closely monitored.

The CITES is considered one of the most successful international wild life conservation treaties because it is so vigorously administered. However, certain loopholes allow significant amounts of legal trade in endangered species to continue. Member countries are permitted to define what constitutes a "readily recognisable part or derivative" of a listed species and can suit their definitions to their purposes. Exemptions are also allowed for trade in wild life products considered "personal or household effects." And, most importantly, parties can take "reservations" with respect to individual species at the time of signing, and so continue trade in those species.

Co-operative monitoring and enforcement programmes were recently established for driftnet fishing in the North Pacific and have been implemented by Canada, Japan and the United States. Similar programmes were adopted by the United States and certain Asian nations. Concern had been expressed by the US salmon industry and conservation interests over the latitudinal location of the 40-mile-long fine mesh nets and the fact that the nets were bringing in not only squid but also salmon, seals, dolphins and sea birds. The problem is not a parochial one: use of driftnets spread to the Mediterranean and the South Pacific in the late 1980s.

To encourage and assist national programmes for conserving biological diversity, the IUCN, the United Nations Environment Programme, and the World Resources Institute in the United States are seeking to organise the development of a Global Strategy for Conserving Biodiversity. The programme will be committed to three linked pursuits: saving the maximum diversity of life, studying its potential use and its role in the biosphere, and using it in sustainable management systems.

5. CONCLUSIONS

Growing public concern for the environment has helped to achieve progress on wild life issues, but intensification of land use and other types of development have put added pressure on wild life. Conservation of wild life must be made a part of economic planning if biological diversity and healthy ecosystems are to be maintained.

Problems addressed

In the course of the 1970s and 1980s some of the wild life problems of OECD countries have been fully addressed and at least partially solved.

- A number of species have been brought back from the brink of extinction: the ibex, whooping crane, trailing arbutus, and Lord Howe Island wood hen are examples;

- Increasing amounts of land have been set aside as protected habitat for wild life;
- A number of highly toxic chemicals (DDT, PCBs, benzene) are no longer manufactured or are strictly controlled; however, they still remain in the environment, largely because of their chemical persistence;
- Commercial farming of certain species – e.g., American alligator, Norwegian salmonids – has taken pressure off wild populations;
- Instruments for intergovernmental co-operation have been created and results have been achieved: wetlands set aside as a result of the Ramsar convention and trade of endangered species forbidden through the CITES.

Problems remaining

Some remaining problems have been partially solved, others not at all:

- Numerous plants and animals remain endangered and the numbers threatened are even larger. The rates at which they are falling into these categories are increasing: some species have become extinct while awaiting classification, and with resources limited, priorities for protection must be established among species;
- Although habitat continues to be set aside, the loss of habitat – through physical alteration or chemical contamination – remains the principal cause of stress on and ultimate loss of wild life;
- Release of pollutants, conventional and toxic, continues to plague wild life: acid precipitation and toxic compounds from the air damage vegetation and aquatic species; pesticides and other chemicals, through biomagnification, can cause harm to individuals at the top of food chains; land runoff generates excessive algal blooms;
- Illegal trade in endangered species continues to be an issue, with inadequate regulation and even differing philosophical views;
- Increasing intensity of resource harvest practices in oceans and seas, particularly where significant resource wastage is involved and endangered species are affected.

Problems emerging

Some emerging problems are genuinely new; others may have existed for some time, but have now become more intense:

- Transboundary issues concerning migratory species of birds, mammals and fish;
- Atmospheric pollution problems, such as excessive CO_2 and other greenhouse gases with potential for climate change, subsequent rise in sea level and attendant vegetative and animal shifts; excessive CFCs in the upper atmosphere destroying ozone that protects living organisms from ultraviolet radiation;
- Increasing intensity of policy differences over use of wild life resources, such as timber production vs. wild life and recreation in forests.

New opportunities

A number of current activities or circumstances offer new opportunities for dealing with wild life issues in the 1990s:

- Genetic engineering, already producing viruses and bacteria beneficial to pest control, will also help create compounds of commercial value in agriculture, sylviculture and wild life management. Maintaining the diversity of species will be important in this effort as will adequate planning for the impact on ecosystems of altered microbes and other modified plants and animals;
- More frequent use of computers, particularly in helping to perform functions such as gene mapping and genetic manipulation exercises, creating data banks, and improving information systems; and development of research into products that may replace wild life products from threatened and endangered species or reduce demand for them;
- Development of national policies, standards and economic incentives in agriculture and sylviculture to promote less environmentally harmful practices (organic farming, integrated pest management and natural fertilizers) whose products are safer to eat;
- Continuing to develop international co-operation towards sustainable development with the focus on managing whole ecosystems, such as alpine or Antarctic ecosystems, species over their entire ranges, and wild life uses and trade.

Chapter 8

SOLID WASTE

Solid wastes are of growing importance economically, since the number of regulations and restrictions on simply dumping them anywhere is rising all the time. Dischargers of solid wastes thus have to take on responsibility for "controlled" disposal of them, and must frequently call on specialised services, public or private, to deal with that. In the OECD area as a whole the average cost of disposing of hazardous waste is now around US$50/60 per tonne, and in Denmark $120 per tonne. For certain waste such as transformers containing PCBs (polychlorinated biphenyls), the cost of disposal can be as high as $3 000-$4 500 per tonne. The controlled disposal of all hazardous wastes cost $19 billion in the United States in 1988. For the OECD Europe area, the annual cost is estimated at $1.2 billion.

One specific aspect of the economic realities of waste is the residual value it may still have in terms of recovery/recycling. For example, a saving of some 1 500 kWh (1.5 barrels of oil) results when one tonne of steel is produced from scrap instead of ore. For copper, the energy saving is spectacular: 11 800 kWh per tonne or 87 per cent. Paper manufacturers, too, can achieve an energy saving of up to 60 per cent by using old paper. Firms engaged in the reclamation of many types of waste have been in business for a long time now. Sizeable quantities of paper, glass, solvents, acids, ferrous and non-ferrous metals are recovered and recycled. At the beginning of the 1980s it was estimated that in the EEC area some 4 200 firms were engaged in the secondary raw materials trade.

On the social and political fronts, too, the question of waste is seen as increasingly important. In the early 1980s the NIMBY (not in my back yard) syndrome developed apace. In other words, countries are sorely tempted to get rid of their waste by exporting it. The waste disposal problem has to be posed in terms of the acceptability of landfills or waste treatment plant.

New principles of major importance for the future were embodied in the 1989 Basel Convention, namely:

- The sovereign right of countries to prohibit the entry of hazardous and other wastes of foreign origin into their territory or their elimination within that territory;
- The elimination of waste in the country in which it was produced insofar as that is compatible with economically rational and efficient management.

It is not easy to define the concept of waste precisely. "Waste" often conveys a negative economic value but this reality varies in space and time. The criterion of legal abandonment is also used frequently but it is not easy to see it taking concrete form. This chapter is concerned with all "solid wastes", defined as all substances undiluted in water or in the air which a holder wishes to or must dispose of, with the exception of radioactive wastes from nuclear activities which are not dealt with in the chapter.

1. WASTE PRODUCTION

The quantity of wastes produced in OECD countries has grown steadily. In 1990, there were some 9 billion tonnes to be managed. This massive quantity included 420 million tonnes of municipal wastes, and close to 1 500 million tonnes of industrial wastes (including over 300 million tonnes of hazardous wastes). In addition about 7 billion tonnes of other wastes include residues from the production of energy, agricultural waste, mining spoil, demolition debris, dredge spoil and sewage sludge. Although some of these wastes are inert, they also raise a number of difficult management problems. (See Chapters on Agriculture, Energy and Inland Waters) These figures are higher than those for the 1970s and the mid-1980s. (Figure 23)

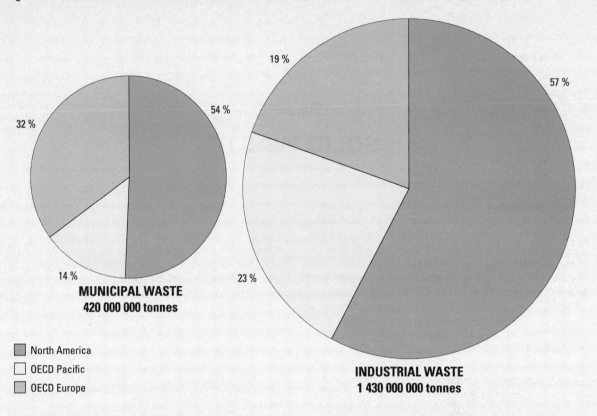

Figure 23. **MUNICIPAL AND INDUSTRIAL WASTE GENERATED, late 1980s**

54 %

32 %

14 %

MUNICIPAL WASTE
420 000 000 tonnes

19 %

57 %

23 %

INDUSTRIAL WASTE
1 430 000 000 tonnes

- North America
- OECD Pacific
- OECD Europe

	Waste Generated, late 1980s (in 1000 tonnes) [a]		
	Municipal Waste	Industrial Waste	Hazardous and Special Waste
Canada	16 400	61 000 [c]	3 300 [c]
USA [a]	208 800	760 000	275 000
Japan	48 300	312 000	. .
France	17 000	50 000	3 000
Germany [b]	20 200	61 400	6 000
Italy	17 300	43 700	3 800
UK	17 700 [d]	50 000	4 500
North America	225 000	821 000	278 000
OECD Pacific	60 000	333 000	. .
OECD Europe	136 000	272 000	24 000
OECD	420 000	1 430 000	303 000
Eastern Europe [e]	. .	520 000	19 000
Rest of the World [e]	. .	180 000	16 000
World [e]	. .	2 100 000	338 000

Notes: a) Inter country comparison should not be made without proper attention to variations in national definitions, in particular with respect to hazardous and special waste (eg. USA' s total includes liquid wastes.)
b) Includes western Germany only.
c) 1980.
d) England and Wales only.
e) Secretariat estimates.

Source: OECD

THE PCB STORAGE SITE FIRE AT SAINT BASILE LE GRAND (CANADA)

PCB Waste Storage Sites: A National Concern

The group of chemicals known as polychlorinated biphenyls, or PCBs, were first synthesized in 1881. Following this, it was discovered that these chemicals were in many ways ideal for a number of industrial uses, especially as cooling and insulating liquids for electrical transformers and capacitors. These properties led to their widespread use in many industrialised countries.

However, almost a century after their development, it was discovered that PCBs put many sectors of the environment at risk. Other properties of these chemicals, such as their persistence, toxicity and capacity to bioaccumulate in the tissues of many species, led, in 1977, to a North American ban on their manufacture and importation, and on most non-electrical uses. Because of the ban, equipment containing PCBs eventually came to be replaced with alternative materials. Over time, as they were removed from commercial and industrial use, materials containing PCBs were stored at numerous sites across Canada.

The PCB Warehouse Fire

In 1979 and 1980 a company called Cie SOTERC Inc. received a license to store PCB wastes in a warehouse at Saint Basile le Grand, located in the province of Quebec. This authorised the company to store a maximum of 90 900 litres of liquid PCB wastes. In 1981 an application by the company to double that capacity to 181 800 litres was refused by the provincial environment department. The PCB-contaminated wastes remained in storage until August of 1988, when the warehouse containing the PCB wastes caught fire. At the time of the fire the warehouse contained approximately 101 800 litres of askarels, stored in 200-litre drums. An undetermined quantity of oils and other contaminated residues was also present at the site, stored in other barrels and in capacitors and transformers.

The health of nearby residents was an immediate concern. Uncontrolled burning of PCBs poses a risk to human health because of the chemical by-products formed when burning occurs at low temperatures. These by-products, such as furans and dioxins, are many times more toxic than the PCBs themselves. For this reason, almost immediately after the fire, about 3 800 residents living in the region were evacuated. The affected communities were those located either close to the fire itself, or within the zone potentially impacted by smoke from the fire. The evacuees lived for 18 days in school gymnasiums, arenas and hotels, returning to their homes only after the results of tests established that it was safe to return.

By quickly evacuating nearby residents, exposure to the smoke plume from the fire was minimised. Tests of the air, soil and water taken in the area following the fire reveal low levels of PCB contamination at the warehouse site itself, and non-detectable levels elsewhere.

Canada

USA

AFFECTED AREA

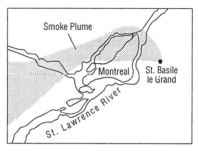

Smoke Plume

Montreal

St. Basile le Grand

St. Lawrence River

Improving the Management of PCB Wastes

In all, 15 different organisations participated in responding to the Saint Basile le Grand emergency. Following this, public concern shifted to the longer-term problem of managing toxic wastes such as PCBs.

The incident at Saint Basile le Grand showed that it was necessary, first of all, to adopt more stringent laws and regulations to manage and control the handling, transportation, storage and destruction of toxic substances and second, to ensure compliance with and enforcement of these laws. Since that time, several concrete steps have been taken while others are being devised to ensure a more permanent resolution of the PCB waste problem:

- A co-ordinated national inventory was carried out to identify PCB waste storage sites across the country;
- Steps were taken under the Canadian Environmental Protection Act to create stringent and legally enforceable requirements regarding PCB waste storage;
- A federal PCB Destruction Program has been established. Under this programme the federal environment department has offered to site mobile PCB destruction facilities in regions of Canada which have sufficient volumes of PCB wastes and which have requested federal assistance.

These measures are expected to improve the management of PCB wastes in Canada and to reduce the risk that a similar environmental incident will occur in the future.

Contribution from Canada

Municipal waste

Municipal waste is one category about which a good deal is known, although methods for estimating its quantities are far from standard. This category generally includes household waste and certain white goods as well as similar wastes from small commercial and industrial firms and the residue from markets and gardens which are collected and processed by or for local authorities. In most countries quantities of municipal waste are steadily rising. (Figure 24) At the end of the 1980s, the average quantity of municipal waste per capita in the OECD countries was 513 kg per annum. That average masks substantial differences between countries: in Italy the average quantity of municipal waste produced per capita was 263 kg, against 864 kg in the United States.

The composition of municipal waste, too, varies widely from one country to another, although some general trends over time can be detected.

Organic waste still accounts for the largest share of municipal waste everywhere. In Europe and the United States, the proportions of glass and metals, though they are tending to fall as recycling efforts are stepped up and as these substances are increasingly replaced by plastics, remain much the same (at between 5 and 10 per cent of all municipal waste). In Japan, there has been a substantial fall in the quantities of glass and metal, which is probably ascribable to strictly selective waste collection. By contrast, there is a marked though variable trend towards a reduction in quantities of paper and board and a clearer trend towards an increase in the proportion of plastics.

Industrial waste

Although in most countries the exact quantities of industrial waste generated are still largely unknown, it is estimated that the OECD area as a whole produced about 1 000 million tonnes annually in the early 1980s, 1 300 million tonnes/year in the mid-1980s, and 1 500 million tonnes in 1990. (Figure 23)

Wastes deemed hazardous are estimated today to total 275 million tonnes per annum in the United States, 24 million tonnes in OECD Europe and 338 million tonnes per annum worldwide. These are, however, rough estimates. More accurate figures ought to be available in future, since several countries now require producers to declare exactly how much waste they generate.

The hazardous and special waste categories comprise a wide variety of substances, but of course roughly 50 per cent of them are chemicals. For OECD Europe, more accurate estimates of the major categories of hazardous wastes exist: solvents comprise 6-7.5 per cent of the total, waste paint 4-5 per cent, waste containing heavy metals 4-10 per cent, acids 30-40 per cent and oily wastes 17-20 per cent.

Specific waste

One particular category of waste produced not only by households and industry but also by educational establishments, the medical world, research laboratories, tradesmen and farmers, deserves special attention. This is the SQHW (small quantities of hazardous waste) category. According to 1986 estimates, SQHW from all OECD-area households amount to some 350 000 tonnes per annum, and 90 per cent of them stem from a mere dozen products: motor oils, batteries, paints, medicines, lacquers, solvents, plant nutrients, products used for maintenance and cleaning, glues, and so on.

The amount of SQHW produced by small businesses may be estimated at between 3 and 20 million tonnes per annum for the United States and between 0.5 and 1 million tonnes for OECD Europe. Some 15 types of business are concerned essentially (dental and photographic laboratories, paint and printing workshops, etc.). Laboratories in schools and other educational establishments, hospitals and research centres also produce significant SQHW.

Where agriculture is concerned, for each sq km of cultivated land, plant protection products account for some 25 kg of SQHW in the form of waste from the products themselves and a further 80 kg in the form of packaging.

2. WASTE DISPOSAL

Disposal of municipal waste

Municipal collection

In the past 20 years, municipal waste collection services have expanded to the point where, in most OECD Member countries, such services are provided for virtually the whole population, although in Finland and Portugal, for instance, these services still collect no more than 75 per cent of waste.

Burial in landfills

Burial in municipal landfill sites continued to be the usual way of disposing of municipal waste throughout the 1970s and 1980s. In the United States about 60

Figure 24. TRENDS IN MUNICIPAL WASTE PER CAPITA

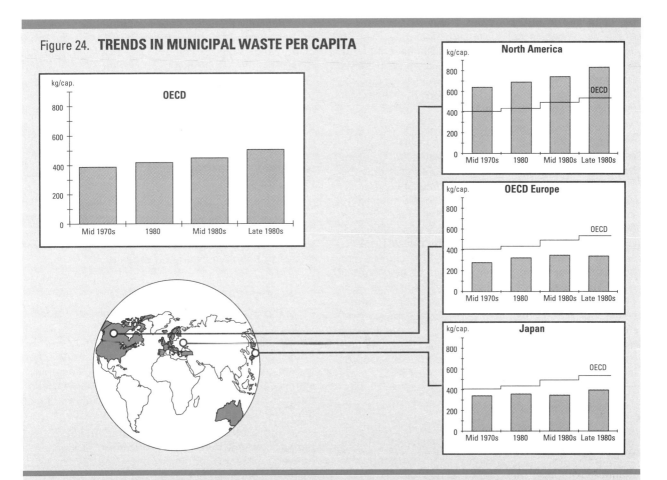

Municipal Waste Generated

	Total (1000 tonnes)				Per Capita (kg/cap.)			
	Mid 1970s	1980	Mid 1980s	Late 1980s	Mid 1970s	1980	Mid 1980s	Late 1980s
North America	151 000	173 000	194 000	225 000	633	687	734	826
Japan	38 000	42 000	42 000	45 000	341	355	344	394
OECD Europe	104 000	110 000	120 000	136 000	277	323	346	336
OECD	302 000	337 000	370 000	420 000	407	436	493	513

Source: OECD

per cent, and in EEC countries about 70 per cent, of municipal waste is still disposed of in this way. In Japan, on the other hand, only about 38 per cent of this waste is sent directly to a landfill site, and in some OECD countries, such as Belgium, France, Italy, Luxembourg, Sweden and Switzerland, more than half of it now goes to some other destination.

Ever stricter technical specifications are now imposed on what are known as "controlled" landfills as regards choice of site, installations, the different parameters involved in running landfill sites and the precautions to be taken on and after closure. Substantial progress has been made in preventing infiltration, for instance by leakproofing and the installation of degasification plants. Nevertheless, burial of municipal waste in landfills faces an uncertain future because existing landfill sites are saturated and citizens are increasingly opposed to the creation of new landfill sites. Municipal waste is also being exported for disposal in a country other than the country of origin. More and more people now consider that only waste that has already undergone some sort of preliminary treatment ought to be buried in landfills. Germany and Switzerland have drafted technical instructions accordingly.

Incineration

Incineration was, after landfill, the next most usual way of disposing of municipal waste in the 1970s and 1980s. Today, in Japan, Sweden and Switzerland over 50 per cent of the waste collected is burned. In some other OECD Member countries (Belgium, Denmark, France, western Germany, Italy, Luxembourg, the Netherlands) the proportion of municipal waste incinerated increased during the 1980s to more than 20 per cent. In 1988 there were 525 incineration plants in EEC countries; 38 per cent of them have a nominal capacity in excess of 6 tonnes per hour, 51 per cent a capacity of between 1 and 6 tonnes/hour and 11 per cent a capacity of below 1 tonne/hour.

In many instances energy is recovered. It is estimated that in the late 1980s, the energy recovered from 17 million tonnes of waste burned in European Member countries amounted to 17 Mboe (million barrels of oil equivalent), and that these countries could recover a potential maximum of 92 Mboe from the burning of household waste. Japan seeks to save as much energy as possible in this way through comprehensive planning. For instance, old people's homes, swimming pools and/or leisure centres could be purpose-built to use energy produced by incineration plants.

Controls on air pollution due to waste incinerators were tightened up considerably in the late 1970s and early 1980s. Incineration plants operating in EEC countries in the mid 1980s were equipped to treat flue gas – in 35 per cent of cases with a mechanical filter, in 36 per cent with an electrofilter and in 7 per cent with both an electrofilter and a gas-scrubbing device.

Recently there has been concern about emissions of polychlorinated dibenzodioxin (PCDD) and polychlorinated dibenzofuran (PCDF). However, the first detailed studies that have been carried out (in western Germany, in particular) show that the ambient concentrations of these substances in emissions from waste incinerators are usually one thousand times smaller than the maximum concentration admissible from the public health standpoint. Control of these emissions depends on the incinerator's operating parameters – combustion temperature, secondary air, anti-pollution filters, and so on.

Incinerators also produce solid wastes (clinker and the substances trapped in filters) which may have a significant effect – especially if these residues have to be treated as hazardous wastes – in the economic analysis of some incineration projects.

Composting and other methods

The role of composting as a method of waste disposal remained fairly modest during the 1970s and 1980s, probably because compost produced from household waste is of fairly low quality and it is hard to find market outlets for it. Composting does play a significant role in the disposal of municipal waste in a number of OECD countries (Austria, Belgium, France, Italy, the Netherlands, Portugal, Spain).

Some other fairly sophisticated methods (systematic sorting, pyrolysis, gasification, production of derived fuels, for example) are also used in some OECD Member countries, but so far not to any great extent. The fall in fossil fuel prices led to a substantial reduction in R & D efforts in this direction. At present Europe has three third-generation pyrolysis/gasification installations and some 30 plants producing fuel from waste products. The EEC has funded 15 or so anaerobic digestion research and pilot projects, and in July 1988 France began to operate an industrial-scale sorting/methanisation plant.

Disposal of industrial wastes

In the early 1970s governments paid little heed to the disposal of waste other than municipal waste, but by the end of the 1980s the situation was quite different. The realisation that old, uncontrolled landfills containing hazardous wastes entailed serious environmental risks and the discovery that illicit international trafficking in hazardous wastes was taking place, coupled with the growing reluctance of the public at large to accept landfills and a fortiori treatment plant for the disposal of hazardous waste, have led to the adoption of more and more stringent regulations on the management of these wastes.

During the first half of the 1980s, above-ground storage and "controlled" burial were far and away the commonest methods of hazardous waste management in Europe, although dumping at sea and recycling also played a certain role (each accounting for some 10-15 per cent of the total amount of wastes concerned). The most recent data available show that landfills still play a predominant role, whereas dumping at sea tends to be less common.

Two trends are clear: in many countries certain methods are being increasingly hedged around by legal restrictions. Some countries (Denmark, Finland, the Netherlands, and the United States) plan to ban landfills as a means of disposing of hazardous waste without some form of pretreatment (e.g. detoxification, insolubilisation, etc.). As for the burning of waste at sea, more and more countries are in favour of a total ban in the 1990s.

There is also an increasing tendency to stipulate exactly what method of treatment must be used for specific waste streams. Austria, western Germany and Switzerland have drawn up indicative lists stipulating, for instance, that all hazardous liquid organic wastes must be incinerated or must receive physico-chemical treatment.

In this context there is likely to be increasing recourse to incineration on land. New incinerators for special waste are planned or indeed are already being built in, for example, Belgium, Denmark, western Germany, Italy, the Netherlands, Spain, Sweden, Switzerland, and the United Kingdom. It seems likely, too, that the use of certain types of waste for extra fuelling in cement ovens will also increase.

3. TRANSFRONTIER MOVEMENTS OF WASTE

A reality that must be kept under control

It was at the beginning of the 1980s that countries became aware that hazardous wastes were being imported and exported. The United States placed such movements under the supervision of a federal agency. In Europe, efforts had to be made to find barrels of dioxin from Soweso.

The first European estimates showed that the following quantities were exported each year: approximately 1 million tonnes of hazardous waste for dumping at sea; 250 000 to 400 000 tonnes for recycling; 700 000 tonnes for disposal in a country other than the country of origin. All in all, more than 2 000 000 tonnes of hazardous wastes (i.e. over 10 per cent of all waste produced) were moving across national frontiers in the OECD-Europe area; this means more than 100 000 frontier crossings a year, of which between 20 000 and 30 000 were probably of extremely hazardous wastes for disposal in a country other than the country of origin. The North American figures available indicate about 200 000 tonnes of hazardous waste exported and 5 000 frontier crossings in 1983, and 9 000 crossings in 1988. (Table 11) There are many reasons for these movements. One may be the need to find a site where the waste can be disposed of safely; but another may be the urge to evade strict standards and consequently higher disposal costs in the country of origin.

The OECD Council consequently decided, on 1st February 1984, "that Member countries shall control the transfrontier movements of hazardous waste and, for this purpose, shall ensure that the competent authorities of the countries concerned are provided with adequate and timely information concerning such movements". Three basic principles were adopted at an OECD conference in Basel in March 1985. These were:

Table 11. **RECORDED EXPORTS OF HAZARDOUS WASTES, late 1980s**

	Amounts of hazardous waste exported	
	Tonnes	Percentage of total
Canada	101 000	3.0
USA	127 000	—
Australia	300	0.1
Denmark	9 000	8.0
Finland	65 000	24.0
France	43 000	1.4
Germany[a]	1 058 000	18.0
Ireland	14 000	70.0
Luxembourg	4 000	100.0
Netherlands	189 000	13.0
Switzerland	108 000	27.0

Note: a/ Includes western Germany only.
Source: OECD

— The principle of non-discrimination, i.e. that OECD Member countries will not apply any less strict controls on transfrontier movements of hazardous wastes involving non-Member countries than they would for movements involving only Member countries;

— The principle of consent, i.e. that they will not allow movements of hazardous wastes to non-Member countries to occur without the consent of the appropriate authorities of the importing country and of any non-Member countries of transit;

– The principle of adequacy of disposal facilities, i.e. that they will not allow such movements to occur unless the hazardous wastes are directed to adequate disposal facilities in the importing country.

These principles have been embodied in EEC law and endorsed by the OECD Council Decision-Recommendation of June 1986 and the Decision of the OECD Council of May 1988. They were included, too, in UNEP's work, which led to 34 countries signing the Basel Convention on the transfrontier movements and the disposal of hazardous waste on 22nd March 1989. Of worldwide scope, the Convention includes both incentive and restrictive measures; the latter include a prohibition on exports to signatory States having informed the secretariat of an import prohibition. The concept of ecologically rational waste management is central to the Convention but the Parties postponed any specific "technical directive" until their first meeting.

West-East and North-South movements

In 1983 large-scale West-East movements of hazardous waste took place. Between 200 000 and 300 000 tonnes of potentially hazardous waste (i.e. probably somewhere between 10 000 and 20 000 loads yearly) were being transported from European market economy countries to East European countries.

More recently it was revealed that attempts had also been made to dispatch hazardous wastes from industrialised to developing countries. Several "shady deals" between American and/or European firms and African governments have been denounced. Indeed, as matters stand at present, it is impossible to justify sending waste from North to South, since in most developing countries neither a waste management policy nor facilities for treating waste exist. Nor have these countries the institutional authorities or the financial resources required.

The risks involved are not negligible: poor waste disposal can be of significant cost to society – 100 to 1 000 times as much as preventive waste management that does not damage the environment. The wastes involved in the kind of traffic described above are the most hazardous ones, those that in the country of origin cost most to get rid of because of their toxic or corrosive nature and because they cannot legally be dumped at sea.

4. OLD LANDFILL SITES

A plethora of "problem sites"

For decades the industrial society continued, heedless of managing the waste it generated. Millions of tonnes of hazardous wastes were tipped or buried without any precautions being taken at all. By the end of the 1970s the problem of managing past mistakes appeared. They take the form of "problem sites" with risks not only for ground waters but also for the health of those who live nearby.

At Love Canal, a small United States locality near Niagara Falls, 20 000 tonnes of abandoned chemical wastes were found. In 1985, 21 512 potentially hazardous landfill sites were inventoried on United States territory, 1 750 of which required urgent remedial action.

At Lekkerkerk, a small village in the Netherlands built on a site polluted mainly by aromatic hydrocarbons, the soil had to be removed and replaced. In 1980 over 4 000 polluted sites were inventoried in the Netherlands, at least 1 000 of which needed to be cleaned up immediately. In Denmark, 3 115 sites possibly containing chemical wastes were identified. At the beginning of the 1970s there were some 50 000 contaminated sites in western Germany; of those about 5 000 required treatment and 10 000 further investigation. In France, a first inventory in 1978 of old hazardous waste disposal sites listed 450 sites, 80 of which required immediate attention. In Belgium in 1982, 8 363 landfills – 148 of them containing chemical and/or infectious wastes – were inventoried in Wallonia (in the south of the country).

The need to step up remedial action

A programme to clean up "problem sites" starts with the adoption of procedures for the pinpointing and description of polluted sites and a preliminary assessment of the risks relating to them. Some OECD countries have already taken steps in this direction, but the global cost of remedial action is extremely high. It is estimated at some $30 billion for western Germany, $6 billion for the Netherlands, and between $20 billion and $100 billion for the United States.

In the United States, the need to clean up old landfill sites has led to the adoption of new regulations on civil liability and the setting up of a fund (the Superfund) to back the campaign against hazardous wastes. The fund is partly financed by taxes levied on producers of certain chemicals and on oil companies.

So far OECD countries in Europe have attempted to raise money to clean up problem sites mainly by prosecuting and fining those presumed to be responsible for the contamination or by calling on the industrial sector to make voluntary contributions. In some countries, however (such as Denmark and the Netherlands), funds have been earmarked in national budgets. The EEC, in the context of the Fourth Community Environment Action Programme, is likely to put forward a series of proposals for measures to remedy soil pollution.

5. RECOVERY, RECYCLING AND PREVENTION

Recyclable waste

By definition, a waste product normally has a negative economic value. Since that value is in principle relative, in time if not in space, a waste product can often be turned (or returned) to profitable account:

- By reuse, i.e. using a recovered product or substance again as it is, for the same purpose as in the first place;
  By using it for a different purpose, i.e. utilising a recovered substance in a production cycle other than the one from which it came;
- By recycling, i.e. putting a recovered substance back into the production cycle it came from.

However, the term "recycling" as used below, in its widest sense, can be taken to mean any waste management operation whose object is to recover energy or secondary raw materials.

Recovery and recycling of municipal waste

Data from OECD countries on the extent to which municipal waste is recovered and recycled are patchy.

For paper/board, the average recovery rate for the OECD area as a whole was approximately 27 per cent in 1975, 30 per cent in 1980 and 34 per cent in the late 1980s. These average figures conceal substantial differences between countries, however. During the period 1980-1989 the recovery rate rose appreciably, particularly in Austria, western Germany and Netherlands (by 7 to 13 per cent).

For glass, the average recovery rate for the OECD area as a whole was 22 per cent in 1980, 29 per cent in 1985 and 32 per cent in the late 1980s. The two extremes among the European countries of the OECD were the Netherlands, with 55 per cent, and Ireland, with only 8 per cent. Today, the target figure of 4 million tonnes of recycled cullet yearly in Europe has almost been reached.

Clearly, selective collection of other wastes (including metals, plastics, batteries, and so on) is also being increasingly adopted in some OECD countries. Sweden, for instance, issued an Order in 1986 setting up a tax scheme with the object of recovering and recycling batteries. Other countries, too (Japan, France, the Netherlands) have been running schemes for the selective collection of miniature batteries for several years now. The fact remains, however, that industrial-scale recycling of these batteries is not easy to develop.

Lastly, mechanical sorting to recover raw wastes has been used since the late 1970s in Austria, Belgium, France, western Germany, Italy, Japan, the Netherlands, Sweden, the United Kingdom, and the United States. Many installations, however, have run into technical difficulties and it has also been hard to market the recovered products. Today the tendency is to concentrate on the sorting of a limited number of household waste items collected separately.

Recovery and recycling of industrial waste

There are no comparable data on the quantity of substances recycled from industrial waste, and virtually no information exists on such trends. It is estimated that in the United States some 2 million tonnes of wastes classified as hazardous were recycled in 1981. In the Netherlands, in addition to the chemical residues recycled on the production site itself, more than 220 000 tonnes of wastes are recycled elsewhere each year including 44 000 tonnes that are exported – 40 000 tonnes of scrap metal, 50 000 tonnes of acids and chemical bases and 130 000 tonnes of organic wastes. As concerns the solvents waste situation in EEC countries, a survey in 1986 showed that 3.13 million tonnes were produced, 474 000 tonnes of which (some 15 per cent) were recycled.

Towards preventing the generation of waste

The best way to manage waste is to prevent its generation, thus avoiding the squandering of resources and raw materials while at the same time reducing public health and environmental risks and helping to offset the inadequacies of treatment, storage and disposal facilities. Preventive action has long been advocated. The idea was at the forefront of international thinking in 1976, as seen in the Recommendation of the OECD Council on a comprehensive waste management policy. But the move from theory to practice has yet to be made when it comes to the prevention of waste formation.

INCINERATOR ASH MANAGEMENT IN JAPAN

Benefits and Costs of Incineration

In Japan waste incineration is an accepted and commonly-used approach to waste management and the proportion of incineration has increased each year. In 1987, of the 44.9 million tonnes of household waste generated, 32.6 million tonnes, almost 73 per cent, was incinerated, creating 5.3 million tonnes of ash residue. Similarly, for industrial wastes such as wood chips, of about 8 million tonnes generated in 1985, 3.3 million tonnes were incinerated, generating some 414 000 tonnes of ash.

The benefits of incineration include a reduction in the volume of waste, hence a lessening of pressure on landfill sites, and, for some wastes, cost efficiency relative to other forms of disposal. Also, in some cases, portions of otherwise useless materials can be reclaimed through incineration. However, one of the problems associated with incineration is the need for safe disposal of its by-product: ash.

Ensuring Proper Ash Disposal

Incinerator ash is frequently contaminated with the residues of the incinerated waste. It may also contain new contaminants formed during the incineration process. When improperly disposed of, these contaminants may leach into and pollute surface and groundwater supplies. Thus, incineration ash must be handled with care. Several techniques are employed in Japan:

- Ash is disposed of in landfills with liners and other features designed to control leaching into soil and water;
- Ash is mixed with cement to minimize the potential for leaching and is pelletised prior to being disposed of in landfill sites;
- Ash from certain wastes, such as sewage sludge, is reclaimed and used to make bricks or other construction material;
- Ash is melted at temperatures of between 1250-1350 degrees Celsius. This technique, which reduces ash volume by two-thirds, also reduces the possibility of leaching, and is becoming more and more widely used in Japan.

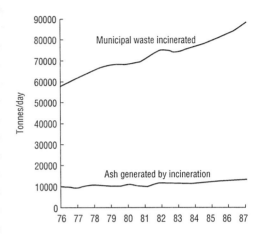

Since 1987, research concerning inorganic hazardous wastes has been aiming for the development of treatment technologies for derived ash or sludge.

The Life Cycle Approach to Waste Management

Incinerator ash management illustrates the importance of adopting a "life cycle" approach to waste management and environmental protection, whereby wastes are managed in every phase of their life cycle. In the case of waste incineration, proper disposal of the ash residue is as important as proper incineration of the original material.

Contribution from Japan

Prevention through the use of "clean" technologies

Minimising waste at the manufacturing stage means introducing improvements or changes in the manufacturing process and moving towards "clean" technologies.

The idea was first officially mooted in the EEC when a Council Decision of 9th April 1979 invited the Commission to launch a research and development programme and a public awareness campaign. A few months later, in November 1979, a Declaration on low- and no-waste technology was adopted by the United Nations Economic Commission for Europe. That led to the publication of an international repertory of non-waste technologies, updated regularly.

In addition to the funding by the EEC of its programme of clean technology pilot projects, governments too have implemented policies offering incentives and financial backing for the development of non-waste technologies. Some countries, for example Denmark, Finland, France, and the Netherlands, now look on these technologies as a means of making businesses more competitive and boosting their exports, while at the same time reducing waste production.

Prevention through the manufacture of "clean" products

Sound preventive policy must, of course, include provision for low- or no-waste products, i.e. seeing to it that the goods marketed contribute as little as possible, during or after their use, to increasing the quantities or noxiousness of wastes as a whole. Product life itself is a variable which may give grounds for government intervention.

For a number of years now, some Scandinavian countries have been encouraging the replacement of potentially hazardous constituents in manufactured products by others that are less harmful. For instance, the use of cadmium or organic solvents in certain paints is now banned. Japan, too, is seeking to reduce the use of mercury and cadmium in batteries.

"Environment-friendly" quality labels have been introduced for certain products in several countries, while others have been awarding an annual "Ecoproduct" prize. The EEC's Fourth Community Environment Action Programme, too, refers to the concept of "clean products", defining them as products which generate no waste when disposed of. The aim is to lay down specific criteria.

6. CONCLUSIONS

Progress

In the past 20 years, *more and more specific policies concerning the management of both municipal and industrial waste have been devised in the OECD countries* and progress has been made with regard to:

- The collection of municipal waste, a service which is now available to virtually the entire population of the OECD countries;
- Disposal and recycling of municipal waste;
- Management of industrial waste, particularly hazardous wastes.

The harmonisation of national policies proved to be a major problem, particularly with a view to avoiding undesirable transfrontier transfers of hazardous wastes. The 1970s brought several important international conventions to regulate the dumping of wastes at sea, and the adoption, at the international level, of a series of fundamental principles applicable first to the management of all categories of wastes, then to specific categories – used oils, polychlorinated biphenyls (PCBs), beverage containers, wastes from the titanium dioxide industry, used paper, toxic and hazardous wastes. Starting in the 1980s, *hazardous and special wastes* and the control of their transfrontier movements were the *main focus of international work in this field.*

Remaining and emerging problems

The amount of waste produced in OECD countries *has consistently increased*, however; by the beginning of the 1990s it had reached more than 10 tonnes per person per year or approximately 420 million tonnes of household waste, 1 500 million tonnes of industrial waste (including over 300 million tonnes of hazardous waste) and 7 billion tonnes of miscellaneous waste (resulting from energy production, agriculture, mining, demolition and dredging, and sewage sludge).

At the beginning of the 1990s, the increase in the quantity of *municipal waste* is far from being under control and preventive policies remain to be perfected. Attention must focus on:

- The installation of certain disposal facilities, particularly landfills and incinerators; this sometimes stirs up controversy concerning the risks involved and is challenged by public opinion, which is becoming more and more sensitive to environmental issues;

- The selective collection of waste and its recycling;
- The avoidance of waste, for instance in packaging.

The adoption of the Basel Convention on the control of transfrontier movements of hazardous wastes marked the culmination of a long trend. But where *industrial wastes* are concerned, a number of unresolved problems remain at the start of the 1990s:

- Pollution of the land as a result of practices in the past (former landfills for solid wastes, former sites of industrial activity);
- The use of the sea in which to dump hazardous wastes or of marine installations in which to incinerate them;
- Liability, insurance and compensation for damage.

In spite of the measures that have been taken, the quantity, the toxicity and/or the complexity of waste have continued to increase, and its processing still places a heavy financial burden on the economy – an average of $50 to 60 per tonne for hazardous waste. It is vital, therefore, that prevention of waste formation or *"reduction of waste produced"* become a major aspect of the concept of sustainable development.

REFERENCES

OECD (1978), *Beverage Containers: Re-use or Recycling,* Paris.

OECD (1979), *Waste Paper Recovery: Economic Aspects and Environmental Impacts,* Paris.

OECD (1980), *Used Tyres in Solid Waste Management,* Paris.

OECD (1981), *Economic Instruments in Solid Waste Management,* Paris.

OECD (1982), *Product Durability and Product Life Extension – Their Contribution to Solid Waste Management,* Paris.

OECD (1983), *Household Waste: Separate Collection and Recycling,* Paris.

OECD (1983), *Hazardous Waste "Problem" Sites – Report of an Expert Seminar,* Paris.

OECD (1985), *The Costs and Benefits of Hazardous Waste Management,* Paris.

OECD (1985), *Identification of Responsibilities in Hazardous Waste Management,* Paris.

OECD (1985), *Transfrontier Movements of Hazardous Wastes: Legal and Institutional Aspects,* Paris.

OECD (1986), *Fate of Small Quantities of Hazardous Waste,* Paris.

OECD (1987), *Control of PCB Wastes,* Paris.

OECD (1990), *Monitoring and Control of Transfrontier Movement of Hazardous Wastes,* Paris.

Chapter 9

NOISE

Noise, no matter what its source – road, rail or air traffic, industry, or neighbourhood activities – remains a key issue in most OECD countries. Its effects on health are now well established. Transport noise is a prime nuisance in towns and in the vicinity of major infrastructures, and many people living in OECD countries feel that it reduces their quality of life and downgrades their surroundings. It is also a major source of stress and can be a cause of the neighbourhood disputes that often arise because of people's differing lifestyles.

Noise also has major economic consequences. Recent studies in western Germany put the social cost of the damage caused by transport noise at nearly 2 per cent of GDP, equivalent to DM 33 billion. Commercial interests are also involved: products, machines and vehicles wishing to penetrate markets cause noise and must comply with national and international regulations on noise levels. Such regulations are also a means of protecting markets. Moreover, expenditure on noise abatement such as investment in infrastructures and acoustic insulation, to mention only the most important, accounts for a substantial share of public and private expenditure today in the environmental area. In the Netherlands, for example, public expenditure on noise abatement exceeded Gld 150 million in 1989 ($70 million), while in France national expenditure on noise abatement amounted to FF 2.3 billion ($360 million) in 1987.

People consider noise to be the main local environmental problem, sometimes even more important than air pollution or the quality of drinking water. Any analysis of the noise environment must take account not only of the physical impact of noise and its physiological effects on the body and on health, but also of its psycho-sociological consequences, including annoyance.

Noise is measured in decibels. In daily life people are generally exposed to noise levels ranging from a minimum of 30-40 decibels to a maximum of 80-90 decibels or even more. Various indices have been developed for assessing the impact of noise and for regulating exposure to it. However, many countries have a marked preference for the Leq in dBA scale ("equivalent sound level" in decibels, A-weighted); this can be used for assessing the impact of noise from most sources and for measuring the related annoyance. For this reason, statistics for noise exposure in this chapter will usually be expressed in Leq in dBA.[1]

The vibrations often associated with noise can also cause annoyance and have physiological effects. However, that problem has not been dealt with in this chapter because it needs to be investigated more closely.

1. THE EFFECTS OF NOISE

This section describes the effects that noise has on people, including the effects on health, communication and behaviour, and psychological annoyance.

Noise can also have a major effect on local wild life. Whether caused by transport or by tourism, noise, together with other types of disturbance such as the severance effects of surface transport infrastructure, disrupts the natural habitat and so reduces the areas in which the various species can live undisturbed. (See Chapter on Wild Life)

Effects on health

The physiological and pathological effects of noise

For a long time it was thought that the body could adjust fairly well to noise, i.e. "get used to" it, but recent observations have shown that this is not the case. For example, Europe-wide research has shown that even after several years of exposure to noise, cardiac response remains high.

Hearing damage is only one of the harmful effects of noise; continuous noise can induce non-auditory physiological and pathogenic effects (such as a rise in blood pressure or an increase in the risk of cardiovascular disorders).

Noise thus comes under the vast category of contributory stress factors in disorders of the cardiovascular and digestive systems. It has been observed that the number of medical prescriptions, psychiatric and psychotherapy sessions, and the level of consumption of tranquilisers and sleeping pills are higher in noisy urban districts than in quieter ones.

Sleep disturbance

Sleep serves to repair the consequences of physical and mental fatigue, and thus helps to maintain the metabolism in good working order and to keep people fit. Research has shown that exposure to noise during sleep both changes the duration of sleep and diminishes its quality by altering the phases (from deep to light sleep) – something the sleeper does not perceive.

Effects on hearing

Of all the effects that noise has on people, deafness can be identified with the greatest certainty. The auditory fatigue caused by noise of a maximum intensity of 75-80 dB raises the hearing threshold (i.e. results in a transitory decrease in auditory acuity). Prolonged exposure to this level of noise, as experienced by certain categories of workers (e.g. road workers, traffic police, drivers and delivery workers), can result in permanent loss of hearing. However, most cases of permanent hearing loss result from working in extremely noisy environments such as forges, bottling factories, textile mills, and so on.

Effects on communication

If conversation, radio, music, television and sound signals of various kinds are unintelligible, an essential part of life is missing. Intelligibility is a prerequisite for the education of children, acoustic comfort in the home and public places, and safety in industry and transport.

Interference with speech occurs at noise levels frequently encountered in the street, in public places, and in areas outside the home such as gardens and balconies. That interference is even greater for a considerable proportion of the population, mainly old people who are hard of hearing due to the effects of age (presbyacusis).

Psychological annoyance and effects on behaviour

The psycho-sociological factors in noise discomfort are complex, being bound up with the perceptive and affective reactions of the people subjected to noise; these reactions in turn determine their behaviour in response to it. For example, at certain levels noise can disrupt home life and prompt people to close windows or to shift activities to rooms that are less exposed to noise, or to decide to sound-proof their homes. Noise also affects the use of outside amenities. For example, it has been observed that less use is made of private gardens for recreation and relaxation, and fewer people visit public gardens, when there is too much noise.

Noise can also fuel personal grievances (such as disputes between neighbours), and sometimes trigger off violent reactions. High noise levels may lead to formal complaints being made to the authorities, sometimes resulting in community action or litigation. However, the number of complaints is not necessarily an accurate guide to the extent of noise pollution, mainly because social and political factors may influence the degree to which the complaints are representative.

Noise abatement objectives

Annoyance is often a general sensation, and the relationship between levels of individual annoyance and noise levels is statistically significant. It is possible to devise noise indices which take into account the degree of annoyance to residents and to establish "threshold values" for defining an acceptable or comfortable environment.

The many studies undertaken in OECD countries on the effects of noise and the behaviour that it induces have shown that, to comply with desirable limits for indoor comfort, the outdoor level of noise should not exceed 65 dBA (day-time Leq). In the case of new residential areas, the outdoor levels should not even exceed 55 dBA (day-time Leq). These levels now frequently serve as the reference for defining noise "black spots" where the levels of exposure to noise exceed 65 or 70 dBA (Leq from 6 a.m. to 10 p.m.), and "grey areas" where the noise level is between 55 and 65 dBA.

LILLE: NOISE ABATEMENT IN PUBLIC BUILDINGS

EXAMPLE OF NOISE ABATEMENT: SWIMMING POOL

Octave Range in Hertz*	Reverberation Time in seconds before treatment	after treatment	Gain in dB
125	2.8	1	4.5
250	3.3	1	5.2
500	4.4	0.9	6.9
1000	4.6	0.9	7.1
2000	4.0	0.85	6.7
4000	3.5	0.8	6.4

* Speech is located in the octaves of 500, 1000 et 2000 Hz.

A Co-ordinated Noise Abatement Policy in Force for many Years

For over twenty years Lille has had a noise abatement policy. This policy aims to reduce noise both at its source and while being transmitted or received. For example, roads in the old part of the town have been re-surfaced and anti-noise screens installed along urban expressways. The oldest public sector housing has also been soundproofed.

In 1983, the town of Lille signed a "pilot town" noise abatement contract with the Ministry of the Environment, setting up an additional local programme jointly financed by the State. A noise "map" of the town was drawn up, and this is now updated at regular intervals. A programme to soundproof public buildings such as schools, day nurseries and health, social and sports facilities (gymnasia, swimming-pools) was also undertaken.

The public facilities and buildings to be soundproofed were selected on the basis of existing conditions, social policy priorities (infant care, etc.), information from users and managers of public buildings (teachers, medical and social personnel) and complaints from users and parents. Noise levels in school canteens were reduced. This example serves to illustrate the noise level to which users of public buildings may be exposed and the inexpensive remedies available to deal with it.

Exposure of Children to Noise in School Canteens

School canteens are often extremely noisy, averaging close to 82-85 dBA, which is high compared to noise levels permitted in the workplace; at 70 dBA, fatigue often starts to appear. Furthermore, the "reverberation time", i.e. the length of time a sound reverberates before fading, was also found to be excessive -- between 2 and 4 seconds -- compared with a recommended duration of 1 second for new school buildings.

Noise of this kind can cause nervous fatigue (headaches, loss of appetite), and result in aggressive or irritable behaviour and psychomotor disturbance. Children find it difficult to talk to each other and may feel isolated, instead of being able to relax, talk and mix with one another, in preparation for afternoon lessons.

Simple but Effective Soundproofing

Soundproofing reduces both the duration of reverberation and the level of sound. In school canteens where it was not possible to use curtains or carpeting because of the difficulty of keeping them clean, sound-absorbing materials were necessary, particularly for ceilings, panels and partitions. Noise was also reduced by partitions between tables and chair legs with rubber tips. These measures are simple and inexpensive.

The soundproofing proved effective. The sound-absorbing materials reduced noise by between 4 and 8 dBA and the duration of reverberation was shortened by between 2 and 3 seconds to 0.6-1.0 second. This meets the standards for new school buildings and gives children a satisfactory acoustic environment.

Contribution from France

2. THE STATE OF THE NOISE ENVIRONMENT SINCE THE EARLY 1970s

Exposure to noise from surface and air transport

It is now estimated that about 130 million people in OECD countries are exposed to unacceptable noise levels, i.e. in excess of 65 dBA (day-time Leq), caused by road, rail and air traffic. Furthermore, 400 million people, i.e. over 50 per cent of the OECD's population, are today exposed to noise levels in excess of 55 dBA, which, though not unacceptable, are considered to be uncomfortable and unsatisfactory.

Over the period 1970 to 1990, the state of the noise environment and the level of exposure to noise stabilized, at best, in the case of black spots, but got worse in the grey areas as far as transport noise is concerned. The major cause of increased noise levels in OECD countries – and which accounts for the scale of the problems with which noise abatement policies have to deal – has been the large growth in transport. The length of motorway networks has increased in North America, OECD Europe and Japan by 61, 146 and 510 per cent respectively, while the number of motor vehicles increased by 68, 110 and 200 per cent. In particular, total road traffic (including all vehicles) increased by 80, 92 and 126 per cent respectively from 1970 to 1988. (See Chapter on Transport)

However, the trend of exposure to noise, as measured by the level of noise at the facade of the dwelling,[2] has varied since the 1970s. During that decade, the situation at every level of exposure worsened, mainly because of the increase in traffic and urban development, and also because the noise abatement policies implemented had only limited success.

Subsequently, from the early to the mid-1980s, there was relatively little overall change, as improvements in noise "black spots" were offset by increase in "grey areas". The effects of slower economic growth, the introduction of more stringent emission standards for vehicles, and the implementation of other noise abatement measures (such as requiring new infrastructures to be designed to certain noise standards, placing noise barriers along the sides of expressways, taking account of the noise factor in planning new districts, and improved sound-proofing of new buildings) took time to make themselves felt, but they compensated to a certain extent, particularly in the mid-1980s, for the increase in traffic. But governments never really came to grips with the problem.

Other relevant factors include urban change – the growth of new suburbs and housing developments in rural areas close to towns – and declining populations in inner city areas, where noise levels are the highest. Nevertheless, while noise abatement measures and the designing of infrastructures aimed at reducing or preventing black spots have helped to eliminate the worst situations, they have not halted the spread of "grey areas".

However, the long-run data give a very imperfect picture of the situation. Moreover, marked variations in the level of exposure to noise can be observed, not only from one OECD country to another (see below), but also within the same country, the same town or even the same district, since noise is a local environmental problem. In addition, the rapid growth in road and air traffic in the last few years has further modified noise exposure trends.

Main sources of traffic noise

Transport is by far the major source of noise to which people in the OECD area are exposed, ahead of other sources such as building or industry. Road traffic is the main offender, but the levels of exposure to road traffic noise vary widely from one country to another; the proportion of the population exposed to more than 65 dBA can vary from 5 per cent in the "quiet" countries (Scandinavia) to 30 per cent in "noisy countries". At the other end of the "noise scale", the proportion of the population that enjoys a satisfactory outdoor noise environment (less than 55 dBA (daytime Leq)) varies similarly, from less than 20 per cent in some countries to over 60 per cent in Scandinavia, for instance.

Aircraft are the next main source of noise to which people are exposed, although the proportion of the population badly affected by aircraft noise is between 3 and 50 times smaller than that affected by the noise of surface transport, depending on the country. The proportion of the population affected by aircraft noise is particularly high in the United States, where about 2 per cent of the population, i.e. 5 million people, is exposed to more than 65 dBa. This proportion is four times higher than in Europe or Japan.

In most countries railway noise affects a smaller proportion of the population, although in some it can rank second to road transport. This is the case in Switzerland and in western Germany, for example, owing to the greater role played by railways in relation to other modes of transport, the density of the rail network and the topographical features of these countries. In Switzerland 6 per cent of the population is exposed to more than 65 dBA, compared with only 0.4 per cent in France.

Other sources of noise and neighbourhood noise

A few figures will give an idea of the relative extent of other sources of noise, such as factories, workshops and building sites. For example, the statistics show that in western Germany an appreciable proportion of the population in heavily-populated areas is exposed to noise from factories in excess of 65 dBA. In most countries, however, policies to reduce noise from these fixed sources have improved the situation considerably over the past 20 years.

ZURICH: MONITORING AIRCRAFT NOISE

RECORDED TAKE-OFF PATHS

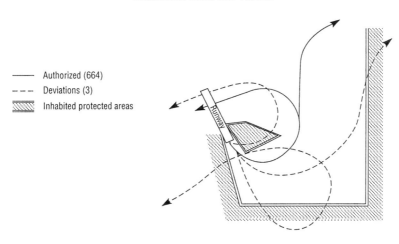

—— Authorized (664)
– – – Deviations (3)
▒▒▒ Inhabited protected areas

A Major Source of Noise

Jet aircraft are major sources of noise, and can be especially irritating for people living near or around airports. Zurich airport is Switzerland's leading international airport and a major European airport. In 1989 it handled more than 210 000 commercial aircraft, carrying 12.2 million passengers and 274 000 tonnes of freight.

The airport is not far from the city and is surrounded by several villages. Therefore planes that do not comply with the assigned take-off paths are a major nuisance.

Monitoring Aircraft Take-Off Compliance

In 1987 airport authorities introduced a radar system to monitor each take-off and a system to measure ground noise levels of aircraft that do not keep to their authorized take-off paths. Every take-off is identified (flight number, type of aircraft, take-off weight) and the noise level at take-off is measured and compared to the authorised level. This flight track and noise monitoring system replaced an earlier noise monitoring installation.

If an aircraft fails to comply with the recommended take-off procedures, a report is sent to the airline concerned, unless there were technical or safety reasons for non-compliance. A list of infringements is published every month and each airline's "performance" is clearly indicated.

As the system is extremely accurate nobody questions it, and most airlines take up infringements with their pilots. The system also monitors landing-approach tracks and associated noise levels.

Take-Off Violations and Noise Nuisance Have Declined

The results of measuring compliance with assigned take-off paths, and co-operation between the airport authorities and the airlines on the basis of the measurements, have been excellent. Since 1987, the proportion of take-offs infringing authorised procedures has remained below 0.4 per cent. This improved compliance has also reduced noise annoyance around the airport.

The success achieved at Zurich airport illustrates how the availability of information on the performance of airlines can lead to their improved compliance with established regulations. This has led to the installation of a similar system at the Geneva airport.

The monitoring system is also used to help establish the "facts" in cases where noise complaints result from flight paths being flown differently from their intended location over ground.

Contribution from Switzerland

Neighbourhood noise includes noise from hi-fi equipment, household appliances, lifts and other equipment in apartment buildings, the sound of dogs barking, and so on. Despite the fact that in many countries the sound-proofing of new dwellings has improved in recent years, along with better thermal insulation, the level of neighbourhood noise is still disturbing because it comes from numerous sources, and they are often increasingly powerful. It is difficult to devise and to implement effective ways of reducing neighbourhood noise, since the problem is often the way people behave and it is this that would have to change. Furthermore, new buildings do not always comply with sound-proofing standards.

Neighbourhood noise is becoming an increasing source of concern, as shown by surveys on the discomfort caused by noise in the home. In 1988 in Japan, about 40 per cent of the total number of noise complaints concerned neighbourhood noise. In 1987 in the Netherlands, 66 per cent of the population said that they were disturbed by neighbourhood noise (compared with 60 per cent disturbed by the noise of road traffic) and 26 per cent said that they were very disturbed (compared with 20 per cent for road traffic noise). The number of people who said that they were disturbed by neighbourhood noise rose by more than 50 per cent from 1977 to 1987.

3. THE NOISE ENVIRONMENT IN THE 1990s

Noise from road transport

Despite the noise abatement measures implemented in many countries, noise from road transport remains a problem. Policies can address it from various angles:

- The source (vehicle testing, introduction of maximum noise emission levels for vehicles);
- Traffic (by means of transport policy, economic incentives, and changing the behaviour of drivers, particularly drivers of two-wheelers);
- Infrastructures (quieter road surfaces, anti-noise barriers, better road layout);
- Land use and buildings exposed to noise (via zoning regulations on use of roadside areas, sound-proofing).

The recent growth in road traffic suggests that the situation is unlikely to improve in the short or medium term, particularly as regards the noise from heavy goods vehicles, despite the introduction of more stringent noise limits and policies restricting traffic. It is well known that heavy goods vehicles account for a good deal of road noise; and since annual growth rates of more than 10 or 15 per cent have been observed in lorry traffic in certain European countries in recent years, such traffic could double in the next five years. The problem is an international one, particularly in Europe because of its network of motorways and the large volume of transit traffic in some countries.

It is to be feared that the effects of the noise emission limits recently introduced in most countries will be partly cancelled out by the growth in traffic if further measures to reduce noise emission levels are not implemented. Limits on the noise levels of vehicles in use could play an important role in this respect.

Noise from rail transport

Prospects for the growth in rail traffic are not the same as for road transport. To a large extent, the noise from rail traffic can be reduced only by installing better protection against noise along track in those urban areas in which the existing level of noise is unacceptable, by shifting from diesel to electric-powered engines, and by lowering noise emission levels, which can be achieved only by improving infrastructures (continuously welded track) and rolling stock. This seems difficult to do in the case of goods trains, particularly in Europe where they operate on an international basis, including Eastern Europe. Furthermore, high-speed trains require the construction of new lines; this creates noise pollution in areas that were formerly little or not at all affected, although today much greater account is taken of noise factors in designing track layout and rolling stock than was the case 10 or 15 years ago.

Noise from air transport

The improvement observed in the 1980s in noise levels around airports was due to the introduction of much more stringent aircraft noise emission levels – the latest and most energy-efficient jets are less noisy – and to the banning of old, noisy aircraft. These noise limits and policies were introduced under the auspices of the International Civil Aviation Organisation (ICAO) in all OECD countries. However, the benefits of more stringent standards are being increasingly eroded by the very steep growth in traffic.

Future levels of aircraft noise will be affected by that growth, by the fact that emission levels are unlikely

REDUCING NOISE FROM MOTOR VEHICLES IN AUSTRALIA

In order to reduce noise from motor vehicles several Australian states have introduced simple tests for measuring noise levels when a vehicle is stationary. These tests can be carried out on automobiles, heavy vehicles and motorcycles, either in the street or in test centres. Vehicles which do not comply with the prescribed noise limits may be subject to legal penalty.

According to surveys, 2 to 3 per cent of all vehicles on the road exceed the limits. Non-compliance for heavy vehicles is estimated at 5 to 8 per cent and for motorcycles at 25 per cent. The main reasons for non-compliance are modified or inappropriately maintained exhaust system components.

Repairs following test failure usually cost in the range of US$11 - $450 for cars, and up to US$55 - $1 350 for heavy vehicles.

Approaches to Controlling Vehicle Noise

Different states apply different approaches to controlling vehicle noise, requiring varying degrees of co-operation between environmental agencies, police and vehicle registration authorities.

In Adelaide, South Australia, police officers encountering vehicles on the road which have safety or noise defects serve the owner a "defect notice" which must be cleared by the vehicle's undergoing a full safety and noise check at a registered inspection station. Vehicles which fail have their registrations cancelled pending satisfactory results. The programme works well, and since noise aspects are built onto a programme set up for safety reasons, the incremental costs for noise control are small.

In New South Wales, noisy vehicles may be stopped and tested at the roadside (where it is safe to do so), and the offenders may be prosecuted. Owners whose vehicles could not be stopped are contacted through their registration numbers and served an inspection notice requiring them to present their vehicle for testing at an approved testing facility. Sufficient time is given owners to effect repairs, so that only a small proportion of vehicles fail. Failed vehicles have their registrations suspended pending satisfactory results.

In the state of Victoria, the Environmental Protection Agency (EPA) has responsibility for vehicle noise enforcement, and has developed its programmes similarly to those of New South Wales. Close co-operation has been developed with the police, who do most of the on-road spotting. Authorised private exhaust specialists conduct tests on vehicles identified as defective, and defect notices can only be cleared by the EPA on presentation of a test certificate. Owners of defective

MAXIMUM NOISE LEVELS ALLOWED IN VEHICLE TESTS

Motor cars

96 dB(A) - manufactured before 1 Jan 1983
90 dB(A) - manufactured after 1 Jan 1983

Motorcycles

100 dB(A) - manufactured before 3 March 1985
94 dB(A) - manufactured after 3 March 1985

Diesel lorries and buses

Limits differ according to gross vehicle mass and year of manufacture

Manufactured after 1 July 1983 the limits range from 95 dB(A) (less than 3 500 kg) up to 99 dB(A) (greater than 12 000 kg).

vehicles may face fines of US$112, and owners who do not clear defect notices may be fined up to US$388.

Effective and Inexpensive Measures

These measures have been very effective. In one state, 1 626 cars which a first on-the-spot noise test had found to be noisy showed an average reduction in noise emissions of 8.7 decibels at the second test, while 236 lorries tested showed a reduction of 9 decibels. The measures were less successful in reducing motorcycle noise. Most of the motorcycles that seemed noisy passed the first test because the noise emission limits for motorcycles dating from before 1984 were too low, and because it is usually the way the motorcyclist drives rather than the machine itself that is responsible for the noise.

The success of these measures in reducing noise from vehicles owes much to the close co-operation between the police and environmental protection agencies. Furthermore, these measures are inexpensive and seem an easy means of implementing international noise limits for new vehicles.

Contribution from Australia

to come down further, and by the fact that it seems difficult in most OECD countries to restrict urban development in the vicinity of airports. Thus, although further operating bans are yet to be placed on the noisiest aircraft in the 1990s, the problems caused by air traffic noise are likely to get worse. However, better traffic management could play an appreciable role in reducing noise levels, as is shown by the experience of some airports.

New sources and sites of noise, and new nuisances

Although traffic is, and is likely to remain, the prime source of noise, changing lifestyles and patterns of consumption are resulting in the emergence of other more limited sources of noise that have a more localised impact and are less easy to pinpoint and control.

The causes include: the expansion of the audiovisual media, leisure activities, tourism, and public entertainment; the growth in recreational "toys" such as trail bikes, snowmobiles, ultra-light aircraft and so on; the use of motorised vehicles and craft in formerly unspoilt country and mountain areas; the growth of air travel, charter flights (particularly at night) and helicopter flights; and the extensive use of high-fi systems and various other acoustic apparatus (personal portable cassette players, speech simulators and so on). As a result, silence is becoming a scarcer commodity. Nonetheless, it should be noted that effective control over some of these sources of noise has been achieved, as is the case with ultra-light aircraft in the United Kingdom and Switzerland.

Paradoxically, although the use of speech simulators for information purposes in a whole range of areas of everyday activity (vehicles, public places) may lead to a proliferation of sound sources, it will at the same time demand a sufficiently quiet environment for the announcements and information to be put across clearly. This can be indispensable for safety purposes, for example when driving.

Population and industrial trends, and multi-exposure to noise

Certain long-term trends in industrial activities, in the types of goods being marketed, and in population have had and will continue to have considerable repercussions on the general development of the noise environment, community exposure and the resulting annoyance or damage.

The decline in the heavy and textile industries and the increased use of robots in the production process are reducing the number of workers exposed to high levels of noise in the workplace, thereby reducing one of the main causes of permanent deafness. Because of the increasing ageing of the population in many OECD countries, a relative increase may be anticipated in certain disabilities and physical disorders that can be directly aggravated by pollution, and particularly by noise pollution.

However, the figures set out above do not give a complete picture of the noise environment. Until now, there has been a tendency to study each type of noise exposure separately and to focus on the Leq at the facade of the dwelling. In practice, each individual is exposed to many sources of noise, either simultaneously (e.g. the noise of cars and aircraft) or successively (in the home, while commuting, at the workplace, etc.). A study carried out in Japan not only showed the size of the "overall dose" of noise but also illustrated how much the degree of exposure to environmental noise varies from one individual to the next: 33 per cent of housewives and 36 per cent of workers were exposed to noise levels in excess of 70 dBA over a period of 24 hours.

Noise exposure at work, outdoors, during commuting, in the home, during recreation, and so on should all be considered when analysing the complex effects of the "overall dose" of noise received by each individual, so that the real level of exposure to noise and its effects are not underestimated. The problem of multi-exposure to noise is likely to become more and more acute in the future.

4. CONCLUSIONS

Noise is a key feature of the environment, from both the social and the economic points of view. By now, the disruption and damage caused by noise – annoyance, disturbed sleep, auditory and non-auditory impairment, stress, impact on inter-personal relations – are fairly well understood. Such damage clearly has an economic cost, even if it is not fully perceived as yet. The economic implications of noise are significant, not only in terms of the direct cost of noise abatement policies but also to the extent that products and

goods marketed internationally are required to comply with national noise regulations.

Today the state of the noise environment can be characterised as follows:

- Altogether about 130 million people in OECD countries are exposed to noise levels in their homes that are considered unacceptable; about 400 million people in the OECD area still do not enjoy a satisfactory acoustic environment in their homes;

- Over the past 20 years, the general noise environment and the level of exposure to noise have gradually worsened, with a spread of the "grey areas" in which the situation is neither unacceptable nor satisfactory; the number of "black spots" with unacceptable noise exposure levels has remained the same despite some progress in the vicinity of major airports;

- Transport is still the main source of noise, ahead of other external sources such as industry or building; road traffic is still by far the main source of traffic noise in the OECD countries. In most countries, noise from aircraft comes second, followed by railway noise and noise from fixed sources;

- However, the situation varies from one OECD country to the next, from fairly "noisy" countries like Japan or southern European countries to fairly "quiet" ones like the Nordic countries. The main sources of transport noise likewise vary from country to country: aircraft noise is high in the United States, and train noise is fairly high in countries like western Germany or Switzerland, compared with the OECD average;

- Outdoor and indoor neighbourhood noise is also a major source of annoyance and, in some countries, of numerous complaints;

- Lastly, noise in the workplace is still the main cause of the most serious auditory damage, although the number of new cases of deafness seems to be declining as a result of changes in industrial activities.

Thus, because of the massive increase in transport vehicles over the past 20 years, noise abatement policies have overall only contained the growth of the damage to the acoustic environment. The main noise abatement policy measures that have had positive effects are:

- The introduction of more stringent noise emission limits for surface and air transport;

- The requirement that noise should be taken into consideration when new transport infrastructures are being designed;

- The introduction of more stringent soundproofing standards for housing and buildings, along with energy-saving measures;

- Limits on noise from fixed sources;

- The introduction of limits on noise from aircraft in some airports, and on road vehicles in countries such as Australia;

- Steps to reduce existing noise, such as the installation of noise barriers or acoustic insulation at the worst black spots.

Nonetheless, remaining problems are:

- The spread of grey areas in cities as a result of the steep growth in traffic in recent years;

- Neighbourhood noise, with an increase in both the number and level of domestic sources of noise because of inadequate policies in this area;

- The fact that aircraft noise has started to increase again as a result of the rapid growth in traffic, and that noise emission limits have stagnated;

- The failure to take effective account of noise pollution in town planning and management;

- The fact that most OECD countries have been slow to bring their standards into line with the most stringent standards of a few countries, and in particular to adopt the noise abatement technology available;

- The general absence of controls over the noise from vehicles in use.

How will the acoustic environment evolve in the 1990s? The answer will depend on whether OECD countries are able to solve these remaining problems and also the following new problems:

- The increase in the number and level of noise sources (vehicles, sources of noise in the home);

- The steep growth of traffic, especially of air and lorry traffic;

- The fact that more areas are being affected by noise, such as rural and unspoilt areas, and for longer periods of time, especially later in the evening, at night, and at the weekend;

- New noise sources, such as the personal portable cassette players and radios, motorised recreational vehicles, and so on;

- Multi-exposure to various noise sources.

NOTES AND REFERENCES

1. The Leq gives the average sound level over a given period.
2. The most commonly used index is the daytime Leq dBA (6 a.m.-10 p.m.), sometimes supplemented by a night-time or evening Leq.

OECD (1978), *Reducing Noise in OECD Countries*, Paris.

OECD (1980), *Noise Abatement Policies*, Paris.

OECD (1986), *Fighting Noise. Strengthening Noise Abatement Policies*, Paris.

OECD (1988), *Transport and the Environment*, Paris.

OECD (to be published), *Noise Abatement Policies for the 1990s*, Paris.

Part II

A CHANGING ECONOMIC CONTEXT

Chapter 10

AGRICULTURE

Agricultural policy and agricultural production should be seen in the light of the general economic climate including international trade and of the economic policies being pursued. Agriculture is bound up with economic development as a result of its greatly increased dependence on suppliers, on the agro-food industry, on world markets for agricultural products and on the capital-intensive structure of farming.

The principal aims of agricultural policy are to achieve food security, through regular and reasonably priced food supplies, possibly to produce export income and to bring satisfactory financial returns for farmers. Agricultural policy in OECD countries stimulates and supports agriculture in various ways: agricultural production is promoted and, where necessary, adjusted through market and pricing policies and international policy. General social and fiscal policies also apply to agriculture. As a result of these policies, radical changes have taken place in the production methods used in OECD countries. Modern agriculture is characterised by economies of scale, mechanisation, intensification and specialisation, all of which are made possible by greater use of inputs external to the farm (e.g. energy, agrochemicals, machinery), based on technological innovations. External inputs represent just over 36 per cent of the value of final agricultural production in OECD countries.

1. AGRICULTURE-ENVIRONMENT RELATIONS

Agriculture is a process of using the soil and altering its vegetational cover, either directly – in arable and cropland agriculture – or indirectly – with grazing animals. The vegetational cover and the ways it is maintained have impacts on the soil itself – modifying its structure and chemical composition – and on the fauna that it supports. Agricultural practices "spill over" on to other land as well since habitats are interlinked and both plants and animals are to varying degrees geographically mobile. Agriculture also involves the introduction of chemicals to the land. Plants may take up some of these chemicals which may then be transmitted through food chains; they may eventually permeate water systems and the air and are lodged in the soil. The environmental impacts of agriculture follow from these basic mechanisms. (Table 12)

Agriculture has had *a long positive association with the environment*. Historically, agriculture has been a major modifier of the natural environment, and ecosystem change is basic to agricultural processes. The drainage of land for farming has undoubtedly been a major cause of the elimination of malaria and probably other diseases in Europe and North America. Drainage and other soil cultivation operations can have diverse beneficial effects on flood control and water purity. Deep soils may moderate flash floods and paddy fields act as reservoirs and sediment settling basins. In older OECD countries, plants and animals have adapted to the agricultural systems to such a point that a substantial number of species are wholly dependent on agriculture. Conservation of the natural environment in these countries is in part a matter of maintaining traditional agricultural practices. In most countries farmers are increasingly providing tourist and recreation facilities, which increase the value of and returns from their land and land maintenance efforts.

Table 12. SELECTED ENVIRONMENTAL EFFECTS OF AGRICULTURE

Agricultural practices	Soil	Ground water	Surface water	Flora	Fauna	Others: air, noise, landscape, agricultural products
Land development: land consolidation programmes	Inadequate management leading to soil degradation	Other water management influencing ground water table		Loss of species		Loss of ecosystem, loss of ecological diversity. Land degradation if activity not suited to site
Irrigation, drainage	Excess salts, waterlogging	Loss of quality (more salts), drinking water supply affected	Soil degradation, siltation, water pollution with soil particles	Drying out of natural elements, affecting river ecosystems		
Tillage	Wind erosion, water erosion					
Mechanisation: large or heavy equipment	Soil compaction, soil erosion					Combustion gases, noise
Fertilizer use:						
Nitrogen		Nitrate leaching affecting water				
Phosphate	Accumulation of heavy metals (Cd)			Effect on soil microflora		
Manure, slurry	Excess: accumulation of phosphates, copper (pig slurry)	Nitrate, phosphate (by use of excess slurry)	Run-off, leaching or direct discharge leading to eutrophication	Eutrophication leads: to excess algae and water-plants	to oxygen depletion affecting fish	Stench, ammonia
Sewage sludge, compost	Accumulation of heavy metals, contaminants					Residues
Applying pesticides	Accumulation of pesticides and degradation products	Leaching of mobile pesticide residues and degradation products		Affects soil microflora; resistance of some weeds	Poisoning; resistance	Evaporation; spray drift, residues
Imput of feed additives, medicines	Possible effects					Residues
Modern buildings (e.g. silos) and intensive livestock farming	See: slurry	See: slurry	See: slurry			Ammonia, offensive odours, noise, residues Infrastructure: Aesthetic impacts

Source: OECD

170

2. CHANGES IN AGRICULTURE: TRENDS AND PROSPECTS

Major changes in agriculture

Two features of agriculture in OECD countries in the 1970s and 1980s are of central significance to any assessment of prospects in the 1990s:

- The trend towards increasing vertical integration of the food sector;
- The growing imbalance between agricultural production and the demand for its output.

Modern agriculture is a sector of production becoming closely linked with input suppliers and with the food processing and manufacturing industries. The consequence of this vertical integration is that the requirements of the post-farm sectors have made their mark throughout the agricultural industry, determining the variety and quality of the commodities produced and the times of harvest and slaughter. About three-quarters of all commodities leaving the farm are subject to some degree of commercial processing before final consumption by households.

The tendency for agricultural production to outstrip demand resulted in increasing surplus stocks of temperate foodstuffs and declining producer prices in real terms during much of the 1980s. In parts of the OECD this has resulted in a re-appraisal of agricultural support policies with the double aim of reducing surplus production and cutting support costs (as in the EEC and the United States) or with reductions in support levels (in Australia and New Zealand).

Since both of these trends can be expected to continue into the 1990s they provide the background for any assessment of the prospects for the environment. Together they mean that agricultural producers could be faced with constraints on output both in terms of quantity and in terms of product specification as determined by the needs of the food processing industry.

Structural changes of environmental significance

The elements of change in agriculture which have significance for the environment may be placed in four groups: the extent of the agricultural area; the product or enterprise composition of agricultural production; the intensity of production; and the degree of specialisation of the basic producing units, i.e. the farms. Changes in these parameters take place under the influence of economic and technological forces reflected in and modified through agricultural policies.

While the *area of land* devoted to agriculture has declined slightly, agricultural production in OECD as a whole has increased over the last decade by 20 to 30 per cent. In Japan, output remained more or less constant, an exception to the general trend in OECD countries. Most recently land set-aside policies have accentuated this decline in the amount of land devoted to agriculture.

The economic and demographic contexts in which agriculture operates are important factors in the rate at which new technology is adopted and disseminated. In almost all OECD countries the promotion of technical progress has been one of the objectives of agricultural policy. Technical progress is in itself not necessarily of great environmental significance. Thus, higher-yielding or more disease-resistant cereal varieties or improved strains of livestock – all of which have been important sources of productivity gains over the recent past – are almost "neutral", environmentally speaking, except for possible effects on the pool of genetic material. In practice, however, technological improvements of this kind have been accompanied by intensification and specialisation. These two primary factors in determining environmental quality have come about through major structural change in the agricultural sector, i.e. a rapid increase in mean farm size so that a declining number of farms now accounts for an increasing proportion of total agricultural area and total output.

The kind of intensive farming practised on modern arable farms, where a limited number of crops is grown continuously with a high cropping frequency (fast crop rotation) and large increases in production, is possible only through the use of fertilizers and pesticides, irrigation or sprinkling and mechanisation, and by improving plant varieties. It has been estimated that in England, for example, plant breeding accounted for about 65 per cent of the increase in wheat yields recorded over the 25 years from 1950 to 1975, while other factors, such as improved use of fertilizers, better harvesting techniques and more effective agrochemicals, accounted for 35 per cent. In the 1970s, however, the yield improvement was mainly attributable to the introduction of superior varieties. Similarly, half of the trebling of maize yields in the United States over the past 45 years is attributed to plant breeding. Comparable developments have taken place in the livestock sector, characterised by intensive farming of pigs, poultry and cattle. This kind of production requires large quantities of feed grain and protein-supplemented feeds. In the EEC over 60 per cent of poultry and pig production is concentrated in about 10 per cent of farms, all of which are highly specialised. The same concentration has occurred in the United States.

As regards cropping patterns, what has mattered most to the environment is probably the shift between arable and permanent cropland, on the one hand, and permanent grassland on the other. Arable and permanent cropland has increased at the expense of permanent grassland in the OECD as a whole. A regression analysis for the separate OECD regions showed that, of annual changes in area of arable and permanent crops 1970-85, 15-20 per cent was at the expense of permanent grassland, while the other 80-85 per cent was

FUR FARMING IN FINLAND

An Important Economic Activity

The breeding of fur animals native to the boreal forest was first developed in Canada. It the 1950s, it was introduced into Scandinavia, where conditions are similar. Today fur farming has become a distinctive feature of Finland, which is the world's second largest exporter of furs in absolute figures. The export value of the Finnish fur industry rose steadily since 1970 and reached its peak in 1987, at 348 000 ECU. Since then the export value has been decreasing and was worth, for mink and fox fur, 158 000 ECU in 1989.

In addition to foxes and American minks, a considerably smaller number of doglike raccoons and polecats are raised. The total number of foxes and doglike raccoons bred on fur farms in 1989-1990 was about 1.9 million, while the number of minks and polecats was about 3.0 million. The animals are fed with Baltic herring, meat offal - mainly chicken waste - and fish offal from Norway.

In 1989-1990 there were about 3500 fur farms in Finland, employing between 5000 and 6000 persons. However, the fur farming industry is presently experiencing the worst crisis in its history. During the last three years the prices of fur have not equaled production costs.

Year	Fur Farm Numbers	Mink(a) Hides (1000)	Fox(b) Hides (1000)
1970/71	2 511	2 841	-
1971/72	2 640	2 613	-
1972/73	2 895	2 691	93
1973/74	2 932	3 023	131
1974/75	3 039	3 190	245
1975/76	2 958	2 987	375
1976/77	2 795	2 803	419
1977/78	2 999	2 960	538
1978/79	3 499	3 424	750
1979/80	4 372	-	1 110
1980/81	5 267	3 855	1 513
1981/82	5 529	3 850	1 705
1982/83	5 588	4 024	2 212
1983/84	5 577	4 137	2 314
1984/85	5 312	4 387	2 164
1985/86	5 573	4 577	2 860
1986/87	5 416	3 717	3 133
1987/88	5 151	3 368	3 175
1988/89	4 852	3 520	2 917
1989/90	3 500	3 000	1 900

a) and polecat
b) and doglike racoon

Environmental Impacts of Fur Farming

The environmental impacts of fur farming comprise the following elements: danger to the indigenous animal populations from escaped animals and from risk of disease; pollution; and odour.

The escape of bred animals into wild populations can have adverse effects; for example the displacement of native species and spread of disease. A noteworthy case of species displacement is the proliferation of mink (*Mustela vison*) having escaped from fur farms, to the detriment of the indigenous mink (*Mustela lutreola*) which, as a result, is no longer found in Finland.

In general, all fur-bearing animals are prone to worm diseases and the large population of farm-bred minks, foxes and other animals make swift contagion a problem, both for reared and wild stock.

Pollution impacts include odour and the disposal of waste. Problems involving slaughter waste can be solved by recycling the carcasses as feedstuffs. Until recently, little attention has been paid to the leaching of residuals in the areas surrounding fur farms. These farms often lie on sloping riverbanks, so that liquid excrement may reach rivers and lakes. In fact, it has been estimated that in 1987, when fur farming was most intensive, water pollution from fur farms equalled 10 per cent of the pollution load from all municipal sewerage in Finland, measured in terms of biochemical oxygen demand. The groundwater near large-scale farms risks contamination by nitrates and phosphates because the accumulated manure is often left in situ until it leaches away.

Managing Impacts from Fur Farming

The great diversity of furs now demanded by the market could never have been produced in the wild. Fur farming is an industry which, if properly managed, can help meet the needs of consumers and export markets while simultaneously alleviating pressure from harvesting of wild stocks. Its environmental sustainability will require a thorough understanding of potential adverse impacts, and more co-ordinated controls over the size and operating conditions of fur farms.

Contribution from Finland

attributable to the reduction in total agricultural area in all regions except North America.

The intensification process can be demonstrated by a number of aggregate indicators which, despite variations in the actual climatic, social and ecological characters of Member countries' agriculture (e.g. humid agriculture in Japan, extensive agriculture in Australia), give an overall view of these trends. (Figure 25) One general summary indicator is *total energy consumption* per unit area. In aggregate the energy intensity of OECD agriculture increased by 39 per cent over the period 1970-88.

A major factor in the growth of energy consumption is *the substitution of machines for manual labour*. The number of machines used per sq km of arable land has continued to rise in Europe and in Japan but has stabilised in North America. The obverse pattern is observable with agricultural employment per sq km, which has declined in Europe and Japan. North America has also experienced a decline in employment per sq km. Thus, over the period 1970-88 each worker was on average replaced by 2 machines in the OECD as a whole, with higher replacement rates in OECD Europe and lower rates in Japan. (Figure 25)

The *use of agricultural chemicals* is a further index of intensity and specialisation; in addition, it is independently relevant to the environment because it shows the quantities of manufactured chemicals released into it. (Figure 25) For the OECD as a whole, consumption of *commercial fertilizers* decreased in the 1980s after steady growth in the 1970s. Consumption continued to rise during most of the 1980s in Europe and Japan. In aggregate there has been a net substitution of nitrogenous fertilizer for phosphate over the last 18 years with, in consequence, a fall in the intensity of phosphate consumption in most countries. Nitrogenous fertilizer application rates grew in all countries over the same 1970-1988 period but stabilised or decreased in most countries in the late 1980s. Phosphate consumption rates are much less variable across the OECD than those of nitrogenous fertilizer use.

Rates of application of *pesticides* vary considerably between OECD countries. The greatest variation in use intensity between countries concerns insecticides but there is a tendency for heavy usage of all types of pesticides. Data on trends in application are sparse, but suggest a fall in application rates during the 1980s except for insecticides.

The final aspect of intensification and specialisation to be examined is *irrigation*. (Figure 26) The proportion of the arable area irrigated in the OECD as a whole reached a maximum in the early 1980s and, while declining since, is still above the level of the 1970s. Continuing growth of the irrigated area has been a feature of OECD Europe.

In summary, the 1970s and part of the 1980s brought agricultural trends that are environmentally deleterious, although they became more moderate in the late 1980s. In North America, while there has been a small extension of the total agricultural area which may have been at the expense of natural habitats, all of the indicators examined show that intensity of production has not increased. In contrast, almost all indicators are adverse for OECD Europe: the loss of permanent grassland, greater intensity of production and increased use of fertilizers. There is some suggestion that the pace of change slowed in the mid-1980s and evidence that the application rate of pesticides is declining, at least in some parts of the OECD. Intensification has proceeded at a faster pace in the EEC than in the rest of Europe and there are fewer indicators in the EEC of a moderation of its growth. On the other hand, there has been in aggregate no loss of permanent grassland in the EEC region.

Prospects

As the statistical facts mentioned above are cast in terms of averages, they perhaps conceal the changing nature of some technologies towards a better integration of environmental concerns. Farm machinery or irrigation system designs, fertilizer application rates and methods, pesticide spectra, composition or dosage changes associated with a better ability to measure environmental stress have tended to shift the damage potential of agrochemical input use, specialisation or intensification in the direction of improvement. To the extent that new technologies embody environmental concerns of society, albeit with a lag, aggregate indicators might underestimate such achievements.

The moderation of the trends towards intensity and specialisation is principally the result of falling real prices and consequent fall in farm incomes; together with increased uncertainty over future prices and markets, they reduce the rate of the return to the producer on his investment in boosting output from his land. Increasingly during the 1980s this factor was reinforced both by policies to contain agricultural production physically and by policies directed at reducing conflicts at the agriculture/environment interface. Indeed, the integration of these two objectives was a feature of the second half of the decade. The set-aside policies of both the United States and the EEC (under the Extensification Directive) attempt to do this either by tying participation in the scheme to conservation practices (USA), or by restricting the alternative uses of set-aside land (EEC). Such policies are most appropriate to conservation of flora and fauna. Further sophistication of these policies may be anticipated during the 1990s. Other types of environmental problems such as chemical pollution require different policy approaches, but the integration of environmental objectives with agricultural objectives in agricultural policy formulation is an important trend that should continue in the coming decade.

Significant structural change within the agricultural sector can be expected in the 1990s. Suggestions as to the most desirable direction for this change

Figure 25. CHANGES IN AGRICULTURAL ENERGY USE, FARM MACHINERY, MANPOWER AND FERTILIZER USE, 1970-1988

ENERGY IN TOE ^{a} PER KM^2 OF ARABLE AND CROP LAND

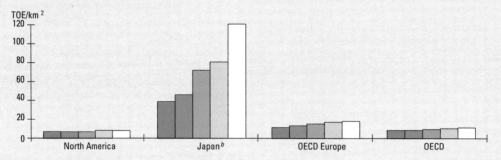

NUMBER OF TRACTORS AND COMBINED HARVESTER-THRESHERS PER KM^2 OF ARABLE AND CROP LAND

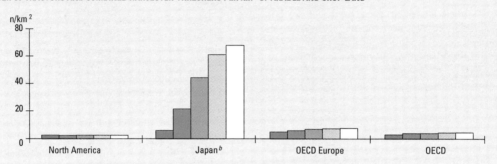

AGRICULTURAL WORKERS PER KM^2 OF ARABLE AND CROP LAND

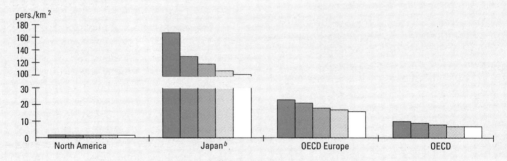

TONNES OF COMMERCIAL FERTILIZERS (NPK)^c USED PER KM^2 OF ARABLE AND CROP LAND

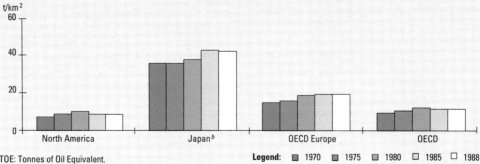

Notes: a) TOE: Tonnes of Oil Equivalent.
　　　 b) Figures are not fully comparable with those of other regions.
　　　 c) NPK: Nitrates, Phosphates, and Potash Fertilizers.

Legend: ▮ 1970　▮ 1975　▮ 1980　☐ 1985　☐ 1988

Source: OECD

Figure 26. **TREND IN IRRIGATED AREAS**

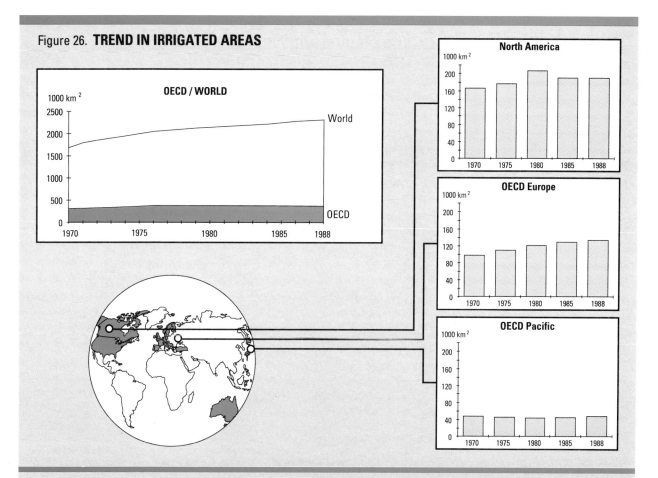

	Agricultural Land				Irrigated Areas			
	1000 km²			% Change	1000 km²			% Change
	1970	1980	1988	1970-88	1970	1980	1988	1970-88
Canada	645	730	785	22	4.2	5.8	8.2	95
USA	4 350	4 282	4 314	-1	159.0	205.8	181.0	14
Japan	58	55	53	-8	34.2	30.6	28.9	-15
France	320	318	313	-2	7.5	10.9	13.7	83
Germany *a*	131	122	119	-9	2.8	3.2	3.3	15
Italy	194	176	171	-12	25.6	28.7	30.8	20
Netherlands	22	20	20	-9	3.8	4.8	5.5	43
Spain	328	312	306	-7	23.8	30.3	33.2	40
UK	189	185	185	-2	0.9	1.4	1.6	76
North America	4 995	5 012	5 099	2	163.2	211.6	189.2	16
OECD Pacific	5 064	4 973	4 916	-3	50.0	47.4	50.1	0
OECD Europe	1 958	1 903	1 858	-5	98.0	122.1	135.3	38
OECD	12 016	11 887	11 872	-1	311.3	381.1	374.7	20
World	45 903	46 649	46 874	2	1 674.0	2 104.4	2 286.7	37

Note: a) Includes western Germany only.

Source: OECD, FAO

PROTECTING ENVIRONMENTALLY SENSITIVE AREAS IN THE UNITED KINGDOM

Farming and the Countryside

It is easy to forget how much of the United Kingdom's countryside, like its cities, has been shaped by man. Its beauty seems natural and enduring, yet many of the features that characterise rural scenery - the hedges and field walls, the ditches and barns - have been created by generations of farmers working to feed the population.

Without agriculture the fields and meadows would eventually revert from grass to scrub and dense woodland. But agriculture itself is constantly changing, in response to changes in consumers' tastes and new scientific techniques. These changes have implications for the appearance of rural areas. A stone wall originally built by farmers to control livestock may have become redundant or simply inadequate to control today's larger breeds. What is to happen to such walls? Land which in the past was suitable only for grazing animals may now, thanks to advances in crop breeding, be capable of growing barley or wheat. What effects will this have on the landscape and on wildlife?

Preserving Unique Rural Areas

In 1987, a new scheme was introduced in the United Kingdom that would help to preserve some of the most beautiful parts of the country from the damage and loss that can come with agricultural change. Although some farming traditions have gone for good, something can be done to help farmers resist the financial pressure to plough up old meadows, to use more chemical sprays or to abandon stone barns and hedges. And advice can be given about managing woodlands, heather moors and ditches in ways that benefit wildlife.

That is what the United Kingdom government is doing in the areas of outstanding landscape, wild life or archaeological interest, under threat from changes in agricultural practices. Nineteen environmentally sensitive areas have thus far been identified in England, Northern Ireland, Scotland and Wales.

With advice from major conservation groups, the farming methods which have made these areas so valuable and that can still be applied in today's world have been identified. Farmers who decide to join the scheme agree to follow those methods.

A wide variety of techniques are employed depending on the region. In Breckland, for example, the pattern of heath, forest, and farmland sustains many rare species of wildlife. To help preserve this region's uniqueness, farmers are

being encouraged to manage the edges of their fields less intensively and, in some cases, to stop cropping them altogether. On river meadows farmers are encouraged to limit their use of agricultural chemicals and to defer haycutting until the flowers have set seed and the birds have nested.

A Co-operative Effort

An important feature of the programme, one crucial to its success, is the co-operation between the farming community, government and the conservation agencies. Farmers joining the scheme agree to do so for a period of at least five years. To offset the costs incurred by farmers who choose to participate, the Ministry of Agriculture pays a sum which recognises the cost of reconciling conservation with commercial farming. This approach underlines that food production and conservation of the countryside can go hand in hand.

Contribution from the United Kingdom

to take vary from country to country and region to region. But in several countries restructuring is increasingly seen as compatible with a desire to improve the environment, promote regional diversification and reduce the dependence of certain rural areas on agriculture.

Opportunities beyond conventional agriculture, which strengthen agriculture's contribution to the environment, are being sought. Farmers are being encouraged, with appropriate incentives, to adopt a greater role in land care and management. Sources of farm incomes are being diversified to include off-farm income and investment. Part-time farming, for example, is being seen, in some countries, as an opportunity to achieve these effects simultaneously: maintain landscape quality, facilitate the further development of tourism, recreation and decentralised industries, and revitalise rural landscapes, rural communities and farming in general.

3. ENVIRONMENTAL IMPACTS OF AGRICULTURAL CHANGES

The development of agricultural production through specialisation and intensification of land use in recent decades has given rise to a wide range of environmental effects, both within the agricultural industry itself and, increasingly, externally to it. The recognition and understanding of these consequences of modern high-technology agriculture developed in the 1970s, and during the 1980s progress was made in addressing these impacts. Some problems still remain, however, and will be of increasing importance during the 1990s.

Effects on soil

These impacts on the soil resource undercut the sustainability of developing agriculture on the land affected. There are several forms:

- *Wind and water erosion* as a result of inappropriate tillage practices. Arable agriculture arrests natural processes of soil formation and exposes the land to erosion. The maximum rate of erosion compatible with maintenance of soil productivity is approximately 10 tonnes per hectare in temperate climate. This rate is exceeded on significant percentages of land in Australia and the United States. Desertification is a severe form of degradation in the arid, semi-arid and sub-humid regions of OECD countries. The countries most susceptible to desertification are Australia, Spain, Turkey and the United States;
- Soil structure can be damaged *from compaction by the use of heavy machinery*;
- Irrigation may cause serious degradation through the *accumulation of excess salts and waterlogging*;
- Chemical fertilizers, manure and other substances, such as sewage sludge, are added to soil to maintain and increase soil productivity. Intensive fertilization aimed at maximising the yield per hectare can give rise to many additional undesirable side-effects. Constituents and impurities in natural and chemical fertilizers, such as phosphates and heavy metals, can accumulate in the soil. Copper, which is added to pig feed to enhance growth and is then found in pig slurry, is another problem. Continuous use of such pig manure as fertilizer will lead to an accumulation of copper in the soil. This makes the cultivation of certain crops difficult and often makes pasture unsuitable for grazing sheep, which are sensitive to copper. The use of other fertilizers can also lead to the accumulation of heavy metals. Cadmium, for example, can accumulate when inorganic phosphates or sewage sludge are applied. In order to prevent this, and to prevent the spread of diseases and intestinal parasites, the use of such substances is subject to restrictions in some countries. In the long term, the accumulation of these elements can lead to lower soil fertility and excessive concentrations of unwanted substances in the crops cultivated;
- To these effects of fertilizers can be added similar effects of pesticides. Pesticide residues can accumulate in the soil, can remain in crops after harvesting and, if ingested by livestock, will appear in livestock products also.

Effects on foodstuffs

The presence of trace elements of pesticides as well as heavy metals in foodstuffs produced on the farm is of increasing concern within OECD countries. This concern has two related targets: identification of the presence of residues through more extensive and sophisticated analysis of products for human consumption; and research into the consequences for human health of these substances, in particular the consequences of long-term exposure to low dosages and the impacts on vulnerable groups such as children. The growth of this problem can be curbed by reductions in the rates at which pesticides and fertilizers are used. But pressure on the food grower to address this issue will increasingly be applied by the consumer through the food processor as a result of the growing

PESTICIDE MONITORING IN THE UNITED STATES

In 1985, the Office of Pesticide Programs (OPP) of the United States Environmental Protection Agency (US-EPA) launched a major new programme to help ascertain the risks and benefits of new and previously-registered pesticides. It developed, for the first time, a comprehensive National Monitoring Plan to gather the essential environmental measurement data to be used in conjunction with the required laboratory animal test data in order to make decisions on pesticide risks and benefits.

Monitoring Within the Context of Pesticide Regulation

The programme includes the collection of exposure-related information, such as chemical use pattern and usage information, the documentation of pesticide-induced illnesses and contamination episodes, the determination of chemical concentrations in humans and the environment, and the collection of information on user and industry compliance with provisions of the Federal Insecticide, Fungicide, and Rodenticide Act.

Within the overall goal of assisting the US-EPA in making its risk/benefit decisions, the pesticide monitoring programme provides data which serve four major objectives in pesticide regulation: 1) assess the risks posed by existing chemicals for specific registration decisions; 2) similarly, assess the risks posed by either proposed new chemicals or new uses of existing chemicals; 3) measure compliance with registration and related regulatory controls; and 4) determine the trends of pesticides in the environment to confirm expected outcomes of regulation and to alert the US-EPA to unanticipated or emerging exposure problems.

A Shared Responsibility for Data Collection

The US-EPA has the leadership role in procuring information on pesticide exposure and effects. However, the responsibility for generating monitoring information on pesticides is shared with other US Federal agencies, states, pesticide registrants, pesticide users, and other parties interested in the consequences of pesticide use.

It is first decided if information needs for a regulatory decision require monitoring data or whether these needs can be fulfilled adequately by less expensive surrogate data or through predictive modeling. The choice depends on the confidence in the available predictive tools and the significance of the decision to be made.

Monitoring and the Re-registration of Existing Chemicals

A first major objective of the programme is to help evaluate the decisions made on previously registered pesticides. This requires the review of the databases for all chemicals registered prior to 1977 when modern data requirements were imposed. The outcome of the review is a "registration standard," a decision document which explains the regulatory position on the use of a given

PESTICIDE MONITORING GOALS AND OBJECTIVES

Goal : Provide Information On Exposure And Effects To Assist In Determining Risks And Benefits From Pesticide Use

OBJECTIVES :

1. Suport Regulatory Decision- Making For Existing Chemicals	2. Support Regulatory Decision-Making For New Chemicals/ Uses

3. Measure Compliance With Regulatory Decisions

4. Determine Trends Of Pesticides In The Environment For Overall Program Evaluation And Exposure Problem Alerts

active ingredient in pesticides and summarises the information available about that chemical.

In some cases, the review of old data or the review of newly generated data will indicate that the pesticide may be causing unreasonable adverse effects on humans or the environment. In these cases, the "special review" decision process is initiated. This is an intensive review of the pesticide's risks and benefits. The US EPA further proposes a regulatory position, and issues a final position which either authorises current uses, restricts some or all uses, or cancels some or all uses.

Monitoring and the Re-registration of New Chemicals and Uses

A second major objective of the pesticide monitoring programme is to support decision-making on registration of new chemicals, and in particular to investigate a number of ways to reduce uncertainty in the new chemicals/new uses programme by establishing requirements early in the registration process.

There are three phases where monitoring data may reduce uncertainties in the risk assessment for full registration: 1) the research and development phase (laboratory or small-scale field testing); 2) the experimental-use permit phase involving large-scale field testing; and 3) the conditional registration or full registration phase.

Contribution from the United States

vertical integration of the food industry. The solutions lie along various lines: reduced use of chemical inputs in agricultural production, development of disease-resistant crop strains and varieties that utilise nitrogen and phosphorous more efficiently, and development of environmentally preferred means of pest control, such as biological means. But the production and marketing of foodstuffs free from chemical residues will remain a major issue of the 1990s.

Other effects of pesticides

The use of pesticides creates another range of environmental effects internal to the agricultural system from the synergy between pests and the mechanisms to control them. Pesticides are an important aid in modern agriculture, particularly in forms of cultivation where the financial value of the crop per hectare is high, such as horticulture, intensive arable farming and fruit growing. In 1980 nearly 80 per cent (in value terms) of all agrochemicals applied were used in seven crop sectors – fruit and vegetables, maize, cotton, rice, soy beans, wheat and sugar beet. Several pests have developed a resistance to certain pesticides. The FAO documents a growing resistance of insects and mites: 182 resistant species in 1965, 288 in 1968, 364 in 1977 and 428 in 1980. Many countries report the resistance of weeds to herbicides. Non-specific pesticides can eliminate benign species – e.g., pollinating insects – and natural predators of pest species, thereby increasing pest problems.

The trend within the pesticide industry is towards the development of pesticides which are finely focused on the specific pests that they are to control and towards utilising natural predators in crop protection. While this should serve to reduce the risk of unintended environmental effects, these risks can never be wholly eliminated. Nor can the problem of pest resistance. Pest control is a continuous battle between the controller and the controlled. The problem is aggravated by the modern practice of large scale continuous cropping of individual crops. Mono-cultures encourage the growth of pest species by providing ideal conditions for their development. In addition, continuous cropping can degrade the soil, necessitating larger quantities of fertilizer to offset these effects. Where production involves concentration on one strain or on a limited range of high-yielding strains, there is another category of environmental risk – that of extensive, even disastrous crop loss from disease or pests whose spread is encouraged by scale and genetic uniformity. There is also the risk that lower-yielding varieties with characteristics that protect against such threats will be eliminated from the available gene pool by the spread of high-yielding strains.

Effects on water systems

A major medium through which agriculture transmits effects to the external environment is *the water system*. Agricultural drainage limits the recharge of the water table in the areas affected and increases the rate at which surface water is removed from the agricultural land. Increased run-off rates may overstrain the capacity of the arterial system to shift water at times of heavy rainfall or snow melt, and thus lead to flooding in urban areas or on other agricultural land. Furthermore, water-borne sediment from eroding agricultural soils can block water courses and silt up reservoirs, reducing storage capacity for water supply and hydro-electric generation. Where drainage systems cut into soil substrata, excessive minerals and salts may be released into the water system. While these direct effects are cause for serious concern in a number of developing countries, they are probably not of as great significance within the OECD, where hydrological principles are well understood and the mechanisms for control and correction generally well established. In Japan, rice paddy agriculture, which covers 54 per cent of agricultural land, even contributes to maintaining water resources, counteracting floods and preventing soil outflow.

Of far greater significance is the leaching of excess agricultural chemicals into the water system. (Figure 27) Agriculture is a major source of *nitrate pollution of water systems*. This arises in several ways:

- The ploughing up of permanent grassland releases large quantities of nitrates into the environment. This was a major source of nitrate pollution in Europe in the 1950s and 1960s but since then, with the stabilisation of the arable area, it has ceased to be one;

- The intensive use of nitrogen fertilizers, over and above recommended rates, can cause large quantities of nitrates to leach into ground water. The amount of leaching will depend on a number of factors, such as the quantity of fertilizer applied and the type used, the soil type, the type of crop and the time of year at which the fertilizer was applied. Little nitrate leaching comes directly from fertilizer applied at recommended levels and under recommended conditions. Leaching from uncultivated land, on the other hand, generally amounts to less than 3 kg of nitrate per hectare;

- Intensive livestock production units result in large concentrations of animal manure. This can be released to the water system through leaching, flooding and breakdown of storage facilities or, where manure is spread on the land, through leaching and run-off.

Nitrate pollution of ground water is causing serious concern about *drinking-water supplies*. Excessive nitrate intake from water and food can give rise to potential health risks: it is suspected of being a factor in the development of *methaemoglobinaemia* in infants and of stomach cancer. The World Health Organisation recommends a maximum limit of 45 mg

Figure 27. APPLICATION OF NITROGENOUS FERTILIZERS ON ARABLE LAND, 1970-1988

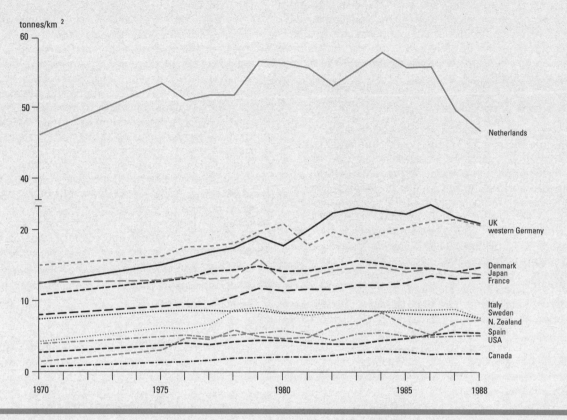

| | Index 1970 = 100 | | | | | tonnes/ km² |
	1970	1975	1980	1985	1988	1988
Canada	100	184	301	403	371	2.6
USA	100	128	147	129	132	5.1
Japan	100	102	101	112	109	13.7
France	100	114	142	156	166	13.3
Germany *a*	100	109	139	136	138	20.6
Italy	100	145	198	209	182	7.6
Netherlands	100	116	122	121	101	46.7
Spain	100	134	161	171	201	5.5
Sweden	100	115	111	111	103	7.6
UK	100	121	143	179	169	20.9
North America	100	130	152	138	140	4.6
OECD Pacific	100	98	99	112	114	2.1
OECD Europe	100	124	153	169	172	9.9
OECD	100	125	148	149	150	5.8
World	100	136	185	212	242	5.4

Note: a) Includes western Germany only.

Source: OECD, FAO, IFA

OVER-FERTILIZATION AND EUTROPHICATION IN THE NETHERLANDS

AGREED REDUCTIONS OF PHOSPHORUS EMISSIONS

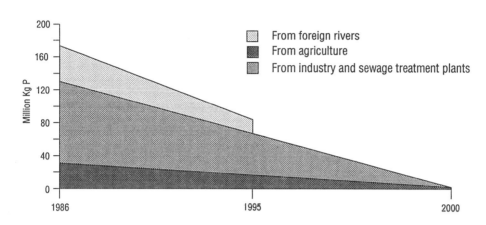

From foreign rivers
From agriculture
From industry and sewage treatment plants

The Over-Fertilization Problem

For a long time the eutrophication of water has been recognised as an environmental problem in the Netherlands. Starting in the 1970s it became increasingly evident that surface waters, groundwaters and soils were being threatened by the increasing use of phosphorus and nitrogen compounds in fertilizers.

Mass-balance studies carried out in the Netherlands show that approximately one-quarter of the 500 000 to 600 000 tonnes of phosphates used in or transported to the Netherlands each year accumulate in the environment, a process which has been going on for twenty years. The accumulation rate for nitrogen, whose inputs range between 4 and 5 million tonnes per year, is 10 per cent.

As a result of this accumulation of nutrients, the Netherlands must cope with adverse environmental effects for years to come. This would be true even if the balance between the supply and removal of phosphorus and nitrogen were to be restored immediately.

The Policy: Reducing Nutrient Inputs

To address the problem of nutrient over-supply, and to restore the nutrient input-output balance, the Netherlands is aiming for a reduction in nutrient discharges of 70 to 90 per cent of 1985 levels by the year 2000. This will be achieved through an integrated approach which includes agricultural measures, more effective sewage treatment plants as well as more effective treatment of industrial wastewater, dredging, more control over the use of phosphates in cleansing agents and detergents, and so forth. All of these measures will be implemented according to the Dutch National Environmental Policy Plan.

Since agricultural practices account for roughly three-quarters of both nitrogen and phosphorus accumulation, the agricultural sector is being given the most attention. As nitrates pose a threat to the quality of groundwater, the policy aims at, among other things, a phased reduction in discharges from nutrients in manure leading to an input-output balance by the year 2000. Legislation is being prepared with regard to the application of other organic fertilizers such as sewage sludge and compost. Chemical fertilizer use is also being studied to determine whether legislation could be introduced to regulate the total amount of nitrogen and phosphorus per hectare in the soil. The content of nitrogen and phosphorus in municipal and industrial wastes will also be reduced.

The policy to combat fertilizer discharge has as its goal the restoration of the balance of phosphorous and nitrogen between supply to the soil and absorption by crops in order to secure the functions of water and soil. It is a major component of the overall Dutch environmental policy aiming at sustainable development.

Financing Over-Fertilization Control Measures

The "Polluter Pays Principle" is the starting point for the financing of these measures. In 1989 approximately ECU 130 million was spent in combatting over-fertilization. This amount will increase to approximately ECU 390 million in 1994, and to ECU 560 million in the year 2000. The cost of the fertilizer discharge policy for consumers will be ECU 10.8 per household in 1994 and ECU 26 in the year 2000.

Contribution from the Netherlands

of nitrate per litre of drinking water; the European Communities' Directive on the Quality of Water for Human Consumption (effective from 1985) gives 50 mg of nitrate per litre as the maximum admissible concentration. Rising concentrations of nitrates in deep ground water have been reported in parts of France, western Germany, the Netherlands and the United Kingdom. This means that for a very long time the aquifers affected will be less acceptable as a source of drinking water. High dosages of nitrogen can lead to higher concentration of nitrogen in certain crops cultivated, which is as undesirable as high nitrate levels in drinking water.

The problem of nitrate pollution of water sources is growing worse in many parts of the OECD and remains one of the most challenging environmenal problems of agriculture in the 1990s.

In general, phosphates are almost entirely absorbed into the topsoil, and in places where there is intensive fertilization and a low absorptive capacity they may start to leach into the ground water and surface water after a few decades. This occurs, for example, in areas where there are a large number of intensive livestock farms; they produce considerable quantities of manure and spread it over a limited area of land.

As a result of fertilization, surface water becomes rich in nutrients that come from ground water (nitrates) or surface run-off (phosphates and nitrates). Such pollution can lead to eutrophication, the excessive growth of algae and water plants, which in turn results in deterioration of the water quality in both lakes and coastal waters. In rural areas in a number of European countries, 70 to 85 per cent of the nitrogen loading and more than 30 per cent of the phosphorus loading of the surface water is of agricultural origin. In more urban areas the corresponding figures are roughly 50 per cent for nitrogen and 5 per cent for phosphorus. Similar problems of pollution and eutrophication can arise from the leakage of slurry from intensive meat-production systems.

Effects on flora and fauna

Agriculture can have a variety of effects on flora and fauna. Programmes of land reclamation and development can directly destroy natural and semi-natural *habitats* with their attendant wild life. In countries with a long agricultural history, such as European countries and Japan, there exist plants and animal communities that are dependent for survival on the continuation of specific agricultural practices; this means that changed cropping patterns within agricultural areas can also destroy flora and fauna. Of particular importance here are the replacement of permanent pasture by arable land and the drainage of pasture land and use of artificial fertilizers on it to raise its productivity. A number of species of palearctic wading birds, for example, are dependent for breeding on the existence of wet pasture; fertilizer use on old pasture can rapidly reduce the diversity of flowering plants. Within Europe, intensive arable production entailing the removal of hedgerows and uncultivated field margins also reduces biological diversity. These problems of habitat loss are to a considerable degree mitigated by reduced pressures for agricultural expansion. In the countries most affected, they are also directly addressed by policies of habitat conservation. One related problem which remains to be solved concerns the drying out of wetlands as a result of agricultural irrigation. Several important European wetlands are at risk in this way.

Pesticide application may also have undesirable effects on flora and fauna. From an environmental viewpoint pesticides may be classified as follows:

- Insecticides, acaricides and nematocides: i) organochlorides are toxic for fish (endosulfan) and birds (dieldrin, DDT), less toxic for mammals. Some are very persistent: DDT and dieldrin produce effects for more than 10 years; they accumulate in food chains and are insoluble in water. A number of these insecticides were banned or restricted to a limited range of applications in the 1970s. ii) Organophosphates and carbamates are moderately persistent; some of them are toxic and/or mobile. These insecticides have replaced the organochlorides. They do not accumulate in man or the environment to any marked degree; however, their improper use and disposal have generated serious problems;
- Fungicides: some are toxic for fish. They are moderately persistent. Mercurial fungicides are toxic and persistent and accumulate in food chains;
- Herbicides: less toxic and moderately persistent.

The extent of the environmental effects of pesticides is governed by:

- The properties of the pesticide (toxicity, biodegradability and potential for bio-accumulation). The information available on some widely used pesticides and their degradation products is not sufficient to permit an adequate assessment of the risk they pose to the environment;
- The quantity used. Unnecessary usage may occur for several reasons;
- The method and frequency of application and the weather conditions during and after application. For instance, 70 per cent of a spray aimed at foliage can be lost in droplets falling to the soil;
- The area to which it is applied.

The way in which a pesticide degrades after application is of crucial significance for its potential effects on the environment. Degradation may be a physiochemical process but in most cases is due to microbiological activity. The mobility of a pesticide or its metabolites in the soil, which determines how readily they can reach ground water or surface water, depends on their physio-chemical characteristics. If a pesticide is degraded reasonably quickly and if both it and its degradation products are sufficiently absorbed by the soil, then, except in the case of accidents or run-off, ground water and surface water will be safe from pollution. Many OECD countries have a licensing system which incorporates an assessment of the environmental effects of pesticides. The application of organochloride and organometal pesticides is restricted. The new pesticides are generally rendered environmentally inactive relatively quickly by degradation processes.

Effects on amenity and life quality

The effects of agriculture on amenity and life quality are similarly diverse. Local effects of intensive livestock production are experienced chiefly in the form of unpleasant smells both from the quantity of manure and slurry and from the concentration of livestock. Ammonia released from stored manure may contribute to the acidification of the environment and affect plant life in the vicinity.

Another local effect concerns *visual amenity*. Cases here concern damage to high-quality rural landscapes by the erection of modern agricultural buildings, e.g., grain silos and barns not in traditional materials, the loss of landscape diversity from mono-cultures, the elimination of features such as hedgerows and the disappearance of ancient permanent grassland. This type of problem mainly occurs in OECD Europe. Of more widespread concern are changes in settlement patterns induced by structural change. While this issue obviously has broader significance, it has an environmental dimension as well, and may be a matter of future concern in those parts of the OECD, such as EEC Europe, where land goes out of agricultural production.

4. IMPACT OF POLLUTION FROM OTHER SOURCES ON AGRICULTURE

While many of the mechanisms of environmental degradation associated with agriculture have only come to be more clearly understood in the past two decades, the state of knowledge about some of the major environmental influences on agriculture is even less advanced. Indeed, many of the phenomena now considered to pose significant long-term threats to agricultural production are only now coming under intense study.

In several countries, pollution from sources other than agriculture has led to regional declines in the quality of food production and, in other cases, the quantity of food produced. Examples include damage to the quality of table grapes caused by acid rain in some parts of western Germany, declines in milk production which in some parts of the Netherlands are believed to have been caused by fluoride emissions from secondary industry, and loss of output following the Chernobyl accident. A growing body of literature describes the impact on agriculture of pollution from these other sources. Most of it, however, is based on extrapolation from the conclusions drawn from laboratory experiments about the implications for regional and national crop estimates of acid precipitation, etc., on crop production. For example, a study in the United States estimated short-term crop yield losses due to ambient ozone concentrations at between $1.9 and $4.3 billion each year. Similarly, Japanese laboratory work suggested that, in some areas, acid rain and other forms of air pollution may be reducing wheat and rice crop production by as much as 30 per cent. However, the nature, intensity, and extent of the effects of acid deposition, photochemical oxidants and sewage sludge on agriculture remain largely unknown. Direct adverse effects on field-grown crops may be limited to a few sensitive species and to areas which experience severe local effects.

Among threats which have been perceived only relatively recently are:

- Increasing concentrations of CO_2 which, in addition to being a factor in the "greenhouse effect" of atmospheric heating, may also directly affect plant metabolism;
- Potential global climate changes caused by greenhouse gases (only part of which come from agriculture), which could have far-reaching effects on growing seasons and precipitation.

5. CONCLUSIONS

In the course of the past 20 years, the agricultural activities of OECD countries have experienced imbalances between production and demand. The result has been growth in surpluses of temperate foodstuffs and decline in producer prices in real terms. In most OECD countries this has led to a reappraisal of agricultural support policies in the latter part of the 1980s. The accompanying structural changes have had far-reaching implications for the environment: increasing vertical integration of the food sector, a slight and then a more marked decline of the amount of land area devoted to food production, increasing intensity and specialisation of food production, emergence of a more environmentally friendly agriculture, and internationalisation of food markets.

Although agriculture has had a long positive association with the environment over this century, the past two decades have mainly witnessed increasing environmental impacts from agriculture which became somewhat more moderate only in the late 1980s:

– The widespread contamination of ground and surface waters and the eutrophication of surface and coastal waters by excess nitrates and phosphates from fertilizers and pesticides;

– The degradation of soil resources in some countries and regions by erosion, salinisation, compaction and pollution;
– Concern with the human health effects of pesticides and fertilizer residues, heavy metals, feed supplements and other contaminants of food products, drinking water and the food chain;
– Pollution problems, including soil, water and air pollution, associated with the growth of intensive animal husbandry and manure spreading;
– The diminution and partition of biotopes valued for nature conservation and wild life habitat;
– Losses in landscape amenity.

In the 1990s, growing world population pressures and rising demand from developing countries for foodstuffs will increase the pressure on agricultural land resources within developing countries and the OECD, which is likely to remain a major exporter of agricultural products:

– OECD countries will have to face the consequences of fertilizer and pesticide residues in

Table 13. AGRICULTURE AND THE ENVIRONMENT: SELECTED INDICATORS

		Canada	USA	France	western Germany	Italy	UK	Japan	North America	OECD Europe	OECD	World
Agricultural land area	1 000 km²	785	4 314	313	119	171	185	53	5 099	1 858	11 872	46 874
of which:												
Arable and crop land	%	59	44	62	63	71	38	88	46	62	34	31
Permanent grassland	%	41	56	38	37	29	62	12	54	38	66	69
Manpower	1 000 pers.	556	3 326	1 437	1 085	2 058	581	4 740	3 882	18 814	28 023	1 082 920
	% change	– 8	– 7	– 48	– 52	– 47	– 26	– 47	– 7	– 29	– 30	23
Farm machinery	1 000	913	5 310	1 670	1 600	1 408	573	3 228	6 223	8 824	18 746	29 872
	% change	20	– 1	22	4	122	12	819	2	47	45	65
Energy consumption	MTOE	3	17	3	2	3	1	6	20	22	49	..
	% change	..	–	25	7	65	– 22	167	17	54	41	..
Nitrogenous fertilizer use on arable and crop land	Tonnes/km²	3	5	13	21	8	21	14	5	10	6	5
	% change	271	32	66	38	82	69	9	40	72	50	142
Pesticide use on arable and crop land	Tonnes/km²	0.09	0.18	0.44	0.42	..	0.58 [a]	1.77	0.16	0.45	0.26	..
Irrigated area	1 000 km²	8	181	14	3	31	2	29	189	135	375	2 287
	% change	95	14	83	15	20	76	– 15	16	38	20	37

Notes: "% change" data refer to the period 1970-1988; all other data refer to 1988 or the latest available year.
   a) Great Britain only.
Source: OECD

foodstuffs and in water supplies; although the consequences on human health are not fully understood at present, pure food and water will be important issues for all regions of the OECD, but even more acute for regions where production intensity is high or will further increase;

— On a regional and local scale, OECD countries will have to ensure that the effects on agriculture of pollution and resource use by both agricultural and non-agricultural activities will not affect the sustainable development of agriculture in larger areas, through, for example, water scarcity or soil erosion;

— More broadly, OECD countries will need to better understand the potential implications for agricultural production of changes in temperature and precipitation regimes which might result from global atmospheric pollution, and the related potential changes in national food balances and international trade;

— OECD countries should benefit from an accelerated transformation of agricultural systems, doubtless in a direction more favourable to the environment with more environmentally conscious agricultural practices, increasing demand for healthier food, and an increasing role for farmers in maintaining landscape, rural ecosystems, and a genetic pool of plant and animal varieties, and in developing rural tourism activities on marginal land.

This prospect makes it necessary to integrate the environment into agricultural policies and practices, by preventing and controlling pollution, by accentuating and enhancing the positive role of agriculture for the environment and by adapting agricultural support policies with proper regard for environmental concerns.

REFERENCES

OECD (1984), *Agricultural Trade with Developing Countries*, Paris.

OECD (1986), *Water Pollution by Fertilizers and Pesticides*, Paris.

OECD (1989), *Agricultural and Environmental Policies, Opportunities for Integration*, Paris.

OECD (1989), *Water Resource Management, Integrated Policies*, Paris.

OECD (1990), *Agricultural Policies, Markets and Trade Monitoring Outlook*, Paris.

Chapter 11

INDUSTRY

Since the start of the 1970s, a marked change has come about in most OECD countries in public attitudes towards industrial activity:

- All OECD countries have realised that production industry is still the driving force behind economic growth and competitiveness, and conversely that the decline of industries can generate acute social and environmental problems;
- Industrial development has become increasingly bound up with the development of science and technology and with the prospect of a new technological revolution, with all the hopes and fears attendant upon it;
- Experience has shown that pollution abatement and less costly use of resources are feasible and that clean industry and clean products can have distinct advantages in international competition.

This development has had two effects: a much closer integration of the objectives of environmental protection and industrial growth, and greater demands on industry to improve its safety record, pollution control and product quality. There is now a realistic prospect of harmonising environmental and economic considerations and thus of gradually incorporating these objectives in policy.

Recent accidents such as those in Bhopal, Mexico City, and Basel focused public attention on the issue of risk. However, this should not be allowed to obscure the emergence of two challenges which will have at least as great an effect on future industrial environment policies: foresight in tackling the problem of long-term accumulation of toxic or harmful substances (for example, CFCs) in the natural environment; and, above all, the inclusion of ecological considerations at as early a stage as possible in the selection and promotion of the new technologies.

1. INDUSTRY-ENVIRONMENT RELATIONS

Because of its place at the heart of economic and scientific development, industry's relations with the environment go far beyond the mere impact of enterprises on their immediate environment or on the resources which they require. There are, in fact, at least four levels of interface between industry and environment:

- *A macroeconomic level*, since industry continues to play a decisive role in determining the rhythms of growth, international trade and technological progress;
- *A public industrial policy level* (financial aid for the location of enterprises or for exports, support for ailing industries, research programmes, etc.). Even if deregulation – rather than more interventionist policies – is now the

order of the day in most OECD countries, these policies still have a clear influence on the restructuring of the industrial fabric, usually by attempting to reconcile the demands of increased competitiveness with higher safety standards or product quality;

- At *enterprise level* a growing number of decisions concern the environment, whether involving investment choices, location strategies, marketing (and product quality) policy or internal health and safety measures;
- A fourth and final level to be borne in mind is that of the *industrial sector concerned with the protection and safety of the environment*, which now employs a not insignificant proportion of the working population and whose

capacity for action and innovation is a vital factor in the success of many industrial environment policies.

The dynamic development of industry-environment relations is increasingly tied up with the very rapid progress of science and technology:

– Progress, first, in our understanding of nature; less than 20 years ago, for example, it would not have been possible to verify the theory of the thinning ozone layer with the scientific instruments available then;

– Progress also in controlling energy and resources. Traditional extraction and exploitation methods are giving way to a genuine prospect of human intervention in the essential ingredients of matter and genetic heritage, and thus of an infinite freedom in the choice of materials. In the recent past, all common materials could be described in a few hundred words; now many thousands are required;

– Progress, too, in the diversification of products and services on the market: computerisation, the dissemination of communication technologies and the ability to carry out increasingly complex chemical or genetic processes will allow scope for an infinite range of combinations in both quantitative and qualitative terms;

– Progress, finally, in changing the production systems themselves, as robotics, the development of flexible workshops and quality circles challenge the old Taylorian concept of work.

Through its decisive role in the choice of products, the size and safety of facilities and the location of activities, *scientific and technological development will henceforth be an essential factor in all OECD countries in the transformation and understanding of the relationship between industry and the environment.*

Quantitative impact of industry on the environment

In 1988/89, industrial output represented approximately one-third, in value terms, of the aggregate GNP of OECD countries, the proportion varying from about 25 per cent for Greece or Denmark to about 40 per cent for Japan or western Germany. This figure of one-third is a rough initial indication of the weight of industry, but on its own it cannot accurately reflect the real impact on resource consumption or pollution emission. There are two reasons: first, the influence of industrial activities clearly extends well beyond the manufacturing sector to embrace agriculture, transport, services and even the location of residential accommodation. Second, the extent of the pressure exerted by industry on the environment is much less closely linked with the general level of economic activity than with the nature of the resources used or products manufactured, the structure and location of activity, the techniques employed and the methods of treating the residues. (Table 14)

Bearing in mind the interdependence of all these factors, pollution emissions or resource requirements in 1987 represented on average for OECD countries:

– 15 per cent of water consumption (excluding cooling);
– 25 per cent of nitrogen oxide emissions;
– 35 per cent of final energy use;
– 40-50 per cent of sulphur oxide emissions;
– 50 per cent of contributions to the greenhouse effect;
– 60 per cent of biological oxygen demand and of substances in suspension (conventional water pollution);
– 75 per cent of non-inert waste;
– 90 per cent of toxic substances discharged into water.

Just a few industrial sectors were responsible for most raw material consumption and pollution, mainly the agro-foodstuffs industry, metals extraction and processing, cement works, the pulp and paper industry, oil refining and the chemicals industry. (Table 14) In Canada it was estimated that only 12 per cent of industrial establishments, belonging to these sectors and representing one-fifth of value added, were responsible for more than two-thirds of all industrial pollution. Fortunately, these are also the sectors which have made the greatest efforts to save energy and raw materials and to control "conventional" types of pollution. This explains why industry's impact on the environment is tending to decrease *in quantitative terms.*

The increasing complexity of risks

Quantitative assessments of annual emissions or consumption are, however, a less and less relevant reflection of the impact of the industrial sector on the environment. Industrial growth in OECD countries will in future be marked far more by a process of qualitative differentiation and by ever-increasing complexity than by quantitative change, which can be expressed in terms of increased consumption of energy or raw materials.

"Dematerialisation" of industrial production

Since 1970 industry has made tremendous efforts to increase its energy productivity: total energy consumption by the industrial sector in the OECD area has fallen since then from 40 to 34 per cent, whereas industry's contribution to GNP has remained more or less stable in volume. In some countries an even more marked reduction in energy consumption was achieved. In the past 20 years, the chemicals industry output has more than doubled while its energy consumption per unit of output has fallen by 57 per cent.

A reduction was also achieved in raw materials consumption. A recent study by the International Monetary Fund states that raw material requirements for a

Table 14. ENVIRONMENTAL EFFECTS OF SELECTED INDUSTRIAL SECTORS

| | Raw material use | Air | Water resources | | Solid wastes and soil | Risks of accidents | Others: noise, workers' health and safety, consumer products |
			Quantity	Quality			
TEXTILES	Wool, synthetic fibres, chemicals for treating	Particulates, odours, SO_2, HC	Process water	BOD, suspended solids, salts, sulphates, toxic metals	Sludges from effluent treatment		Noise from machines, inhalations of dust
LEATHER	Hides, chemicals for treating and tanning		Process water	BOD, suspended solids, sulphates, chromium	Chromium sludges		
IRON AND STEEL	Iron ore, limestone, recycled scrap	Major polluter: SO_2, particulates, NO_x, HC, CO, hydrogen sulphide, acid mists	Process water	BOD, suspended solids, oil, metals, acids, phenol, sulphides, sulphates, ammonia, cyanides, effluents from wetgas scrubbers	Slag, wastes from finishing operations, sludges from effluent treatment	Risk of explosions and fires	Accidents, exposure to toxic substances and dust, noise
PETRO-CHEMICALS REFINERIES	Inorganic chemicals	Major polluter: SO_2, HC, NO_x, CO, particulates, odours	Cooling water	BOD, COD, oil, phenols, chromium, effluent from gas scrubbers	Sludges from effluent treatment, spent catalysts, tars	Risk of explosions and fires	Risk of accidents, noise, visual impact
CHEMICALS	Inorganic and organic chemicals	Major polluter: organic chemicals (benzene, toluene), odours, CFCs		Organic chemicals, heavy metals, suspended solids, COD, cyanide	Major polluter: sludges from air and water pollution treatment, chemical process wastes	Risk of explosions, fires and spills	Exposure to toxic substances, potentially hazardous products
NON-FERROUS METALS (e.g. aluminium)	Bauxite	Major local polluter: fluoride, CO, SO_2, particulates		Gas scrubber effluents containing fluorine, solids and hydrocarbons	Sludges from effluent treatment, spent coatings from electrolysis cells (containing carbons and fluorine)		
MICRO-ELECTRONICS	Chemicals (e.g. solvents), acids	Toxic gases		Contaminations of soils and groundwater by toxic chemicals (e.g. chlorinated solvents) Accidentual spillage of toxic material			Risk of exposure to toxic substances
BIO-TECHNOLOGIES			Used for effluent treatment		Used for clean-up of contaminated land		Fears of hazards from the release of micro-organisms into the environment

Source: OECD

given unit of output have fallen by an average of 1.25 per cent a year since the start of the century. Since 1970, consumption per unit of GNP of cement, paper, steel, aluminium, chlorine, ethylene and ammonia has fallen in most industrial countries, and in the United States it, in fact, started to fall per capita in the early 1980s. In Sweden, the paper industry's water requirements halved between 1960 and 1980, whereas output doubled; industry is the only sector in most OECD countries where water requirements are expected to remain stable or decline. These trends will no doubt be accelerated by future innovation in the fields of new materials, biotechnology and electronics, which will naturally have significant effects on quantitative raw material consumption and pollution emission levels.

Pressure increasingly determined by qualitative industrial changes

Progress in organic chemistry and the metals processing industries has led or is likely to lead to a remarkable *diversification of products*: if present trends continue, 50 per cent of the products which will be used in 15 years' time do not yet exist! The pace at which such new products are created gives rise to doubts as to whether there can ever be systematic control of their toxicity. The following figures give some idea of the problem:

- There are at present 7 million known chemical substances;
- Some 100 000 are available on the market;
- 1 000 new substances are put on sale each year;
- These products, and other substances (chromium, cadmium, etc.), are used in a growing number of consumption or production sectors: pigments for paints, lubricants, fertilizers, food additives, stabilizers, cleaning or anti-corrosion agents, solvents, medicines, etc.;
- By using all existing laboratory resources, a maximum of 500 products could be tested each year, at enourmous expense (a single carcinogenicity test can require three years of work and cost around US$500 000);
- The US Environmental Protection Agency lists some 500 substances as hazardous, but in practice scarcely more than 100 are covered by standards (the EEC list runs to no more than about 30 items).

Many other examples could be cited in the new materials or electronics fields; they show that everywhere, increasing complexity and diversity accompany a reduction in the overall consumption of natural resources.

Risks arising from malfunction of installations

Whereas the last 20 years have seen consistent improvements in pollutant emission control methods at entreprise level, a parallel development has been the increase in public awareness of risk situations and accidental discharges arising from malfunction of installations. Concerns about major accidents from chemical plants have come increasingly to the fore through the twentieth century. This has been particularly so since the 1940s due to the new materials and processes which have been developed. Intensification of production throughout this period has led to economies of scale but has also caused substantially greater quantities of substances to be held in storage and process. This has led to an increase in the potential hazard facing the community at large. At the same time, there has been an increasing public perception as to the hazards that may be present and a similarly increasing awareness as to what may or may not be acceptable in terms of risks to the community and, more latterly, the environment. Whilst statistical data over the last 20 years are difficult to interpret and do not show a significant increase in the number of accidents or in the number of deaths from industrial accidents, major ones such as those in Bhopal and Mexico City have had a substantial effect on public perception and government response.

The major risks are in the main connected with manufacture, storage or transport of:

- Inflammable or explosive substances, mainly fuels, common hydrocarbons and military explosives;
- Unstable or highly reactive substances (certain nitrates, liquid oxygen and hydrogen);
- Large quantities of common toxic substances, which are inputs or by-products of processing industries (chlorine, ammonia and many others in smaller quantities or of lesser significance);
- Smaller quantities of highly toxic and persistent chemical products (PCBs, dioxin, etc).

It is estimated that the resources devoted to preventing or controlling accidental risks are already comparable (in investment and operational costs) to those devoted to reducing continuous pollution.

Accumulation of stocks of harmful products or residues

Any reduction in the flow of industrial pollutants will simply serve progressively to highlight the problem of the accumulation (or reabsorption) of stocks of harmful and persistent products or residues: CO_2 or CFCs accumulate in the upper atmosphere, heavy metals or non-biodegradable substances in water, soils or sediments, waste dumps, etc. Since the average life of CFCs is about one hundred years and since three-quarters of the hazardous waste produced by industry is simply buried in the ground or discharged at sea, it is clear that annual production trends are not in themselves sufficiently good indicators of the impact of industry on the environment. We have generally satisfactory statistics on current output of persistent residues, but there are almost no statistics for the stocks accumulated in the environment.

Displacement of risks from production to product use or destruction

There is, lastly, a noticeable trend towards the displacement of the risks connected with industrial activity from the production sector, where they can be managed with increasing efficiency (except in the event of an accident), to the product use or destruction stage.

This is the case, for example, with PCBs, where the quantities which can be removed at enterprise level are obviously far smaller than those which must be destroyed downstream (from capacitors and transformers); within the EEC, the ratio is 1 to 10 000. Replacement of PCBs by substitute products will not solve the problem of the risks associated with old products or equipment still containing PCBs. The same situation applies for mercury, lead, CFCs, cadmium, etc. OECD statistics for mercury, for example, show:

- An overall decline in apparent consumption;
- A marked reduction of emissions connected with sodium chloride production;
- An increase in risks connected with the consumption of mercury batteries.

As a result, almost 60 per cent of mercury emissions are currently produced at the consumption stage in the United States. This compares with Canadian data for lead which likewise attribute two-thirds of emissions to the use of the products (fuels, paints, etc.) and with Dutch data on cadmium.

This downstream displacement of environmental problems in the production-consumption-residue process considerably broadens the responsibility of *industry, which can no longer remain oblivious to the fate of the products which it markets (their transport, storage and destruction)*. The nature of the risks is also rather different, since they are no longer concentrated but spread over a very wide area. In short, the recent phase of industrialisation in the OECD countries has been characterised by a very marked *qualitative differentiation* of risks: they are now less probable but potentially more serious, more diffuse, more varied and more international and they cannot be effectively managed without a radical change in traditional patterns of industrial action. This qualitative differentation, which is also marked by the increase in accumulation levels, of course means a *looser tie between the trend of industrial activity and the growing seriousness of environmental problems*. In the long run, however, changes in the structure of industry become very important once more.

2. CHANGES IN INDUSTRY: TRENDS AND PROSPECTS

From the early 1970s to the middle of the 1980s, industry in the OECD area had to adjust to particularly demanding circumstances:

- Demand saturation for consumer non-durables, and a booming services economy;
- Accumulation of overcapacity in traditional sectors;
- Changing energy costs;
- Competitition from newly industrialising countries with low labour costs;
- Currency instability;
- Emergence of new technologies with far higher efficiency than traditional ones.

As a result, the industrial output growth rate fell by two-thirds in 20 years, from an average of 5.5 per cent in the years 1960-1968 to 1.8 per cent between 1973 and 1979 and then between 1979 and 1985. In other words, whereas between 1960 and 1973 industrial output had doubled, between 1973 and 1986 it rose by only 25 per cent. Similarly, the rate of growth of industrial investment, which averaged 6 per cent in the 1960s, fell below 2 per cent in the first half of the 1980s. (Figure 28 and Figure 29) As a result, and taking into account the more rapid rate of obsolescence of old equipment, the growth rate of capital stock fell as well, until the mid-1980s, except in Japan.

These trends, characteristic of a large part of the 1970-90 period, merely constitute an average for the OECD countries as a whole. But even in the most dynamic countries, such as Japan, then the United States, the growth rate was a far cry, for nearly 15 years, from the exceptional rates of the decade following the last World War, and far from the rates achieved during that same period by the manufacturing sector of many countries in the Middle East and in Southeast Asia (China, India, Korea, Taiwan, Thailand, Singapore).

This trend towards slower growth has been fundamentally reversed in recent years, and it is no longer possible to view the years from 1970 to 1990 as a homogeneous whole. Launched in Japan, the United States and the Nordic countries in 1984, economic recovery reached most OECD countries by 1986-87 and especially 1988: in that year industrial output grew by more than 6 per cent in the OECD area as a whole. Thanks to this very strong acceleration during the 1984-90 period, investment by industry doubled, or more than doubled, in the United States and Japan, as well as in Belgium, Denmark, and Iceland, during the 1980s and grew by 30 to 50 per cent in the other countries of the EEC.

The most recent forecasts give grounds for supposing that this recovery of industrial growth will last. Hence pressure by industry on the environment must be expected to intensify once again, particularly in such sectors as chemicals and wood pulp, where investments have risen steeply.

Figure 28. **TRENDS IN INDUSTRIAL PRODUCTION, Volume Index**

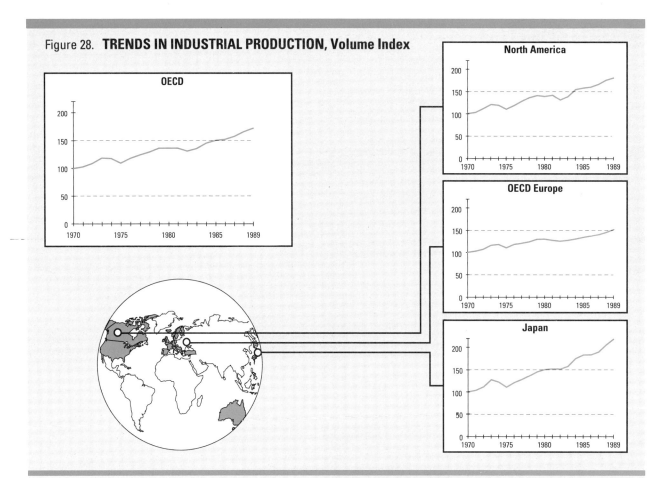

	Volume Index				
	1970	1975	1980	1985	1989
Canada	100	121	143	163	187
USA	100	108	138	158	181
Japan	100	109	150	183	219
France	100	114	135	133	149
Germany *a*	100	103	121	126	141
Italy	100	108	139	134	159
Netherlands	100	119	133	140	149
Spain	100	137	158	164	190
Sweden	100	113	109	121	129
UK	100	102	111	120	132
North America	100	109	139	158	181
OECD Europe	100	110	129	134	152
OECD	100	109	136	150	172

Note: a) Includes western Germany only.

Source: OECD

Figure 29. **TRENDS IN INDUSTRIAL INVESTMENT** *a*

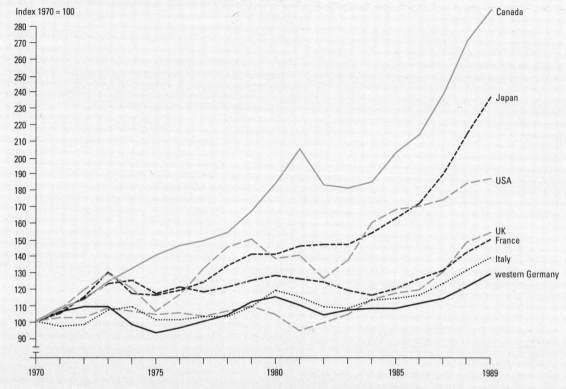

Note: a) Gross Fixed Capital Formation for ISIC 2, 3 and 4 industrial categories in constant 1980 prices.

| | Index 1970 = 100 | | | | |
	1970	1975	1980	1985	1989
Canada	100	140	184	203	290
USA	100	106	138	168	187
Japan	100	116	141	163	237
France	100	117	128	120	150
Germany *a*	100	93	115	108	129
Italy	100	101	119	114	138
UK	100	104	104	117	154
North America	100	109	142	172	195
OECD Europe	100	107	118	117	148
OECD	100	110	132	147	183

Note: a) Includes western Germany only.

Source: OECD

Put into historical perspective, the 1970s and 1980s became a long transition period towards a new state of balance, marked by:

- Radical redeployment of productive structures;
- A trend towards worldwide markets;
- Emergence of a new "technological system";
- Genuine though selective inclusion of environmental considerations in industrial strategies.

De-industrialisation is only relative

Historical statistics show that the weight of industry in the GNP of OECD countries fell overall in value terms from 40 to 30 per cent between 1960 and 1988, while the services sector increased its GNP share. Despite appearances, this trend does not mean that Daniel Bell's 20-year old hypothesis of a transition to a post-industrial society has come true, for at least two reasons:

- Even in value terms, the weight of industry has recently increased in a considerable number of less industrialised OECD countries, such as Greece, Ireland, Portugal, Spain and Turkey;
- Above all, the apparent de-industrialisation mainly results from divergent trends in relative prices: at constant prices the share of manufacturing industry in GDP remained relatively stable.

There is no evidence that this trend has changed in recent years; on the contrary, since 1980, the growth rate of industrial output by volume has consistently exceeded that of GDP. Despite the surge in services, the economies of the OECD countries are still dominated by trade in manufactured goods.

A continuous and radical redeployment of structures

The most significant development in the 1980s is intensified industrial restructuring towards the electronics and electrical industries, telecommunications, data processing and fine chemicals and away from heavy industry; in less than ten years, the growth of the dynamic sectors will have been double that of the crisis-ridden sectors. (Figure 30)

The decline of traditional industries such as textiles, non-ferrous metals processing, iron and steel, cement and petroleum refining in fact continued during the 1980s: in 1988 their production by volume was lower overall in the OECD area as a whole than in 1980. On the other hand, outputs in the mechanical and electrical industries more than doubled in Japan, for example, between 1980 and 1988.

The differentiation of structures and techniques also accelerated within the major industrial sectors; the boom in fine chemicals and pharmaceutical products contrasted with stagnation in minerals and fertilizers; continuous casting, electric steelmaking and second-melt aluminium are increasing in importance at the expense of more traditional metal processing techniques.

This radical shift in production structures has been matched by a redeployment of investment and capital structure. There was a one-third reduction in capacity investment between 1970 and 1985, but a doubling of modernisation investments, a notable boom in "non-material" investment contrasted with stagnation in material investment, industrial gross fixed capital formation concentrated on high-demand sectors (electrical equipment and plant, pulp and paper mills, etc.) and, lastly, the rate at which old equipment became obsolete accelerated.

All these trends resulted in a marked renewal of capital stocks, even if this movement was slowed down at local level to save jobs.

Furthermore, the relative decline in output by traditional industries, efforts to improve productivity in these sectors in order to stand up to international competition and the increase in the pace of obsolescence have exacerbated the decline of old heavy-industry regions and the rise of urban centres with a large skills pool or a high research potential and of regions which have developed more recently and offer attractive living environments.

In addition, the same process of redeployment of industrial production and relocation of activities can be observed throughout the OECD countries, some of which have been better able to adapt to changes in demand and the conditions of international competition than others. The indications are that the industrial geography of the 1990s will be very different from that of the 1970s.

Development of worldwide industrial markets

It is not only within the OECD area that the industrial landscape is changing: the maps are having to be redrawn on a worldwide scale as markets expand. In spite of a relative slowdown in the growth of international trade, imports and exports of manufactured goods have continued to grow within the OECD much faster than either output or investment. Thus, despite the economic difficulties of the Third World and the difficulty in funding investments, *the trend towards international specialisation has continued unabated in recent years*.

This opening up of trade has been tempered by a trend towards increased trade within regions and towards the polarisation of activities within highly integrated economic regions enjoying customs protection and common standards (EEC, North American market, etc.). There is no reason to suppose, however, that this trend will result in an increase in protectionism in the long term: it is far more likely that trade will continue to be the driving force behind world industrial growth.

The trend towards the relocation of heavy industry, a direct consequence of international specialisation, has continued, to the advantage of countries with low labour costs or rich energy or raw materials resources,

Figure 30. CHANGES IN INDUSTRIAL STRUCTURE, 1970, 1975, 1980, 1985, 1989

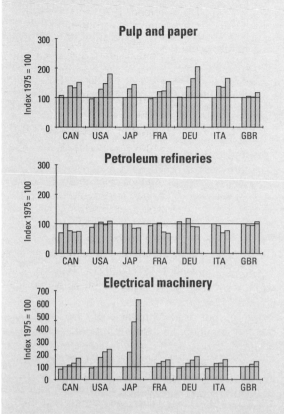

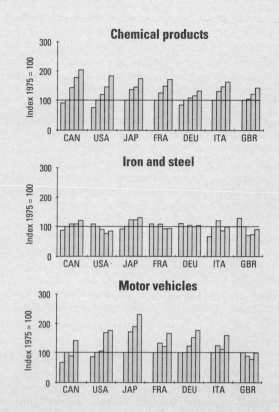

		Pulp, Paper + Paperboard	Chemical Products	Petroleum Refineries	Iron and Steel	Electrical Machinery	Motor Vehicles
Canada	1970	110	98	71	89	83	68
	1980	142	153	76	111	113	89
	1985	136	188	71	109	129	143
	1989	153	217	76	122	167	..
USA	1970	96	81	90	111	90	86
	1980	130	128	106	94	169	108
	1985	150	153	98	77	218	170
	1989	180	193	108	82	235	177
Japan	1970	..	..	..	94	..	..
	1980	130	144	102	125	212	170
	1985	145	152	85	125	453	190
	1989	..	183	86	134	629	231
France	1970	99	..	94	109	..	..
	1980	121	133	105	110	125	133
	1985	126	156	71	88	141	123
	1989	156	181	68	91	152	166
Germany [a]	1970	101	89	107	111	90	100
	1980	138	111	117	106	125	125
	1985	169	122	91	100	149	151
	1989	206	133	89	103	178	174
Italy	1970	..	..	..	68	85	..
	1980	142	135	93	121	127	125
	1985	139	149	72	87	128	114
	1989	167	172	80	99	155	158
UK	1970	..	..	..	132	..	..
	1980	103	107	96	67	101	88
	1985	102	127	96	70	117	76
	1989	123	149	108	86	138	96

Volume Indices 1975 = 100

Note: a) Includes western Germany only.
Source: OECD

despite the growing indebtedness of developing countries and the falling income of oil producers. Thus the OECD share of world steel production dropped from 66 per cent in 1970 to 50 per cent in 1988 and is expected to fall to approximately 40 per cent within 15 years. Aluminium manufacture is gradually concentrating in cheap electricity countries, such as Australia, Brazil, Canada and Venezuela. The petrochemicals industry, particularly ammonia, ethylene and methanol production, is tending to concentrate in gas- or oil-producing countries, such as North America, the Netherlands, Norway, the Middle East, the Soviet Union, China, Saudi Arabia and Kuwait; Saudi Arabia's production capacity is already able to meet 7-8 per cent of world demand for ethanol and methanol, and the forecast for the year 2000 is that non-OECD countries will increase their production from 55 to 70 per cent for ammonia and from 25 to 35 per cent for ethylene – two of the main components in organic chemistry. This trend naturally contributes to speeding up the decline of traditional regions of OECD counries, as stated previously. But it also leads to modernisation and rationalisation of existing facilities, the adoption of new production techniques (automated workshops) and emphasis on the manufacture of higher quality products in most OECD countries.

The emergence of the newly industrialising countries is not the only factor in the development of worldwide markets. In order to withstand competition, adapt to demand changes, reach the critical size required and reduce production costs, a growing majority of enterprises are having to strengthen their international expansion strategies and to organise their activities on a worldwide basis, either by investing abroad or, more often in recent years, by buying existing enterprises, signing co-operation agreements or establishing subsidiaries.

It is now quite common for a number of countries to be involved in the manufacture of a single product (up to 15 countries for the manufacture of cars) in a kind of "world factory" where each country performs the tasks in which it is most competitive.

Multinational enterprises naturally play a decisive role in the structuring of such worldwide production: it is estimated that they currently control some 40 per cent of world industrial production and that at the start of the 1980s the contribution of multinational subsidiaries to foreign trade was something like 30 per cent for Korea and Mexico, 40 per cent for Brazil and as much as 90 per cent for Singapore. Several of the larger multinationals are involved in some of the more energy-intensive industries such as chemicals production, iron and steel, and ore refining, which are important environmentally.

The trend towards the development of worldwide markets and the interdependence of national economies therefore seems to be irreversible. Nevertheless, there is no evidence as yet to suggest that the outcome in the long term will be a large-scale relocation of industry outside the OECD area:

- Investment in industry in developing countries over the last ten years has represented only slightly over a quarter of total foreign investment by the richer countries;
- Over the 15-year period from 1973 to 1988, the Third World share in industrial output increased by only two percentage points (from 16 to 18 per cent);
- Even in traditional industries such as iron and steel, textiles or petrochemicals, automation and technological progress could in the long term put a brake on the relocation process, which is more rapid at the moment in these sectors than in others.

Transition to a new technological system

Successful application of the new technologies in the future is one of the major challenges posed by the industrial restructuring in progress; for this reason, R&D expenditure has grown markedly more rapidly since 1980 than output or investment – at 7 per cent a year (12 per cent for Japan) as against 1.8 per cent for value added.

There is general agreement that the present time is one of *transition to a new technological system* which will transform the world economy as radically as the changes brought about in the 1930s to 1960s by oil, chemicals and motor vehicles. As it is currently taking shape, the new system is likely to focus on four main areas: information and image technologies (data processing and transmission, robotics, artificial intelligence, etc.), biotechnology (genetic engineering, cell culture, enzyme and fermentation engineering), new materials (polymers, alloys, ceramics, composites, etc.) and "new" energy sources (methane/hydrogen, controlled fusion, methanol conversion technology, coal gasification, voltaic cell, lasers, superconductors, etc.).

In contrast to the continued stagnation of traditional raw materials output, very high growth rates are being achieved in new materials production: 17 per cent for ceramics, 8 per cent for composites, 7 per cent for technical plastics. They already hold 10 per cent of the world market, and plastics production by volume has overtaken that of steel. The development of communications and information technology – which alone accounts for more than a quarter of all industrial R&D in OECD countries – has been even more rapid: in the five years from 1983 to 1988, the software and robotics markets saw a fourfold and the components market a threefold increase, and the expansion in the microcomputer market has reached 25 per cent a year. With a few exceptions, biotechnology has not yet reached the stage of commercial application, but it seems set to revolutionise agriculture, foodstuffs and the pharmaceutical sector from early in the 1990s.

REDUCING HAZARDOUS WASTE GENERATION
WITH LOW-WASTE TECHNOLOGIES (GERMANY)

Hazardous Waste Generation

Hazardous wastes, and their safe disposal, are a problem common to all industrialised countries. In Germany, some 4.9 million tonnes of toxic hazardous wastes were disposed of in 1983. The main sources of these wastes are the chemical industry and the use of chemical products in different industrial processes; for example, the use of acids, solvents or paints in the metal finishing and coating industries.

About 40 per cent of the waste was sulphurous waste consisting of 1.4 million tonnes of diluted sulphuric acid - mainly from the titanium dioxide industry - and about 800 000 tonnes of gypsum contaminated with organic compounds from different chemical processes. The category of sulphurous wastes also includes other wastes such as acid tars.

Waste emulsions are another important group; they contributed about half a million tonnes to the total amount of hazardous wastes. Other waste categories are paint sludges and solvents from many different industrial sources which, together, total 600 000 tonnes. Galvanic sludges of different types and salt slags from the secondary aluminium smelting industry were, in 1983, in the range of 200 000 tonnes each. The remaining 1.2 million tonnes are comprised of many different waste categories.

WASTE REDUCTION POTENTIAL

	1983 Amount (million tonnes)	Reduction Potential %
Sulfurous wastes (acids, gypsum)	2.2	80
Waste emulsion	0.5	40-50
Dyes and painting residues	0.3	60-70
Solvents	0.3	60-70
Galvanic sludges	0.2	60-70
Salt slags	0.2	100
Other wastes	1.2	low
TOTAL	4.9	50-60

The Potential for Waste Reduction

Waste reduction at source is one way in which the waste problem can be addressed. Studies in Germany indicate that a total reduction of between 50-60 per cent should be possible. In the solvent, galvanising and spray painting industries a reduction of between 60 and 70 per cent can be achieved while, mainly through recycling, the diluted waste acids in the sulphurous waste category can be reduced by about 80 per cent. A 100 per cent reduction of salt slags generated by the secondary aluminium industry can also be achieved.

A new evaluation of the waste reduction potential, based on the years 1984 and 1985, is being made. It will probably confirm that the earlier estimates are attainable and realistic. The category "other wastes" is being looked at in further detail; some groups in this category also appear to have a high potential for waste reduction.

Encouraging the Use of Low-waste Technologies

To accelerate implementation of low-waste technologies a variety of policy instruments are available: statutes, regulations, economic incentives, training and education programmes and dissemination of information. Each instrument must be tailored to individual situations.

In Germany, all of these instruments are used simultaneously. For example, in 1986 the Air Pollution Control Act and Waste Management Act were amended to foster the use of low-waste technologies. A main objective of the new legislation is to give low-waste technologies priority over customary waste disposal methods. The Acts state that the production of waste must be avoided as far as technically possible and economically acceptable, and wastes must be recycled unless such recycling is economically unfeasible. The German system requires that the best technologies available for source reduction and recycling be applied for all media. Only waste that cannot be avoided nor used with reasonable cost can be disposed of, in an environmentally sound way.

A crucial point with respect both to industry, and to the authorities who must enforce the new regulations, is the circulation of information on low-waste technologies and proper co-operation between industry and administrative authorities.

Contribution from Germany

All these developments can be summed up in one final figure: between 1980 and 1989 growth in the high-technology sectors averaged 8-10 per cent a year compared with the 2 per cent achieved by the rest of industry in the OECD area.

It should be emphasized that the technological change under way is not confined to the gradual establishment of new sectors of activity; its effects will be felt in all production and consumption sectors, even the most traditional, such as foodstuffs and textiles, the main consequences being an increase in productivity and a vast qualitative diversification of products and processes (for example, where about a hundred materials are traditionally used today, several thousand will be in common use in the future).

Selective inclusion of environmental considerations in industrial strategy

It is becoming less and less possible to dissociate the environment from the modernisation effort of the industrialised nations. Better integration of environmental considerations into product design will avoid needless expenditure (such as the payment of high compensation) and also secure a possibly decisive advantage over competitors in a context in which safety, silence, lack of pollution and biological product quality are gradually acquiring a market value. In the last few years, many OECD countries have thus seen an increasing trend towards incorporating pollution concerns and natural resource conservation concerns into enterprise strategy.

One of the effects of this trend has been the development of a specific industrial sector with a market currently worth between US$70 and $100 billion and a workforce of approximately 1.5 million.

While this trend cannot be challenged, it is nevertheless still selective:

- It mainly involves products or the installation of end-of-pipe systems rather than processes; a recent OECD report highlighted the difficulties facing the development of truly clean technology (inappropriateness of regulations and incentives, competition from "conventional" solutions, reluctance by industrialists to take risks, untested techniques, etc.);

- It takes place more slowly in old installations than in new ones, in small or medium-sized firms than in large ones;

- It is, quite clearly, very sensitive to economic conditions; although the Swedish paper industry succeeded under favourable circumstances in halving its SO_2 missions and cutting its discharges into water by 75 per cent between 1960 and 1980 whilst at the same time doubling its output, many industrial sectors in difficulty have recently had to check their efforts to install and particularly to maintain anti-pollution equipment;

- It still has little effect on investment or products exported to developing countries, which are poorly protected by regulatory standards;

- It has, of course, made much greater headway in environmental fields which have been covered by regulations for some time than in those connected with the new technologies or with unregulated risks.

3. ENVIRONMENTAL IMPACT OF INDUSTRIAL CHANGE: APPRAISAL AND CHALLENGES

Until the mid-1980s, the slowdown, the stagnation or relative decline of the most heavily polluting industries, the further rationalisation of energy consumption and the renewal of capital equipment were all factors which led to environmental improvement, even though in some countries economic stagnation delayed the replacement of old equipment and thus investment in "cleaner" technology. On the basis of that twofold observation, the OECD, in 1984, predicted that industrial pollution would increase by only 10 to 20 per cent in the 1980s except in the Mediterranean countries. Although, because of the economic recovery, the increase will be closer to 33 per cent, that does not alter the overall diagnosis for the 1970s and 1980s as a whole: a quantitative moderation of the pressures placed directly on the environment by industry between the beginning and the end of that period. In some fields, the implementation of strict regulations and indeed the imposition of outright bans have allowed an even greater reduction in pollution at plant level; this has been the case, for example, with cement dust and mercury emissions connected with the production of sodium chloride, which have been cut by a factor of ten in ten years, and for lead, PVC and industrial asbestos waste, which have been cut by a factor of 100.

The developments described in the previous section – radical structural change, emergence of new technology, selective incorporation of environmental considerations into industrial strategy – have also accentuated the trend towards more qualitative problems in the industrial environment: although pressure has been relatively reduced, the risks have become more varied. Conventional pollution problems have not vanished, but they have become commonplace. In contrast, new challenges have emerged:

- Coping with the decline of old industrial regions;
- Successfully applying new techniques;
- Managing increasingly complex risks;
- Coping with the steady internalisation of the field of industrial environment policies.

The consequences of the old industrialisation in declining regions

The environmental repercussions of abandoning or running down traditional industrial activities can be just as serious as the effects of sustained growth: contamination of water by toxic substances which have accumulated in abandoned waste dumps; higher water tables after mine pumping has ceased; land slips; deterioration in the living environment as more industrial sites are abandoned; relaxation of environmental standards in remaining factories; replacement of obsolete machinery. Many studies have shown that soil contamination on former factory sites may be very high and that rehabilitating disused sites or making waste storage areas safe for use again is usually extremely costly. The scale of the problem is shown in the OECD estimate that some US$10 billion must be devoted over a 20-year period to cleaning up abandoned industrial waste tips in Europe and North America (assessed at 400 million and 2 billion tonnes respectively). The destruction, recovery or recycling of toxic substances now banned, for example PCBs, poses similar financial and technical problems. Here too, the cost of "cleaning up" is so high as to provide *a posteriori* justification for implementing active prevention policies.

The ambivalence of technological progress: opportunities and risks for the environment of the future

We already know that these technologies will effect major changes in the ways in which pollution and natural resources are managed in future. Biotechnology should pave the way for significant progress in integrated biological control methods, optimum utilisation of agri-foodstuffs wastes, the restoration of damaged environments, water pollution abatement and treatment of dangerous residues (bacteria which can break down or digest toxic molecules, etc.). Wider use of electronics will also permit major advances: remote monitoring and measuring techniques, sensor-linked controls and automated handling of dangerous products. Lastly, the development of new materials opens up the prospect of more resource-efficient and pollution-free replacement of conventional products (for example, ceramics or polymers in place of metals and optical fibres in place of copper wire, etc.).

The potential risks of the new technologies are, however, less well known. The risks associated with the new materials appear to be limited, even if the increasing use of carbon fibres, glass fibres or industrial plastics might be an environmental hazard to some extent at the workplace or in the recycling and incineration phases (Kevlar, epoxy resins). As for the consequences of automation, the only risk is the vulnerability of the automated processes to breakdowns or industrial accidents. The prospects for the electronic industry and communications technologies are also very good, at least in terms of conventional pollution and natural resource consumption.

However, the industrial experience of the last few years, in Japan and the United States especially, has shown that quite significant problems can arise from the growing use of materials which are not readily biodegradable (silicon, gallium arsenide, thermoplastics, ceramics, precious metals, rare earth, zirconium, etc.), and from the nature of the production processes involved, which require high-quality air and water and are relatively polluting at plant level.

The worst fears associated with the new technologies focus at present on biotechnology and in fact have less to do with hazards in the handling or containment of the "product" at the production stage than with the conjectural risk of triggering uncontrolled environmental changes through the release into the environment of genetically-engineered species, viruses or bacteria. Most OECD countries have devised structures for assessing these hypothetical risks; nevertheless, there is still a significant gap at present between the efforts invested in developing the new technologies and the efforts devoted to forecasting and understanding their potential impact on the future environment.

Increasing complexity of risk management

New technology development adds an extra dimension to the growing complexity of risks that is the unavoidable counterpart of the development by industry, particularly the chemicals industry, of an ever wider range of processes and products.

The inevitable result is *a growing uncertainty as to the risks involved; increasingly rarely will risk management simply take the form of an outright elimination of risks*:

- First, it will no longer be possible to base the probability assessment of a major accident on past experience with operating installations, particularly as risk management moves away from individual machines which either work or do not work towards interdependent or interconnected systems whose overall vulnerability is hard to assess; (Table 15)
- Second, current experiences with the effects of exposure to small doses of toxic pollutants, coupled with the ever greater number of products, mean that a zero risk threshold cannot be determined simply on the basis of statistical observations or laboratory results;

Table 15. SELECTED ACCIDENTS INVOLVING HAZARDOUS SUBSTANCES, 1970-1989

Date		Country and location	Origin of accident	Products involved	Number of		
					Deaths	Injured	Evacuated
1970	24.01	Indonesia, Java	Tankfire	Kerosene	50	..	..
	17.12	Iran, Agha Jari	Explosion	Natural gas	34	> 1	..
	—	Japan, Osaka	Explosion in a subway	Gas	92	..	—
1971	11.01	English Channel	Ship collision	Petrochemicals	29	..	..
	3.02	USA, Woodbine	Explosion	Magnesium	> 25	61	..
	26.06	Poland, Czechowice	Explosion	Oil	33	..	..
1972	22.01	USA, St Louis	Explosion (rail transport)	Propylene	—	230	> 100
	30.03	Brazil, Duque de Caxias	Process failure	LPG	39	51	..
	6.04	USA, Doraville	Fire	Gasoline	2	161	..
	1.07	Mexico, Chihuahua	Explosion (rail transport)	Butane	> 8	800	..
1973	10.02	USA, Staten Island	Explosion	Gas	40	2	..
	29.08	Indonesia, Djakarta	Fire, explosion	Fireworks	52	24	> 10
	—	Czechoslovakia	Explosion	Gas	47	—	—
1974	26.04	USA, Chicago	Leakage (storage)	Silicium tetrachloride	1	300	2 000
	29.04	USA, Eagle Pass	Road transport	LPG	17	34	—
	30.04	Japan, Yokkaichi	Transshipment	Chlorine	—	521	—
	1.06	UK, Flixborough	Explosion	Cyclohexane	28	104	3 000
	19.07	USA, Decatur	Rail transport	Isobutane	7	349	—
	21.09	USA, Houston	Explosion (rail transport)	Butadiene	1	235	1 700
	31.01	India, Allahabad	Explosion (rail transport)	Fireworks	42	..	—
	9.11	Japan, Tokyo Bay	Collison, explosion	Naphta	33	..	—
	27.12	Spain, Malaga	Leakage	Chlorine	4	129	..
	—	*Japan, Mitzushima	Release near the sea	Heavy oil	—	—	—
1975	31.01	USA, Markus Hook	Transshipment	Crude oil, phenol	26	35	..
	11.05	USA, Houston	—	Ammonia	6	178	..
	16.06	Germany, Heimstetten	Warehouse fire	Nitrogen oxide	—	—	10 000
	14.12	USA, Niagara Falls	Explosion	Chlorine	4	176	—
	—	India, Chasnala	Industry	—	431	..	..
1976	23.02	USA, Houston	Explosion in a silo	Grain dust	7	..	10 000
	03	USA, Deer Park	Road transport	Ammonia	5	200	—
	13.04	Finland, Lapua	Explosion	Gunpowder	43	> 70	..
	11.05	USA, Houston	Road transport	Ammonia	6	178	..
	10.07	*Italy, Seveso	Air release	TCCD (Dioxine)	—	> 200	730
	10.12	USA, Baton Rouge	Explosion (plant)	Chlorine	—	—	10 000
	12	Colombia, Carthagene	Explosion	Ammonia	30	30	..
1977	7.03	Mexico, Cuernavaca	Leakage	Ammonia	2	500	2 000
	19.06	Mexico, Pueble	Leakage	Vinyl chloride	1	5	> 10 000
	13.07	USA, Rockwood	Road transport	Hydrogen bromide	1	30	> 10 000
	7.10	USA, Michigan	Leakage	Chlorine	—	> 50	> 13 000
	23.12	USA, Westwego	Explosion (storage)	Corn dust	35	9	..
	12.11	South Korea, Iri	Explosion (rail transport)	Dynamite	57	1 300	—
	—	Colombia, Pasacabalo	—	Ammonia	30	22	..
1978	02	USA, Youngstown	Leakage (rail transport)	Chlorine	8	138	..
	2.03	Canada, Ontario	Pipeline	LPG	—	—	20 000
	12.06	Japan, Sendai	Storage	Crude oil	21	350	..
	06	USA, Covington	Leakage (storage)	Chlorine	—	240	..
	7.07	Tunisia, Manouba	Explosion	Ammonium nitrate	3	150	..
	11.07	*Spain, San Carlos	Road transport	Propylene	216	200	—
	15.07	Mexico, Xilatopec	Explosion (road transport)	Gas	100	200	—
	3.08	Italy, Manfredonia	Plant	Ammonia	—	—	10 000
	2.11	Mexico, Sanch. Magal.	Pipe explosion	Gas	41	32	..
1979	8.01	Ireland, Bantry Bay	Explosion (marine transport)	Oil, gas	50	..	..
	02	Poland, Warsaw	Leakage, explosion	Gas	49	77	..
	28.03	*USA, Three Mile Island	Reactor failure	Nuclear	—	—	200 000
	12.04	Pakistan, Rawalpindi	Explosion	Fireworks	> 30	100	..
	3.06	Thailand, Phangnga	Explosion	Oil	50	15	..

Date		Country and location	Origin of accident	Products involved	Number of		
					Deaths	Injured	Evacuated
1979	3.06	*Mexico, Gulf	Eruption at platform	Oil	—	—	—
	5.07	USA, Memphis	Explosion	Methylparathion	—	150	> 2 000
	20.07	Tobago, Caribbean Sea	Fire	Crude oil	26	..	..
	1.10	Greece, Suda Bay	Explosion (transshipment)	Propane	7	140	—
	1.11	USA, Galveston Bay	Explosion	Crude oil	32	..	..
	11.11	Canada, Mississauga	Explosion (rail transport)	Chlorine, LPG	—	—	220 000
	15.11	Turkey, Istanbul	Explosion (marine transport)	Crude oil	52	> 2	—
	25.12	USA, Kendrick Bay	Navigation	—	30	..	..
	—	USSR, Novosibirsk	Plant	Chemicals	300	..	..
1980	11.03	Africa	Explosion	Crude oil	36	..	..
	3.04	USA, Sommerville	Rail transport	Trichlorophosphate	—	418	23 000
	3.05	India, Mandir Asod	Plant explosion	Explosives	50	..	—
	5.06	Malaysia, Port Kelang	Fire	Chemical products	3	200	> 3 000
	16.08	Japan, Shizuoka	Explosion	Propane	14	199	—
	19.08	Iran, Deh-Bos Org	Fire, explosion	Dynamite	80	45	..
	16.11	Thailand, Bangkok	Armament explosion	Explosives	54	353	—
	24.11	Turkey, Danaciobasi	Use/application	Butane	107	..	..
	29.11	Spain, Ortuella	Explosion	Propane	51	90	—
	—	USA, Alaska	Platform fire	Oil	51	—	—
	—	Italy, Rome	Ship collision	Oil	25	26	—
1981	13.02	*USA, Louisville	Leakage, explosion	Hexane	—	4	> 100
	19.05	USA, Puerto Rico	Leakage	Chlorine	—	200	1 500
	1.06	USA, Geismar	Release	Chlorine	—	125	..
	23.07	USA, Blythe	Leakage (road transport)	Nitric acid	—	—	15 000
	4.08	Mexico, Montanas	Rail transport	Chlorine	28	1 000	5 000
	21.08	USA, San Francisco	Road transport	Silicon tetrachloride	—	28	7 000
	25.08	USA, San Francisco	Leakage (pipe)	Lubrif. oil, PCB	—	—	30 000
	—	*USA, Binghampton	Fire in office building	PCB	—	—	—
1982	5.03	Australia, Melbourne	Transport	Butadiene	—	> 1 000	—
	25.04	Italy, Todi	Explosion (use/application)	Gas	34	140	..
	28.09	*USA, Livingston	Derailment and fire	Chemicals	—	—	3 000
	11.12	USA, Taft	Explosion	Acrolein	—	—	20 000
	19.12	Venezuela, Tacoa	Tank explosion	Fuel oil	> 153	500	40 000
	22.12	USA, Vernon	Leakage	Methylacrylate	—	355	—
1983	05	Egypt, Nile River	Explosion (transport)	LPG	317	44	—
	7.05	Turkey, Istanbul	Explosion (use/application)	—	42	50	..
	31.08	Brazil, Pojuca	Fire, explosion	Gasoline	42	> 100	> 1 000
	29.09	India, Dhulwari	Explosion	Gasoline	41	> 100	..
	10.10	Nicaragua, Corinto	Tank explosion	Fuel oil	—	17	25 000
	3.11	India, Dhurabari	Fire	Oil	76	> 60	—
1984	22.01	USA, Sauget	Industry	Phosph. trichloride	—	125	—
	25.02	Brazil, Cubatao	Pipeline explosion	Gasoline	89	..	2 500
	10.05	USA, Peabody	Fire in leather tannery	Benzene	1	125	> 100
	16.08	Brazil, Rio de Janeiro	Leakage, platform fire	Gas	36	19	—
	3.09	USA, Omaha	Leakage (storage)	Nitric acid	—	—	10 000
	6.10	USA, Linden	Tank overheat	Malathion	—	161	—
	30.10	Indonesia, Djakarta	Fire	Ammunition	> 14	> 200	10
	19.11	Mexico, St. J. Ixhuatepec	Explosion (storage tank)	Gas (LPG)	> 500	2 500	> 200 000
	3.12	*India, Bhopal	Leakage	Methyl isocyanate	2 800	50 000	200 000
	17.12	Mexico, Matamoros	Transport	Ammonia	—	182	3 000
	12	Pakistan, Gahri Dhoda	Explosion pipe	Gas	60	..	—
	—	Romania	Factory	Chemicals	100	100	..
	—	*USA, Denver	Leakage (storage)	Gasoline	—	—	..
1985	21.01	USA, Linden	Industry	Dimethoate	—	200	—
	03	Indonesia, Djakarta	Leakage (factory)	Ammonia	—	130	—
	13.04	*Canada, Kenora	Road transport	PCB	—	—	—

Table 15. SELECTED ACCIDENTS INVOLVING HAZARDOUS SUBSTANCES, 1970-1989 *(Cont'd)*

Date		Country and location	Origin of accident	Products involved	Number of		
					Deaths	Injured	Evacuated
1985	14.05	India, Cochin	Release	Hexacyclopentadiene	—	200	..
	19.05	Italia, Priolo	Leakage	Propylene	—	—	> 20 000
	26.05	Spain, Algeciras	Transshipment	Oil	33	37	..
	22.06	USA, Anaheim	Fire (storage)	Pesticides	—	12	10 000
	26.06	USA, Coachella	Fire	Pesticides	—	236	2 000
	16.07	USA, Cedar Rapids	Sewage plants	Polyvenyl chloride	—	56	10 000
	15.08	USA, Institute	Leakage	Aldicarboxime	—	430	3 100
	26.08	USA, South Charleston	Release	Hydrogen chloride	—	135	—
	09	India, Tamil Nadu	Transport	Gasoline	60	..	..
	1.11	India, Padaval	Fire	Gasoline	> 43	82	..
	4.12	India, New Delhi	Release	Sulphuric acid	1	340	> 10
	—	India	—	Chlorine	1	150	—
1986	26.04	*USSR, Chernobyl	Reactor explosion	Nuclear	31	299	135 000
	8.07	USA, Miamisburg	Fire (rail transport)	Phosphorus acid	—	400	40 000
	19.09	UK, Hemel Hempstead	Road transport	Lead oxide	—	150	—
	25.12	Mexico, Cardenas	Leakage (pipeline)	Gas	—	2	> 20 000
	1.11	*Switzerland, Basel	Warehouse fire	Chemicals	—	—	—
	—	*USA, Northville	Leak in oil terminal	Gasoline	—	—	—
1987	24.03	USA, Nantichoke	Fire	Sulphuric acid	—	—	18 000
	4.04	USA, Minot	Fire	Parathion	—	20	10 000
	11.04	USA, Pittsburgh	Derailment	Phosphorus oxychloride	—	14	16 000
	14.04	USA, Salt Lake City	Leakage	Trichlorethylene	1	6	30 000
	7.07	USSR, Annau	Rail transport	Chlorine		200	..
	17.07	*Germany, Herborn	Road transport	Gasoline	6	24	—
	29.10	France, Nantes	Fire	Fertilizers	—	24	25 000
	30.10	USA, Texas City	Process failure	Hydrofluoric acid	—	255	4 000
	5.12	Spain, La Corogne	Fire at sea	Sodium	23	..	20 000
	15.12	Mexico, Minatitlan	Process failure	Acrylonitrile	—	> 200	1 000's
	21.12	Egypt, Alexandria	Explosion	Smoke bombs	8	142	> 1 000
	—	China, Shangsi	Misuse	Fertilizers	—	1 500	30 000
1988	2.01	*USA, Floreffe	Release (storage)	Diesel oil	—	—	—
	10.04	Pakistan, Islamabad	Explosion (storage)	Explosives	> 100	3 000	..
	22.04	Canada, at sea	Explosion (marine transport)	Gasoline	29	—	..
	5.05	USA, Henderson	Explosion, fire	Perchlorinated ammonia	2	350	17 000
	6.05	China, Liu Pan Shui	Explosion	Coal gas	45	5	..
	23.05	USA, Los Angeles	Fire	Chemicals	—	—	11 000
	25.05	Mexico, Chihuahua	Explosion (storage)	Oil	—	7	15 000
	4.06	USSR, Arzamas	Explosion (rail transport)	Explosives	73	230	90 000
	8.06	France, Tours	Fire	Chemicals	—	3	200 000
	15.06	Italy, Genoa	Explosion	Hydrogen	3	2	15 000
	17.06	USA, Springfield	Leakage, fire	Sodium hypochlorite	—	275	20 000
	23.06	Mexico, Monterrey	Explosion	Gasoline	4	15	10 000
	4.07	USSR, Chakhnounia	Leakage (transport)	Pesticides	—	—	20 000
	6.07	UK, North Sea	Explosion, fire (platform)	Oil, gas	167	—	—
	23.08	*Canada, St-Basile-le-Grand	Fire	PCB	—	—	3 800
	3.09	USA, Los Angeles	Process failure, leakage	Sodium hypochlorite	—	37	27 000
	4.09	USA, Los Angeles	Second release	Sodium hypochlorite	—	7	20 000
	23.09	Yugoslavia, Sibanik	Process failure, fire	Fertilizers	—	—	> 60 000
	4.10	URSS, Sverdlovsk	Explosion (rail transport)	Explosives	5	1 020	—
	22.10	China, Shanghai	Explosion in refinery	Petrochemicals	25	17	..
	9.11	India, Bombay	Fine in refinery	Oil	35	16	..
	10.11	North Atlantic	Explosion (marine transport)	Crude oil	27	..	—
	15.11	UK, West Bromwich	Leakage	Nitric acid	—	22	50 000
	31.11	Bangladesh, Chittagong	Explosion	Flammable vapours	33	..	..
	1.12	China	Explosion	Gas	45	23	..
	11.12	Mexico, Mexico City	Explosion	Fireworks	62	87	..
	22.12	India, Jhurkully	Leakage	Sulphur dioxide	—	500	..

Date		Country and location	Origin of accident	Products involved	Number of		
					Deaths	Injured	Evacuated
1989	5.01	USA, Los Angeles	Release	Chlorine	–	–	11 000
	17.01	India, Bhatinda	Leakage	Ammonia	–	500	..
	19.01	China, Henan	Explosion	Fireworks	27	22	..
	20.03	USSR, Ionava	Explosion fire	Ammonia, NPK fertilizer	6	53	30 000
	5.05	India, Brittania Chowk	Leakage	Chlorine	–	200	..
	4.06	USSR, Acha Ufa	Explosion pipeline	Gas	575	623	..
	21.09	USSR, Yurga	Explosion	Ammunition	1	3	20 000
	23.10	USA, Pasadena	Explosion	Ethylene	23	125	1 300
	16.11	Pakistan, Garan Chashma	Explosion	Ammunition	40	> 20	..

Notes: Inclusion criteria:
- 25 deaths or more; or
- 125 injured or more; or
- 10 000 evacuated or more; or 10 thousand people or more deprived of water;
- 10 million US$ or more damages to third parties referred to by *.

Exclusion of:
- Oil spills at sea from ships (see Table 6);
- Mining accidents;
- Voluntary destruction of ships or airplanes;
- Damage caused by defective products.

Sources: OECD, MHIDAS, TNO, SEI, UBA-Handbuch Störfälle, SIGMA

– The uncertainty is even greater when an attempt is made to take into account the interactions and synergies within the natural environment itself; the Basel accident in 1986 involving the release of 33 tonnes of toxic substances into the Rhine provoked significant scientific debate, but far greater uncertainty will persist for a long time about the sources and effects of the 10 000 or so tonnes of toxic substances discharged annually into this same river.

For these reasons, and in view of the escalating economic cost of safety precautions, the OECD countries seem likely to move towards a point where industrial risks cannot all be covered by conventional means of prevention such as licences and standards. The situation faced instead is one where the organisation of information and research, the dissemination and plurality of experience, the capacity to evaluate and grade risks, the ability of institutions and enterprises to control accident situations and the effectiveness of insurance and compensation schemes will all play as important a role as legislation. This was, moreover, the direction taken by a set of initiatives adopted recently by the OECD, in particular at the conference on risks in February 1988.

Irreversible internationalisation of industrial environment problems

In addition to structural change, the internationalisation of trade and the growing integration of the world economy are further aspects of recent industrial development which have a major impact on the environment.

At least four factors are at work in giving industrial environment problems an increasingly international dimension:

– With the opening up of frontiers and increasing international specialisation there has been a substantial increase in the movement of goods and waste and thus in the risks associated with their transport and storage; in the European Community alone, for example, more than 100 000 border crossings of hazardous substance shipments are recorded each year. As long as the current wide divergences in waste treatment costs and in standards persist, it is likely that the problem of concentrations of industrial waste will become a major international challenge in the coming years;

– Owing to the very nature of the products manufactured and discharged, the spread of pollution knows no national barriers: CFC emissions in the northern hemisphere affect the ozone layer in the Antarctic; 70 per cent of the acidification of Swedish lakes is the result of SO_2 emissions from outside Sweden; 50 to 60 per cent of the cadmium discharged into the environment in the Netherlands is "imported" (in the form of batteries and pollution transported by the Rhine); in short, transfrontier pollution is becoming more and more frequent;

OECD WORK RELATED TO ACCIDENTS INVOLVING HAZARDOUS SUBSTANCES

After the accidents which occurred in Bhopal in 1984 and Basel in 1986, where large quantities of chemicals were released, causing, respectively, many deaths and much damage to the environment, it was felt by OECD Member countries that chemical safety should be improved and that the OECD should take a leading role in achieving this. In early 1988, at the initiative of France, Ministers and high level government officials met at the OECD Conference on Accidents Involving Hazardous Substances in order to decide what should be done. The Conference agreed on an outline of policies and proposals for national and international action aimed at improving prevention of, preparedness for and response to such accidents and called for a programme of work in OECD to assist Member countries with improving chemical safety.

Improving Accident Prevention and Response

The two main activities involved in the OECD work on accidents are the development of common principles, procedures and policy guidance related to accidents and the establishment of mechanisms for effective exchange and provision of information.

Concerning policy guidance, the focus is on the preparation of guidance related to accident prevention and response, including guiding principles concerning investments and aid programmes with respect to hazardous installations in non-OECD countries. This guidance will be based on the results of discussions at three workshops held in 1989 and 1990 concerning the roles of industry, workers and public authorities in preventing accidents, and an additional workshop which dealt with emergency response.

Regarding the provision and exchange of information, the work aims at developing a framework for the provision of relevant information to persons having a responsibility in the area of accident prevention and response, and to those who might be potentially affected by an accident in a hazardous installation.

Wide Dissemination of Information

Two OECD Council Acts have been adopted relating to information provision: one on the exchange of information among countries concerning accidents capable of causing transfrontier damage; another dealing with the provision of information to the public and public participation in decision-making related to the prevention of, and response to, accidents involving hazardous substances.

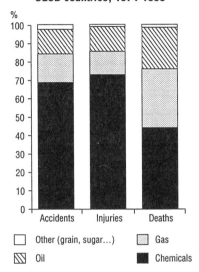

ACCIDENTS INVOLVING 25 OR MORE INJURIES OECD countries, 1974-1985

Legend: Other (grain, sugar...); Gas; Oil; Chemicals

The work aimed at making accident-related information more widely available will be facilitated through the preparation of:

- A user's guide on chemical databases;
- A user's guide on information systems which are of use to emergency planners and responders;
- An international inventory of emergency response centres.

In addition, accident case histories are collected, analysed and disseminated.

All the work is undertaken in close co-operation with other international organisations such as the United Nations Environment Programme, the World Health Organisation, the International Labour Office and the World Bank. Through such co-operation, duplication in effort among international organisations is avoided and information which is gathered as part of the OECD work can be disseminated and used worldwide.

Source: OECD

- The environment is proving more and more to be a factor in international competition, either as an instrument of price competition (for countries with less strict regulatory standards) or as a disguised tariff barrier or an instrument of commercial promotion;
- Above all, standards themselves are becoming international.

The Montreal Ozone Agreement, the Basel accident, the increasing number of initiatives on acid rain, European efforts to harmonize provisions on risks, and negotiations on the discharge of toxic waste at sea, all point up different aspects of the transition from what was a local issue to a now thoroughly international set of environmental problems. Much still remains to be done, particularly with a view to improving relations between the OECD and non-Member countries: a code of conduct for enterprises investing abroad must be drawn up, exports of toxic products monitored, high risk technology transfers regulated, etc. Major efforts to achieve harmonization in all these fields are clearly necessary, either between enterprises themselves or through international organisations.

4. CONCLUSIONS

In the course of the past 20 years, the industrial activities of the OECD countries experienced moderate growth and then more rapid growth and, above all, structural changes that were of significance for the environment: a relative decline of the most polluting sectors (iron and steel, non-ferrous metals, cement) and the emergence of innovating sectors (electronics and telecommunications, data processing and transmission, chemicals, biotechnology, and new materials); obsolescence of old equipment along with the modernisation and increased productivity of firms; the rise of non-material investments; and the globalisation of industrial markets.

Even though industry continues to contribute a sizable share of overall pollution, there has nonetheless been a tendency for industrial pollution to decline gradually, thanks to several factors:

- The replacement of old equipment and the growth of investment in "clean" technologies – especially where the conventional pollutants are concerned – and in technologies that are more effective in their use of natural resources;
- The implementation of more and more restrictive environment policies concerning certain plants, and the remarkable responses which have been provided, in certain countries, by the principal industrial sectors contributing to the polluting load;
- A more demanding attitude on the part of public opinion with regard to industry, particularly as concerns safety, pollution control and quality of products;
- The gradual inclusion of environmental considerations in industrial strategies. This inclusion has been genuine but selective: very sensitive to economic circumstances, focusing more on recent installations than on old ones, still concentrating on end-of-pipe adjustments rather than on transformation of the technical processes used in production.

Nonetheless, in the 1990s:

- Although the OECD countries are in better control of the quantities of resources used and pollutants emitted, they will have to deal with the pressure placed on the environment by what is likely to be continuing industrial growth as well as with marginally higher costs for each unit of pollution eliminated or of waste treated;
- The OECD countries will also have to face types of industrial risk that will be far more complex to manage: risks associated with the new technologies, the risk of accidents, the cumulative effects of widely disseminated or trace pollutants and the unforeseeable repercussions of inadequate treatment of toxic waste;
- The OECD countries should benefit from an accelerated transformation of production systems, doubtless in a direction that will be more favourable to the environment (with more effective recycling, for instance), as industry, science and technology work more and more closely together;
- The OECD countries should benefit from the development of an industrial sector specifically devoted to environment protection and safety, and from the development of clean products.

This prospect makes it necessary to integrate the environment into business strategy as early as possible, step up the monitoring of high-risk industrial installations, and define a set of common rules for use at international level. This is not unrealistic, for:

- On the one hand, the environment is gradually becoming a major concern for the most developed industrial systems and a decisive element in international competition;

- On the other hand, industry's responsibilities have expanded greatly in the past 20 years. What industry needs to do is no longer merely to treat pollution or wastes produced by each individual firm but rather, to manage collectively a set of rare resources while taking into account the spatial and temporal interrelationships that exist on several scales (regional, planetary and between generations).

The central role which industry in the OECD countries plays in economic innovation and organisation throughout the world means that it must bear a special responsibility in the implementation of a sustainable development strategy both within the OECD region and outside of it. The quality of the efforts made by industry in the coming decade to integrate the environment into research, investment, the choice of products and of raw materials, siting policies, etc., will determine the degree of success in managing such complex problems as the treatment of toxic wastes, chemical risks and risks of accident, the greenhouse effect, and the reproduction of the resources that will be indispensable to the generations of the twenty-first century.

REFERENCES

OECD (1985), *Biotechnology and Patent Protection*, Paris.

OECD (1985), *Environment and Economics*, Paris.

OECD (1985), *Environmental Policy and Technical Change*, Paris.

OECD (1986), *Science and Technology Indicators*, Paris.

OECD (1987), *Environmental Data 1987*, Paris.

OECD (1988), *Industrial Structures Statistics* , Paris.

OECD (1990), *Indicators of Industrial Activity*, Paris.

OECD (1990), *Main Economic Indicators*, Paris.

Chapter 12

TRANSPORT

Transport systems play a major positive role in the economic life of industrialised countries and in the daily lives of their citizens. The production and maintenance of transport infrastructures and mobile equipment, on the one hand, and their use, on the other hand, bulk large in the economies of industrialised countries, accounting for 4 to 8 per cent of GDP and 2 to 4 per cent of jobs. Their balances of payments are also strongly influenced by international trade in transport equipment and invisible transport services. The purchase of transport services and personal transport equipment makes up a significant percentage of outlays by businesses and of household consumption expenditure (around 10 per cent in Europe, more in North America, less in Japan). A substantial share of tax revenues also goes towards public expenditures on transport, particularly for capital investment and service subsidy.

The negative effects of transport activities mainly include accidents, congestion, air pollution and noise due to road transport, oil pollution by maritime transport, noise from aircraft, energy consumption, and the consumption of land and of other natural resources for the production of vehicles and infrastructures. For instance, the non-internalised social costs of road transport amount to several per cent of GDP for industrialised countries.

1. THE INTERFACE BETWEEN TRANSPORT AND THE ENVIRONMENT

The demand for transport is largely a "derived demand" and mainly reflects the level of economic activity. The market for passenger transport depends particularly on the travel demands of households while the market for freight transport depends on productive activities.

The kinds of impacts that transport activities have on the environment and their importance depend on:

- The production of transport infrastructure and mobile equipment and their regular servicing and maintenance;
- The operation of transport modes (that is, the intensity of use of infrastructure and mobile equipment);
- The type of transport mode (for example, air, sea, inland waterway, rail, road, pipeline); and
- The technologies used.

Major environmental consequences of transport activities can be summarised and classified as follows: (Table 16)

- Pollution problems are mainly concerned with air pollutants, their associated health risks in urban areas, and ecological impacts at regional levels. Emissions from the transport sector represent a high proportion of overall man-made emissions in industrialised countries – about 90 per cent of all CO emissions, about 50 per cent of NO_x emissions, 50 per cent of total HCs in urban areas; at least 50 per cent of atmospheric lead emissions, and around 80 per cent of all benzene emissions (see Chapter on Air);
- In recent years concerns have increased with respect to global atmospheric issues. Transport emits almost 25 per cent of the world's total CO_2 emissions. In industrialised countries, this percentage may grow to 40 per cent. Transport also contributes to CFC emissions (from air conditioning and foams), which cause stratospheric ozone depletion (see Chapter on Global Atmospheric Issues);
- Noise disturbance, particularly due to road and air traffic, is a common nuisance, especially in densely built-up residential areas and at night. Transport is by far the largest source of noise (see Chapter on Noise);

Table 16. SELECTED ENVIRONMENTAL EFFECTS OF PRINCIPAL TRANSPORT MODES

	Air	Water resources	Land resources	Solid waste	Noise	Risks of accidents	Other impacts
MARINE AND INLAND WATER TRANSPORT		Discharge of ballast water, oil spills, etc. Modification of water systems during port construction and canal cutting and dredging	Land taken for infrastructures; dereliction of obsolete port facilities and canals	Vessels and craft withdrawn from service		Bulk transport of fuels and hazardous substances	
RAIL TRANSPORT			Land taken for rights of way and terminals; dereliction of obsolete facilities	Abandoned lines, equipment and rolling stock	Noise and vibration around terminals and along railway lines	Derailment or collision of freight trains carrying hazardous substances	Partition or destruction of neighbourhoods, farmland and wild life habitats
ROAD TRANSPORT	Air pollution (CO, HC, NO_x, particules and fuel additives such as lead). Global pollution (CO_2, CFC)	Pollution of surface water and groundwater by surface run-off; modification of water systems by road building	Land taken for infrastructures; extraction of road building materials	Abandoned spoil tips and rubble from road works; road vehicles withdrawn from service; waste oil	Noise and vibration from cars, motorcycles and lorries in cities, and along main roads	Deaths, injuries and property damaged from road accidents; risk of transport of hazardous substances; risks of structural failure in old or worn road facilities	Partition or destruction of neighbourhoods, farmland and wild life habitats; congestion
AIR TRANSPORT	Air pollution	Modification of water tables, river courses and field drainage in airport construction	Land taken for infrastructures; dereliction of obsolete facilities	Aircraft withdrawn from service	Noise around airports		

Source: OECD

— Land consumption by transport infrastructures (roads and railways, pipelines and associated facilities) may be in conflict with other land uses and also influence access and property values. New and obsolete transport facilities (such as canals, railway lines, stations and tunnels, and port facilities) give rise to difficult problems concerning land acquisition or derelict land reconversion;

— Solid waste problems mainly involve the disposal of earth and rubble during the building of new transport infrastructures, the recover and recycling of metals from scrapped vehicle and the disposal of certain non-recoverabl materials (see Chapter on Solid Waste);

— Accident risks mainly concern the daily oper ation of road transport modes. Although dis astrous accidents in other transport mode occasionally result in heavy tolls, take together these generally represent only small fraction of the deaths, injuries and prop erty damage attributable to road transport;

INTERNATIONAL LORRY TRAFFIC TRANSIT THROUGH AUSTRIA

Austria at the Crossroads in Central Europe

Because Austria is located in central Europe, it is at the crossroads of many international transport routes of significance, whether concerning road or rail traffic or inland navigation. Among these, road infrastructures across the eastern part of the Alps link the northern with the southern regions of Europe, as well as the eastern and western countries.

The road infrastructure which links Germany and Italy, via the Inn Valley/Brenner route, belongs to the European network of motorways, and plays a vital role as one of the major economic links of international status in Europe.

Growing Importance of International Lorry Traffic

Currently the volume of road freight transit through Austria amounts to approximately 22 million tonnes per year. Over the past 15 years it has increased at the rate of about 1 million tonnes per year. One of a very limited number of routes through the Alps, the Inn Valley/Brenner route concentrates 75 per cent of the total road transit traffic, representing a daily traffic volume of 14 000 cars and more than 4 000 lorries.

During the same 15-year period, the volume of freight transit through Austria by rail, which is far less detrimental to the environment, has remained at a constant yearly level of 8 to 10 million tonnes. The relative market share of rail transit versus road transit decreased sharply: whereas in 1970, the railways held a 70 per cent share of freight transit, at present road freight transit accounts for more than two-thirds of the total transit volume.

Environmental Consequences and Public Complaints

This rapid growth of road freight traffic and of its current daily volume has created many negative environmental effects; among these, noise is one of the most detrimental to the quality of the environment of local populations.

On an average weekday, the level of noise (expressed in daily leq) may reach as much as 67.4 dB(A) along certain portions of the Inn Valley/Brenner motorway. A significant number of dwellings and inhabitants located along this motorway are therefore exposed to daily leq in excess of 65 dB(A), the level above which most people are severely bothered by noise. Obviously, other environmental and safety consequences also arise from this heavy traffic: among these are air pollution, traffic congestion, and reduced safety for the neighbourhood.

For many years, protests have arisen from local populations exposed to these ever-increasing environmental and safety hazards. In response, Austria has endeavoured to point out the physical limits of road traffic in the Alpine region. However, the dialogue with other countries in Europe which are concerned and in search of a solution, taking into account the legitimate interests of the population in the transit areas as well as the transport requirements of European countries' economies, has achieved no tangible results. In 1989, this led the Austrian Federal Ministry for Public Economy and Transport to take

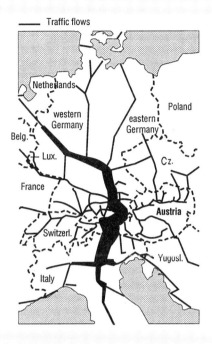

— Traffic flows

measures to prevent people living in the transit areas from taking uncontrollable actions against road traffic.

Night-time Lorry Traffic Ban

Since 1st December 1989, a selective night-time lorry traffic ban has been in force on a limited number of Austrian motorways, including the Inn Valley/Brenner route.

Trucks with a maximum weight exceeding 7.5 tonnes are banned between 10 p.m. and 5 a.m. Several exceptions are, however, provided for. They include, among others, vehicles carrying perishable foodstuffs, milk or cattle and, in particular, noise-reduced trucks, which are generally exempted from these restrictions on night-time traffic.

Concrete results have been achieved through this selective lorry freight traffic ban. The traffic between 10 p.m. and 5 a.m. decreased from 900-1000 trucks for one night on Alp-transit routes to 35 per cent of the former value after the ban. At the same time, the combined rail/road transport traffic grew sharply, with 115 per cent increase for unaccompanied combined transport, and 250 per cent increase for accompanied, during the first 4 months of operation. Side effects, such as shifts of traffic to smaller roads or changes in the traffic market, have not been noticeable. Thus, Austria does not consider the ban alone as a long-term solution for this international traffic problem. Such a long-term strategy certainly includes combined road/rail transport of freight. This means, in particular, that new capacity for rail traffic should be developed, and that improved rail/road combined systems should be promoted throughout Europe. Similar strategies are being studied in Switzerland.

Contribution from Austria

- The pollution of the marine environment by the routine or accidental discharge of oil products is also a cause for concern (see Chapter on Marine Environment);

- The risks caused by the transport of hazardous substances (e.g. chemicals) or hazardous waste represent an increasing problem because of the potential scale and intensity of the damage;

- The consumption of energy resources by the transport sector is also a major concern because of its high dependence on petroleum. The consumption of metals and other non-fuel minerals for the construction of transport infrastructures and mobile equipment raises longer-term issues of resource utilisation and recycling (see Chapter on Energy);

- High levels of congestion in urban and suburban road transport as well as in major air transport nodes result in heavy losses of time.

Although other modes have important impacts in one or two fields, road transport is responsible for much of the transport sector's impact on the environment in almost every aspect except water pollution.

The nature of the problems relating to the impact of transport on the environment is international for several reasons and goes far beyond the general need to harmonise environmental policies among OECD countries:

- Transport vehicles are products subject to international trade, and various standards and related regulations (e.g. noise standards and emissions standards) should not be used as non-tariff barriers to trade;

- Transport vehicles contribute to the emission of air pollutants which are transported across borders (e.g. NO_x) or contribute to global atmospheric pollution (CO_2);

- Transport vehicles themselves cross national borders and imply some harmonisation in fuel provision and in environmental standards.

2. TRANSPORT TRENDS OF ENVIRONMENTAL SIGNIFICANCE

Importance of different transport modes

OECD countries have experienced two "energy shocks" since 1970. Although economic growth has been affected by them, countries have overcome the crises and since 1970 have, on average, achieved steady economic growth.

Freight transport reflects this sustained economic growth. In terms of tonne-kilometers, it increased by 58 per cent in OECD Europe and by 37 per cent in Japan between 1970 and 1988. The various modes of transport have not all benefited to the same extent from the overall increase in freight transport. While road transport showed the highest increase, railway transport declined. Consequently the share of the road sector has increased in OECD countries. (Figure 31)

Passenger transport has made further progress since 1970. In terms of passenger-kilometers, passenger transport by railways and roads increased by 72 per cent in European OECD and by 70 per cent in Japan between 1970 and 1988. Again, road transport grew very rapidly and increased its share. (Figure 31)

In the future, social and economic conditions are not likely to change radically, and thus current transport trends are likely to continue. Both freight and passenger transport will grow steadily and the role of the aviation sector is expected to increase.

Transport infrastructures

In OECD Europe and the United States, annual investment in transport infrastructure is decreasing while expenditure on maintenance is increasing, partly reflecting the competition between investment and maintenance for the financial resources allocated by countries to transport infrastructures.

As a result of the closure of unprofitable lines, the total length of rail networks diminished by 4.1 per cent in OECD Europe and by 1.8 per cent in Japan between 1970 and 1985. However, the length of electrified lines increased and the proportion of electrified lines in the overall network rose from 29.3 per cent to 38.6 per cent in OECD Europe and from 42.1 per cent to 52.8 per cent in Japan between 1970 and 1985.

After 1970 the road network continued to expand, but at a much slower rate than before. However, the motorway network developed more rapidly: over the period 1970 to 1988 it more than doubled in Europe and increased more than sixfold in Japan, whereas North America experienced much slower growth. (Figure 32)

The construction of some large-scale projects has been completed or started recently in OECD countries. In Europe, several high-speed train lines have been constructed in France or are under construction, and the Channel Tunnel and connections through the Alps and between Danish islands are also examples of the revival of large-scale projects. In Japan the double-deck bridge connecting Honshu and Shikoku islands by road and rail was completed in 1988, as was the Tsugaru Strait Tunnel connecting Honshu and Hokkaido islands by railway. Kansai International Airport is under construction on the reclaimed land of Osaka Bay.

Transport activities in OECD countries will undoubtedly continue to increase, although only part

Figure 31. STRUCTURAL CHANGES IN FREIGHT AND IN PASSENGER TRAFFIC, 1970-1988

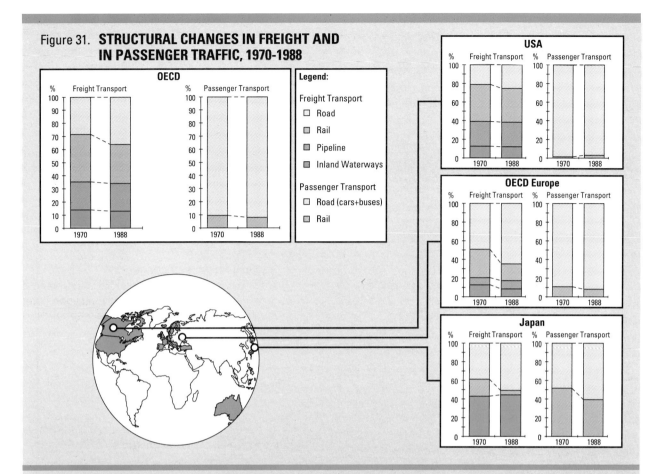

	Freight Transport Changes 1970-1988 (%)			Passenger Transport Changes 1970-1988 (%)		
	Rail	Road	Total	Rail	Road	Total
USA	30.3	69.7	44.0	401.2	56.9	80.3
Japan	-62.7	79.4	37.2	25.3	107.3	69.9
France	-22.6	68.6	13.9	54.4	81.1	78.2
Germany *a*	-17.0	94.1	27.4	8.3	52.3	48.4
Italy	8.3	179.4	124.5	33.5	121.6	111.2
UK	-25.7	46.8	37.0	13.1	62.0	57.7
North America	27.0	72.0	..	328.3	..	..
OECD Europe	-6.3	105.0	57.7	26.2	77.6	72.3
OECD	21.0	84.0	46.0	38.0	68.0	77.0

Notes: Data refer to surface transport only, and are expressed in tonnes-kilometers and passenger-kilometers.
   a) Includes western Germany only.

Source: OECD, ECMT

Figure 32. TRENDS IN ROAD NETWORK LENGTH

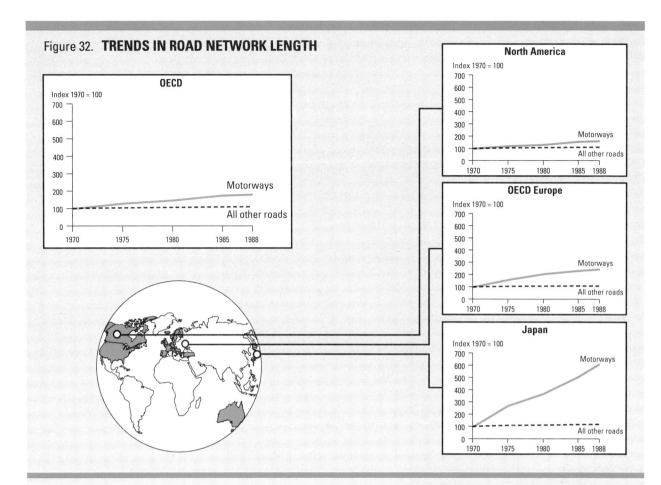

	Total Road Network Length			Motorway Network Length		
	1970 1000 km	1988 1000 km	1970-1988 % change	1970 1000 km	1988 1000 km	1970-1988 % change
Canada	830	930	12	2.76	7.45	170
USA	6 000	6 650	11	53.70	83.21	55
Japan	1 000	1 130	12	0.70	4.28	511
France	790	810	2	1.55	6.57	324
Germany *a*	440	490	12	4.46	8.72	96
Italy	280	300	6	3.91	6.08	55
UK	320	350	9	1.06	2.98	181
North America	6 830	7 580	11	56.46	90.66	61
OECD Pacific	1 980	2 070	5	1.83	5.52	202
OECD Europe	2 880	3 130	9	14.53	35.73	146
OECD	11 690	12 790	9	72.82	131.91	81

Note: a) Includes western Germany only.

Source: OECD

of this increase will be accommodated through new infrastructures because of their high cost, particularly within already urbanised areas. The United States will focus on the construction of airports while European countries will make an effort to build a network of high-speed trains.

Increasing motorisation and mobility in road transport

As already mentioned, road transport plays a major role in transport and is responsible for much of the transport sector's impact on the environment. The stock of passenger cars in use has continued to increase since 1970. In the 18 years to 1988, it multiplied by a factor of two in OECD Europe, by 3.5 in Japan and by 1.6 in North America. The average level of motorisation is now about 80 cars per 1 000 inhabitants worldwide but as much as 550 in the United States and 330 and 250 in OECD Europe and in Japan respectively. The stock of commercial vehicles in use also grew during this period. (Figure 33)

The growth of the vehicle stock was accompanied by structural changes significant to the environment:

- A progressive introduction of cleaner vehicles;
- A growing number of diesel vehicles, particularly in Europe;
- An increase of the share of heavy duty trucks in the stock of commercial vehicles in almost all countries.

Over the period 1970 to 1988 the total distance travelled each year by passenger cars grew. (Figure 34) Average vehicle use (in terms of kilometres travelled per year) is, however, decreasing because of the extension of multiple vehicle households (since second or third cars are used less than the first), a stabilisation in the time spent on urban travel and some possible adaptation to motoring costs. North America shows especially high growth in both total distance and average distance travelled.

Energy consumption by road transport

Transport activities account for about 30 per cent of total energy consumption in OECD countries and are almost entirely dependent on oil. (See Chapter on Energy)

Road transport is by far the biggest energy consumer within all transport sectors (82 per cent of total consumption by transport), whereas air, rail and inland navigation respectively account for 13 per cent, 3 per cent, and 2 per cent. Oil demand by the road transport sector is determined by three major factors: the vehicle stock, the distances travelled, and the fuel efficiency of the fleet.

In the past two decades road transport has become an increasingly important determinant of the level of oil consumption, and its share will continue to increase. In OECD countries, for example, the road transport sector accounted for 714 MTOE, or 48 per cent of total final oil consumption in 1988, compared with 445 MTOE, or 34 per cent, in 1970.

Since 1970 progress has been made in the area of fuel efficiency, and average oil consumption per vehicle-kilometre was markedly reduced as a consequence of the two oil shocks in the 1970s. Although several countries introduced voluntary or mandatory fuel efficiency standards for passenger cars, motor vehicle oil consumption in OECD countries increased by 61 per cent between 1970 and 1988. The main reasons for that increase were the continued growth of road traffic (by 86 per cent over the same period), the growth of the motor vehicle stock (by 94 per cent), and the easier oil market situation in the late 1980s which reduced the rate of decline in oil consumption by cars.

With regard to gasoline consumption by road transport, there has been an average increase of about 38 per cent in industrialised countries since 1970. The growth in gasoline consumption was particularly high in Japan (97 per cent) and relatively low in North America (28 per cent).

With regard to diesel fuel consumption by road transport, the trends over the last two decades show an even higher rate of increase than for gasoline (191 per cent), thus reflecting the continuous increase of the diesel vehicle stock in many countries. The share of diesel in oil consumption by road transport is particularly high in Japan (42 per cent in 1988), but also in OECD Europe (40 per cent in 1988). In North America, however, diesel accounts for only about 17 per cent. (Figure 35)

Emission control for motor vehicles

In order to protect public health and the environment, regulations on motor vehicle exhaust and noise have been introduced. In terms of exhaust emissions, engine modifications such as increasing the air/fuel ratio and delaying ignition timing have been the main devices used to meet emission control standards, especially at the early stage. Recirculating part of the exhaust gas back into the incoming air/fuel mixture (EGR) is also frequently used as a technique for lowering NO_x emissions. However, tighter emissions standards require other techniques and exhaust after-treatment devices such as catalytic converters and thermal reaction. Today virtually all passenger cars sold in Canada, the United States and Japan are equipped with three-way catalyst converters. While various technical problems associated with reducing emissions from gasoline-fueled vehicles have been solved, diesel-fueled vehicles are receiving more attention because they are significant sources of particulates and NO_x. (See Chapter on Air)

As regards noise emission control technologies, the most successful include:

- Redesign of the engine for lower engine speeds and greater displacement;
- Redesign of engine structure and configuration;
- Engine encapsulation. (See Chapter on Noise)

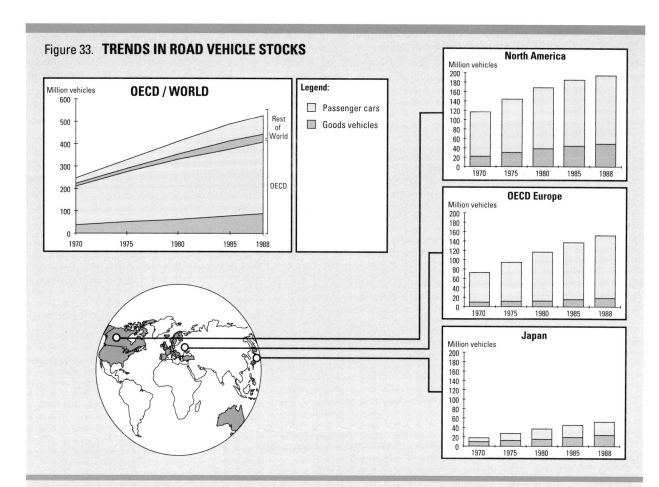

Figure 33. **TRENDS IN ROAD VEHICLE STOCKS**

	Passenger Cars in Use			Goods Vehicles in Use			Vehicles/1000 inhabitants	
	1970	1988	1970-1988	1970	1988	1970-1988	1988	1988
	1000 vehicles		% change	1000 vehicles		% change	Passenger cars	Total Motor Vehicles
Canada	6 600	11 930	81	1 440	3 590	149	460	600
USA	89 240	137 280	54	18 800	42 180	124	560	730
Japan	8 780	30 780	251	8 280	21 440	159	250	430
France	12 280	22 520	83	2 070	4 360	111	400	480
Germany *a*	13 940	28 580	105	1 030	1 330	29	470	500
Italy	10 190	25 250	148	900	1 990	121	440	490
UK	11 800	20 900	77	1 660	1 956	18	370	400
North America	95 850	149 220	56	20 240	45 780	126	550	720
OECD Pacific	13 480	39 820	195	9 400	23 850	154	280	450
OECD Europe	63 880	136 480	114	8 150	15 800	94	330	380
OECD	173 210	325 520	88	37 790	85 430	126	390	500
World	193 520	405 700	110	52 850	121 600	130	81	100

Note: a) Includes western Germany only.

Source: OECD

Figure 34. TRENDS IN ROAD TRAFFIC

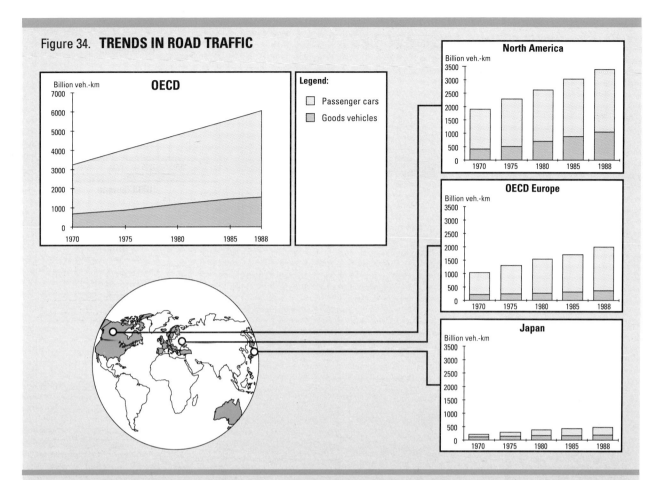

	Passenger Cars			Goods Vehicles			Total Traffic per capita
	1970	1988	1970-1988	1970	1988	1970-1988	1988
	billion veh.-km		% Change	billion veh.-km		% Change	veh. km/cap.
Canada	101	153	52	24	66	173	8 510
USA	1 434	2 240	56	345	927	168	13 110
Japan	121	322	167	100	166	66	3 920
France	165	305	85	42	90	117	7 140
Germany *a*	201	377	87	27	37	37	6 780
Italy	123	237	93	23	45	99	5 060
UK	141	270	92	35	54	55	5 740
North America	1 535	2 394	56	370	993	168	12 670
OECD Pacific	194	448	131	118	208	76	4 570
OECD Europe	856	1 647	93	178	335	89	4 930
OECD	2 584	4 489	74	666	1 536	131	7 420

Note: a) Includes western Germany only.

Source: OECD

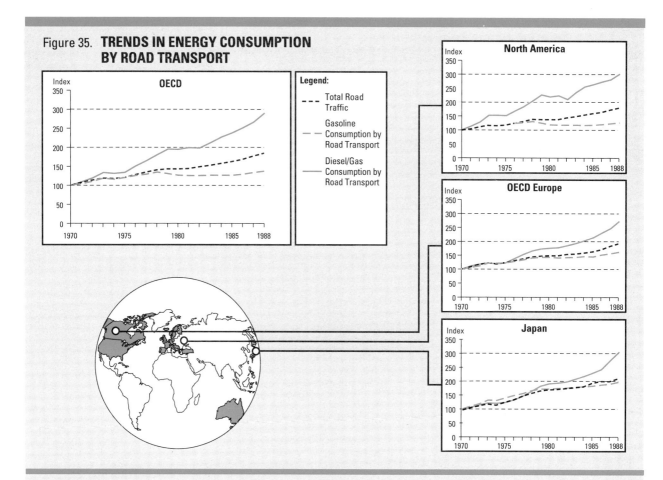

Figure 35. **TRENDS IN ENERGY CONSUMPTION BY ROAD TRANSPORT**

| | Energy Consumption by Road Transport | | | | | | Total Road Traffic | | |
| | Gasoline Consumption | | | Diesel/Gas Consumption | | | | | |
	1970 MTOE	1988 MTOE	1970-88 % Change	1970 MTOE	1988 MTOE	1970-88 % Change	1970 billion veh-km	1988 billion veh-km	1970-1988 % Change
Canada	21.0	26.8	28	1.1	6.0	447	125.9	220.8	75
USA	256.0	326.5	28	22.8	66.2	191	1787.3	3228.7	81
Japan	15.8	31.1	97	7.5	23.3	210	226.0	480.9	113
France	13.1	19.9	51	4.4	14.5	233	208.0	399.0	92
Germany *a*	16.8	28.1	67	6.7	14.2	112	234.2	416.5	78
Italy	9.6	12.5	31	4.0	15.0	279	146.4	290.8	99
UK	15.2	24.9	63	5.2	9.7	86	178.9	327.5	83
North America	277.0	353.4	28	23.9	72.2	203	1913.2	3449.5	80
OECD Pacific	25.0	40.3	61	16.8	32.6	94	318.2	650.4	104
OECD Europe	76.7	124.3	62	31.0	84.2	172	1056.9	2026.1	92
OECD	378.7	523.6	38	63.3	183.8	190	3288.3	6126.0	86

Notes: MTOE = Million Tonnes of Oil Equivalents.
   a) Includes western Germany only.

Source: OECD

Table 17. **TRANSPORT AND THE ENVIRONMENT: SELECTED INDICATORS**

		Canada	USA	France	Western Germany	Italy	UK	Japan	North America	OECD Europe	OECD
INFRASTRUCTURE											
Motorways	% change[a]	170	55	323	95	55	182	513	61	146	81
ROAD VEHICLE STOCK	% change	92	66	87	104	151	68	198	68	111	94
Total ownership	Veh./1 000 inh.	600	730	480	500	490	400	430	720	370	500
TRAFFIC											
Total road traffic	% change	75	81	92	78	99	83[b]	113	80	92	86
Road freight traffic	% change	107	70	69	94	179	47	79	72	105	84
Rail freight traffic	% change	11	30	−23	−17	8	−26	−63	27	−6	21
ENERGY CONSUMPTION											
Total final energy consumption by the transport sector											
Total	MTOE	42	482	40	49	32	43	66	523	254	868
of which: Air	%	11	15	9	10	5	15	4	15	11	13
Road	%	80	82	86	87	91	80	85	82	83	82
Rail	%	5	2	3	3	2	2	4	3	3	3
Diesel consumption by road transport	% change	447	191	233	112	279	86	210	203	172	191
Share of total	%	18	17	42	34	52	28	42	17	40	26
NOISE FROM ROAD TRAFFIC											
Population exposed to > 65 dB	Million	2	17	9	8	10	6	37	19	63	120
AIR POLLUTION											
Share of transport emissions in total emissions											
NO_x	%	61	41	76	65	52	49	44	43	60	49
CO	%	66	67	71	74	91	86	..	67	78	71
HC	%	37	33	60	53	87	32	..	33	50	39
SO_x	%	3	4	10	6	4	2	18	4	4	4

Notes: a) All "% change" data cover the period 1970-1988. Other data refer to 1988 or the most recent year available.
   b) England and Wales only.
Source: OECD

3. CONCLUSIONS

Over the past 20 years, transport activities in OECD countries have grown in three ways:

- New infrastructures: motorway length expanded by 61 per cent in North America, 150 per cent in Europe, and 500 per cent in Japan;
- Vehicle stocks: the number of road vehicles grew by about 70 per cent in North America, 100 per cent in Europe, and 200 per cent in Japan;
- Traffic volume: road traffic, for example, grew by 80 per cent in North America, close to 100 per cent in Europe, and 130 per cent in Japan.

Despite the overall expansion of the transport sector, some progress has been made over the past two decades in the implementation of environmental, energy and transport policies:

- Motor vehicle standards and technology in industrialised countries advanced with the

TRANSPORT AND THE LOS ANGELES AIR QUALITY MAINTENANCE PLAN

A Serious Air Pollution Problem

The Los Angeles region has 13.5 million residents, a population greater than all but two of the states in the United States. The most serious air pollution problems in the entire country are found in this area. Maximum ozone and carbon monoxide levels exceed by nearly three times the national standards set to protect public health. Poor atmospheric ventilation, frequent sunshine and bordering mountains combine to produce record-breaking air pollution levels in a basin that long ago exceeded its carrying capacity. While individual automobiles emit fewer of the traditional pollutants than in the past, booming population increases and even greater growth in vehicle use make mobile sources responsible for roughly 87 per cent of carbon monoxide emissions, 59 per cent of the nitrogen oxides and 46 per cent of the hydrocarbons. By the year 2010 the number of vehicles is expected to increase by 35 per cent, but vehicle usage will grow by twice that amount as more affordable housing is sought at a greater distance from the workplace.

An Ambitious Management Plan

In the absence of preventive policies, these trends will exacerbate current pollution and congestion problems, thus presenting a major challenge to air quality and planning agencies. In response, these agencies have developed the Air Quality Maintenance Plan. The transport component of this plan proposes radical changes to mobility, private auto usage, travel behaviour and patterns, and development trends. The overall objective is the attainment of federal air quality standards within 20 years. To achieve this three categories or "tiers" of measures are envisaged:

- Tier 1 transport measures will expand application of known control technologies and management approaches. For example, a Trip Reduction ordinance affecting 8000 employers region-wide and aiming to increase average occupancy of employee automobiles by a minimum of 35 per cent was implemented in 1988;
- Tier 2 transport measures comprise demonstrated but not yet widely applied controls and "on the horizon" technologies requiring further advances in the near future. They focus on widespread use of both technologies and vehicle fuels which result in lower emissions, and could include conversion to clean fuels such as methanol or electric power. Specific goals are to ensure that, by the year 2000, 40 per cent of passenger vehicles, 70 per cent of freight vehicles and 100 per cent of buses are low-emitting and to achieve a 50 per cent reduction of off-road vehicle emissions;
- Tier 3 transport measures will rely on technologies anticipated in the more distant future: for example, conversion of almost all automobiles to electric power.

Technological measures cannot by themselves solve the region's air quality problems. Behavioural and lifestyle changes will also be needed and measures designed to encourage such changes are included in the plan. For example, a mobility plan includes measures which aim to eliminate three million daily work trips by encouraging work-at-home and telecommuting. Through

PROJECTED AIR QUALITY TO 2010

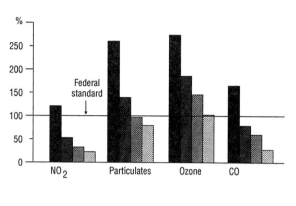

■ No new controls
▨ Tier 1
▧ Tier 2
▒ Tier 3

growth management measures, development patterns and powers would be radically shifted. The future distribution of housing and employment would be altered by regional policies aimed at reducing vehicle congestion and emissions and would no longer be determined solely by local governments.

Implementation: A Challenge for Policy-makers and Citizens

While Tier 1 measures of the Air Quality Maintenance Plan are being implemented, Tiers 2 and 3 are a complex collection of planned but uncertain future actions. Several kinds of uncertainties will have to be addressed in such a future-oriented undertaking; these include: whether new technologies and fuel systems can be developed and implemented; willingness of local governments to manage growth consistent with regional goals; and perhaps most importantly, securing public support for the more controversial yet-to-be-developed measures. It is also important to ensure that emission reductions realised in the Los Angeles region are not achieved at the expense of another region, i.e. by transferring pollution elsewhere.

The planning process has raised basic questions about the quality of life in an urban area -- about the inter-relationships and trade-offs between economic development, air quality and transport. The measures eventually implemented will reflect how Los Angeles residents choose to balance their environmental, mobility and economic concerns.

Contribution from the United States

implementation of standards for air pollution (CO, NO_x, HC) and their progressive tightening. Significant declines in CO and HC emissions have been achieved in Canada, the United States and Japan, and lead levels have fallen appreciably almost everywhere. In the case of noise, progress on emission standards has been slow, and has not compensated for the increase in noise due to the growth in traffic volumes;

– Environmental impact assessment is now fairly common practice in the design of new infrastructure projects, and has helped prevent environmental disruption.

Motor vehicle fuel efficiency and fuel quality have improved:

– Actual average energy consumption per vehicle has been markedly reduced as a consequence of the oil crises in 1973 and 1979 through major technological improvements in the energy efficiency of vehicles. However, recent evidence shows that these improvements have not continued, partly because of changes in the fleet structure and partly because of the decrease in the price of fuel. With regard to fuel quality, the lead content of petrol has been reduced and most countries have already introduced unleaded petrol. This has contributed to reducing lead emissions and thus reducing the exposure of the population to lead;

– Transport systems management has also contributed to environmental progress through public transport development, particularly in Europe and Japan, car traffic management, and the creation of pedestrian and traffic quiet zones in urban areas.

At the beginning of the 1990s, however, and despite this progress:

– The contribution of the transport sector to total emissions of air pollutants is higher than in the past, and high compared to the contribution of other sectors;

– In urban areas, people are exposed to high levels of ozone and noise, and inside their vehicles they are also subjected to high levels of pollution from traditional air pollutants;

– Regional and global pollution problems, to which the tranport sector contributes substantially, are of growing concern;

– The stock of vehicles and related traffic volumes grow continuously, leading to excessive levels of traffic congestion in urban areas and around major air hubs.

These problems have received a greater impetus in recent years with renewed sectoral growth, and they are expected to continue. They are accompanied by structural changes with immediate environmental implications:

– The rapid increase in the number of diesel vehicles, including heavy duty trucks;

– The growth of road transport in absolute and relative terms.

Faced with these prospects of environmental damages, congestion and financing difficulties, the development of the sector will be sustainable if and only if transport and environmental policies are better integrated. This implies:

– Some containment of the growth of traffic demand, particularly for road transport;

– Adjustments in sectoral structures (increasing the shares of more environmentally friendly modes, and adapting fiscal charges on vehicles, fuels and the use of vehicles);

– Technological progress in the short and long terms to achieve quiet, clean and energy-efficient vehicles;

– Developing a sound economic approach based on the polluter pays principle, reducing overall subsidies and eliminating charges and taxes inconsistent with environmental and economic efficiency;

– Rigorous implementation of the legislation and measures adopted.

REFERENCES

OECD (1975), *Better Towns with Less Traffic*, Paris.

OECD (1978), *The Automobile and the Environment*, MIT Press, Cambridge.

OECD (1979), *Urban Transport and the Environment*, 3 volumes, Paris.

OECD (1979), *The Cost and Effectiveness of Automobile Exhaust Emission Regulations*, Paris.

OECD (1982), *Photochemical Smog – Contribution of Volatile Organic Compounds*, Paris.

OECD (1983), *Report from a Workshop on Polycylic Aromatic Hydrocarbons*, Paris.

OECD (1983), *Long-Term Outlook for the World Automobile Industry*, Paris.

OECD (1983), *Impacts of Heavy Freight Vehicles*, Paris.

OECD (1985), *Environment and Economics*, Paris.

OECD (1985), *The State of the Environment*, Paris.

OECD (1989), *Compendium of Environmental Data 1989*, Paris.

OECD (1985), *Report of Toxic Substances in the Atmosphere: Benzene*, Paris.

OECD (1986), *Environmental Effects of Automotive Transportation*, Paris.

OECD (1978), *Reducing Noise in OECD Countries*, Paris.

OECD (1980), *Noise Abatement Policies*, Paris.

OECD (1986), *Fighting Noise*, Paris.

OECD (1988), *Cities and Transport*, Paris.

OECD (1988), *Transport and the Environment*, Paris.

ECMT/OECD (1990), *Transport Policy and the Environment*, Paris.

Chapter 13

ENERGY

Energy is a major component of OECD economies, both as an industrial sector in itself and as an essential factor input to most other economic activities, whether it be agriculture, industries or services, including transport.

Energy also plays an essential role in the everyday life of citizens, heating their houses and supplying power for most domestic services (household appliances and other electrical goods), as well as providing them with the capacity to travel to their workplace and business or holiday activities.

Furthermore, energy plays an important economic and political role in the world context, as a major "raw material" traded worldwide. The locations of major energy resources, such as oil, gas and coal fields, relative to the large consuming countries, give rise to complex relationships between producers and consumers.

Finally, energy is directly concerned by worldwide preoccupations with sustainable development and the "greenhouse effect", as well as energy security and economic growth.

The energy sector refers here to the extraction, conversion, transport and consumption of energy and the disposal of energy wastes; it also encompasses coal and other solid fuels, oil, gas, nuclear power, hydropower and other renewable energies (such as solar, wind, tidal, and biomass energies) and their conversion products such as electricity. In this chapter, only energy consumption from electricity generation will be covered in some detail; the utilisation of other energy sources for different end uses is described elsewhere. (See Chapters on Agriculture, Industry and Transport)

Environmental issues related to the use of energy are discussed in the sections concerned. (See Chapters on Global Atmospheric Issues, Air, Inland Waters, Marine Environment, Land and Solid Waste)

This chapter initially reviews the major trends of environmental significance in the energy balance of OECD countries and in the energy sector; it then goes on to consider the environmental concerns related to energy production and use.

1. ENERGY CHANGES: TRENDS AND PROSPECTS

***Growth in energy requirements
and indigenous energy production***

The trends in energy requirements and consumption in OECD countries over the last two decades, as well as those relating to national production and net oil imports, are attributable to three major factors: the price of energies and especially of oil; economic growth, technological and structural changes in OECD economies; and the energy policies pursued in OECD countries, particularly those aimed at energy conservation. Environmental issues and public debates on energy policies (e.g. the Chernobyl accident, greenhouse effects) have also played an important role in many countries, especially in recent years.

The beginning of the 1970s saw the end of a period of fast economic growth and low energy prices in the OECD area. The rate of increase in energy requirements and consumption, the volume of oil imports (which had expanded rapidly up to the beginning of the 1970s) were all slowed down by the first major oil price rise in 1973. The upward trend then resumed until the second big oil price hike in 1979. After that, slower, and in some cases, negative growth in OECD economies led to another downturn. Since the mid-1980s and until 1990 however, the energy scene has been dominated by the restoration of economic growth in OECD countries and little progress in energy intensity.

As a consequence of these trends, total energy requirements, defined as the total energy needed for both final use and for energy transformation (e.g. from fossil fuel to electricity), did not rise regularly over the past two decades: two periods of decline, after the two oil price shocks, punctuated the periods of growth. Overall, the total energy requirements of OECD countries have increased by almost 30 per cent over 20 years. (Figure 36) Total final energy consumption followed a similar pattern over the period.

With oil prices high and newly- or recently-developed sources of different types of energy in OECD countries (oil and gas in the North Sea and Alaska, nuclear energy in France, for instance) reaching operational maturity, the indigenous energy output of OECD countries expanded, especially in the mid-1980s. Total production is now almost 40 per cent higher than in 1970. (Figure 37) Oil imports by OECD countries, which grew slowly but not regularly during the 1970s, fell back in the mid-1980s, but then picked up again towards the end of the decade.

The consequences of these energy trends on the environment are not easy to describe in general terms, since they also depend upon the mis of energy sources, the technologies adopted and the policies implemented to control pollution and risks. Nevertheless, it may be possible to draw some general conclusions as to the environmental impact of some of these energy changes, especially as regards indigenous energy production.

The growth in indigenous energy production in OECD countries over the last 20 years means that a higher proportion of this part of the energy sector activity is now taking place within OECD countries or in nearby marine areas. In fact almost all the increase in primary energy requirements by OECD countries over the past 20 years has been covered overall by a 40 per cent increase in energy production in OECD countries. (Figures 36 and 37) Over the same period, total imports of primary energy from non-OECD countries remained stable but with increased imports of gas and decreased imports of oil.

Over the last two decades there have been increases in the OECD countries' production of all fuels, although at very different rates: the fastest growth has been in nuclear energy production, coal and oil. (Figure 37) There have also been marked differences between countries, with, for instance, Norway and the UK boosting oil and gas production; Australia and the USA, coal production; and France, nuclear power production.

As a result, there have been shifts in the type and sometimes the magnitude of the environmental effects of the energy sector. There have been changes, for instance, in environmental risks and the types of pollutants emitted, as well as occupational risks to workers, mainly relating to coal production and nuclear energy. The location of risks and pollution has also shifted: over

the past 20 years, energy production has developed and intensified in formerly unexploited wild life and natural areas – for instance, oil production in the North Sea, Alaska or coastal waters. (See Chapters on Land and Marine Environment)

Hence, OECD countries are potentially faced with risks and pollution which would otherwise be supported by non-OECD exporting countries, had the ratio of imports to indigenous production of energy remained unchanged since 1970. On the other hand, the pollution and risks at the energy production and transport stages are usually under better control in OECD countries than in many developing countries. All in all, therefore, those "shifts" in environmental effects around the planet may be beneficial to the world environment as a whole.

The contribution of environmental policies and of public awareness

Environmental policies, which developed greatly over the past 20 years, as well as greater public awareness of environmental issues, have had a significant effect on energy policies.

Because many governments implemented new and stricter anti-pollution policies in the energy sector during the period, there have been substantial reductions in the emission of air and water pollutants from energy facilities in several countries, despite an increase in the level of activity. (See Chapters on Air and International Responses) Further action is planned in several countries, including Canada, Sweden, Switzerland, the USA and the European Community, regarding power plants and large industrial and domestic boilers.

Technological change has also had a major impact. Alongside the effects of environmental policies and economic changes, new anti-pollution technologies and industrial processes have had significant, and almost always positive, consequences for the rate of pollutant emissions associated with a given activity. This is particularly true of technologies such as sulphur control in coal and oil use. Further improvements are possible through a more general use of those technologies and the implementation of recently developed ones such as fluidised bed combustion. (See Chapter on Industry)

General policy instruments such as environmental impact assessment are now better integrated into the development of energy policies and investment, for instance when it comes to choosing technology or siting new energy facilities.

Major events, such as the Three Mile Island and Chernobyl accidents, have had significant impacts on the energy sector. First, they have led some countries to cancel the further development of nuclear energy or to carry out a comprehensive review of their nuclear policy. Second, through the growing concern for the safe use of nuclear energy, these events have brought

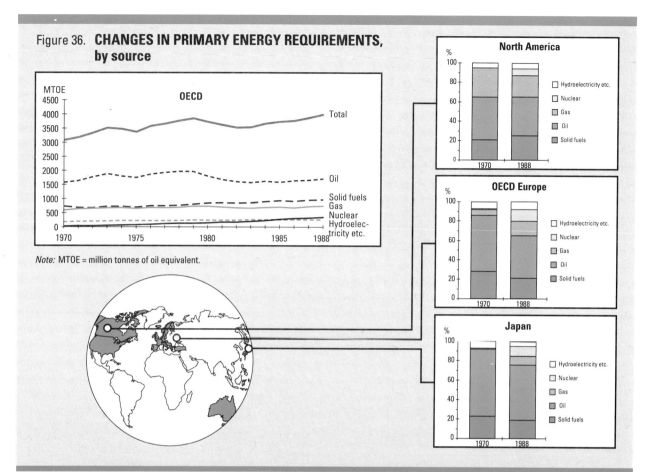

Figure 36. **CHANGES IN PRIMARY ENERGY REQUIREMENTS, by source**

Note: MTOE = million tonnes of oil equivalent.

	Changes 1970 - 1988, in MTOE						TOTAL 1988 MTOE
	Coal	Oil	Gas	Nuclear	Hydro [a]	TOTAL	
Canada	17.4	6.4	22.6	18.3	33.1	85.8	249.5
USA	201.0	99.6	-70.2	119.6	-3.3	277.1	1 928.4
Japan	12.0	41.8	34.6	38.9	3.8	104.0	398.8
France	-15.8	-7.7	15.5	60.3	4.8	53.7	208.9
Germany [b]	-14.8	-11.6	32.7	31.1	0.7	34.8	274.1
Italy	4.2	7.1	23.5	-0.7	0.6	34.0	151.7
Netherlands	3.0	-4.6	15.0	0.7	0.0	14.7	64.5
Spain	7.3	19.0	3.2	11.0	1.8	35.2	84.6
Sweden	3.4	-12.7	0.3	15.5	6.5	12.8	56.2
UK	-23.0	-21.9	36.1	8.4	0.3	0.8	208.5
North America	218.4	106.0	-47.6	137.8	29.8	362.9	2 177.9
OECD Pacific	23.9	47.0	50.3	38.9	7.7	138.4	495.8
OECD Europe	-3.7	-18.8	141.5	144.9	36.3	287.3	1 329.3
OECD	238.7	134.2	144.2	321.7	73.7	788.6	4 002.9
World [c]	816.7	866.4	755.6	403.5	221.6	3 068.9	7 956.5

Notes: a) Hydroelectricity and other.
b) Includes western Germany only.
c) 1970 figure refers to a Secretariat estimate.

Source: OECD - IEA

Figure 37. TRENDS IN INDIGENOUS ENERGY PRODUCTION

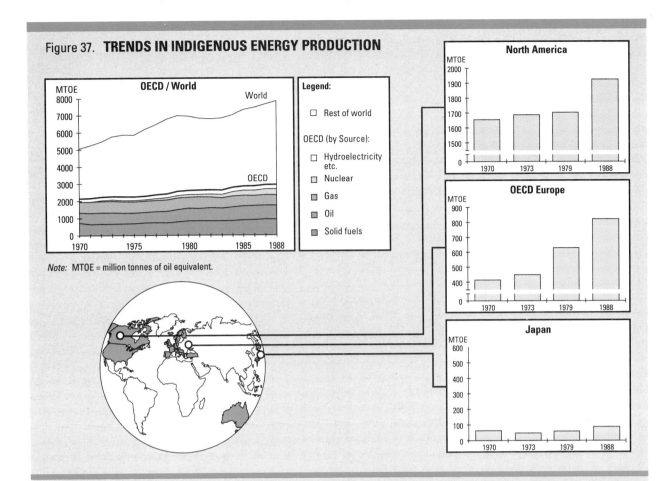

Note: MTOE = million tonnes of oil equivalent.

	Indigenous Energy Production (MTOE)				Changes (%)
	1970	1973	1979	1988	1970-1988
Canada	159.0	216.3	239.8	308.4	94.0
USA	1 475.2	1 478.6	1 546.7	1 616.0	9.5
Japan	50.6	39.2	48.2	70.6	39.5
France	50.3	42.4	49.2	98.4	95.9
Germany a	122.5	120.6	124.1	130.1	6.2
Italy	25.0	25.6	25.8	30.2	20.6
Netherlands	29.2	56.9	73.4	55.0	88.2
Spain	13.5	15.2	21.8	33.5	148.0
Sweden	12.2	17.4	22.3	36.9	202.4
UK	101.7	108.4	192.4	231.3	127.5
North America	1 634.2	1 694.9	1 786.5	1 924.4	17.8
OECD Pacific	103.7	114.1	142.7	223.2	115.2
OECD Europe	410.4	454.0	628.7	821.8	100.3
OECD	2 148.2	2 263.0	2 557.9	2 969.4	38.2
of wich: - Solid fuels	704.4	677.8	790.3	927.4	31.5
- Oil	642.0	662.1	714.2	800.8	25.5
- Gas	602.0	683.3	690.2	646.1	4.9
- Nuclear	16.3	42.0	125.2	338.0	1 810.8
- Hydroelectricity etc.	183.4	197.8	238.0	257.2	38.9
World	5 051.7	5 774.6	6 896.2	7 945.9	57.3

Note: a) Includes western Germany only.

Source: OECD -IEA

about (and will continue to spur) improvements both in nuclear reactors and in their safe operation, thereby reducing the risk of incidents and accidents. Improvements in the control and safety of oil or gas transport have also been implemented in the wake of major tanker accidents (Amoco Cadiz, Exxon Valdez).

Finally, public and governmental concern with regional and global environmental issues, which has grown enormously in recent years, is of utmost importance for the energy sector and future energy policies. Increasing pressure is being put on fossil fuel users to contribute to the reduction or prevention of problems such as the accumulation of CO_2 and other gases in the atmosphere and the related greenhouse effect. (See Chapters on Global Atmospheric Issues and on Air)

Improvement in the energy intensity of economies

During the 1970s and 1980s, and especially in the past 15 years, the relationship between economic growth and energy demand has weakened. Technological and structural changes in economies, higher energy prices and governments' energy conservation policies played a major role in modifying trends that existed up to the early 1970s. Energy intensity (measured as total energy requirement per unit of GDP) improved considerably in the most energy-consuming OECD countries and in the OECD as a whole over the period. Nevertheless, there have not been improvements in all countries, and since the mid-1980s the rate of improvement has tended to diminish. (Figure 38)

Energy prices played a major role. The improvement in energy intensity was triggered by the oil price shock of 1973, and given a further boost by the 1979 oil price rise. During the 1970s and early 1980s the price of oil was high, motivating governments to develop energy-saving programmes. After 1983, the real price of energy fell, first slowly, then sharply in the second half of the 1980s, and governmental energy-saving programmes were wound down. That sharp decline in oil prices, and the ensuing general reduction in most energy prices, made energy savings efforts less profitable in strict financial terms.

At the same time, environmental policies have in many cases reduced the environmental impacts of each unit of energy consumed. (See Chapters on Air, Inland Waters, and Marine Environment) However, continuing growth in energy demand has prevented total environmental stress from decreasing substantially. This means that the benefits for the environment have been less important than might have been expected had the efforts to improve the energy intensity of OECD economies continued at the same pace. Furthermore it is important to recognise that today the energy intensity of OECD regions varies considerably, from 0.45 in North America to 0.41 in Europe and 0.27 in Japan.

Further improvements in energy intensity will depend on a combination of factors, and there is still much uncertainty as to their relative importance. In most countries, the factors involved include the structure of industrial production (see Chapter on Industry) and the general and/or structural changes of economic activities, as well as changes in energy systems and in technologies. In addition to economic criteria such as the price of oil, energy markets and the rate of growth, governments' regulatory and fiscal policies and energy conservation policies will also play a major role.

While great efforts have been made and substantial energy savings have been achieved in the last 20 years, there is still considerable scope at the OECD level for further improving energy intensity under acceptable economic conditions and, for environmental reasons, this scope needs to be exploited. That would also enhance the safety of energy supply and reduce the risks of uncertain energy markets.

Structural changes in energy supply

Over this 20-year period, the relative roles of both oil and gas were largely reduced in the OECD's energy requirement balance, while the role of coal and nuclear energy steadily grew. These long-term trends nevertheless conceal widely varying responses to the oil price shocks, to the renewed growth of economies in the 1980s, and to oil price decreases observed at the end of the 1980s. (Figure 36) Nevertheless, by then all sources of energy were increasingly in use.

Energy consumption trends differed sharply from one country to another. The structure of primary energy requirements, i.e. the relative contribution of different sources of energy, changed over the two decades in accordance with trends in final demands by industry, transport and household. (See Chapters on Industry, Transport and Socio-Demographic Changes) These changes in the mix of energy were also related to the efforts made by each OECD country to develop its national energy resources so as to continue reducing its imports of oil wherever it was considered more economical to do so, and to diversify its sources of energy. The availability of national energy resources in each country played a significant role in these trends; this also appears clearly at OECD regional level.

Coal increased its share in most OECD countries (chiefly in the USA, Australia and some European countries), essentially in substitution for oil in the production of electricity, thanks to improvements in mine productivity, the development of national production of coal, the reduction of trade quotas and trade barriers for imported coal in several countries and technical advances that helped reduce the environmental consequences of its use. Coal consumption nevertheless declined in a few countries, particularly France, western Germany and the UK.

Oil use also expanded in some countries and diminished in others. In the USA, Japan, Greece and Turkey, for instance, oil energy requirements increased, whereas they declined in France, western Germany,

Figure 38. TRENDS IN ENERGY REQUIREMENTS BY UNIT OF GDP

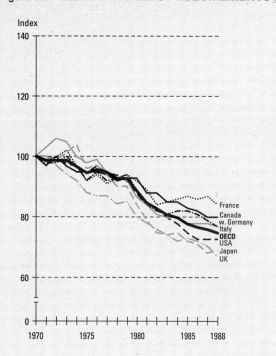

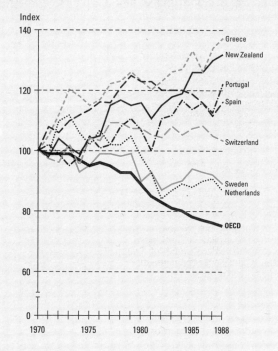

Notes: - Indices (base 100 in 1970) are calculated from the ratio: Total Primary Energy Requirements / Gross Domestic Product (GDP)

- GDP values are expressed in US$ at 1985 prices and exchange rates.

	Trends 1970 - 1988, Index 100 =1970							State TOE/1000 US$ [a]
	1970	1973	1975	1979	1980	1985	1988	1988
Canada	100	97	95	93	93	83	80	0.64
USA	100	98	95	92	88	75	73	0.44
Japan	100	101	96	90	84	72	69	0.27
Australia	100	97	99	99	98	89	87	0.47
N. Zealand	100	101	104	115	116	126	132	0.63
Austria	100	98	91	93	90	86	84	0.41
Belgium	100	100	89	91	83	75	74	0.53
Denmark	100	87	81	83	77	68	64	0.32
Finland	100	101	92	97	95	86	84	0.49
France	100	102	92	94	92	87	84	0.37
Germany [b]	100	100	92	94	89	82	77	0.41
Greece	100	120	115	126	123	133	137	0.58
Iceland	100	113	95	90	85	85	84	0.50
Ireland	100	99	87	92	86	80	79	0.48
Italy	100	105	98	92	87	78	77	0.32
Luxembourg	100	91	79	71	66	51	47	0.87
Netherlands	100	112	102	105	98	88	87	0.48
Norway	100	99	91	92	87	82	78	0.44
Portugal	100	95	105	111	107	114	122	0.67
Spain	100	110	113	125	123	119	116	0.45
Sweden	100	101	95	99	90	94	89	0.52
Switzerland	100	102	104	107	107	107	103	0.28
Turkey	100	161	154	156	163	158	161	0.79
UK	100	94	88	85	80	73	67	0.41
North America	100	98	95	92	89	76	74	0.45
OECD Pacific	100	101	97	91	86	74	72	0.44
OECD Europe	100	101	94	95	91	85	81	0.41
OECD	100	99	95	93	89	78	75	0.41

Notes: a) GDP expressed in 1985 prices and exchange rates.
b) Includes western Germany only.

Source: OECD - IEA

ELECTRICITY PRODUCTION AND DISTRICT HEATING IN HELSINKI

The manner in which energy is produced and used has important implications for the state of the environment. Electricity is one example. Often in the past, and still today, electricity production from fossil fuel is characterised by low efficiency and excess heat loss. Thus a need exists for more efficient energy production and utilisation processes.

Increasing Energy Efficiency through "Combined Energy Production"

In Finland, "combined energy production" normally refers to the joint production of electricity and heat for district heating. Thermal power plants are therefore conceived, wherever possible, so that they produce electricity together with heat, which is then used to heat offices, industries and households instead of being disposed of as waste heat. Significant improvements in energy efficiency are realised in this way.

Moreover, in the late 1960s and early 1970s, the efforts to develop peat as an indigenous source of energy led to the construction of peat-fired thermal power plants with combined energy production in areas where this source is more economical than imported oil or coal; peat now provides 20 per cent of the total energy used for combined energy production. The capacity of combined heat and power plants is such that they now produce, for all of Finland, more than 60 per cent of the total energy needed for district heating.

District Heating in Helsinki

The energy supply system in Helsinki is based primarily on the combined production of electricity and heat in three thermal power stations located in the city area. Combined production has been found to have two advantages: it is the most economical solution, permitting large-scale electrical and district heating systems, lower-than-average energy prices, and considerable fuel savings compared with conventional heating systems; and it allows closer control of environmental impacts.

District heating is expanding and by 1989, 95 per cent of the buildings in Helsinki which could be connected economically to the system had been integrated. Similarly, at the end of 1989, about 90 per cent of all buildings in Helsinki were supplied by district heating and in this same year district heating sales amounted to 5249 GWh. Small-scale systems, using oil or coal, designed to heat individual buildings or groups of buildings, were rapidly disappearing.

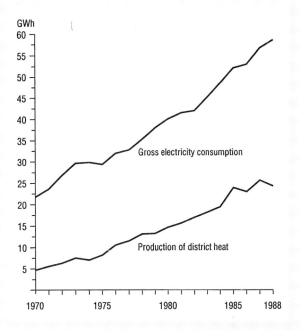

Energy Efficiency Yields Environmental Benefits

Recapturing and utilising waste heat from energy production makes sense in terms of economics, energy policy and environmental protection. Increased efficiency of energy use slows down depletion rates of non-renewable fuels, and can result in lower fuel imports. The environment benefits from the fact that combined heat and power production decreases both consumption and the amount of flue gas. Moreover, flue gases from district heating plants are filtered and diluted through high chimneys.

In the Helsinki metropolitan area, district heating has already had a positive effect on air quality. In 1989 combined energy production in Helsinki resulted in fuel savings equivalent to 390 000 tonnes of heavy fuel oil. Consequently, the emissions from energy production were clearly lower than would have been the case if combined energy production had not been used.

Contribution from Finland

Sweden and the UK. Gas energy requirements increased in almost all OECD countries but the USA; gas has been used in many countries as a substitute for oil and many national sources of gas have been exploited, as in the Netherlands, Norway and the UK. (Figure 36)

Nuclear power production has expanded the most in the USA, France and, to a lesser extent, western Germany and Japan, while the share of nuclear energy relative to other fuels has also greatly increased in other countries (Canada, Spain, Sweden and Switzerland). France is now the country where this form of energy plays the most important role in the overall national energy balance, a situation which allows significant exports of electricity to other European countries. Though its use in the OECD area grew sharply in the early 1980s, the strategic and economic choices concerning nuclear energy vary widely from one country to another.

The mid-1980s appear to have marked a high point for nuclear energy. In some countries, following the Chernobyl accident, governments had second thoughts about existing policies and/or public support for nuclear energy declined, while other countries confirmed their choice. Development of nuclear energy by the USA, Canada, Japan, France, and the UK is continuing, although rates of development are different. Decisions to develop nuclear energy further have been postponed in Italy and the Netherlands; in Italy a referendum organised in late 1987 showed broad opposition on the part of the public to further development of nuclear energy and even the wish to see its current minor role decrease. Opposition to nuclear energy has been confirmed in Austria, Australia, Denmark, New Zealand, Norway and Sweden.

The contributions of hydropower and other renewable sources of energy have increased slightly in OECD countries, which means their share of the overall energy balance fell slightly. In a few countries such as Canada, Norway and Sweden, the contribution of these sources increased significantly, however.

When considered at OECD or national level, the contribution of other renewable energy sources (geothermal, solar, biomass or wind energies) remains very low in all countries, and the potential for increasing their share of the energy balance significantly is still considered to be limited for most of them, essentially for economic reasons. Moreover, in many cases, there are technical, physical and environmental constraints which might ultimately discourage significant expansion of even economically viable renewables.

The consequences of these changes in the relative share of energy sources in the energy balance between 1970 and 1990 were considerable for the OECD as a whole, shifting the nature of environmental effects since these differ significantly from one source of energy to another. These changes have been particularly important in countries such as France, western Germany or the UK where the consumption of some energy sources declined over the period while that of other sources increased significantly. (Figure 36)

Development of electricity

The market share of electricity as an end-use energy source for industry, services and households increased in almost all OECD countries over the period. The volume of electricity produced almost doubled over the two decades. The structure of power generation has also shown a significant change, with the use of oil, gas and hydroelectricity decreasing while the shares of nuclear energy and coal have increased. (Figure 39)

The changes have varied considerably in OECD regions and in individual countries, illustrating differences in national energy strategies and in the availability of national resources. Coal's share in power generation has increased in the USA, Japan and Italy, while it has declined in France and western Germany. Oil's share has decreased in almost all countries and sometimes, as in Japan or Italy, by a very large percentage. The use of nuclear energy has increased in almost all countries concerned, especially in Belgium and France, but also in Japan, western Germany, Sweden and Switzerland.

The increasing share of electricity as an end-use energy form may have both desirable and less desirable impacts on the environment. For instance, shifts from fossil fuel to electricity in industry can have a beneficial effect on the environment, particularly if associated with utilisation of waste heat and with switching to low-polluting fuels like natural gas. This is also true of the commercial and residential sectors.

Nevertheless, these effects depend more generally on the type of the substituted fuel, the type of fuels used for electricity generation, the extent of emission control of alternative energy forms and the possible savings in end-energy by switching to electricity. Without such savings, primary energy demand generally rises with the production of electricity. Pollutant emissions can therefore rise or fall according to circumstances.

Energy "markets"

Throughout the 1970s and 1980s, the regulatory and fiscal context established by OECD governments and other countries had major impacts on energy markets – on their size, their evolution, and the way they operated. This is still true to a very large extent. In most countries, government policies still in effect mean that the energy markets still do not operate freely, although many steps in that direction have been taken. There remain, for instance, barriers in several European coal markets and the price of energy is still regulated at varying rates in a number of OECD countries. Moreover, new policies may be introduced. For instance, following the sharp decline in world oil prices in 1986, fiscal measures were taken in several countries for budgetary

Figure 39. ELECTRICITY GENERATED BY PRIMARY ENERGY SOURCE

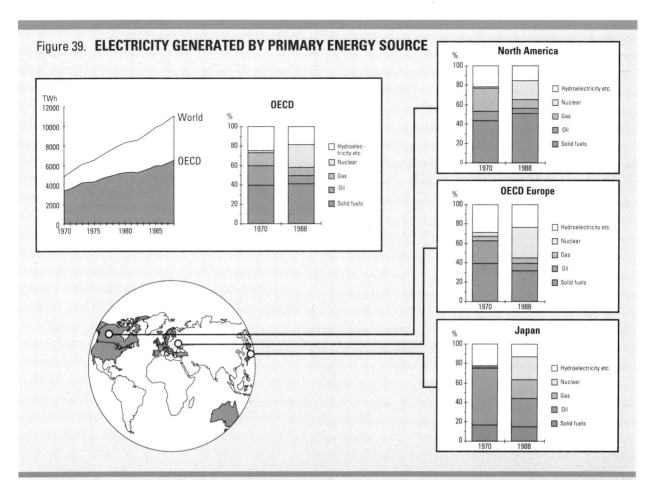

State 1988	Total Electricity Generated (TWh)	of which:				
		Solid Fuels	Oil	Gas	Nuclear Energy	Hydroelectricity + other
Canada	504.3	18.9%	2.4%	1.4%	16.4%	60.8%
USA	2 872.0	57.4%	5.5%	9.4%	19.5%	8.2%
Japan	753.7	14.9%	29.1%	19.4%	23.7%	12.9%
France	391.9	7.5%	1.5%	0.6%	70.3%	20.1%
Germany [a]	431.2	52.2%	2.6%	6.8%	33.7%	4.8%
Italy	203.6	17.1%	44.1%	15.9%	-	22.9%
UK	308.2	67.1%	9.5%	0.6%	20.6%	2.3%
North America	3 376.3	51.6%	5.1%	8.2%	19.0%	16.1%
OECD Pacific	922.7	23.8%	24.0%	18.0%	19.4%	14.8%
OECD Europe	2 179.4	33.5%	7.8%	5.6%	31.8%	23.3%
OECD	6 478.4	40.9%	8.7%	8.7%	23.4%	18.3%
World	11 046.6	63.0%			17.1%	19.9%

Changes 1970-1988 (in %)	Total	Solid Fuels	Oil	Gas	Nuclear Energy	Hydro + other
OECD	90.4%	97.7%	-18.0%	21.8%	1 924.0%	41.1%
World [b]	109.9%		78.5%		1 598.6%	75.7%

Notes: a) Includes western Germany only.

b) 1971 - 1988.

Source: OECD - IEA

or balance-of-trade purposes, but the overall effects of those policies on energy markets are not yet clear.

Uncertainty surrounds energy markets at both world and national levels, therefore, as regards not only the world price of oil but also the regulatory and fiscal policies of governments. Hence, both governments and private energy enterprises find it more and more difficult to develop clear long-term strategies.

This uncertainty may have negative impacts on the environment in that it generally reduces the means and the incentive, especially in private industry, to develop strong R&D activities including R&D for energy conservation, and to invest in anti-pollution equipment. For instance, research, development and demonstra-

tion resources for all but nuclear energy were reduced in the mid-1980s, under pressure from private oil companies coping with lower profits, from reduced public budgets and lower public priorities placed on the energy sector. On the other hand, uncertainty may also help to generate in public authorities a greater effort to intensify R&D so that countries can become less dependent on uncertain energy prices.

The relatively low world price of oil may also induce OECD countries to scale back energy-saving efforts and to rely proportionately more on imported energy, thereby reducing, in the latter case, indigenous production of energy and the related environmental consequences or risks within OECD countries.

2. ENVIRONMENTAL IMPACTS: APPRAISAL AND CHALLENGES

Major achievements

An analysis of changes in the energy sector and an assessment of environmental problems over the last two decades show that important progress has been achieved. In the seven largest OECD countries SOx emissions have decreased by 40 per cent and the growth of CO_2 and NOx emissions have been limited over a 20-year period which witnessed a 26 per cent increase in energy requirement and a 73 per cent GDP growth. (Figure 40)

The most important reason has been the significant improvement in the energy intensity of most OECD countries, essentially related to structural changes in economic activities and to important energy savings over the period. The reduced energy intensity of OECD economies, added to environmental policies and technological improvements, led to significant reduction in the emission of traditional air pollutants such as SO_2 and particulates in several countries. (See chapter on Air) Similarly, other types of environmental policies, e.g. environmental impact assessment, have helped to improve control of environmental problems and risks related to new energy facilities. (See Chapters on Inland Waters and Marine Environment)

Environmental issues

Nevertheless, not all changes in the environmental impacts of energy have been positive ones; for instance, the emissions of some air pollutants, such as for NOx or CO_2, have not been reduced. Moreover, policy-makers are increasingly examining pollutants previously thought to be of lesser importance (e.g. methane) as well as longer-term strains on the environment. Numerous environmental problems have cumulative components or very long-term resilience aspects, such as acidification of soils and lakes, trace metal accumula-

tion in soil, or buildup of CO_2 in the atmosphere, and these have obviously increased over the period.

Finally, the energy/environment relationship in the 1990s needs to be assessed in a very different context than did the situation 20 years ago. This relationship has clearly shifted from the pollution-based approach of the early 1970s, to a global and system approach of complex interaction between economies, energy and the environment. This provides the context for an assessment of remaining or emerging environmental issues related to energy.

Today it is increasingly recognised that the energy/environment relationship must not be studied solely from the standpoint of the impact of energy activities on the environment. There is now a clearly articulated and generally increasing public and governmental concern about the implications both for energy activities (increased costs, perceived risks) and for economic activities. Energy, through its effects on the environment, is clearly one of the key variables of sustainable economic development.

It is evident, therefore, that environmental issues add a new dimension to the formulation of energy and economic policies and the development of the energy sector, besides those which already existed, such as energy prices and the security of energy supplies.

In this context, major environmental issues related to the energy sector can be summarised as follows:

- Potential climate change relating to the use of fossil fuels may have major impacts on the sea level, agricultural production and other aspects of human activity;

- Pollution arising from the combustion of fossil fuels, especially oil and coal, concerns mainly air, with pollutants such as SOx, NOx, hydro-

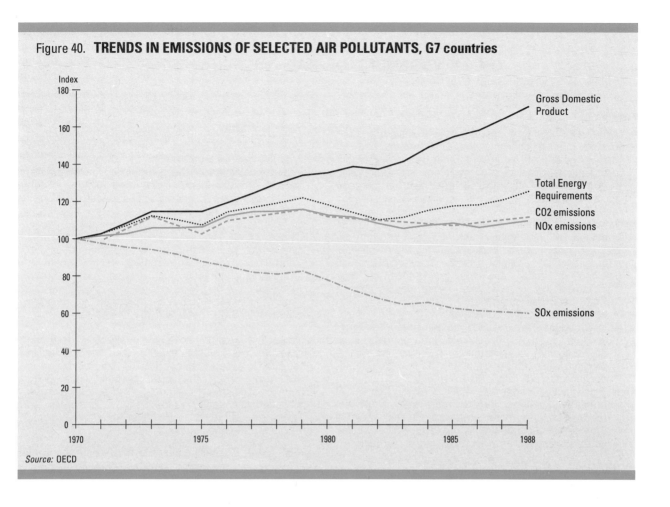

Figure 40. **TRENDS IN EMISSIONS OF SELECTED AIR POLLUTANTS, G7 countries**

Index

Gross Domestic Product

Total Energy Requirements

CO2 emissions

NOx emissions

SOx emissions

Source: OECD

carbons and others, e.g. trace elements released at the stack;

- High-level radioactive wastes for which long-term disposal policies have yet to be fully implemented. Although with the technology currently used in OECD countries the probability of a nuclear reactor accident causing a significant release of radioactive products into the environment is very low per reactor-year of operation, the number of reactor-years is growing and with them the probability of accidents; its consequences could be very serious for the workers, the population and the environment. Safe decommissioning of nuclear installations will also be important.

Other important concerns are:

- Risks to the health of coal miners and risks to other workers and the environment during the extraction of gas and oil, their transport in pipelines or tankers and during terminal operations;

- The release of oil products into fresh and sea water and the thermal pollution of rivers, as well as the salted and acid drainage from coal mines;

- The long-term safe disposal of low and intermediate radioactive wastes, since siting issues involve opposition from local populations;

- The extraction and processing of coal and uranium, which create land-use problems related to mines, waste tips, plants, and the transport of materials;

- Proper solid waste disposal, including ash and flue gas desulphurisation sludges, which is increasingly difficult and costly;

- Land consumption by hydro-electricity and other renewable sources of energy (e.g. flooding, firewood taken from forest land, solar collectors);

- Potential effects of exposure to the radiations of electro-magnetic fields from electricity distribution;

231

THE MANAGEMENT OF RADIOACTIVE WASTES

Limiting discharges of radioactive effluents from nuclear installations into the environment was an early goal of nuclear energy development programmes. One of the results of this systematic policy to reduce effluent discharges was an increase in the production of solid or solidified wastes which could not be diluted or dispersed readily into the environment. Thus, during the 1970s and 1980s, methods of managing such wastes had to be devised that would correspond to their inherent characteristics, chiefly their concentration of radioactive matter and the persistence of their radiological toxicity over time. These wastes can be divided into three categories:
- Low-activity short-lived wastes;
- Intermediate level wastes contaminated by long-lived radionuclides, essentially alpha emitters, such as plutonium and transuranic elements, which produce little heat because of their moderate concentration of radioactive elements;
- Highly active long-lived wastes consisting chiefly of irradiated fuel discharged from reactors (if not reprocessed in order to recover the residual uranium and plutonium) and highly active vitrified wastes produced after reprocessing of the fuel.

Regardless of the category to which they belong, all radioactive wastes are temporarily stored at production facilities, awaiting disposal with the following goals:
- Protecting the public and the environment -- both current and future generations -- from the possible effects of radiation exposure;
- Minimizing the ways in which the presence of radioactive waste repositories could limit the activities of future generations, especially where the exploitation of natural resources is concerned, and, more broadly speaking, respecting the general principles of environmental protection and ethics, in both the short and long term.

In practice, systems for the disposal of radioactive wastes were devised for each category of waste; these systems relied on containing the radioactive matter and isolating it from the natural environment.

Low-activity short-lived wastes

Their volume, the result of several decades of accumulation, can amount to several tens of thousands or even several million cubic metres, depending on the national programmes involved. Two types of installations have already been established or planned which take into account the relatively fast radioactive decay over time:

- Surface or near-surface installations. Through a system of institutional control measures to be carried out for a maximum of 300 years, and a strict verification of the composition of the waste, safety requirements can be met. Such installations are in operation in France, the United Kingdom and the United States;
- Underground installations built at a certain depth; since access is more difficult over a prolonged period of time, the need for institutional control and verification of the content of the waste in long-lived elements is limited. One such installation is operating in Sweden, and others are being constructed or are planned in western Germany, Switzerland and the United Kingdom.

Radioactive wastes packaged in specially designed containers were also dumped at sea (particularly in the Atlantic Ocean, under OECD control, between 1967 and 1982); the practice has since been suspended, following the adoption of a resolution by the contracting parties to the London Convention on the Prevention of Marine Pollution from the Dumping of Waste and Other Matters.

Intermediate and highly active long-lived wastes

Their chief characteristic to be taken into account is that the radioactive toxicity can persist over very long periods of time: several tens of thousands of years, or more. The systems used for isolating them have to be effective enough so that radionuclides can only be released gradually into the biosphere and in conditions such that they do not constitute an unacceptable radiation risk, even for populations living thousands of years from now. The containment system must comprise multiple and relatively independent barriers with a certain degree of redundancy, so as to ensure a quasi-total confinement for times of between 10 000 to 100 000 years, or perhaps longer. Given the length of the containment period required, disposal systems must be passive, that is, long-term safety should not depend on human control or surveillance.

Various types of solutions have been suggested: sending radioactive wastes into space, nuclear transmutation (this involves destroying the long-lived radioactive nuclei by nuclear bombardment), and burial at great depths in stable geological formations either on land or under the ocean floor. Currently the burial of long-lived wastes in geological formations on land at minimum depths of several hundred metres is the only solution being seriously investigated. However, over ten years of research by the international scientific community, under the auspices of the OECD, have shown that sub-seabed geological formations could probably also provide satisfactory safety conditions.

National research programmes are currently investigating stable formations on land, such as granite, salt, clay, shale and tuff. In the first phase, considerable means were devoted to developing methods by which to investigate these geological formations so as to ensure that their stability was satisfactory and, particularly, that the risks of seismic activity and the flow of underground water (which constitute the main means by which radionuclides are transported) were reasonably small. In this context the OECD, in 1980, launched an international project in a former iron mine at Stripa (Sweden) in which nine OECD Member countries have participated. On the national level, "underground research laboratories" were also created for the purpose of conducting detailed research into the different types of formation that were envisaged. Aside from the Stripa project, such underground laboratories exist at Mol (Belgium), investigating clay; Grimsel (Switzerland) and the Lac du Bonnet (Canada) investigating granite; and Asse (Germany), investigating salt. In the future these undergound laboratories will be replaced by so-called "second-generation" laboratories whose chief aim will be to "validate" specific sites where repositories for long-lived wastes could be built.

The timetables for these programmes extend over several decades. The first facilities capable of receiving long-lived wastes either as irradiated fuel or as vitrified wastes are planned in France, Germany and the United States by approximately 2010. Although the specialists do agree that knowledge about disposing of nuclear waste in geological formations is now firmly established, they find it advisable to proceed with caution and to ensure that for each facility, the site, design and safety aspects are examined with the utmost care.

In this context, the emphasis is currently placed on two types of activities:
- Long-term safety studies and the use of scientific models to illustrate the potential long-term behaviour of radioactive waste repositories. Such modeling is the principal means of evaluating long-term safety. Considerable progress has been made through international multidisciplinary co-operation and today scientists have available adequate tools with which to analyse long-term safety;
- Field investigations and research, in underground laboratories and at the surface at potential sites, which gather data to be used in carrying out safety studies. Close international co-operation has been established in this area as well.

Prospects

The major technical and scientific difficulties facing radioactive waste management at the time the most important nuclear programmes were launched in the 1950s and 1960s have been or are about to be resolved, regarding low-activity short-lived wastes, and are in the process of being resolved regarding long-lived wastes. Concerning the latter type of waste, specialists are confident that deep, stable geological formations offering adequate isolation capability can be found.

The programmes now under way have two goals: to find suitable sites and to propose facilities in such a way that technical, safety and cost aspects are considered together and optimized. Timetables for repository development cover large spans of time and caution is being used in their implementation.

The most acute problems at this stage concern the way radioactive wastes are perceived by the public. Hence efforts have been made to inform the public more fully in order to improve general understanding. Progress is slow, however, even though all national programmes are now devoting considerable attention to informing and communicating.

Despite the intricate technical, scientific, social and political considerations involved, there is reason to believe that the problems of managing radioactive wastes will find practical and safe solutions by the beginning of the next century.

Source: OECD-NEA

Table 18. SELECTED ENVIRONMENTAL EFFECTS OF THE ENERGY SECTOR[a]

Energy sources	Air	Waters (surface, underground, inland and marine)	Land and soils	Wild life	Risks	Others: wates, human health, noise, visual impacts
FOSSIL FUELS EXTRACTION, TREATMENT, TRANSPORT, WASTE DISPOSAL						
COAL	SO_x, NO_x particulates CO_2 CH_4	Acid and salted mine drainage Mine liquid waste disposal Water availability Wash water treatment Water pollution from storage heaps	Land subsidence Land use for mines and heaps Land reclamation of open cast mines	Natural habitat disturbed Exploitation of wilderness or natural areas for surface mining	Occupational risks	Noise of rail transport of coal Dust emission Visual impact of coal heaps
PETROLEUM PRODUCTS	H_2S production SO_4, NO_4, CO_4, CO_3, HC_2, CH_4, ammonia, particulates, trace elements CO_2	Oil spills Water availability	Land use for facilities and pipes	Natural habitat disturbed Pipeline impact on wild life Wild life polluted through leaks or spills	Blowouts, explosions and fires	Odour Pipeline leaks Spills (accidental and operational) Visual impacts of pipelines
GAS	HC emission (mainly methane) NO_x, CO_2 H_2S and combustion emissions	Liquid residual disposal	Land use for facilities and pipes	Natural habitat disturbed Impacts of pipelines on wild life	Blowouts High leak potential General safety	Spills and explosions Visual impacts of pipelines
ELECTRICITY GENERATION FROM FOSSIL FUELS (excluding nuclear energy)						
	SO_2, NO_2, CO, CO_2, HC, trace elements, particulates, radionuclides Long-range transport and deposition of pollutants "Greenhouse effect"	Water availability Thermal releases	Land requirement	Secondary effects on water, air and land	Occupational risks	Visual impact of cooling towers and power lines Solid wastes Ash disposal Noise
URANIUM FUEL CYCLE AND ELECTRICITY FROM NUCLEAR POWER PLANTS						
	Radioactive dust Gaseous effluent (radionuclides, F, NO_x) Noble gas, H-3, I-131, C-14 Local climatic impact of cooling towers	Mine drainage Underground water contamination Water availability Thermal releases Liquid radionuclide emission (H-3, CO-60, Sr-90, I-131, Ru-106, Cs-136 and 137)	Land subsidence (mine) Land reclamation of open cast mines Land use for mines	Secondary effects of impacts on water, land and air	Occupational risks Plant accidents Disposal of high level radioactive wastes	Radioactive products Mine water Mill tailing water (toxic metal, liquid and solid chemical wastes, radiological wastes) Recycled fission products Visual impact of cooling towers and power lines Noise Decontamination and decommissioning of nuclear power plants

Table 18. SELECTED ENVIRONMENTAL EFFECTS OF THE ENERGY SECTOR[a] *(Cont'd)*

Energy sources	Air	Waters (surface, underground, inland and marine)	Land and soils	Wild life	Risks	Others: wates, human health, noise, visual impacts
RENEWABLE ENERGY						
HYDROPOWER	Local climatic effects of large installations	Effect on hydrological cycles Water quality and resources	Land irreversibly flooded Landslide risks	Wild life habitat of rivers Change in ecosystems Fish migration affected	Risk of dam rupture	Visual impacts
OTHERS: Biomass, geothermal, wind and solar energies	Biomass combustion: air pollution, particulates Geothermal: air pollution	Biomass conversion: water pollution ; water availability Geothermal: water pollution	Land use for energy plantations Land requirement of solar energy	Biomass: ecosystem disruption by energy plantations	Biomass risk to workers	Noise of wind generators Visual impact of wind generators Photovoltaic toxic pollution when decommissioning

Note: a) Excluding energy use in transport, agriculture (see chapters on Transport and Agriculture) and other uses (heating, etc.)
Source: OECD

— Environmental impacts of renewable energies other than hydro-power, which are generally felt to be limited, but which could nevertheless be important if these renewable energies were to be used on a large scale.

In addition, energy sector activities have other impacts on different components of the environment (air, water, land and soil, wild life, etc.). These may appear more limited, but they can be important at local level, raising problems of siting for large energy facilities. These impacts also concern solid wastes, noise and risk issues. (Table 18) The future development of environmental effects and issues will depend essentially on two aspects: future energy supply and demand, and future environmental and energy policies.

Future energy supply and demand

Forecasting future energy demand and supply at both world and OECD levels is clearly a difficult exercise when attempted in quantitative terms only. A qualitative review of major variables in this field is useful.

The analysis of past trends has shown that the energy situation in OECD depends on several such variables: the rate of growth of OECD countries' economies; the world price of oil, which itself depends on many factors, including strictly geopolitical ones; governmental policies, including environmental policies; and technological changes.

Furthermore, with the world concern for the long-term effects of energy on the environment (such as greenhouse effects), this forecasting analysis must now be performed at world level so as to better consider the relative weight of OECD energy production and consumption in a world context, along with other world regions or groups of countries. It must also take into account the consequences of the global dimension of environmental issues on policies such as development assistance, trade policies or transfers of technology.

At the world level, the major variables of the energy scene in the 1990s and in the early twenty-first century therefore appear to be:

— The relative economic growth and industrial development of the various regions of the world;
— The growth in population, which has a major impact on energy demand in developing countries when coupled with economic growth and with limited potential for energy savings;
— The relative energy intensity of economies, related to energy prices, technology changes and national energy policies;
— The long-term availability of different energy resources and energy prices; their spatial distribution throughout the world, and the relative capacity of countries to master their use (especially for nuclear energy);
— The relative constraints which environmental policies place on national energy policies, with specific impacts on different fuels in their production or consumption stages.

235

In the worldwide context it is important to stress that, over the long term, i.e. up to 2010-2020, the energy demand of developing countries may exceed the demand of the industrialised countries. The weight of the OECD, measured in total energy requirements, which was reduced from more than 60 per cent of the world total in 1970 to less than 50 per cent at the end of the 1980s, will fall still further in percentage terms, clear evidence that management of such global environmental problems as the greenhouse effect now has a worldwide dimension.

Future environmental and energy policies

The environmental consequences of the evolving energy situation will depend on the strength and speed at which technological changes and environmental policies are developed and implemented. The end of the 1990s and beyond will also see the full effects of environmental regulations and policies decided in the mid-1980s, in line with international agreements on SOx and NOx reductions.

Nevertheless in the short or medium term it can be expected that the increased reliance on indigenous sources of energy, except for oil, is likely to increase the pressures on the environment, as will the resumption of GDP growth, and reduced annual gains in the energy intensity of economies, compared to development in the 1970s and the early 1980s.

More generally, the uncertainty surrounding both the future rate of growth of the OECD and world economies and the future levels of world oil prices means that continuous improvements in the environmental impacts of the energy sector may depend more on explicit and reinforced environmental policies

Table 19. ENERGY AND THE ENVIRONMENT: SELECTED INDICATORS

		Canada	USA	France	Western Germany	Italy	UK	Japan	North America	OECD Europe	OECD	World
Total primary energy	MTOE	250	1 928	209	274	152	209	399	2 178	1 329	4 003	7 957
Requirements	% change[a]	62	22	35	16	32	–	49	26	29	30	63
Net oil imports	MTOE	– 19	341	86	114	90	– 38	230	322	402	958	. .
	% change	– 545	112	– 13	– 9	– 5	– 135	15	95	– 36	– 6	. .
Indigenous energy	MTOE	308	1 616	98	130	30	231	71	1 924	822	2 969	7 946
Production	% change	94	10	96	6	21	128	40	18	100	38	57
Total final consumption	MTOE	159	1 379	141	198	114	149	279	1 538	951	2 833	5 549
of energy	% change	45	14	15	13	31	3	40	16	23	21	. .
Electricity	TWh	504	2 872	392	431	204	308	754	3 376	2 179	6 478	11 047
generated	% change	141	77	167	78	73	24	110	84	90	90	128
Energy intensity	TOE/1 000 $	0.64	0.44	0.37	0.41	0.32	0.41	0.27	0.45	0.41	0.41	. .
(requirements/GDP)[b]	% change	– 21	– 27	– 16	– 23	– 23	– 33	– 31	– 26	– 19	– 25	. .
Air SOx	1 000 tonnes	3 800	20 700	1 335	1 306	2 070	3 600	835	24 500	13 200	39 900	99 000
pollutant	% change	– 43	– 27	– 55	– 65	– 27	– 42	– 83	– 30	– 42	– 38	. .
emissions: Particulates	1 000 tonnes	1 709	6 900	298	532	413	533	. .	9 000	4 000	13 000	57 000
	% change	– 16	– 63	. .	– 60	25	– 49	. .	– 57	– 43	– 52	. .
NOx	1 000 tonnes	1 943	19 800	1 766	2 872	1 570	2 513	1 176	21 700	12 700	36 600	68 000
	% change	42	8	34	21	11	5	– 29	10	25	13	. .
CO2	1 000 t. of C	124	1 433	103	198	108	163	272	1 557	886	2 793	6 256
	% change	32	19	– 18	– 5	17	– 13	25	20	4	15	32
Waste from nuclear fuel	Tonne of heavy metals	1 300	1 900	950	360	–	900	770	3 200	3 800	6 989	. .

Notes: a) "% change" figures refer to the period 1970-1988; all other data refer to 1988 or the latest available year.
b) GDP values refer to 1985 prices and exchange rates.
MTOE: Million Tonnes of Oil Equivalent; TWh: Tera Watt hours.
Source: OECD

236

adopted by governments when energy prices do not provide sufficient information to the consumers. On the other hand, economic expansion, structural changes, and relief from pressures of energy costs on budgets could permit the financing of preventive measures to benefit the environment in the longer term.

Therefore, and in the context of global issues, the environmental impacts of the energy sector will depend greatly on the future capacity of governments to:

– Better integrate environmental concerns into the development of energy policies at the earliest possible stage. This is of particular importance with respect to global environ-

mental problems related to energy, and will increasingly have to be accomplished in a world context;
– Adopt policies that anticipate and prevent environmental problems created by trends in the energy sector, and introduce and enforce environmental protection measures at all stages of energy production and use;
– Help develop environmental technology adapted to the energy sector;
– Encourage more efficient use of energy;
– Ensure that energy costs reflect the full environmental costs, with appropriate consideration for the costs borne by countries outside the OECD.

3. CONCLUSIONS

Over the past 20 years, economic growth has been much higher than energy demand growth and consequent environmental effects in OECD countries: while the GDP of those countries increased by 72 per cent, their energy requirements grew by 30 per cent and some environmental consequences have been reduced (by about 40 per cent in SO_2 emissions) or contained (+15 per cent in CO_2 emissions).

That development was due to:

– The emergence and implementation of environmental policies;
– Structural changes in the energy supply induced by changes in real energy prices and government energy policies; and
– Structural changes in OECD economies.

The following factors have played a major role in reshaping this relationship:

– Technologies needed to meet certain environmental concerns (such as sulphur control for coal or oil use) have been mastered and widely, although not yet fully, implemented;
– Continuous strengthening and broadening of environmental policies (such as environmental impact assessments and risk assessment studies) particularly in the 1980s, have helped the integration of environmental concerns into energy policies and projects;
– Improvements in the energy efficiency of OECD economies have been achieved (25 per cent overall), particularly in the years after 1973 and 1979. Although this progress did not extend to all countries nor to the latter part of the 1980s, it helped to limit the emission of pollutants. Energy efficiency is still considered to be the most cost-effective solution for

reducing the environmental effects of energy, and there is considerable potential in that regard at OECD level;

– The growing reliance on indigenous sources of energy (+38 per cent), within OECD countries or adjacent marine areas, increased a number of environmental impacts such as those associated with oil, coal and nuclear energy production;
– Shifts in energy use, mainly from oil to coal and nuclear energy, have changed the type, location and extent of the environmental impacts of the energy sector, with both positive and negative effects.

In the 1990s OECD countries will have to contend with major environmental issues related to energy production and consumption of a markedly changed nature:

– Concerns with traditional atmospheric pollution arising from the combustion of fossil fuels remain at local and regional levels (urban smog, acid rain), but are supplemented by:
– Concerns with global atmospheric pollution by greenhouse gases such as CO_2 with its potential impacts in terms of climate changes and further sea level rise, modified water cycles and agricultural impacts;
– Risks relating to the various stages of the nuclear fuel cycle and problems of disposal of high-level radioactive wastes for which long-term policies have yet to be implemented;
– Risks relating to fossil fuel extraction, transport and use such as risks to coal miners, oil spills from oil production, transport or refining.

The magnitude of these environmental impacts of the energy sector will largely depend on the rate of economic growth, geopolitical changes, and efforts by government, industry and households to save energy and implement cleaner and safer technology.

They also have to be placed in an international context of environmental, energy and economic interdependence. Through increased cost and/or risk perception for specific energy cycles or systems, these environmental impacts, if not contained, may become a limiting factor for energy development and therefore impair sustainable economic development.

Future demographic and economic growth in different regions of the world will lead to a decrease in the relative importance of OECD countries in the emission of pollutants related to energy, such as greenhouse gases. This suggests that it is of utmost importance to integrate environmental concerns into aid and development assistance policies, trade policies and international technology transfers.

REFERENCES

IEA (1985), *Electricity in IEA Countries, Issues and Outlook*, OECD, Paris.

IEA (1987), *Coal Environmental Policies and Institutions*, OECD, Paris.

IEA (1987), *Energy Conservation in IEA Countries*, OECD, Paris.

IEA (1987), *Renewable Sources of Energy*, OECD, Paris.

IEA (1988), *Electricity, Nuclear Power and Fuel Cycle in OECD Countries, New data 1988*, OECD, Paris.

IEA (1989), *Energy and the Environment: Policy Overview*, OECD, Paris.

IEA (1989), *Energy Balances of OECD Countries*, OECD, Paris.

IEA (1989), *Energy Policies and Programmes of IEA Countries, 1988 Review*, OECD, Paris.

IEA (1989), *Energy Statistics*, OECD, Paris.

IEA (1989), *World Energy Statistics and Balances*, OECD, Paris.

OECD (forthcoming, 1990), *Review of Energy and Environmental Policies*, Paris.

Chapter 14

SOCIO-DEMOGRAPHIC CHANGES

This chapter analyses the environmental impact of socio-demographic changes. Population, household structure, and time use patterns have changed very quickly during the past few decades in OECD countries. As a result, consumption and leisure activities, including tourism, have changed, with many immediate environmental consequences: exploitation of natural resources, increased disposal of wastes, landscape and ecological deterioration, congestion, extension of pollution and noise in time and space. Although the development of consumption and leisure patterns reflect economic and institutional conditions, they are socially determined and cannot be explained purely by economic rationality.

In addition, by posing new types of problems for which current policies have not been framed, the management of consumption and leisure activities will be a challenge for future environmental policies. Since emissions originating from consumption and leisure activities are more widely dispersed than emissions from stationary sources, they will be very difficult to manage and control. Traditional measures like economic incentives may turn out to be ineffective because of the many non-economic functions which consumption and leisure serve. In some cases, technological achievements on the one hand are cancelled out by socio-demographic developments on the other.

Environmental effects related to socio-demographic changes, often accompanied by profound economic changes, will not only be the subject of environmental protection policy but will also influence other policy sectors, such as urban planning and physical planning.

1. SOCIO-DEMOGRAPHIC CHANGES: TRENDS AND PROSPECTS

Slower population growth

Although since 1970 the total OECD population has grown by some 100 million people, during the same period of time the OECD population relative to the total world population has declined from roughly 19 per cent to 16 per cent. Thus, population growth within the OECD area has been very slow compared with population growth in non-OECD countries. The (unweighted) average annual population growth rate of OECD countries is now less than 0.7 per cent, reflecting the current remarkably low levels of fertility in the great majority of OECD countries. Some countries, mainly in Europe, have already reached or are approaching the zero population growth rate. As soon as the largest industrialised countries, i.e. Japan and the United States, reach stationary population growth, the growth of the total OECD population will be negligible.

Meanwhile, the population of some other parts of the world has doubled or will do so in a few decades.

The world's population reached the 5 billion mark in 1987 and is increasing by 80-85 million each year, whereas OECD countries needed some 15 years to add that number to their population. In many places in the Middle East, Africa and Latin America, the population has been growing at an explosive annual rate of 3 per cent or more. As nearly all of the additional inhabitants of developing countries earn their living directly from their physical surroundings, thus putting stress on the immediate environment, population growth will constitute one of the main obstacles to protecting the environment on a global scale and to integrating it with socio-economic development in a more sustainable way.

Ageing of the population and changing household structure

The slowing of population growth is accompanied by two significant socio-demographic trends common to almost all OECD countries: ageing of the population and an increase in the number of small households. Mainly because of low fertility and mortality rates, there has been an increase in the proportion of elderly people (defined as those aged 65 or more) over the past few decades. (Figure 41) This has caused an upward shift in the age structure of the population as a whole and of elderly people themselves. Between 1950 and 1980, the average proportion of people aged 65 or more grew over 40 per cent to reach 12.2 per cent. In the same period, life expectancy at birth increased, on average, by more than seven years. Although the pace of ageing varies from country to country, the trend is very clear.

Since the 1960s the average size of households has diminished drastically, especially in OECD countries with lower than average population growth. This trend is closely related to the ageing process. The proportion of the population in one-person households has more than doubled in most Member countries and amounts to one quarter or more of the total population in some countries: in the Netherlands, for example, the average size of household dropped from 3.2 in 1971 to 2.5 in 1985, and 22 per cent of the population was in one-person households by 1980. This development has been especially pronounced in urban areas: in Sweden and Switzerland the average size of households in urban centres has fallen below two, and nearly half of urban households in 1980 were one-person households.

Although the increasing proportions of old people and smaller households seem to have only a limited direct impact on the environment, their cumulative effects can be substantial. As they alter the composition of future populations and households, these changes extend their effects to the environment by creating new forms of time use, consumption, and related behavioural patterns. Ageing, for instance, can be expected to cause an increase in the proportion of people who spend more time at home and consume fewer waste-producing goods. Splitting the stock of households into smaller units may, on the other hand, result in an inefficient use of energy resources and encourage wasteful consumption patterns.

Diverse trends in urban areas

Urban populations account for 70-80 per cent of the total OECD population. The growth rates of urban populations have clearly been falling since 1970 in almost all OECD countries and the differences between Member countries in the levels of urbanisation have been narrowing. This general trend conceals, however, the considerable differences that exist in the urbanisation process within and between countries. In southern European countries, urbanisation levels have continued to rise and the trend has been a movement towards the largest cities. Even in those OECD countries where urbanisation has slowed down in general, the largest conurbations have continued to grow in some instances. To the extent that this development

has been attributable to rural-to-urban migration, it has contributed to further depopulation of the countryside in many OECD countries.

On the other hand, the deterioration of the urban environment has contributed to a counter-urbanisation process which can be seen in two trends:

- The on-going depopulation of many urban areas and especially of the *centres* of big cities in all OECD countries except Canada, Japan and the southern European countries;
- The growth of medium-sized urban areas in several OECD countries as people in inner-city areas move, not only to the suburbs, but also to smaller urban communities beyond the bounds of metropolitan areas.

It is clear that these trends in urban areas have interacting effects on the environment:

- The spatial expansion of the largest cities seriously conflicts with other uses of the surrounding land and will no doubt put additional stress on ecosystems outside these areas;
- As a result of increased traffic, congestion, higher pollution levels, littering, reduced green spaces and the loss of other environmental amenities, living conditions in many large urban areas in the OECD region have become worse in the past 20 years;
- By boosting interest in more single-family housing, counter-urbanisation may result in diminishing economies-of-scale, increase energy consumption and cause further dependence on public infrastructure; one result may be water shortages such as those that are occurring in the Southwest of the United States.

Social values and attitudes

People's attitudes and commitment to social goals and ideals determine their preferences and behaviour to a large extent. In recent decades, particularly in the Western industrial countries, the social trend towards liberal behavioural norms and conventions combined with an increased material well-being has been accompanied by an increase in interest in the environment. Opinion polls in several OECD countries show high levels of concern over the environment during the past two decades. Today, the public's support for environmental programmes appears stronger than ever, judging from the manner and degree of urgency with which environmental issues are addressed at the political level in many OECD countries.

People do not always seem to be willing to act on their preferences, however, either because they believe that an individual cannot influence matters very much or because they think that they may enjoy such collective goods as clean air without making any contribution themselves. In addition, people are not always fully

Figure 41. POPULATION TRENDS, 1970-1988

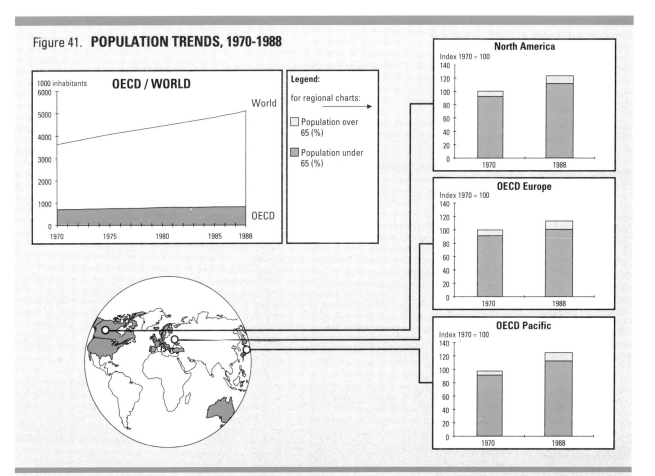

	Total Population		Population over 65	
	1000 inhabitants 1988	Growth (%) 1970-1988	1000 inhabitants 1988	Growth (%) 1970-1988
Canada	25 950	21.8	2 879	69.8
USA	246 329	20.1	30 367	51.0
Japan	122 613	18.2	13 680	86.6
France	55 873	10.0	7 646	17.0
Germany *a*	61 451	1.3	9 348	17.0
Italy	57 441	7.0	8 385	50.9
UK	57 065	2.6	8 883	22.5
North America	272 279	20.3	33 246	52.5
OECD Pacific	142 477	19.4	15 833	83.8
OECD Europe	410 890	11.2	53 403	29.2
OECD	825 646	15.5	102 482	42.9
World	5 114 979	38.5	..	..

Note: a) Includes western Germany only.

Source: OECD

aware of the environmental consequences of their behaviour. Therefore, the conflict between individual utility-seeking behaviour and commitment to social goals can be expected to persist in the near future. However, recent consumer campaigns for environmentally friendly products, for example, carried out in several Member countries show that people are able to change, and will change, their attitudes and behaviour if they are given proper opportunities to do so. This applies especially to consumption, which, according to polls, is usually the lowest priority in people's value hierarchy. People's attitudes and behaviour can also be influenced by several means, such as economic incentives and institutional arrangements.

Prospects

Despite the uncertainty inevitably surrounding projections of such socio-demographic variables as migration and household structure, and the often considerable differences in the rate and scale of changes between countries, it is possible to identify some broad socio-demographic trends for the 1990s:

- The decline in population growth rates will continue in the OECD area, although the population of most Member countries is expected to grow until the end of the century. Some 95 per cent of the projected increase in the world's population from 5 billion today to over

6 billion by the year 2000 will take place in developing regions;
- Net migration will remain at the recent relatively low level, depending, however, on the particular socio-economic, environmental and political conditions in the countries of origin and on the immigration policies of host countries;
- The OECD population will continue to age, but the proportion of the elderly will generally grow slowly during the 1990s. However, there will be a sharp increase in the proportion of elderly people from 2000-2010 to 2040, when the average proportion is projected to be almost 22 per cent. The general ageing of the population will be accompanied by the ageing of the elderly population itself;
- The trend towards smaller households will probably continue, although there may be variations in the rate of this development;
- Time use will follow patterns rather similar to those in the past two or three decades: fewer hours of work, more leisure, less time used for domestic chores, more out-of-home recreation;
- Public attitudes will be very much in favour of environmental protection. As incomes and material welfare increase, people will be more concerned about the quality of their well-being, including the quality of the enviroment.

2. THE ENVIRONMENTAL SIGNIFICANCE OF CONSUMPTION AND TOURISM ACTIVITIES

Consumption patterns: A new focus for environmental protection policies

Whilst developing countries face environmental problems largely because of their rapid population growth, the populations of the OECD countries affect the physical environment mainly through their consumption and affluent lifestyles. Most consumption activities have a direct impact on the environment – by consuming natural resources, by generating wastes, by contributing to pollution, by occupying land and space, and so on. Traditionally, however, environmental pressures and damage in developed countries have been associated with production, whether in industry, agriculture or energy. Accordingly, decisions made by households and individuals in the final consumption phase have largely been neglected.

From 1970 to 1988, the increase in final consumption expenditure in major OECD countries ranged from 50 per cent to 110 per cent, with an OECD average of nearly 80 per cent. (Figure 42) Despite considerable uncertainty over the development of the major determinants of consumption growth, it can be estimated

that real consumption in OECD countries will continue to grow in the near future, although the rate of growth will vary from country to country. In the United Kingdom, for instance, consumer spending is projected to increase by 40 per cent from the mid-1980s to the year 1999.

The consequences of massive and ever-increasing consumption can clearly be seen in the effect developed countries have on the world's resources. The average person in the developed world consumes natural resources at a rate which is at least 10-20 times as high as the corresponding figure for the poorest countries. The average per capita consumption of paper is around 120 kg a year in developed countries compared with 8 kg in the Third World, of steel 450 kg compared with 43 kg, and of purchased energy equivalent to coal almost 6 tonnes compared with 0.5 tonnes.

Consumption also results in a massive output of wastes – more than 30 million kg in Tokyo, 14 million kg in New York, and 9 million kg in Paris every day. Furthermore, environmental risks related to the use of products and to the disposal of goods seem to be growing

Figure 42. PRIVATE FINAL CONSUMPTION EXPENDITURE, 1970-1988

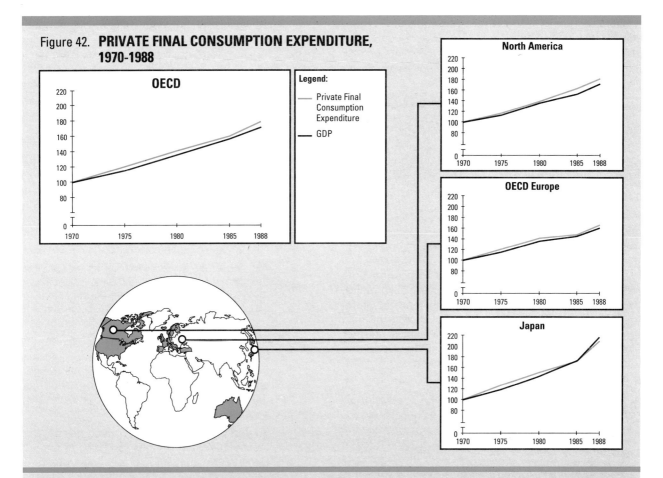

	Index 1970 = 100				
	1970	1975	1980	1985	1988
Canada	100	136	162	184	209
USA	100	116	135	160	177
Japan	100	131	161	185	209
France	100	121	141	155	170
Germany *a*	100	117	138	142	156
Italy	100	119	151	165	187
UK	100	113	125	139	165
North America	100	117	137	162	179
OECD Europe	100	119	138	148	165
OECD Pacific	100	130	158	182	203
OECD	100	120	140	160	178

Note: a) Includes western Germany only.

Source: OECD

in OECD countries. CFCs in aerosols, additives in food, lead in petrol, and so on are just a few examples of harmful substances now generated and discharged into the environment at the final consumption stage of the material cycle.

Changes in consumption structure and patterns, including their social, cultural and subjective determinants, have significant environmental implications. First, the proportion of miscellaneous goods and services, prepared food products, and restaurant and café services in the household budget has increased in most OECD countries during the past two decades. (Table 20) The consequences can be seen not only in the amount of household waste produced but also in the composition of this waste. The increased use of highly processed prepared food, for example, is directly related to the increased proportion of *containers and packaging in household waste* which, measured by volume, may represent nearly half of the total post-consumption waste in an industrialised country. In particular, the rapid growth in the use of containers during the past few decades has meant an increase in metals, plastics, and other synthetic materials in household wastes that are difficult to collect and recycle or dispose of. (See Chapter on Solid Waste)

Second, the steady growth in the proportion of consumption expenditures allocated to *durable goods* in most OECD countries has led to a rapid growth in the stock of durable goods. An example: around 1960 in the United Kingdom about 20 per cent of households owned a refrigerator, 30 per cent a washing machine, and 60 per cent a TV set, while in 1987 nearly all households owned a TV set and a refrigerator, and more than 80 per cent owned a washing machine; in addition, half the households owned a video recorder and 30 per cent a micro-wave oven, durables of which nothing was known 20 years ago. Some of the social changes, such as the trend towards smaller households combined with the ageing process, will no doubt reinforce the growth of the stock of durable goods. The impact of this development and of enriched consumption in general can be seen in the increased rates at which goods are disposed of and hence in the growing amounts of waste. (See Chapter on Solid Waste)

Third, *the increasingly dominant position of the private automobile among the different modes of transport* is an example of an environmentally harmful consumption pattern which is difficult to explain without reference to the social and individual functions that car ownership performs. Roughly 60 per cent of households in OECD countries now own a private car and the number of multi-car households has been rising steadily. In France, for example, more than one household out in five owns two or more cars. The car stock of most Member countries is projected to continue growing up to the year 2000, although at lower rates than previously. In addition, shifts to larger models in Japan and Europe are noticeable. (See Chapter on Transport)

The increased time spent on leisure activities, the dispersion of shopping, recreation and education services, will increase the use of the private automobile for domestic trips. By lengthening the distance between home and work, the current patterns of urban sprawl are likely to increase the need for private automobiles for work and related trips. The increasing number of smaller households is also likely to stimulate the growth of the overall stock of cars and reduce the number of passengers per car, thus cancelling out the favourable effects of new cars' increased energy efficiency and cleaner technologies on the environment.

What could be done to prevent or offset the negative environmental effects of changing consumption patterns?

- Economic incentives through pricing and taxation policies, for instance, should be used in two ways: to prevent general increases in income from being transformed into environmentally harmful consumption patterns, and to support people's willingness to adopt new ways of life;

- Consumers should be provided with information on the consequences of their consumption choices and behaviour, so as to encourage demand for environmentally sound products and use of products;

- Environmentally aware product design and technological innovations should be promoted. Consumers should also be encouraged to assert themselves by demanding such changes in products and in production technologies;

- In some cases, rules and regulations will also have to be used to direct consumers towards more environmentally friendly behaviour.

Tourism: A need for sustainable development

Tourism is an important economic activity in the OECD area. It represents 26 per cent of the total export of services of Member countries, creates and maintains a number of direct, indirect and induced jobs, employing up to 14 per cent of the workforce in the service sector of certain countries, and it contributes to sustaining the economic development of many parts and regions of the OECD.

Today, tourism forms a complex in which economic, socio-cultural and environmental aspects interrelate in a number of ways. The impact of tourism on the economy can be very great; so too are its effects on the physical and socio-cultural environment. Paradoxically, tourism threatens the quality of the environment in many ways yet, perhaps more than any other sector, it depends on a sustained high quality of the environment, the basic "raw material" of the tourism industry.

Tourism is a fast-growing business. After a flattening of demand at the beginning of the 1980s, world

Table 20. STRUCTURE OF HOUSEHOLDS' CONSUMPTION EXPENDITURES

Percent of households' consumption

	Food, beverages and tobacco		Clothing and footwear		Gross rent, fuel and power		Furniture, furnishing, household operation		Health expenses	
	1970	1988	1970	1988	1970	1988	1970	1988	1970	1988
Canada	21.9	16.5	8.0	5.9	19.7	21.7	9.5	9.6	3.7	4.3
USA	18.6	13.1	8.2	6.4	18.0	19.5	7.3	5.6	9.4	15.0
Japan	30.4	20.2	7.7	6.0	16.2	18.7	7.6	5.5	7.9	10.8
Australia	27.6	21.4	8.9	6.5	15.4	20.5	7.7	7.4	6.0	7.1
Austria	34.5	22.1	12.6	10.3	11.6	19.0	10.0	7.8	3.7	5.3
Belgium	31.4	22.6	7.4	6.3	15.2	16.5	14.0	12.9	6.3	10.0
Denmark	30.3	22.2	7.8	5.8	18.3	26.0	9.7	7.1	2.0	2.0
Finland	32.1	23.7	8.3	5.5	17.9	16.8	6.9	7.2	2.8	3.8
France	26.0	19.7	9.6	6.8	15.3	18.9	10.2	8.2	7.1	9.3
Germany[a]	29.8	22.1	10.2	8.6	16.2	20.3	10.1	9.4	2.6	3.4
Greece	42.2	40.0	12.7	9.6	14.3	12.2	7.5	8.7	4.2	3.8
Iceland	30.9	22.2	10.4	10.0	17.1	13.2	10.8	10.7	2.6	1.6
Ireland	46.2	40.6	10.0	6.5	11.8	11.0	7.7	7.4	2.3	3.4
Italy	39.1	23.0	8.9	9.7	12.3	14.5	7.1	8.8	3.8	6.1
Luxembourg	28.4	21.8	9.4	6.7	17.5	20.8	9.4	10.5	5.4	8.0
Netherlands	25.8	18.2	10.6	6.9	12.4	18.2	11.5	8.0	8.4	12.3
Norway	32.3	25.4	10.5	7.3	14.1	17.9	8.4	7.2	4.0	4.1
Sweden	28.0	21.8	7.6	7.2	20.5	24.3	7.8	6.2	2.1	2.5
Switzerland	31.4	26.9	6.6	4.4	17.2	17.8	7.7	5.0	6.2	9.3
UK	26.4	17.9	8.8	7.1	17.2	20.0	7.9	6.7	0.9	1.3

	Transport, communication		Recreational, entertainment, education, culture		Miscellaneous goods and services		Personal care		Restaurants, cafes, hotels	
Canada	13.7	15.7	9.4	11.3	13.9	14.6	2.5	2.5	6.3	6.5
USA	15.0	14.8	8.6	9.9	14.2	15.6	3.2	2.7	5.9	6.0
Japan	7.8	9.7	9.2	10.2	13.1	17.9	..	..	..	..
Australia	15.4	13.6	7.3	9.0	11.4	15.1	..	..	..	..
Austria	13.1	16.0	6.5	7.0	16.8	17.6	3.5	2.7	11.4	12.0
Belgium	10.4	12.8	4.0	5.3	11.1	14.1	2.8	2.6	4.8	4.8
Denmark	15.1	15.5	8.3	9.9	9.7	11.0	1.6	1.6	5.3	5.8
Finland	15.3	18.5	6.4	9.9	10.9	12.9	1.4	1.7	5.1	7.9
France	13.4	16.9	6.9	7.5	11.7	13.5	1.5	1.9	6.1	6.6
Germany[a]	14.0	15.7	10.2	10.0	6.3	8.7	1.9	1.6	..	..
Greece	8.5	12.9	4.9	6.8	7.7	10.7	1.1	1.9	4.5	6.7
Iceland	14.1	17.9	6.3	8.2	7.4	12.5	1.5	1.7	3.3	8.2
Ireland	10.4	12.0	8.0	10.4	6.7	8.9	0.8	2.2	1.6	1.7
Italy	10.3	12.9	7.8	8.7	12.0	17.4	2.8	3.0	7.1	10.2
Luxembourg	10.9	17.9	4.0	4.4	15.1	13.0	..	..	..	..
Netherlands	9.3	10.8	8.4	9.5	12.8	13.7	2.8	2.5	5.3	4.9
Norway	11.7	13.3	7.7	8.9	9.9	11.7	1.7	2.2	3.6	4.9
Sweden	13.4	18.8	8.2	9.6	7.0	7.9	2.5	2.5	3.5	4.1
Switzerland	10.9	10.9	9.0	9.8	7.7	10.3	2.1	2.0	..	..
UK	12.7	16.7	8.7	9.5	17.7	21.0	1.8	1.9	12.3	12.8

Note: a/ Includes western Germany only.
Source: OECD

tourism expanded again at an annual average growth rate of around 6 per cent. Within the OECD area, the evolution of international demand over the period 1980-1988 was characterised by well above average growth rates in the Pacific basin (+103 per cent in tourist flows, and +172 per cent in receipts in real terms), and more modest though important increases in North America (respectively +34 per cent and +29 per cent) and in Europe (+24 per cent and +38 per cent). (Figure 43) Of the total of 340 million international travellers worldwide, about 75 per cent visited OECD countries, with 50 per cent going to European countries. Domestic tourism in OECD countries has also grown steadily during the past two decades, although generally at lower rates than international tourism.

Tourism makes a significant contribution to the national economies of several OECD countries: 7.8 per cent of Austrian GDP, 5.5 per cent for Portugal, 4.9 per cent for Spain and 6.4 per cent for Switzerland. By providing countries with a means of building up their less developed regions, tourism also has an outstanding positive impact on local economies and employment which is of great importance in marginal rural areas. (See Chapter on Agriculture)

The environmental impact of tourism is substantial and widespread, and not always harmful. On the positive side, tourism has stimulated measures to protect the physical environment, landscapes, historic sites and wildlife. In some cases, it has benefited the environment by helping to improve the level of local infrastructure. On the negative side:

— Tourism can cause a significant amount of air and noise pollution, mainly because of motor traffic;

— Locally, tourism can be a major source of water pollution due to high concentrations of populations over short periods in areas poorly equipped in sewage treatment facilities;

— Other harmful effects include littering and waste disposal problems, loss of natural landscape due to construction or restricted public access, damage to flora and fauna, degradation of landscape and of historic sites and monuments, and congestion.

Much of the pollution and environmental damage attributable to tourism is caused by an *inadequate infrastructure* — lack of water supply, sanitation and solid waste treatment, insufficient transport networks, and so on. This in turn is partly due to the difficulty of amortizing such infrastructures over only a short period of the year.

Many tourist areas in OECD countries are located in *critical zones with vulnerable ecosystems*. Cases in point include mountain areas in the Alpine region, natural parks and wilderness areas in the United States and Canada, islands in the Mediterranean and coastal zones in several OECD countries. The degree of environmental damage caused to these areas by tourism depends to a large extent on the carrying capacity of the resort, i.e. a certain threshold level beyond which physical deterioration of the resource or damage to natural ecosystems will occur.

Too many tourists in the same place at the same time, a situation typical of the *seasonal nature and geographical concentrations of mass tourism*, is one of the fundamental causes of environmental damage. Already more than 40 per cent of all tourist arrivals in Europe each year — a quarter of the world total — are concentrated around the Mediterranean, increasing the risk of overloading some of the existing developed tourist sites in that area. During the busiest season in the European Alps, population density in some places is higher than the density of many industrial districts and puts major strains on mountain ecosystems.

The impact of tourism on the environment is likely to increase as tourism itself grows. The overall growth of tourism arrivals in OECD countries in the 1990s is expected to continue at a somewhat higher rate than GDP, not far from the general rate of 5 per cent recorded annually during the 1980s. Domestic tourism, which has proved to be less sensitive to general economic fluctuations than international tourism, is also very likely to continue to grow steadily, along with an increasing interest in outdoor activities. In the near future, the increased number of retired people will also mean that more people will have opportunities to make use of tourist services. In OECD countries, in which the nature of work is changing and the amount of non-working time is increasing fast, tourism has become and will increasingly be an important concern in the daily lives of individuals.

There is little doubt about the increasing awareness of the interrelations of tourism and the environment; nearly all Member countries reported tourism-related environmental protection measures and actions in recent years. It is too early to tell, however, whether these measures will be enough to prevent the deterioration of environmental quality — the basic tourist asset — and thereby secure the continuation of tourism itself on a sustainable basis.

Figure 43. **TRENDS IN INTERNATIONAL TOURISM**

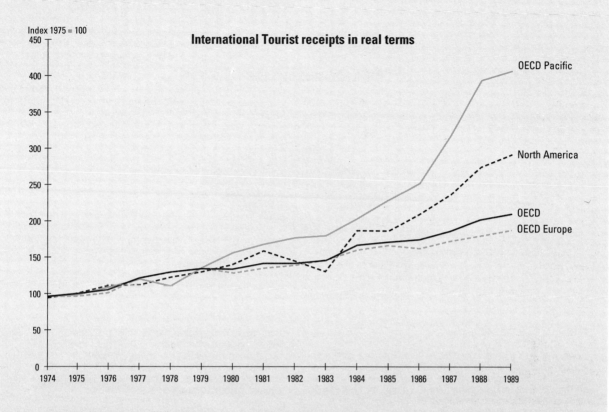

Index 1975 = 100

International Tourist receipts in real terms

International tourist receipts in real terms

| | Index 1975 = 100 | | | | million US $ [a] |
	1975	1980	1985	1989	1989
Canada	100	116	132	155	4 100
USA	100	147	201	329	31 030
Japan	100	143	233	363	2 920
France	100	141	185	242	16 480
Germany [b]	100	121	157	175	8 700
Italy	100	192	230	191	11 330
Netherlands	100	87	120	138	3 110
Spain	100	110	169	185	13 910
Sweden	100	116	185	243	2 300
UK	100	126	164	170	9 930
North America	100	140	186	291	35 130
OECD Pacific	100	157	229	407	6 400
OECD Europe	100	131	167	187	98 410
OECD	100	134	172	211	139 940

Notes: a) In 1987 prices and exchange rates.
b) Includes western Germany only.

Source: OECD

COASTAL POPULATION GROWTH IN THE UNITED STATES

POPULATION DENSITY, 1960 - 2010

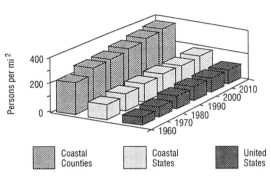

Note: Does not include Alaska

A Rising Coastal Population

Since the 1940s, Americans have been moving in greater and greater numbers to the nearest major body of water: whether to the shoreline of the Atlantic Ocean, the coast of the Gulf of Mexico, the Great Lakes, or the Pacific Ocean. Already, more than half of the population of the United States -- 52.9 per cent as of 1987 -- lives within 80 kilometres of the coast, where people are densely packed -- especially in the East -- onto less than ten per cent of the nation's land.

Projections regarding future population growth in coastal areas vary, but demographers do agree that coastal populations in the United States are increasing in absolute terms and will continue to rise in virtually all regions in the years ahead. Economic factors, recreational opportunities and the benefits of communing with nature at the ocean's edge are all contributing to this movement towards the coast.

Increasing Pressure on Coastal Resources

This growth in coastal populations is exerting strong pressure on the marine environment and its resources. Estuaries, wetlands, beaches, coastal waters and the fauna and flora which these support are being threatened by the pressures of pollution and habitat loss. The coastal development boom has erected few new cities, but many a cluster of houses, stores, offices and marinas. This pattern has spared the environment the worst intensity and scale of urban pollution, but it has subjected a disproportionally large area of the coast to disruptive human settlement.

These new human communities, once settled, become constantly growing sources of pollution. Each day point-sources such as sewage treatment plants and industrial and commercial facilities discharge some 48 billion litres of effluent directly into estuaries and near-coastal waters. In some areas, non-point source pollution causes even greater problems than pollution from point sources. Point sources, since they are large, can be easily located, and thus regulated. Non-point source pollution, on the other hand, originates in thousands of hard-to-pinpoint places. Most often it takes the form of toxic runoff from city streets, suburban developments or agricultural land. Another problem is habitat loss, which threatens near-coastal flora and fauna.

The economic ramifications of coastal population growth are significant. Already, on any given day, one-third of United States shellfish beds are closed to fisherman, whether sport or commercial, largely because of pathogen contamination from sewage or agricultural waste. Near-shore fisheries are also threatened by spawning-habitat loss, a result of coastal pollution and declining wetlands.

Strategies to Manage Coastal Population Growth

Knowledge and understanding of the impacts of the coastal population boom on the environment is increasing, as are efforts to manage this growth. The challenge is to develop approaches to coastal development that protect the health of both coastal inhabitants and of the environment as a whole. Some of the more widely discussed strategies include pollution prevention (waste reduction, recycling and treatment), volunteerism, land-use planning, community consensus-building, tax incentives and user fees.

Many of these complementary strategies can, and are, being implemented through integrated management schemes which focus on particularly vulnerable or valuable areas. Prime wetlands now benefit from better protection under United States law and a national estuary programme is helping to implement integrated management schemes in important estuaries like Chesapeake Bay (Atlantic coast) and Puget Sound (Pacific coast). Concern about the state of the coastal environment, and debate about how best to reconcile its protection with population growth, continues in virtually all coastal areas under pressure. In all, 29 states recently adopted or are preparing coastal zone management programmes.

Contribution from the United States

3. CONCLUSIONS

Over the past 20 years, the population of OECD countries has grown by 116 million inhabitants, but declined from 19 to 16 per cent of the world population; it has become richer, it has aged rapidly and the size of households has declined dramatically. Consumption patterns have increasingly become dependent on services, packaged goods, durable goods and the automobile; consequently, they have generated more waste and pollution and generally consumed more natural resources, such as oil, water and wood. Time use patterns have been marked by a rapid increase in leisure and tourism activities. This has been partly beneficial for the environment, by stimulating improved protection of the physical environment, landscapes, historic sites and wild life in a number of countries, but it has also generated increased pressures (air pollution, water pollution from sewage, littering, environmental restructuring with second homes and tourism-related buildings and infrastructures) often concentrated in environmentally sensitive areas such as lakes, seashores and mountains.

In the 1990s the decline in population growth in OECD countries will continue. Although foreigners will constitute a growing proportion of the total population, net migration will remain at a relatively low level. The OECD population will continue to age and live in ever smaller households. Time use patterns will follow the recent trends of fewer hours of work and more leisure. The tourism industry will continue to grow. In the first half of the next century, the ageing process will accelerate and the rapid population growth of developing countries will probably stimulate migration from less developed to more developed countries.

This has several implications for the environment and for future environmental policies:

- Despite the slowdown in its growth, the population of OECD countries will place a major strain on the world's resources and on the state of the environment through its increased consumption and its use and disposal of final products. Consequently, a critical issue is how to prevent the general increase in disposable incomes from being transformed into environmentally harmful consumption patterns and how to support people's willingness to adopt environmentally friendly consumption patterns and ways of life;

- The socio-demographic development of OECD countries seems to encourage the preference for private cars over other modes of transport. Increased private transport will lead to, among other things, increased congestion and wider dispersion of leisure activities and related environmental problems;

- The impact of tourism on physical resources and the environment is substantial and is expected to increase. But since a high-quality environment is an essential prerequisite for tourism, there is a growing concern with the sustainable development of the tourism industry. This issue is of crucial importance for all countries and in particular for southern Europe.

REFERENCES

OECD (yearly), *Tourism Policies and International Tourism in OECD Member Countries*, Paris.

OECD (1989), *National and International Tourism Statistics, 1974-1985*, Paris.

Part III

MANAGING THE ENVIRONMENT: TOWARDS SUSTAINABILITY

Chapter 15

ECONOMIC RESPONSES

This chapter reviews the relationship between economic development and environmental quality within OECD countries and the policy responses of governments to this. The relationships involved are quite complex:

- The growth of OECD economies, accompanied by structural and technical change and changes in the practices of individual households and of private and public enterprises, affect the environment through the generation and disposal of pollutants and through the abstraction and use of natural resources;
- Changes in environmental conditions affect the economy through changes in the quality and quantity of natural resources available, through the performance of such environmentally-sensitive economic sectors as agriculture, forestry and tourism, and through damage to the built environment and human health.

Public concern over these consequences, which tends to intensify as material standards of living and educational standards rise, triggers the pressure to protect and conserve the environment – but to do so without undermining the development which has brought about the concern. (Figure 44) This is the policy challenge which has faced Member countries over the past 20 years and will continue to face them during the 1990s.

In response to this challenge, Member governments have:

- Stimulated work on estimating and measuring environmental benefits, pollution control expenditures and their economic effects;
- Supported the appropriate use of economic instruments, alongside cost-effective regulatory instruments, in accordance with the polluter pays principle (PPP);
- Encouraged the progressive adoption of anticipatory, rather than exclusively reactive, instruments of environmental policy, encouraged more effective integration of environmental and economic sectoral policies, and adopted the goal of sustainable economic development, encouraging the development of policy instruments to improve natural resource management as well as pollution control.

1. MEASURING BENEFITS, COSTS AND ECONOMIC IMPACTS OF ENVIRONMENTAL POLICIES

The formulation and implementation of environmental policies should be informed by comparable economic data on the benefits that may be achieved, on the direct costs of implementing them, and on the wider economic repercussions which may result.

Environmental benefits

The main purpose of measuring environmental benefits (or their obverse, environmental damage) in monetary units is to make it feasible to establish direct comparisons between the costs and benefits of existing or proposed environmental policy measures, or to assist in setting the levels of pollution charges or other economic instruments.

The methods used fall into two broad categories: *direct* methods, which involve directly estimating, in monetary terms, the environmental gain or loss under consideration; and *indirect* methods, which typically

Figure 44. PUBLIC OPINION: ENVIRONMENTAL PROTECTION VS. GROWTH TRADE OFF, late 1980s

COUNTRY

USA (1990)

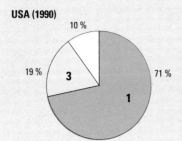

- USA:
"Here are two statements which people sometimes make when discussing the environment and economic growth. Which of these statements comes closer to your own point of view?"
1) Protection of the environement should be given priority, even at the risk of curbing economic growth.
3) Economic growth should be given priority, even if the environment suffers to some extent.

(sampling: 1223 pers.)

JAPAN (1990)

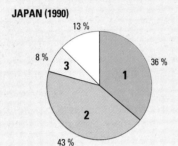

- Japan:
Respondents were asked to choose one of the following:
1) The protection of the global environment should be given priority as it is essential to human beings, even if a certain amount of economic growth is sacrificed.
2a) Environmental protection and economic growth are both possible.
2b) Global environmental protection should be deliberately harmonized with economic growth.
3) Economic growth should be given priority as it is most important for a rich and happy life.

(sampling: 3753 pers.)

EEC EUROPE (1988)

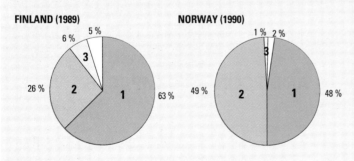

- EEC:
"I will mention certain opinions that are sometimes expressed concerning environmental problems. Which of these opinions are you most in agreement with?"
2) Protecting the environment and preserving natural resources are necessary conditions to assure economic development.
3) Development of the economy should take priority over questions of the environment.
4) Sometimes it is necessary to make a judgement between economic development and protection of the environment.

(sampling: 11729 pers.)

FINLAND (1989)   NORWAY (1990)

- Finland and Norway:
"I will quote three opinions concerning environmental protection and economic growth and would like to know which of these you are most in agreement with."
1) Environmental protection should be given priority even if economic growth suffers somewhat.
2) Environmental protection and economic growth are both possible.
3) Economic growth should be given priority even if the environment suffers somewhat.

(sampling: Finland: 1985 pers.; Norway: 1506 pers.)

Legend:

1	Priority to environment	**3**	Priority to economic growth
2	Both are possible		Do not know

Source: OECD

involve first estimating the gain or loss in physical terms and then converting from a physical to a monetary measure. Although there have been very considerable advances in methodologies for the development of environmental benefit estimates, a great deal more is needed before the "state of the art" is generally satisfactory. Benefit estimates are easier to establish in the case of aircraft and road traffic noise than in the case of the preservation of rare habitats or unique landscapes. Inevitably, attempts to calculate aggregate monetary values for the environmental damage in an entire country are fraught with even greater difficulties and invariably are very incomplete in their coverage.

Where this has been attempted, however, the resulting values are quite high – in the range of 1.6 per cent of GDP as regards air and water pollution control benefits. These estimates do not usually cover damages related to accidental pollution, to uncertain pollution effects (e.g. climate change relating to greenhouse gases) and to issues of natural resources management (e.g. floods), and thus provide only a minimum assessment.

Environmental control costs

Annual environmental *expenditure* data[1] provide useful information on the level of resources devoted to environmental maintenance and improvement at the national and sectoral levels, compared with the level of resources being devoted to other policy areas. Comparisons made over time between changes in environmental expenditure and changes in the state of the environment can be useful in evaluating the cost-effectiveness of environmental policies. Expenditure data are also needed when assessing the macro and sectoral economic impacts of environmental policies.

Available data relate only to pollution abatement and control (PAC) expenditure (Table 21); no comparable expenditure data have been collected relating to conservation of the natural and built environment. A small number of Member countries were able to provide comprehensive annual estimates for a recent year and some of them have provided estimates on a continuing basis. *Although a standardised OECD questionnaire was used to collect data, there are differences in the scope and definition of the data actually supplied.* This means that any comparisons between Member countries and over time have to be interpreted with caution.

Total PAC expenditure ranges between 0.8 per cent and 1.5 per cent of GDP. (Table 21) In the case of western Germany and the United States for which there are reasonable time series data, the relative importance of PAC expenditures appears to have risen

Table 21. POLLUTION ABATEMENT AND CONTROL (PAC) EXPENDITURES, mid 1980s

	PAC expenditures as percentage of GDP			PAC investments as percentage of total national investment			Budgeted R&D expenditures as percentage of total budgeted R&D expenditures
	Public	Private	Total	Public	Private	Total	Public
Canada	0.89	0.36ª	1.25ᵇ	. .	1.52	. .	2.2
USA	0.60	0.86	1.47	1.14	1.62	2.76	0.5
Japan	1.17	0.08ª	1.25ᵇ	2.87	0.28	3.15	0.4ᵈ
Finland	0.52	0.64	1.16	1.06	1.12	2.18	. .
France	0.56	0.33	0.89	0.83	0.46	1.29	0.7
Germanyᵉ	0.78	0.74	1.52	1.54	1.54	3.09	3.4
Italy	0.13	. .	. .	0.24	. .	. .	1.9
Netherlands	0.95	0.30	1.26	. .	0.85	. .	3.8
Norway	0.54	0.27	0.82	0.85	0.44	1.28	2.7
Sweden	0.66	0.27	0.93ᶜ	1.10	0.73	1.83	2.5
UK	0.62	0.62	1.25	. .	. .	. .	1.3

Notes: Althrough a standard questionnaire was used to collect the data, these data are not fully comparable.
　　a) Excludes running costs.
　　b) Partial total.
　　c) Composite total.
　　d) OECD estimate.
　　e) Includes western Germany only.
Source: OECD

modestly in real terms from the 1970s to the mid 1980s. With the exception of the USA, PAC expenditure has tended to be greater in the *public* sector than *in private enterprises*; the former has been more concentrated on water and waste pollution control and the latter on air pollution control. Further, expenditures by *households* might represent an additional 20-25 per cent of the total. The incidence of PAC expenditures differs between industries, the most important being electricity, gas, and water, mining and quarrying, chemicals, petroleum, iron and steel, metal products and machinery, wood products, non-ferrous metals, textiles and leather, paper and printing, food and tobacco.

The adoption of the polluter pays principle by OECD countries places the initial responsibility for paying the cost of pollution abatement on *enterprises* causing the pollution. These costs are passed on to consumers in the form of higher prices. Private investment expenditures appear to be quite high in the early years of an aggressive pollution control programme (e.g. in the 1970s in the United States and Japan), but diminish or stabilise over time as the installation of the required pollution control equipment is completed. Private operation and maintenance expenditures, on the other hand, should continue to increase, partially offsetting any reduction in investments. Depending on the industrial structure of countries, estimates of total pollution control expenditure by industry may vary from 1 per cent or less to 2 per cent of the country's gross industrial domestic product.

The *public* ultimately pays the costs required to accomplish environmental improvements. These costs may be paid directly by households or indirectly through higher taxes, higher prices, and lower increases (or even reductions) in government services in other areas.

Given the importance of satisfactory PAC expenditure and cost data for policy-making, there is a need to develop more consistent approaches to the estimation of PAC expenditures and costs, and to encourage a more transparent presentation of those expenditures and costs.

Indirect economic impacts

The two preceding sub-sections have reviewed the *direct* economic impacts of environmental policy. However, the policies are also likely to have some *indirect* repercussions on Member country economies. The nature of these repercussions, in both direction and magnitude, became a matter of debate in the late 1970s and early 1980s. One viewpoint was that stricter environ-

mental controls and increased PAC expenditures were contributing significantly to the slowdown of these economies. Others argued that these measures were having favourable economic effects, notably through job creation and the stimulation of certain forms of technical change.

These indirect economic effects have been examined by comparing the experiences of six Member countries – Austria, Finland, France, Netherlands, Norway and the United States – with some additional information obtained from Italy and Japan. In interpreting the findings summarised below, it should be noted that the scope and levels of PAC expenditures, whose economic repercussions were assessed, varied considerably between countries and that the macro-economic models used to predict indirect impacts also differed.

Despite these differences, the conclusions to be drawn from the country studies are broadly similar: at the aggregate level, the indirect economic impacts, whether negative or positive, were very small and were indeed an insignificant factor in the overall performance of the OECD countries studied. There were both positive and negative small impacts on national output, with the favourable effects most apparent early on. The effect on prices was ranging between +0.1 per cent and +0.5 per cent price increase per year, while the foreign trade effect was small in magnitude and mixed in direction. Similarly, the employment effect was small in magnitude and variable in direction, while productivity – as measured conventionally – generally suffered a slight decrease.

In concluding that the indirect economic impacts, as estimated in these studies, were relatively insignificant, caveats should be added. Firstly, analysis at a sectoral and/or regional level may reveal more significant economic consequences which are concealed in the national aggregate analyses. Secondly, more recent results indicate that the crowding-out effects of environmental control policies may have been underestimated in previous studies. It is quite likely that low-cost measures have been taken to date, and further abatement could involve higher costs. There is certainly concern that both damage and abatement costs in the future may increase significantly, in particular with regard to some global issues such as climate change. Hence, an important issue is whether or not the current economic expansion path is sustainable in the long run. This underlines the importance of continuing and extending these economic impact studies, and relating them to the kinds of environmental policies being implemented during the 1990s.

2. INSTRUMENTS OF ENVIRONMENTAL POLICY

Over the past 20 years, member countries have used a variety of policy instruments to protect and conserve the environment. These may be broadly categorised as *regulatory* and *economic* instruments. *Regulatory* instruments are institutional measures aimed at directly influencing the environmental performance of polluters by regulating processes or products used, by prohibiting or limiting the discharge of certain pollutants, and/or by restricting activities to certain times, areas, etc. through licensing, setting standards, zoning, and so on. *Economic* instruments aim to affect the costs and benefits of the alternative actions open to polluters and to influence their behaviour towards choosing those actions which are environmentally more desirable.

In developing their approach to the use of environmental policy instruments, Member countries have taken a variety of steps. They have supported the application of the polluter pays principle and, more recently, the resource pricing principle, in the formulation and application of these instruments; they have acknowledged that a combination of both regulatory and economic instruments is needed; they have encouraged the formulation and implementation of economic and regulatory instruments in accordance with these principles and in a cost-effective and efficient manner.

Economic instruments

The main types of economic instruments in use in Member countries are:

- *Charges*, including effluent charges, user charges, product charges, and administrative charges, used to discourage polluting activities and/or to provide financial assistance to achieve reductions in pollution;
- *Subsidies*, in the form of grants, soft loans and tax allowances which may be used to encourage less polluting behaviour;
- *Deposit-refund schemes* (for example, on beverage containers) to encourage re-use and/or more "environmentally friendly" disposal;
- *Market creation arrangements*, such as trading arrangements to encourage more efficient and cost-effective use of emission permits;
- *Financial enforcement incentives*, such as non-compliance fees and performance bonds which provide an additional financial inducement to comply with existing environmental regulations.

A 1988 survey of OECD Member countries showed that 153 economic instruments were in use, of which 81 took the form of charges, 41 consisted of some type of subsidy and 31 fell within the other three categories. Since then, additional economic instruments have been approved or been submitted for approval in a number of Member countries (including Austria, Belgium, Canada, Denmark, Finland, France, Germany, Italy, Norway and Sweden).

This is indicative of the relatively large number of economic instruments in existence or envisaged. However, such statistics in themselves provide little indication of the true policy significance of different instruments. A number of other criteria are needed to provide a proper evaluation, such as:

- *Environmental effectiveness*: does the instrument provide an effective financial incentive to restore and preserve environmental quality at the required level?
- *Cost-effectiveness*: does the instrument help to achieve the required environmental quality at least resource cost?
- *Administrative feasibility*: is the use of the instrument feasible in terms of its information requirements, administrative demands and political acceptability?
- *Institutional compatibility*: is the instrument compatible with the environmental policy approach and the administrative framework within which it must operate?

These criteria need not be fully compatible with each other and therefore it would be unrealistic to expect instruments to conform fully with all of them.

Additionally, a fundamental guiding principle for environmental policy is the polluter pays principle (PPP) which relates to each of the four criteria above and therefore deserves consideration in its own right. Recommendations on PPP, which have been approved by Member countries, date back to 1972 when it was stated that polluters should, subject to certain exceptions, bear the full costs of pollution-reduction measures decided upon by public authorities to ensure that the environment is in an acceptable state. Most recently the PPP has been extended to accidental pollution.

Charges

The most common types of charges applied in Member countries are user charges and administrative charges. (Table 22) Typically, user charges relate to the collection of household waste and the discharge of waste-water in municipal sewage. Administrative charges mainly take the form of licence and authorisation payments. Product charges are used in many countries (e.g. for oil and lubricants, batteries, beverage containers and fertilizers) to encourage the return of waste materials or the more economical use of potentially polluting substances. A number of countries also operate some form of tax differentiation scheme, especially in the transport sector (e.g. tax differentiation between leaded and unleaded petrol). On the whole,

THE POLLUTER PAYS PRINCIPLE

As environmental policies began to be formulated in the late 1960s, it was proclaimed, to the public's satisfaction, that polluters would be made to pay for the costs of pollution. Politically, the "Polluter Pays Principle" , or PPP, was born, but few slogans or concepts have been as controversial or misunderstood.

An Economic Principle

In economic terms, the basic tenet of the PPP is that the price of a good, or service should fully reflect its cost of production and the cost of the resources used, including environmental resources. Use of air, water or land for the emission, discharge or storage of wastes is as much a use of resources as are other, "conventional" factors of production such as use of labour and material inputs. In the absence of payment for their use, these environmental resources are wasted, degraded and even destroyed.

For economists, it is the free use of such resources which is the prime cause of environmental degradation. The PPP seeks to rectify this by making polluters "internalise" the costs of use or degradation of environmental resources. The objective is therefore to fully integrate use of the environment into the economic sphere through the use of price signals.

What should the polluter pay? In theory, the polluter should pay the full cost of damages caused by his activity. This would create an incentive for the reduction of such damage, at least to the level where the cost of pollution reduction is equal to the marginal cost of the damage caused by such pollution. However, such costs are often extremely difficult to determine and in practice, polluters are often made to pay for the cost of pollution control.

International Application of the Polluter Pays Principle

Effective international use of the PPP requires a co-ordinated approach. This is because environmental regulations can become a source of distortion if some countries subsidise private investment in pollution control while others do not, thus placing the subsidised enterprises in an advantageous position relative to their non-subsidised competitors.

To encourage uniform application of the PPP, in 1972 the OECD Council stipulated that the PPP should constitute a fundamental principle of pollution control in Member countries. Although many other ways exist whereby the environment can become a source of distortion in trade (for example, through imposition of non-tariff barriers), internationally the PPP has become a fundamental principle of non-subsidisation of polluters.

Nonetheless, in certain circumstances it was desirable that the state encourage or accelerate the adoption of pollution reduction measures. Thus it was recognised that certain

OECD RECOMMENDATIONS ON THE PPP

26th May 1972	Guiding Principles concerning International Economic Aspects of Environment Policies
14th Nov. 1974	The Implementation of the PPP
7th July 1989	The Application of the PPP to Accidental Pollutions

exceptions could be tolerated in applying the PPP. To this end, another OECD Recommendation stipulated that aid could be made available to polluters under specified conditions: aid should be given only if the polluting sector cannot afford to pay the costs of pollution control because of economic difficulties; aid should be given for a fixed amount of time in a clearly defined programme; and aid should not distort conditions of international trade.

The PPP was also endorsed by the European Community in a 1975 Recommendation which attached conditions similar to those of the OECD concerning its application.

An Evolving Approach to Pollution Control

The PPP should continue to evolve to address new and changing environmental issues. In 1989, the OECD adopted a Recommendation on the Application of the PPP to Accidental Pollution which links the economic prinicple and the legal principle relating to damage compensation. Similarly, the question of how the PPP could be extended to address global pollution issues such as climate change bears further investigation. Regardless of how the PPP evolves in the future, there can be no doubt that integrating the costs of environmental resource use into economic price mechanisms is an important step towards ensuring that such resources are better managed for future generations.

Source: OECD

effluent charges are less widely used than the other types of charges, being most frequently applied to water, noise in a few cases and least frequently to atmospheric emissions. They are sometimes criticised on grounds of administrative feasibility and political acceptability.

Table 22. TYPES OF CHARGE SYSTEMS

| | Type of charges | | | | | | | Tax differen-tiation |
| | Effluent | | | | User | Product | Adminis-trative | |
	Air	Water	Waste	Noise				
Canada					X	X		X
United States				X	X	X	X	
Australia		X	X		X		X	
Japan	X			X				
Austria		X			X			X
Belgium		X	X		X		X	X
Denmark		X			X	X	X	X
Finland					X	X	X	X
France	X	X		X	X	X		
Germany		X	(x)	X	X	X	X	(x)
Greece	X				X		X	X
Italy		X			X	X		
Netherlands	X	X	X		X	X	X	X
Norway					X	X	X	X
Portugal		X					X	
Spain			X		X		X	
Sweden	X				X	X	X	X
Switzerland	(x)			X	X	(x)		X
Turkey			X					
United Kingdom		X		X	X		X	X

Note: x = applied, (x) = under consideration.
Source: OECD (1989), Economic Instruments for Environmental Protection, Paris

The types of charges levied are very diverse. Their overall coverage of polluting activities is fairly limited; for instance, product charges are limited to a small range of products and effluent charges are limited to a small number of residues. Where charges are applied, they are (with the partial exception of certain user charges) often set at fairly low levels relative to the full pollution control cost incurred by the polluter and the residual pollution damage incurred by the polluter. Whilst this situation reduces the likelihood of significantly adverse, economic repercussions occurring, the potential benefits from charges are not fully realised because the incentive effects to environmental improvement and cost-effective pollution control are weakened.

Subsidies

The majority of Member countries for which data are available appear to provide financial assistance, in one form or another, for certain pollution control activities. In a number of cases these payments are linked to charges where, for example, the revenues are used to help finance investment in pollution control equipment. In other cases, subsidies may be concealed in "below cost" charges for environmental services or take the form of grants, soft loans or special tax allowances.

For a number of years OECD has operated a procedure for the Notification of Financial Assistance Systems for Pollution Prevention and Control. The levels of subsidy notified are between 0.0006 per cent and 0.1 per cent of GDP and do not appear to constitute significant departures from the PPP nor to imply discernable effects on international trade. However, the subsidy estimates may not be comprehensive: assistance specifically for pollution control probably accounts for only a small part of the aid received by industry compared with that from other programmes such as employment and regional development. The incidence of the financial assistance may be uneven between economic sector. Non-responding Member countries may provide different levels of financial assistance.

Although there are some potential welfare losses arising from these subsidies, Member countries would often claim that they are permitted exceptions within the PPP and that tangible benefits do result. For example, it is suggested that they help to speed up the replacement of old plant by cleaner technologies and, in the transitional phase, to deal with the financial pressures of adjusting to stricter pollution controls. With less certainty, it is also stated that the availability of financial assistance plays a positive role in negotiating and imposing stricter direct regulations. Hence, provided subsidies are kept within strict bounds and the PPP is not significantly undermined, this type of economic instrument may continue to have a positive role to play in environmental policy.

Other economic instruments

Deposit-refund schemes appear to work reasonably well, particularly in the case of beverage containers, and are broadly consistent with the PPP. However, in terms of environmental effectiveness, it is not clear that they have been a major factor in influencing the proportion of containers returned for re-use or correct disposal.

The best-known example of *market creation* is the establishment of an emissions trading system which is mainly found in the United States and, to a lesser degree, in western Germany. One of the purposes of this instrument is to achieve a measure of technological and administrative flexibility in pollution control which, in some other countries, may be achieved through using more flexible regulatory instruments.

Non-compliance fees are an example of *enforcement incentives* which are used in a number of countries. In some cases they are set at a fairly nominal and somewhat arbitrary level; in other cases they are related to the profits gained from non-compliance or to the social cost resulting from non-compliance. There is some evidence to suggest that their practical value is often limited because fee levels are lower than strict conformity with the PPP would suggest and the lower the fee, the lower its degree of environmental effectiveness.

Overall role of economic instruments

The practical use made of economic instruments in pollution control has grown over the past 20 years. There remains, however, a considerable untapped potential to make greater and more effective use of these types of instruments in the future. At the same time it has to be recognised that in the main pollution control objectives both now and in the foreseeable future will be achieved primarily through reliance on regulatory instruments of a "command and control" nature, supplemented by the use of economic instruments.

Regulatory instruments

In general, regulatory instruments perform relatively well as regards their institutional compatibility, administrative feasibility and environmental effectiveness, but may perform less well in terms of economic efficiency, cost effectiveness and enforcement. Member countries have thus been encouraging better performance in these specific areas, for example by encouraging appropriate technological development and improving the enforcement of environmental policies.

Technical change

The relationship between environmental protection and technical change is complex. The process of technical change which accompanies economic development may, if uncontrolled, ease or intensify environmental problems. Environmental controls, depending upon their formulation and implementation, may slow or quicken the overall pace of technical change within the economy as well as modify its direction. In itself, technical change, as regards pollution control techniques, can make significant contributions to cost-effective improvements in environmental quality.

There were some fears during the late 1970s and early 1980s that environmental regulatory mechanisms were inhibiting technical change and innovation and thereby retarding productivity and general economic growth. However, a series of studies has shown that any such effects are minimal and any slow-down in economic growth is primarily due to other factors. It was found that, for the regulatory system to support the overall rate of technical innovation and advances in pollution control technology, regulatory instruments should, as far as possible:

- Stipulate performance standards without specifying the process or technology to be used;
- Establish reasonable deadlines (i.e. neither excessively long nor short term) and time-tables for compliance with performance standards;
- Use economic instruments in a supplementary role to build into the market an incentive to innovate;
- Encourage consultations with industry to help identify the most effective points in the production cycle at which to tackle the environmental problems under consideration;
- Review the requirements of environmental regulations so that contradictory technological requirements may be eliminated wherever possible;
- Encourage the dissemination of technical information and the provision of technical advice about methods of pollution control and strengthen the sources of finance for environmental sector innovations.

The promotion and diffusion of "clean" technologies within industry in Member countries has also been examined. The review showed that, despite the potential benefits of such technologies relative to end-of-pipe treatment, their use had been relatively limited. The reasons for this relate to both market and regulatory failures: existing markets for clean technologies are perceived to be relatively small; in some areas, few appropriate clean technologies are available; higher initial capital costs may be an inhibiting factor, even where subsequent operating costs may be lower; additional risks and uncertainties are perceived to flow from the newer clean technologies; there may be a lack of support for the development of clean technologies from the manufacturers of anti-pollution equipment; and ill-suited regulations may implicitly encourage use of "end-of-pipe" treatment systems.

Enforcement of environmental policies

During the 1980s studies were undertaken covering a number of Member countries which showed that enforcement of environmental policy instruments is often a weak point in their implementation. This has led to a number of suggestions for improvement. For example, enforcement mechanisms should be established at every stage in the environmental quality management cycle as well as at the regulatory level and should be periodically reviewed. Regulations should, where possible, be rationalised and simplified and permitting procedures streamlined. Compliance monitoring should be strengthened, self-monitoring extended, and environmental auditing by industry encouraged. Industry should be invited to co-operate in the rule-making process to facilitate greater co-operation in subsequent rule enforcement. Controls and sanctions for non-compliance should be strengthened by imposing tougher fines and simplifying legal and administrative procedures for applying sanctions. Regulations should be supported with economic instruments which increase the financial incentives to compliance. Lastly, fuller information and wider publicity should be provided both to polluters about control requirements and pollution abatement technologies and to the public about discharges and penalties for non-compliance.

Such measures need not result in increased expenditure on enforcement. Through re-allocation and redeployment, existing resources may be used more effectively than they are now. There is certainly considerable scope for achieving greater efficiency and cost effectiveness in the formulation and implementation of regulatory instruments.

3. SUSTAINABLE AND INTEGRATED DEVELOPMENT

In recent years the approach to environmental policy in Member countries has been extended beyond the traditional concern over pollution control, through an appropriate mix of regulatory and economic instruments. Greater emphasis has been placed on formulating an overall objective of sustainable development encompassing concerns over the reduction of the natural resource capital stock as well as over pollution control and on the need to achieve sustainable development by strengthening the anticipatory element in environmental policy and adopting a more integrated approach to environmental protection and economic development.

Sustainable development

The notion of sustainable development has become widely accepted, particularly since publication of the Report of the World Commission of Environment and Development in 1987. A number of key elements central to the "sustainable development" concept have been identified.

The *increasingly international and indeed global nature of environmental problems*, as well as increased trade and financial linkages among countries, suggests that local and national decision-makers cannot ignore the effects on the larger collectivity. For instance, an individual nation which maximises its economic growth by means which increase pollution and deplete natural resources elsewhere might not only undermine growth prospects in countries outside its boundaries, but also see its own longer term growth prospects threatened by the interdependence of ecological and economic systems.

Decision-making has too often been geared to the short term, ignoring *a longer term view* and the consequences for future generations of natural resource depletion and increasing pollution. There is not only a need to consider the ability of individuals and nations to share in the benefits of economic growth and natural resource amenities in the present but also a need to consider the legacy to future generations. Maintaining or increasing this legacy in a key element of sustainable development.

Sustainable development requires recognising that well-being depends not only upon the quantity of economic growth but also upon its quality. It is important to distinguish between the various forms of capital that contribute to well-being and make up the legacy to be passed on to future generations. "Man-made" capital (e.g. basic infrastructure) and "human capital", including the skills and educational levels of the work force, have long been recognised as major contributors to meeting present and future needs. However, *stocks of natural resources and pollution control* might also be seen as comprising *"natural capital"*. To prevent the undue depletion of "natural capital" necessary for sustainable development, policy measures must address both the management of natural resources and the control of pollution. A key issue is the extent to which there may be substitution between different forms of capital consistent with maintaining overall well-being; some degree of substitutability between stocks of "natural" capital versus "man-made" and "human" capital can be expected.

Priority for sustainable development in the 1990s

With the adoption of the objective of sustainable development, the *overall approach* to environmental policy is changing. Attention is now being focused on ensuring that all dimensions of environmental problems are considered, including pollution control, resource management and broad quality-of-life considerations, on developing more effective institutional arrangements for the formulation and implementation of environmental policies, on promoting technological change towards "clean, green" growth, on using economic instruments to provide market signals for environmental protection that better reflect relative scarcities, on streamlining regulatory instruments for

ENVIRONMENTAL DIMENSIONS OF THE
1992 EUROPEAN COMMUNITY INTERNAL MARKET

Harmonisation of Economic Policies

The 1957 Treaty of the European Economic Community provides for the establishment of a common market and the progressive harmonisation of member states' economic policies. The revision of this treaty in 1987 established a target date of 1992 for completion of the Community's internal market by the removal of barriers to movement between member states. A 1985 White Paper by the Commission of the European Communities sets out a detailed programme of almost 300 measures necessary for the removal of physical, technical and fiscal barriers.

In parallel with this initiative, the Community has also decided that expenditures from its structural funds - the social, agricultural guidance and regional development funds - should be doubled in the period up to 1993. The economic consequences of completion of the internal market have been analysed in a report (the "Cecchini Report") which suggests that these consequences will be a one-time gain of 4 to 7 per cent of Community national income, additional to the economic growth which would otherwise occur. There is also likely to be a considerable "second round" economic growth effect in the longer term, associated with far-reaching changes in economic structure, in the size and location of production units and in technologies.

Environmental Implications of an Integrated Market

The environmental implications of "1992" (the completion of the internal market and associated developments) have been examined separately by a Task Force of experts, drawn from different member states of the Community. The report concludes that the European Community will have opportunities and additional resources to secure environmental improvement, while facing a challenge to ensure that the economic growth generated by the Internal

Market is consistent with a course of sustainable development. The Task Force stressed that a high quality environment is, to an increasing degree, an essential condition for economic development and a key factor in the Community's position in world trade.

The Report identifies a number of priority areas for the future development of policy:

- Increased use of market mechanisms including environmental charges and taxes, coupled with strict allocation responsibility and liabilities for environmental damage, so as to promote efficient use of resources, limit the generation of wastes and, as far as possible, avoid negative environmental impacts;
- Action to ensure that Community measures relating to the Internal Market take full account of the environmental dimension;
- Monitoring of the environmental impacts of structural fund expenditures and encouragement of investment in pollution abatement and clean technologies;
- Environmental information, including development of data collection networks, in conjunction with anticipatory policies, and provision of information on environmental risks to consumers and local communities;
- An enhanced Community role, following completion of the Internal Market, in international environmental protection issues: global issues such as ozone depletion and climate change, regional issues such as pollution in the Mediterranean Sea, and the environmental problems facing developing countries, such as promotion of sustainable use of natural resources.

Developing harmonised policies which address these priorities is an important challenge to the European Community and its Member states.

Contribution from the European Commission

ENVIRONMENT-ECONOMY INTEGRATION IN FINLAND

The environment and the economy of Finland are interdependent. Finland's economy still depends heavily on its forests and lakes and on the direct and indirect uses of their products: for example, this is the case of industry, the pulp and paper industry, mechanical engineering and chemicals, tourism and recreation. Similarly, the quality of the environment is affected by economic growth, changes in industrial structure and technology and changing patterns of consumer spending.

Principles for Environment-Economy Integration

The establishment of a Ministry of the Environment in 1983 provided the opportunity and impetus to reflect on the interdependency of the environment and the economy. To explore ways of achieving environment-economy integration, a review of environmental policy was carried out jointly between the OECD Secretariat and Finnish authorities in 1986 and 1987. The review concluded that such interdependency could be woven into environmental policy if policy-making adhered to the following set of principles:

- Fuller integration of the different components of environmental policy;
- Fuller integration of environmental policy as a whole within other sectoral policies and programmes;
- Strengthening of the implementation of environmental policies.

Specific Integration and Implementation Measures

To further the integration of environmental protection within economic development, environmental protection has been included in the responsibilities of various government ministries, and the co-operation between government ministries has intensified significantly.

Examples of other steps include extension of the Polluter Pays Principle (PPP) and use of environmental impact assessment (EIA) procedures. To apply the Polluter Pays Principle, two environmental taxes - the carbon dioxide tax on fossil fuels and the phosphorus tax on mineral fertilizers - were introduced in January 1990. Activities to further the use of EIA have so far concentrated on the development of EIA procedures and on analysing their prospects for application. As permit and notification procedures are harmonised and combined, EIA will become an integral part of the new system.

As for strengthening the implementation of environmental policies, several tools were identified by the OECD Review: improving regulatory and economic instruments, adopting a multi-media and co-ordinated approach to policy implementation, promoting environmental information and research and encouraging public participation and the dissemination of information.

To further the co-ordination of pollution-control procedures, a new Environmental Permits Procedure Act is being considered; it would harmonise the processing of permit applications and facilitate the assessment of pollutant emission effects on the environment.

To improve the development and distribution of environmental and related economic information, an Environment Data Centre was established within the National Board of Waters and the Environment. An Environmental Information Board was created in 1990, to direct and co-ordinate activities related to environmental research and monitoring and to environmental information systems.

A Long-term Process

The Finnish experience shows that environment-economy integration is a complex but achievable process. Although a number of measures have been enacted, the full target is a long-term process which cannot yet be considered as achieved. The studies on policy integration which have recently been published in Finland will continue to guide the evolution of Finnish environmental policies towards sustainable development.

Contribution from Finland

greater efficiency and cost effectiveness, on modifying production/consumption patterns to maintain the stock of scarce resources and lessen pollution, on making greater use of anticipatory approaches in the formulation and implementation of environmental policies, on developing more integrated approaches to environmental policy, both within the environmental sector and between the environmental sector and other sectors of the economy, and on analysing linkages between the environment and the economy and developing environmental indicators for measuring environmental performance.

The *anticipatory approach* to environmental policy was endorsed by Member governments in the OECD Declaration of 1979 and was re-affirmed in their Declaration of 1985.

The anticipatory approach has been developed through a variety of mechanisms over the past 20 years. These have included forecasting studies of growth and technical change in environmentally sensitive sectors and of natural resource consumption and waste levels, more use of the PPP and resource pricing, greater use of environmental impact assessment in project planning, and tighter control over the production and use of chemicals.

The full extent to which the anticipatory approach has been and is being encouraged by Member countries is perhaps not sufficiently widely appreciated because of the fragmented nature of the many different situations in which it is applied.

The *integrative approach* is often closely associated with the anticipatory approach since the two tend to be mutually re-inforcing. This has been given special emphasis by Member countries since the 1985 Declaration. Integration is used in this context in two senses: in the formulation of policy *goals* and in the development of *means* to achieve those goals, both within the environmental sector itself and at the interface between the environmental sector and other sectors of the economy.

Whilst integration is being supported at the level of aggregate economic development policy (e.g. by attempting to integrate environmental considerations into economic development policy models), the main integrating initiatives are at the sectoral level, notably in such sectors as energy, industry, transport and agriculture, but also in trade or aid policies. (See Chapters in Part II and Chapter on International Responses in Part III)

4. CONCLUSIONS

OECD Member countries have achieved progress over the last 20 years in protecting environmental quality and, at the same time, permitting substantial economic development and change to take place. At one level this has been secured mainly through extending and strengthening the traditional pollution "command and control" system. According to available evidence, pollution abatement policies have not been unduly costly. Their direct cost is estimated in the range of 0.8 to 1.5 per cent of GDP. Available estimates of the benefits of these pollution abatement policies, that is the consequent reduction in the damage caused by pollution, are significantly higher. Only moderate consequences for overall prices and economic growth have been identified; and even positive ones for total employment in several countries. Meanwhile, in the more advanced countries, there is a noticeable shift in the relative importance of capital expenditure and operating cost items in environmental budgets, with operating costs now increasingly important. However, countries which have deferred pollution abatement and which now face an important backlog might have to consider relatively costly options in order to restore their environment, although they might rely on more cost-effective approaches based on prevention and economic instruments.

There have also been many innovations in thinking and practice which have resulted in the overall approach to environmental policy being very different at the beginning of the 1990s from what it was at the beginning of the 1970s. Today's approach emphasises:

- Broader objectives for environmental policy based upon the concept of sustainable development, and focuses upon resource conservation as well as pollution control;

- More effective institutional arrangements for the formulation and implementation of environmental policy;

- More use of economic instruments to provide appropriate market signals for environmental protection; and improvements to the efficiency and cost effectiveness of regulatory instruments;

- Wider use of anticipatory approaches to the formulation and implementation of environmental policy;

- Development of more integrated approaches to environmental controls, both within the environmental sector and between the environmental sector and other sectors of the economy.

The extent to which innovations in thinking have been translated into practice has varied and much remains to be accomplished.

Sectoral and general economic policies continue to have a significant influence on the environmental policy agenda: fiscal policies are often not neutral for the environment; subsidies in sectors such as agriculture and transport shape the nature and extent of these sectors as well as their environmental impacts; trade policies cover such environmentally significant products such as chemicals and automobiles, and the trade in natural resources such as wood and wild life products; foreign investment policies and practices related to private financing and bilateral or multilateral aid have environmental impacts, whether they take environmental concerns into account or not; while economic factors influencing exchange rates may have a dramatic effect on the prices of natural resources.

In view of the environmental challenges facing Member countries, at both national and international levels, *a new generation of policy actions is needed in the 1990s to realise sustainable development in practice.*

NOTE AND REFERENCES

1. The principal difference between expenditure and cost data is usually that the former include the actual capital expenditure incurred in a given year whilst the latter include the annualised capital costs of the capital assets employed in that year.

OECD (1985), *Environment and Economics*, Paris.

OECD (1985), *The Macro-Economic Impact of Environmental Expenditure*, Paris.

OECD (1985), *Environmental Policy and Technical Change*, Paris.

OECD (1986), *Information and Natural Resources*, Paris.

OECD (1986), *Environmental Monograph No. 4: Environmental Assessment and Development Assistance*, Paris.

OECD (1987), *Environment Monograph No. 8: Improving the Enforcement of Environmental Policies*, Paris.

OECD (1987), *Environment Monograph No. 9: The Promotion and Diffusion of Clean Technologies*, Paris.

OECD (1987), *Pricing Water Services*, Paris.

OECD (1988), *Environmental Policies in Finland*, Paris.

OECD (1989), *Environmental Policy Benefits: Monetary Valuation*, Paris.

OECD (1989), *Economic Instruments for Environmental Protection*, Paris.

OECD (1989), *Renewable Natural Resources: Economic Incentives for Improved Management*, Paris.

OECD (1989), *Environment Monograph No. 24: Accidents Involving Hazardous Substances*, Paris.

OECD (1989), *Agricultural and Environmental Policies: Opportunities for Integration*, Paris.

OECD (1990), *Pollution Abatement and Control Expenditure in OECD Countries: Statistical Compendium*, Paris.

OECD (1990), *The Economics of Sustainable Development*, Paris.

Chapter 16

INTERNATIONAL RESPONSES

1. TRANSFRONTIER POLLUTION

In the course of the last 30 years, countries have become increasingly concerned by transfrontier pollution. It involves two or more countries; it affects primarily the quality of surface or underground waters (rivers, lakes), of coastal waters, or of air and, more generally, it requires environmental management in frontier regions and in relevant countries. This phenomenon was first observed in surface waters and in industrialised frontier regions. During the early 1970s it was established that long-range transfrontier air pollution was prevalent in Europe, at first in relation to sulphur oxides and, subsequently, nitrogen oxides.

On the basis of the results of scientific studies countries negotiated and implemented a large number of multilateral agreements to combat transboundary pollution. Numerous bilateral agreements were also negotiated and implemented on the basis of the main principles brought out in the 1970s. In North America, for instance, several environment protection agreements were signed by the United States with Mexico and Canada. Among the most important multilateral agreement were the agreements for the protection of the Rhine and its tributaries against pollution (1963, 1976); the Bonn agreement for the protection of the North Sea (1969, amended in 1983); the Nordic convention on environmental protection (1974); the conventions on the prevention of marine pollution from land-based sources (Atlantic Ocean and Baltic Sea, 1974; Mediterranean Sea, 1980); the convention on transfrontier co-operation of collectivities or territorial authorities (1980); the convention and protocols on long-distance transboundary air pollution (1979, 1985, 1988). (Table 23)

Liability and compensation in the event of serious environmental damage, in particular beyond a country's borders, were covered in conventions concerning nuclear installations (1960 and 1963), activities in space (1972), oil tankers (1969, 1971, 1984), maritime transport (1976) and road and rail transport of dangerous goods (1989).

International transport of hazardous goods and wastes was made subject to new regulations: in 1989, a convention was adopted to avoid certain transfrontier movements of hazardous wastes and to regulate those movements which do not endanger the environment.

The elaboration of many conventions was facilitated by the work of a number of international organisations – in particular, by the Recommendations and Decisions of the OECD on transfrontier pollution (1974, 1976, 1977, 1978) and on hazardous wastes (1984, 1985, 1986, 1988). The oldest convention on strict liability was negotiated within the framework of the OECD, and the signature of the Basel convention on hazardous wastes was preceded by intensive negotiations within the OECD. Directives by the European Community also played a major role in the creation of a new approach to the problem of transfrontier pollution.

These agreements have in common the following main characteristics: they specify the general principles applicable to transfrontier pollution, identify very harmful pollutants, create prohibitions and, in certain cases, require permit delivery procedures. The first steps for governments were to acquire the necessary jurisdiction, to design the means with which to regulate activities affecting the environment beyond national boundaries, to set up consultation procedures with other countries, and to assign officials to international tasks. Gradually, international obligations became clearer and, in certain cases, they took on more concrete form through quantified pollution reduction goals. In the field of transport, the specific nature of hazardous wastes as distinct from hazardous goods was recognised. In the field of liability, the transport of hazardous substances is now covered by a regime of strict liability.

INTERNATIONAL CO-OPERATION AND THE RHINE RIVER

Pollution of the Rhine River

The population growth and industrial expansion that have taken place in Western Europe over the last 40 years and the concentration of activities in central Western Europe have led to more and more pollutants being discharged into the River Rhine. The quality of the water has deteriorated accordingly. At the beginning of the 1970s, oxygen depletion of the Rhine was severe and massive fish kills occurred regularly. Furthermore, an alarming increase in the discharge of heavy metals and organic micropollutants threatened various water uses, in particular the supply of potable water.

Early International Restoration Efforts

The riparian countries - Switzerland, France, Germany, Luxembourg and the Netherlands-, aware of the gravity of the situation, decided to co-operate. In 1963 they established the International Commission for the Protection of the Rhine against pollution (IRC). In 1976 the European Commission joined the IRC. In the same year the Rhine Chemical Treaty and the Treaty for the Protection of the Rhine against pollution by chlorides were concluded.

As a result of these efforts and of national discharge control programmes within riparian countries, water quality in the Rhine has improved markedly over the past 15 years. After declining for many years, the oxygen content has increased steadily since 1970, while the concentrations of almost all heavy metals have been reduced. Significant reductions have also been achieved for organic micropollutants and for oil. Despite this progress, however, and in view of recent industrial accidents which have contributed to additional pollution in the Rhine, authorities from the riparian states and the European Comission recently set new objectives for reduction of pollution in the Rhine.

The Rhine Action Plan

Through the Rhine action plan the participants have committed themselves to meeting four objectives by the year 2000:

- The return to the Rhine of important species no longer present, such as salmon;
- Maintaining a level of water quality suitable for the supply of potable water;
- Reducing pollutant levels in river sediments;
- The health of the North Sea ecosystem.

First, riparian states are focusing their control efforts on 42 toxic substances found in the river. The contributions from each country of 27 of these pollutants have been identified. Results show that industrial establishments are

NUMBER OF WASTE TREATMENT PLANTS

Switzerland	1985	147
	1995	147
Germany	1985	1 468
	1995	1 558
France	1985	83
	1995	116
Luxembourg	1985	15
	1995	19
Netherlands	1985	80
	1995	81
TOTAL	1985	1788
	1995	1921

not the sole sources of pollution; diffuse sources such as urban and agricultural runoff are also important. Countries have committed themselves to accomplishing significant annual reductions in pollutant loads to the river by 1995: 1-2 dichloroethane will be reduced from 580 tonnes to 65 tonnes and chloroform from 110 tonnes to 40 tonnes. Lead inputs, already reduced to 280 tonnes per year, will be further reduced by 15 per cent.

Concerning urban wastewater treatment, important efforts already made in the past will be supplemented. In 1985 more than 1800 wastewater treatment plants were operating in the Rhine basin, with a treatment capacity of some 82 million "person equivalents." By 1995, 100 additional stations will be constructed, with a treatment capacity of over 5 million person equivalents. A concerted effort will be made in the French sector of the river basin to bring the level of wastewater collection and treatment up to 80 per cent of the total amount generated.

The riparian states have recently tightened water quality objectives concerning biochemical oxygen demand (BOD), ammonia and phosphorus. Fewer than half of the existing installations are capable of meeting the new objectives for BOD and ammonia, and even fewer - 10 per cent - are capable of meeting the objectives for phosphorus.

Source: OECD

Table 23. **LIST OF MULTILATERAL CONVENTIONS**

	Subject	Type[a]	Place and date	No. of OECD country signatures	No. of OECD country ratifications or accessions	Entry into force
	SEA POLLUTION					
1-1.	Prevention of pollution of the sea by oil (OILPOL)	Conv.[b]	London, 1954	15[c]	19	26.07.1958
1-2.	Limitation of liability of owners of sea-going ships	Conv.	Brussels, 1957	14	15	31.05.1968
1-3.	Pollution of the North Sea by oil	Agr.	Bonn, 1969	8	8	09.08.1969
1-4.	Civil liability for oil pollution damage (CLC)	Conv.	Brussels, 1969	15	19	19.06.1975
1-4a.	Protocol to amend No. 1-4	Prot.	London, 1984	10	3	Pending
1-5.	Intervention on the high seas in case of oil pollution (INTERVENTION)	Conv.	Brussels, 1969	18	17	06.05.1975
1-5a.	Protocol to No. 1-5 (substances other than oil)	Prot.	London, 1973	8	14	30.03.1983
1-6.	Co-operation against pollution of the sea by oil	Agr.	Copenhagen, 1971	4	4	16.10.1971
1-7.	International fund for compensation for oil pollution damage (FUND)	Conv.	Brussels, 1971	12	15	16.10.1979
1-7a.	Protocol to No. 1-7 (FUND)	Prot.	London, 1976	3	11	Pending
1-7b.	Protocol to No. 1-7 (FUND)	Prot.	London, 1984	. .	2	Pending
1-8.	Prevention of marine pollution by dumping from ships and aircraft	Conv.	Oslo, 1972	20	20	07.04.1974
1-9.	Prevention of marine pollution by dumping of wastes + other matter (LDC)	Conv.	London, Mexico, Moscow Washington, 1972	22	21	30.08.1975
1-10.	Prevention of pollution from ships (MARPOL)	Conv.	London, 1973	11	5	Pending
1-10a.	Protocol to No. 1-10 (MARPOL PROT) (segregated ballast)	Prot.	London, 1978	8	15	02.10.1983
1-11.	Protection of the Marine environment of the Baltic Sea	Conv.	Helsinki, 1974	4	4	03.05.1980
1-12.	Prevention of marine pollution from land-based sources	Conv.	Paris, 1974	13 (+EEC)	11 (+EEC)	06.05.1978
1-13.	Protection of the Mediterranean Sea against pollution	Conv.	Barcelona, 1976	5 (+EEC)	5 (+EEC)	12.02.1978
1-13a.	Protocol to No. 1-13 (dumping from ships and aircraft)	Prot.	Barcelona, 1976	5 (+EEC)	5 (+EEC)	12.02.1978
1-13b.	Protocol No. 1-13 (pollution by oil/cooperation in emergency cases)	Prot.	Barcelona, 1976	5 (+EEC)	5 (+EEC)	12.02.1978
1-13c.	Protocol to No. 1-13 (protection against land-based sources)	Prot.	Athens, 1980	4 (+EEC)	2 (+EEC)	17.06.1983
1-14.	Limitation of liability for maritime claims (LLMC)	Conv.	London, 1976	8	8	01.12.1986
1-15.	Law of the Sea	Conv.	Montego Bay, 1982	24 (+EEC)	1	Pending
1-16.	Protocol concerning Mediterranean specially protected areas	Prot.	Geneva, 1982	4	. .	Pending
1-17.	Coop. in dealing with pollution of the North Sea by oil + other subst.	Agr.	Bonn, 1983	8 (+EEC)	. .	Pending
1-18.	Protection + development of the wider Caribbean region	Conv.	Cartagena, 1983	4 (+EEC)	0	Pending
1-18a.	Protocol to No. 1-18 (oil spills)	Prot.	Cartagena, 1983	. .	. .	Pending
1-18b.	Protocol to No. 1-18 (specially protected areas and wild life)	Prot.	1990	. .	. .	. .
1-19.	Protection of the natural resources and environment of the South Pacific	Conv.	Noumea, 1986	3	. .	Pending

Table 23. LIST OF MULTILATERAL CONVENTIONS (Cont'd)

Subject	Type[a]	Place and date	No. of OECD country signatures	No. of OECD country ratifications or accessions	Entry into force
NUCLEAR					
2-1. Third party liability for nuclear energy	Conv.	Paris, 1960	16	14	01.04.1968
2-1a. Protocol to No. 2-1	Prot.	Paris, 1982	17	13	07.10.1968
2-2. Liability of operators of nuclear ships	Conv.	Brussels, 1962	5 (+EEC)	2	Pending
2-3. Supplementary to No. 2-1 (third party liability for nuclear energy)	Conv.	Brussels, 1963	13	11	04.12.1974
2-3a. Additional protocol to No. 2-3	Prot.	Paris, 1982	13	10	Pending
2-4. Banning nuclear weapons tests in the atmosphere, outer space and under water	Conv.	Moscow, 1963	23	23	10.10.1963
2-5. Prohibition of nuclear weapons on the seabed, ocean floor, and sub-soil	Conv.	London, Moscow Washington, 1971	22	22	18.05.1972
2-6. Civil liability in maritime carriage of nuclear material	Conv.	Brussels, 1971	10	8	15.07.1975
2-7. Early notification of a nuclear accident	Conv.	Vienna, 1986	22	8	27.10.1986
2-8. Assistance in the case of a nuclear accident or radiological emergency	Conv.	Vienna, 1986	21	4	26.02.1987
2-9. Joint protocol relating to the application of the Vienna Convention and the Paris Convention	Prot.	Vienna, 1988	15	1	Pending
FAUNA AND FLORA					
3-1. Preservation of fauna and flora	Conv.	London, 1933	6	4	14.01.1936
3-2. Regulation of whaling	Conv.	Washington, 1946	7	17	10.11.1948
3-3. Conservation of the living resources of the South East Atlantic	Conv.	Rome, 1969	6	7	24.10.1971
3-4. Wetlands of international importance especially as waterfowl habitat	Conv.	Ramsar, 1971	13	22	21.12.1975
3-5. Protection of world cultural and natural heritage	Conv.	Paris, 1972	17	17	17.12.1975
3-6. Antarctic seals	Conv.	London, 1972	8	7	23.11.1972
3-7. Polar bears	Agr.	Oslo, 1973	4	4	26.05.1976
3-8. Fishing and conservation of the living resources in the Baltic Sea	Conv.	Gdansk, 1973	4	EEC	28.07.1974
3-9. International trade in endangered species	Conv.	Washington, 1973	17	20	01.07.1975
3-10. Future multilateral cooperation in the North West Atlantic Fisheries	Conv.	Ottawa, 1978	6 (+EEC)	3 (+EEC)	01.01.1979
3-11. European wild life and natural habitats	Conv.	Bern, 1979	18 (+EEC)	17 (+EEC)	01.06.1982
3-12. Conservation of migratory species of wild animals	Conv.	Bonn, 1979	13 (+EEC)	12 (+EEC)	01.11.1983
3-13. Conservation of antarctic marine living resources	Conv.	Canberra, 1980	9 (+EEC)	9 (+EEC)	07.04.1982
AIR POLLUTION					
4-1. Long range transboundary air pollution	Conv.	Geneva, 1979	21 (+EEC)	21 (+EEC)	16.03.1983
4-1a. Protocol to 5-7 on the reduction of sulphur emissions or their transboundary fluxes by 30%	Prot.	Helsinki, 1985	13	12	02.09.1987
4-1b. Protocol to 5-7 concerning the control of emissions of nitrogen oxides or their transboundary fluxes	Prot.	Sofia, 1988	14	4	Pending
4-2. Transfrontier co-operation	Conv.	Madrid, 1980	9	11	22.12.1981

Table 23. LIST OF MULTILATERAL CONVENTIONS *(Cont'd)*

	Subject	Type[a]	Place and date	No. of OECD country signatures	No. of OECD country ratifications or accessions	Entry into force
4-3.	Protection of the ozone layer	Conv.	Vienna, 1985	. .	. .	Pending
4-4.	Protocol to 5-9	Prot.	Montreal, 1987	. .	. .	01.01.1989
RHINE POLLUTION						
5-1.	Protection of the Rhine against pollution	Agr.	Bonn, 1963	5 (+EEC)	5 (+EEC)	01.05.1965
5-2.	Rhine chloride pollution	Conv.	Bonn, 1976	4	4	1985
5-3.	Protection of the Rhine against chemical pollution	Conv.	Bonn, 1976	5 (+EEC)	5 (+EEC)	01.02.1979
MISCELLANEOUS						
6-1.	International carriage of dangerous goods by road (ADR)	Agr.	Geneva, 1957	14	. .	29.01.1968
6-2.	Restriction of use of detergents	Agr.	Strasbourg, 1968	9	10	16.02.1971
6-2a.	Protocol amending No. 5-2	Prot.	Strasbourg, 1983	5	3	01.11.1984
6-3.	International liability for damage caused by space objects	Conv.	London, Moscow, Washington, 1972	15	22	17.08.1972
6-4.	Nordic environmental protection	Conv.	Stockholm, 1974	4	4	05.10.1976
6-5.	Prohibition of military use of environmental modification techniques	Conv.	Geneva, 1977	19	11	05.10.1978
6-6.	Protection of workers against air pollution, noise + vibration (ILO 148)	Conv.	Geneva, 1977	. .	6	11.07.1979
6-7.	Control of transboundary movements of hazardous wastes and their disposal	Conv.	Basel, 1989	. .	. .	. .
6-8.	Civil liability for damage caused during carriage of dangerous goods by road, rail, and inland navigation vessels (CRTD)	Conv.	Geneva, 1980	. .	. .	. .

Notes: a) Abbreviations: Agr. - Agreement;
                             Conv. - Convention;
                             Prot. - Protocol.
    b) No longer fully operational, because superseded from October 1983 by the MARPOL Protocol.
    c) Denounced by several countries in 1983 and 1984.
Source: OECD, Beitraege zur Umweltgestaltung · Internationales Umweltrecht · Multilaterale Vertraege, IMO IUCN · Environmental Law Center

2. GLOBAL COMMONS

Atmospheric issues

Until the mid-1980s, atmospheric issues were still largely perceived as urban and regional. Two issues then emerged on the forefront of the international agenda which make clear the global nature of atmospheric problems.

The first of these issues was the alarming deterioration of atmospheric ozone levels. Scientific evidence that the earth's ozone layer (which protects the earth from the sun's radiation) was becoming thinner led to the Vienna Convention of 1985, and then to the Montreal Protocol of 1987 based on this Convention. This Protocol called for the reduction of ozone-threatening chlorofluorocarbons (CFCs) over an agreed time period. Although the major CFC-producing nations signed this Protocol, key developing nations did not. At the London Conference of June 1990, however, the provisions of the Montreal Protocol were strengthened, and an agreement was reached on financial arrangements; this has already led to the participation of some developing nations in the accord. (See Chapter on Global Atmospheric Issues)

The second issue was global warming. A series of scientific conferences pointed to the buildup of "greenhouse gases" in the environment. The most important of these gases are carbon dioxide (CO_2), chlorofluorocarbons (CFCs), methane (CH_4) and nitrous oxides (N_2O). Taken together, these gases contribute about 96 per cent of total greenhouse gas emissions in the world today. These emissions occur in both developed and developing countries, and they quickly spread into the atmosphere, where they form an international "blanket" that is suspected of raising global temperatures, altering important rainfall patterns, and increasing sea levels. (See Chapter on Global Atmospheric Issues)

International concern about perceived global warming trends eventually led the United Nations to establish the Intergovernmental Panel on Climate Change (IPCC) in 1988. This body undertook a detailed review of the scientific aspects of global warming and looked at the potential environmental and economic impacts that might result from future emissions. The Panel then reviewed the policy options available to national governments for dealing with the problem. A number of independent initiatives related to the IPCC process have also taken place in recent years. For example, several major international conferences dealing with different aspects of the climate change problem have been held. The conferences in Noordwijk, Washington, The Hague, London, Cairo and Bergen were particularly important in helping to crystallise political thinking on this complex issue.

The IPCC's first assessment report, and the Second World Climate Conference (autumn 1990), are expected to call for an international framework convention on climate change. That convention is likely to focus on ways of controlling greenhouse gas emissions, and protecting and increasing greenhouse gas sinks such as forests; on development and transfer of technology for improving energy use efficiencies; on adaptation strategies; and on how to involve developing countries in the climate change response process. If it is possible to achieve such a broadly-based international convention, detailed protocols will then be negotiated covering the technical aspects of the accord. Many countries have specifically called for the conclusion of a framework convention on climate change by 1992.

The international legal regime for dealing with global atmospheric problems remains inadequate for the time being. Nevertheless, the model of establishing a framework convention, followed by a detailed protocol or protocols, has been successfully used for the ozone issue, and will soon be applied to the climate change problem. Although it is encouraging that the international community is seeking ways to co-ordinate its response to climate change, the road ahead will not be easy. It is not yet clear that an internationl agreement on global warming (or the protocols necessary to give substance to such an agreement) is actually a feasible objective. Furthermore, even if an agreement is signed, it will be several years before its actual implementation and even longer before actual improvements in the state of the world's atmosphere become visible.

Marine environment

Ocean management encompasses national, regional and international actions, strategies and agreements. Since the 1950s the legal regime has evolved on all three levels.

Due to the diversity of pressures affecting the marine environment, its effective management is dependent on the successful integration of many different environmental protection strategies and policies. The essential issue in marine management is the need to balance the multiple uses made of the oceans with the need to maintain their ecological integrity. Because of the potential conflict between many of these uses, ocean management often involves controversies.

Early concerns focused on ocean pollution by oil, and the International Convention for the Prevention of Pollution of the Sea by Oil (OILPOL) was formulated in 1954 to combat oil pollution from shipping. This convention was replaced by a broader agreement in 1973, the International Convention for the Prevention of Pollution from Ships (MARPOL), which deals more generally with pollution from shipping.

Concern about the uncontrolled dumping of wastes at sea culminated in the signing in 1972 of the Convention on the Prevention of Marine Pollution by Dumping of Wastes and Other Matter (usually referred to as the London Dumping Convention).

To help conserve wetlands of international importance from restructuring and other pressures, the Convention on Wetlands of International Importance Especially as Waterfowl Habitat (The Ramsar Convention) was adopted in 1971. Over 400 wetland sites in some 51 countries have been designated, many of them being in estuaries and coastal zones.

Subsequently, the legal framework for protection of the marine environment evolved with a more regional focus. After the Oslo and Paris Conventions concerning the North Atlantic and North Sea regions and the Helsinki Convention for the Baltic Sea area, UNEP launched its Regional Seas Programme. This has led to regional marine protection agreements among states concerned in 11 marine areas of the world. In 1982 the United Nations Convention on the Law of the Sea (UNCLOS) was adopted, providing a global framework through which both pollution and harvesting pressures can be addressed; however, it is not yet in force.

The comprehensiveness of the legal regime can be evaluated by reviewing how agreements address major pressures. Early agreements focused on specific substances (e.g. oil) and practices (e.g. ocean dumping). Subsequent agreements have adopted a more regional and comprehensive approach to deal with a larger number of pollutants and activities. However, while progress has been made in the control of some specific substances, in many areas the problem of land-based pollution sources, which account for most of the pollution entering coastal zones, remain largely uncontrolled, particularly in the case of non-point sources such as agricultural runoff but also to a lesser extent in the case of industrial and municipal discharges.

3. OUTLOOK FOR INTERNATIONAL ENVIRONMENTAL LAW

Whereas the period from 1960 to 1989 was a period of gestation for international environment law, it would seem that the years to come will witness the development of international co-operation through a number of new conventions with innovative ideas and regulations. Already, Member countries are negotiating a dozen new important international agreements on environmental protection, not to mention actions at bilateral levels or within the European Community. There are also attempts to review the state of international environmental law and identify gaps to be filled in the future. The outlook for international law in the area of environmental protection and transfrontier or global pollution can be characterised by the following five main trends.

The first one will be to implement, complete and *reinforce the many existing agreements*. This trend will be especially clear with regard to transfrontier air pollution, with new agreements on volatile organic compounds (VOCs) and stricter measures to protect the ozone layer. Similarly, the convention on international movements of waste will have to be ratified, implemented and possibly improved.

The second trend will be to *extend* to central and eastern Europe, many principles already agreed by OECD Member countries – for example, by adopting a convention on transboundary impact assessment, international bodies of water and accidents with transboundary impacts. The texts of such conventions under negotiation are based on existing agreements, on OECD Recommendations and Decisions and on European Community Directives. Another type of co-operation will consist of creating and strengthening networks for the exchange of data and resource information (for example on accidents at the ECE level). As regards dangerous installations, greater importance will be given to existing information and consultation procedures concerning the location of such installations in frontier regions. International borders should progressively cease to prevent the environment of frontier regions from being managed in an integrated fashion in accordance with the principles of non-discrimination and international solidarity.

The third trend will be to rely more frequently on *quantified targets* in order to describe more precisely the undertakings of the contracting parties with respect to environmental protection. This means the adoption at regional or worldwide level of specific standards (relating to emissions, products and/or quality) and undertakings as to goals to be achieved (for example, reduction by x per cent of emissions or of the production of a given chemical by a given date). These quantified commitments should become internationally verifiable. Sanctions could even be provided in order to discourage inaccurate reporting, and conversely, economic incentives might be introduced in order to induce countries to implement their undertakings fully.

The fourth trend will consist of *specifying liability* in the event of accidental pollution and ensuring that victims of transfrontier accidents receive compensation. Work on this issue is under way within most international organisations and should lead to new agreements on maritime transport, on dangerous installations and even on hazardous wastes. The ceilings on the amounts available for payment as compensation will need to be increased, given the effects of inflation and the financial extent of the latest disasters – and of the even greater ones that might occur in the future.

Lastly, ideas have been put forward to attempt to define the concept and content of a sort of *fundamental right to a sound environment* and to ensure that ways will be sought to create international mechanisms to foster better protection of the environment in those countries which fail to manage it appropriately.

Recognition that the vessel Earth is in danger might have repercussions on the right of countries to use their natural resources without regard to the need to achieve sustainable development and protect resources which are of world interest. On a worldwide level, limits might be placed on types of conduct which are in too flagrant contradiction with the goals of environmental protection recognised by the world community.

4. TRADE AND THE ENVIRONMENT

OECD countries account for about 76 per cent of world trade – 73 per cent of chemical exports, 88 per cent of automobile exports, 73 per cent of imports of forestry products and 80 per cent of imports of primates. Some of this trade is concentrated within the OECD area itself, while part of it involves other economies such as those of developing countries and Eastern European countries. With the development of the international dimensions in both trade and environmental issues, it appears that the potential for conflicts in the 1990s between trade and environmental objectives is on the rise. At the beginning of the 1990s, however, issues concerning trade and the environment have been addressed only, and mostly indirectly, through international agreements (e.g. the Montreal Protocol Concerning the Protection of the Ozone Layer, the Basel Convention on the Control of Transfrontier Movements of Hazardous Wastes and their Disposal).

A number of concerns have to do with the relationship between trade and the environment; among them are trade concerns about environmental regulations, concerns about natural resource depletion and trade practices, as well as broader economic aspects of trade and the environment.

Trade and environmental regulations

Firstly, some attention is being given to international differences in *environmental standards* concerning products such as automobiles and chemicals, in order to avoid their leading to non-tariff barriers to trade. Concerning motor vehicles, OECD countries have adopted exhaust emission standards over the past 20 years. These standards have evolved over time, with different levels, schedules and test cycles in Japan, North America and Europe. Guidelines have also been adopted by UNEP for application by developing countries. International trade in motor vehicles would benefit from internationally harmonized emission standards, although environmentalists fear that this would result in the adoption of weak standards. (See Chapter on Transport) Present differences in standards stem largely from the number of countries involved in negotiations and from differences in environmental goals and industrial structures. Trade in chemicals has prompted the OECD to develop an extensive programme to induce Member countries to adopt common procedures for testing the impact of new and existing chemicals on man and the environment. The programme seeks to discourage non-tariff barriers to trade in chemicals and share (and hence reduce) testing costs for OECD countries.

Secondly, the increasing trade in "green products" calls for international co-operation to avoid undesirable effects on trade stemming from differences in national *labeling* of those products. Industries which have been able to develop products that are environmentally friendly and cost-efficient have gained a competitive advantage both nationally and internationally. Markets for products such as "clean" household products, substitutes for batteries and CFCs are growing fast. Together with the development of the green consumer market, green product advertising and environmental labelling have developed in a frequently uncontrolled and misleading fashion. That is why in many OECD countries national labelling schemes have been adopted or are at present under discussion. Differences in national labelling schemes may, however, be a potential obstacle to international trade in environmentally friendly goods. Consequently, enhanced levels of international co-operation are essential.

Largely driven by environmental regulations, the world *market for clean technology and pollution abatement equipment* has developed strongly over the past decade. Countries with the most stringent environmental legislation have taken an early lead in the development of environmental technology and are now the main exporting countries. Recently, new markets in Eastern Europe and some developing countries have started to open up. The development of the environmental technology market so far has been dominated by end-of-pipe processes, the main reason being that the demand for integrated technologies (clean production processes) depends to a large extent on the renewal of capital stock.

From the trade policy point of view, an examination of impacts of environmental measures may be essential in order to prevent trade conflicts, even though studies so far have not found any significant international trade distortions relating to environmental policies. The Trade Committee of the OECD has started a comprehensive examination on this issue. In particular, it intends to further consider, within the framework of the existing GATT rules, how concepts such as transparency, national treatment and non-discrimination, legitimacy and proportionality should be applied in the context of environmental regulations.

Trade and sustainable development

Trade by industrialised countries and their trade-related policies indirectly affect the environment and the use of natural resources in developing countries. A number of factors, such as developing countries' debt and/or balance of payment problems, industrialised countries' protectionism against goods manufactured in developing countries, preferential treatment of raw materials and agricultural products from developing countries, and price fluctuations on the world market, have contributed to an unsustainable use of natural resources, soil degradation, excessive use of fertilizers and pesticides, and pollution in many developing countries.

INFORMATION EXCHANGE RELATED TO THE EXPORT OF HAZARDOUS CHEMICALS

The Need for Information Exchange

All countries need to be properly informed about the potential risks to human health and the environment involved with hazardous chemicals. This need has emerged as a priority among international policy objectives.

While importing countries have the primary responsibility for protecting humans and the environment from the hazards associated with chemicals imported into their territories, exporting countries have a responsibility to assist importing countries in doing so. If the exporting country has made the judgement that a given chemical should be banned or severely restricted, it is in possession of the information on which that judgement is based.

The OECD Programme for Information Exchange

OECD Member countries, being among the major producers, exporters and importers of chemicals, have established an information exchange scheme related to export of banned or severely restricted chemicals. The OECD programme contains two recommendations directed at Member countries:

- First, if a chemical which is banned or severely restricted in a Member country is exported, information should be provided to allow the importing country to make timely and informed decisions concerning the chemical;

- Second, Member countries should take into account a set of guiding principles governing the provision of information to importing countries. These principles provide a general framework to assist Member countries in developing their national schemes. They identify the minimum information needed to alert the importing country and describe a two-step mechanism for carrying out the information exchange. The first step calls on the exporting Member country to make relevant information available when it bans or severely restricts a chemical. The second step involves an alert notification to the importing country the first time such a chemical is exported. The guiding principles also call on exporting countries to provide additional information to importing countries on request.

The programme relates only to those chemicals which have been the subject of a regulatory action by an exporting Member country to ban or severely restrict domestic use; thus only a small number of the many thousands of chemicals in commerce are affected.

However, these chemicals have great potential to impose heavy costs on societies in the form of health effects and environmental damage. Among the chemicals banned or severely restricted in more than one OECD Member country are Dieldrin, Chlordane, DDT, and PCBs. Use of these chemicals in importing countries has, in fact, in many instances, caused serious damage to human health and the environment.

Information relating to banned or severely restricted chemicals is to be provided not only to OECD Member countries, but to non-Member countries as well. Therefore, information will be available to those less developed countries with perhaps the greatest need for assistance in relation to imports of hazardous chemicals.

Two reviews have been carried out to examine actions taken by OECD Member countries in accordance with the programme. The results of these reviews indicate that most, if not all, of the major OECD chemical exporting countries now have in place, or are in the process of establishing, systems to provide export-related notifications.

Towards Global Co-operation on Information Exchange

The OECD information exchange scheme related to export of banned or severely restricted chemicals has been adopted on a worldwide basis. The United Nations Environment Programme's (UNEP) London Guidelines for the Exchange of Information on Chemicals in International Trade, and the Food and Agriculture Organisation's (FAO) International Code of Conduct on the Distribution and Use of Pesticides, establish similar export notification systems. They also introduce the Principle of Prior Informed Consent, whereby the export of a banned or severely restricted chemical should not proceed without the agreement of the importing country. As with the OECD recommendations, these two schemes are voluntary.

Since the scope of these export notification schemes goes beyond that of the OECD, the OECD activities in the future will focus on working with UNEP, FAO and other international organisations to facilitate implementation of these schemes.

Source: OECD

An example of an international trade flow with a negative environmental impact in a developing country is the importation by the European Community of cassava from Thailand. Thailand indeed exports its entire cassava production, and 90 per cent of it goes to the European Community. This production, taking up about 1.5 million ha of land, has led to the rapid degradation of natural resources in Thailand. Production takes place on deforested land, giving rise to erosion and declining soil fertility. Since 1982 the EC has tried to restrict its imports from Thailand, but thus far this has not led to a decrease in production. It is feared that further restrictions on imports of cassava would result in a drop in foreign currency earnings for Thailand and stockpiling of the product. If, as a result, new land were to be reclaimed for the cultivation of alternative crops, deforestation would be accelerated and might be even more harmful to the environment than the present cassava production.

While in many cases, international trade practices only affect the environment of the developing country or countries involved, there are also cases where trade flows have a regional or even global impact. This has induced countries to use trade instruments unilaterally or multilaterally for environmental objectives. International concern over the destruction of the tropical forests and the sustainable use and management of forest resources, for example, has induced a growing number of countries to introduce import or export restrictions on tropical timber. Although partly motivated by the wish to develop local processing industries, several producer countries have banned the export of raw logs. (See Chapter on Forest)

Trade in endangered or threatened wild life species and in products from such species is monitored by the United Nations' Convention on Trade in Endangered Species of Wild Fauna and Flora (CITES), which has been signed by 109 states. CITES operates on the basis of lists, updated every two years, covering animals and plants threatened by extinction. Trade in these species is either banned or controlled. The implementation of the Convention is the responsibility of the individual contracting parties, and the quality of its implementation varies greatly. In October 1989 CITES contracting parties decided to ban all trade in ivory in order to save the African elephant. (See Chapter on Wild Life)

Environmental conservation at national, international and global levels will necessitate the management of trade in such a way as to prevent international trade from having major environmental impacts. To achieve a sustainable development of international trade, both environmental and trade policies should be designed so that prices of internationally traded products, services or natural resources fully reflect the environmental cost of their production, consumption or disposal.

Broader economic aspects of international trade and the environment

Already in the 1970s, concerns had been expressed about the impact of national environmental policies on international competitiveness. Industries in countries without environmental regulations or with relatively lenient ones might incur lower costs than their international competitors. A number of studies, concerning some OECD countries, on the macroeconomic and trade effects of environmental policies have shown negligible trade effects. However, the recent upsurge in public environmental awareness and the increasing priority placed on environmental policies in many countries, has given rise to renewed concern about the potential impact of those policies on international trade performance. OECD countries recognise the benefits of some international harmonisation of environmental policies. Harmonisation with developing countries or with Eastern European countries might, however, be more difficult in the years ahead.

Just as environmental concerns are becoming more prominent on the agenda of many countries, international trade liberalisation is also an increasingly important policy question. For example, the European Community has set 31st December 1992 as a target date for the completion of its Internal Market and in 1987 the United States and Canada signed a Free Trade Agreement in which they decided to eliminate all their bilateral tariff barriers. These agreements may have considerable consequences for the environment. Trade liberalisation should allow for the full exploitation of comparative advantages, which will lead to international specialisation, increased competition, cost reductions, economic growth, and increases in international trade flows. Fears have been expressed that this might lead to increased freight and passenger transport, energy consumption and some environmental degradation. However, higher economic welfare levels may have a positive impact on an individual's preferences for a better environment and consumers may demand environmentally friendlier products. The net environmental impact is uncertain, and will largely depend upon environmental policy developments.

Large-scale Trade in Wild Life

The world market for wild life is surprisingly large. Worth at least US $5 billion in wholesale, one year's international trade includes at least 1 million orchids; some 40,000 primates; until recently, ivory from at least 90,000 African elephants; 4 million wild birds; 10 million reptile skins; 15 million pelts from furbearers; over 300 million tropical fish and other items as diverse as kangaroo leather and tortoiseshell trinkets. The market is growing steadily, due to advances in transportation, expanding demand in consumer countries and more effective wild life hunting and exploitation techniques.

Products from wild life are usually sold as luxury goods, such as fur coats and reptile-skin accessories or, in the live trade, as pets. Price tags can be enormous, especially for endangered species. The glandular scent from Himalayan musk deer is worth up to four times its weight in gold in Far Eastern medicinal markets. Extremely rare giant pitcher plants from Borneo can be sold for US $1,000 each on the black market. Rare Peruvian butterflies may retail for upwards of US $3,000 apiece and horn from endangered Asian rhinoceros species is worth over US $28 600 per kilogram in Taiwan.

A Threat to Wild Life

For most wild plants and animals the most immediate threat to survival is habitat loss. Nevertheless, international wild life trade - the import, export or re-export across national borders of live animals and plants, as well as their parts and products - remains a destructive force. It has been estimated that almost 40 per cent of all vertebrates that now face extinction do so largely because they are hunted by human beings for trade.

Already, the list of species that have disappeared as a result of human exploitation includes, among others, the Stellar's sea cow, the West Indian monk seal, the Great Auk, the sea mink and the passenger pigeon. Many other species, such as rhinoceros, sea turtles, macaws and certain species of cacti are threatened by unsustainable exploitation for international markets. At least two of the three chimpanzee sub-species in Africa are threatened by dwindling habitats and by hunting for their meat; losses to trade may tip the balance towards extinction. Similarly, black market demands in some parts of the world encourage hunters to kill tigers, jaguars, grizzly and black bears, saltwater crocodiles and other species that are already subjected to other pressures from human activities. Commercial hunters and collectors frequently kill or remove these and other species with little regard for how many individuals can be replaced through natural reproduction.

Ecological and Economic Consequences

Uncontrolled wild life trade can have far-reaching ecological consequences. Once a species is eliminated, natural food chains and delicate predator-prey relationships may be upset. For example, in Bangladesh, India and Indonesia, malaria infestation has been partly attributed to annual harvests of some 250 million bullfrogs - natural insect predators - for the frog-leg trade. The lack of wild

REPORTED TRADE IN WILDLIFE AND WILDLIFE PRODUCTS

	Africa	Asia	Europe	North & Central America	South America	World
Mammals *(in thousands)*						
Live I	-	7	15	17	-	42
Primates E	7.8	22	3	5	3.8	43
Cat I	6.7	7	116	43	1.0	175
Skins E	7.7	60	15	87	3.4	179
Raw I	14.2	505	133	26	.1	679
Ivory(kg) E	303.7	280	134	2	-	720
Birds *(in thousands)*						
Live I	13.2	67	196	322	6.2	606
Parrots E	160.3	89	55	36	265.3	607
Reptiles *(in thousands)*						
Reptile I	3.4	2 480	3 908	2 436	80.7	8 910
Skins E	359.7	4 198	1 539	930	1 900.3	8 953

I = Imports
E = Exports

Source: World Resources Institute

frogs may necessitate increased reliance on DDT and other harmful pesticides.

The economic effects of overexploitation of wild life may also be severe. Developing countries, which provide the bulk of wild animals and plants in trade, depend on wild life for important foreign exchange. If wild life resources are not properly managed, they simply will not be available to future consumers, hunters, fishermen, sightseers, nature lovers and other wild life "users" who provide important financial income to developing nations' economies.

Managing Wild Life Trade Sustainably

If properly controlled, wild life trade need not threaten plant and animal species. Instead, trade can be a strong force for conservation, providing countries with the economic incentive to protect habitat and manage wild life on a sustainable-use basis. For example, some reptiles reproduce rapidly and respond well to captive breeding and ranching efforts. Several successful ranching operations exist for threatened African and Asian crocodile species; in Latin America, conservationists and traders are exploring possibilities for sustainable-use management of the spectacled caiman, the Tegu lizard and the green iguana.

More and more examples are available to demonstrate how sensible utilisation of species and their products can aid wild life conservation efforts by providing needed financial resources. Most importantly, well organised wild life management schemes may generate income that can be used to help administer national parks and to support local human communities.

Contribution from IUCN

5. AID AND THE ENVIRONMENT

The problems

Environmental concerns vary considerably within and among developing countries. However, despite the particularities of each individual developing country, environmental problems are, generally speaking, of two kinds.

The first, arising primarily from a combination of poverty and population growth, are those which lead to the degradation of renewable natural resources. The most dramatic example in this category is the destruction of tropical forests, wetlands and other critical habitats. The last official statistics from the U.N. Food and Agriculture Organisation (FAO) estimated a loss of 11 million hectares of tropical forest per year between 1981 and 1985. Current, preliminary estimates suggest, however, that 17 million hectares of tropical forests vanish each year. Other examples of natural resource destruction include: soil erosion and loss of soil fertility, desertification, loss of biological diversity and over-utilisation of water resources (e.g. through over-fishing, dragnet fishing, and so on).

The second category includes problems, arising from increased industrialisation and urbanisation, which lead to the pollution of water, air and soil through urban and industrial activities, waste disposal and destructive tourism development.

Together with the environmental destruction taking place in developed countries, these problems are contributing to such global environmental threats as climate change and the depletion of the ozone layer.

Addressing the problems: 1970-1990

Twenty years ago development assistance agencies and financial institutions gave little attention to environmental protection. In the last 10 years, however, both the aid agencies of OECD Member countries and multilateral financial institutions such as the World Bank have devoted increasing attention to the "environment".

The environmental policies for development assistance which are currently being developed by these organisations are characterised by three central elements. They are:

Environmentally beneficial projects designed to protect existing environments, or upgrade and rehabilitate degraded ones.

Just as the environmental problems in developing countries can be divided between those resulting from natural resource degradation and those arising from industrialisation and urbanisation, so environmentally beneficial projects can be aimed at improving the rural and the urban environment. In practice, however, most of the environmental projects which have

been undertaken to date have been implemented in rural rather than urban areas. Examples of such projects include those related to soil conservation, erosion and desertification control; afforestation and fuelwood production; creation of nature and wildlife reserves; protection and rehabilitation of water resources; pesticide control programmes and waste management schemes.

Environmental impact assessment (EIA) procedures for ensuring that traditional development aid projects and programmes are assessed for their potential environmental impact and carried out in an environmentally sound manner.

At present, nine members of the OECD's Development Assistance Committee (DAC – Australia, Canada, Denmark, Germany, the Netherlands, Norway, Switzerland, the United Kingdom and the United States), together with the major multilateral development institutions such as the World Bank, Inter- American Development Bank and Asian Development Bank have established formal procedures for assessing the environmental impacts of their development assistance activities. Most of the other bilateral and multilateral donors are in the process of drafting such procedures.

Generally speaking, these procedures provide for: a screening of project types to determine which ones need to be assessed; an initial environmental examination to determine whether or not a full-fledged environmental impact assessment (EIA) needs to be undertaken; the EIA itself, followed by mitigation measures to reduce the negative environmental impacts of projects which are implemented; and monitoring of completed projects to ensure that they conform with any environmental provisions called for in the EIA.

The types of projects most frequently being assessed for their environmental impact include highways and other transport projects, large dams and irrigation/drainage schemes, industrial activities, extractive activities such as mining, oil and gas extraction, and projects which result in substantial changes in renewable resource use, such as the conversion of forests or natural areas to agricultural production or pastureland.

Most bilateral aid agencies have only just begun to establish procedures for EIA and have, therefore, not yet acquired much experience in actual implementation. The same applies to multilateral agencies. The World Bank, for example, adopted formal procedures in October 1989 and estimates that 20 to 25 per cent of its projects will be subject to a full environmental assessment. Whereas the bilateral agencies take responsibility for their own EIAs, assessments of World Bank projects will be the borrower's (i.e. the developing country's) responsibility, as part of the project preparation. The Bank, in its environmental clearance process,

SWAPPING DEBT FOR CONSERVATION

Debt and the Environment

A country's indebtedness can have highly adverse effects on its environment, restricting the ability of indebted countries to manage their natural assets in a way that promotes sustainable development. The same is true of fluctuations and downward trends in commodity prices, especially when these are coupled with lower inflows of foreign capital and growing debt service.

These effects have been felt most strongly in Africa and Latin America. The rising cost of oil imports has forced some African countries to clear forests for wood fuel. In Latin America, in attempting to service their debt, many countries have made impressive efforts to develop new products for export - raw materials, foodstuffs, and resource-intensive manufactured goods - thereby accentuating pressures on their natural resources and on the environment as a whole.

How Debt-for-Nature Swaps are Made

A debt-for-nature swap is an arrangement by which an indebted country undertakes, in exchange for cancellation of a portion of its foreign debt, to establish local currency funds to be used to finance a conservation programme. The mechanism brings a number of partners together: the debtor government, the creditor, and a non-governmental organisation (NGO), often international, concerned with the environment.

The first step involves establishing the terms of the debt conversion. All parties must agree on the exchange rate for converting dollar-denominated debt to local currency, the percentage of face value at which to redeem the loan, the types of financial instruments to be issued and the conservation programme to be set in motion. Next, the money to acquire the discounted debt must be found. Creditor banks are generally reluctant to make outright donations; funds are usually secured from private donors or bilateral aid agencies. Last, acquiring debt titles requires an experienced agent to enter into a formal exchange agreement with the creditor bank, which will transfer custody of the title to the debtor country's central bank. The central bank then converts the title into cash, local currency funds or some other instrument with which to fund the agreed conservation work.

The mechanism is advantageous for all of the participants:

- For the debtor country it is an opportunity to buy back part of its debt and raise funds for conservation without ceding any part of its sovereignty, since the debt-for-nature swap does not result in a foreign stake in a local corporation;
- For the creditor bank, it is a means of relinquishing claims that may well be unrecoverable;
- For the NGOs, it generates additional funding for conservation work.

Implementing Debt-For-Nature Swaps

Bolivia was the first country to sign a debt-for-nature agreement, in 1987. This has resulted in enhanced

SELECTED EXAMPLES

Bolivia	-	$650 000 of debt swapped
	-	135 000 ha protected in Beni biosphere reserve
Costa Rica	-	$72 million of debt swapped
	-	numerous conservation initiatives
Ecuador	-	$10 million of debt swapped
	-	numerous conservation initiatives
Madagascar	-	$2 million to $3 million of debt swapped
	-	re-afforestation and training
Philippines	-	$2 million of debt swapped
	-	park management, environmental education, training and research

protection for the Beni biosphere reserve, an area of 135 000 hectares containing several threatened species of wild animals and a group of nomadic hunter Indians. Three adjacent areas with a wealth of flora and fauna - the Yacuma regional park, the Cordebeni watershed and the Chimane forest - will also be protected. Since then, other countries have taken part in debt-for-nature-swaps, such as Costa Rica, Ecuador, Madagascar and the Philippines.

The country which has made the largest volume of debt-for-nature swaps is Costa Rica. Between 1987 and 1989, through donations totalling US $10.1 million, the country converted US $72 million of its foreign debt into US $36 million of local currency bonds. The money has gone to finance purchases of land to enlarge parks and maintain them, to strengthen public and private institutions and to re-forest thousands of hectares of small holdings.

Prospects for Debt-for-Nature Swaps

Debt-for-nature swaps are still too recent and modest in scope for firm conclusions to be drawn about their outcome. They should be regarded neither as a miracle solution for the indebtedness of developing countries, nor as the sole means of helping these countries to promote policies of sustainable development. If the debt problem is to be solved, additional policies designed to attract international finance will have to be devised and implemented. Nevertheless, for the environment, both local and worldwide, debt-for-nature swaps are an important step forward.

Source: OECD

will indicate when there is a need for an environmental analysis, provide technical support, and review the final assessment.

Measures for strengthening the capability of developing countries to deal with environmental issues.

Ultimately, the responsibility for protecting the environment and managing the natural resource base of developing countries rests with the developing countries themselves. Many of them, however, are presently ill-equipped to undertake that management on their own. In recognition of this fact, many donors have begun to realise that their environmental programmes must go beyond the provision of "environmentally beneficial projects" and the implementation of "environmental impact assessment" to include measures which "help developing countries help themselves".

Specific activities being undertaken in this regard include the development and strengthening of environmental ministries, agencies and institutes in developing countries through the provision of short- and long-term experts and advisors as well as environmental training for government officials. The latter may range from general courses on environmental management to specific seminars and workshops on pollution control techniques and environmental impact assessment. In addition, both bilateral and multilateral development institutions are giving increased attention to strengthening the environmental database in developing countries. The World Bank, for example, has prepared "issues papers" for the majority of its active borrowing members which are designed to identify key environmental problems and their underlying causes. It is also preparing a number of "action plans" for developing countries which include both an overall strategy and recommendations for specific action with descriptions of the environmental policies, investment strategies and legislation required.

These three elements together currently make up the environmental "policy" of most bi- and multilateral donors. In some cases that policy is a formal one in the form of legislation or legally binding administrative rules or procedures. In other cases, the policy is more informal, based on non-binding statements of intent or in-house suggestions for incorporating environmental concerns in decision-making.

As with the adoption of an environmental policy, the establishment of environmental offices or departments, together with provisions for "environmental personnel", is in various stages of implementation among development assistance institutions. Among the multilaterals, the World Bank has gone furthest in administrative restructuring through the creation of a central Environment Department and four regional Environment Divisions to oversee and promote environmental activities in its work.

Agenda for the future

To a certain extent, future activities in the field of "aid and environment" will be related to expanding and improving the responses to the following three questions:

- What kind of environmentally beneficial projects are most needed in which developing countries?
- How can environmental impact assessments be carried out in the most cost-efficient manner?
- What are the most effective measures to be taken to "help developing countries help themselves" in managing their environment?

In addition, however, there are three new aspects to the aid and environment issue which will be receiving increasing attention in the future. The first of these relates to clarifying the overall economic aspects of the environment. While progress has taken place in integrating environmental concerns into *project* work, increased efforts will need to be made in the future to integrate the same concerns into *non-project* aid. Research into environmental economics, especially the methodological issues concerning the valuation of the environment and the role of macro-economic policy, is becoming a high priority. Specific activities being examined in this regard include the means to ensure appropriate pricing of environmental costs and the benefits of policy making and programme and project design, the use of market-oriented instruments to enhance environment protection, and financial incentives for environment protection, including debt swaps.

The second aspect is that of global environmental problems. There is a growing realisation that the industrialised nations, which account for the major share of global pollution, have a special responsibility to help developing countries respond to such issues as climate change, ozone layer depletion and biodiversity. Beyond that, however, the exact type of assistance needed or the way in which it should be provided are yet to be specified and made operational. Apart from these multilateral efforts, the bilateral development agencies are beginning to address global issues through their existing programmes, particularly in the forestry and energy sectors.

Because of the multiplicity of actors – bi- and multilateral development institutions, NGOs, host governments – involved in developing country environments, the solutions to national, regional and global environmental problems must be jointly arrived at and carried out in a co-ordinated manner.

The need for coordinated action is particularly relevant to the third new aspect of the aid and environment issue, namely that of Eastern European countries. Their environmental problems are somewhat different from those of developing countries, being more associated with industrial and urban pollution. For that

Table 24. PUBLIC OPINION ON ENVIRONMENTAL PROBLEMS, percent of persons "very concerned"

LOCAL ENVIRONMENTAL PROBLEMS

	Year	Number of interviews	Lack of access to open space and countryside	Loss of good farmland	Deterioration of the landscape	Waste disposal	Drinking-water quality	Air pollution	Noise	Water pollution (rivers, lakes...)
Japan	1990	3 753	29	n.a.	n.a.	n.a.	n.a.	n.a.	n.a.	n.a.
Finland	1989	1 985	2	n.a.	15	11	9	20	13	22
Norway	1990	1 506	1	2	4	5	5	6	5	15
Belgium	1988	1 022	4	6	12	44	6	9	8	n.a.
Denmark	1988	1 009	1	3	5	2	2	5	4	n.a.
France	1988	993	6	11	12	6	8	7	6	n.a.
Western Germany	1988	1 007	6	6	11	6	8	14	14	n.a.
Greece	1988	1 000	17	15	28	29	14	26	20	n.a.
Ireland	1988	992	1	1	3	10	6	6	3	n.a.
Italy	1988	1 021	10	12	20	15	20	15	11	n.a.
Luxembourg	1988	300	3	5	13	7	6	14	12	n.a.
Netherlands	1988	1 023	2	5	10	8	3	4	5	n.a.
Portugal	1988	1 000	9	13	14	15	12	11	12	n.a.
Spain	1988	1 017	12	11	17	9	15	14	14	n.a.
United Kingdom	1988	1 345	3	5	11	10	4	6	5	n.a.
EEC	1988	11 729	7	8	14	10	10	11	9	n.a.

NATIONAL ENVIRONMENTAL PROBLEMS / INTERNATIONAL ENVIRONMENTAL PROBLEMS

	Year	Number of interviews	Accidental damage to the marine environment	Nuclear waste disposal	Industrial waste disposal	Water pollution	Air pollution	Extinction of plant or animal species in the world	Depletion of world forest and natural resources	Possible climate changes brought about by carbon dioxyde
USA	1990	1 223	52	46	n.a.	64	58	n.a.	40	30
Japan	1990	3 753	42	24	32[a]	41	41	25	37	43
Finland	1989	1 985	64	44	43	35	61	43	63	44
Norway	1990	1 506	45	n.a.	43	42	39	64	65	65
Belgium	1988	1 022	32	n.a.	39	32	34	37	28	29
Denmark	1988	1 009	55	n.a.	56	50	45	44	45	54
France	1988	993	47	n.a.	44	38	36	40	32	34
Western Germany	1988	1 007	46	n.a.	50	46	45	45	32	48
Greece	1988	1 000	55	n.a.	47	44	53	41	38	45
Ireland	1988	992	36	n.a.	38	38	30	27	28	34
Italy	1988	1 021	59	n.a.	58	62	62	43	39	48
Luxembourg	1988	300	38	n.a.	45	36	40	49	37	39
Netherlands	1988	1 023	57	n.a.	62	56	54	48	32	36
Portugal	1988	1 000	41	n.a.	43	44	41	43	38	43
Spain	1988	1 017	53	n.a.	53	54	52	58	55	50
United Kingdom	1988	1 345	40	n.a.	47	38	32	39	36	40
EEC	1988	11 729	48	n.a.	50	47	45	44	35	43

Notes: n.a. = not asked
a/ Pollution by hazardous chemicals.
Source: OECD

reason, environmentally beneficial projects in Eastern Europe, at least in the short term, will need to concentrate on the clean-up and rehabilitation of environmental resources which have suffered from decades of industrial pollution. At the present time aid to Eastern Europe is being undertaken outside official bilateral development assistance budgets and is not, therefore, subject to the same "environmental policy" described above for developing countries. But just as with developing countries, environmental impact assessment and institutional strengthening will need to be incorporated into future development assistance for Eastern Europe which, in the immediate future, will most likely be provided through new and existing multilateral institutions such as the European Bank for Reconstruction and Development and the World Bank.

6. CONCLUSIONS

A growing number of environmental issues are international by nature. First, some problems relate to *transfrontier pollution*. Among these are long-range pollution, the management of international river basins, the international transport of hazardous wastes, and risks associated with installations located close to international frontiers.

Second, some problems concern *regional or global commons*. They can only be resolved through concerted action on the part of OECD countries. This applies not only to planet-wide problems, such as the protection of the stratospheric ozone layer and potential climate changes as a consequence of CO_2 and other greenhouse gas emissions, but also to problems such as the management of regional seas.

Third, a number of environmental issues are *trade*-related. OECD countries account for a large part of world trade in chemicals, automobiles, natural resources such as forestry products or endangered species of wild flora and fauna. In many cases, trade and trade-related policies of industrialised countries indirectly affect pollution and the use of natural resources in developing and developed countries.

Fourth, environmental problems in non-OECD countries such as developing countries or central and Eastern European countries need to be handled in conjunction with *bilateral and multilateral aid and financing*. In the last ten years, development assistance agencies of OECD Member countries and multilateral financial institutions have progressively assessed the potential environmental impacts of traditional development aid projects, financed specific environmentally beneficial projects, and stimulated the capability of receiving countries to deal with environmental issues.

Although some interest has been shown by environmentalists and several international organisations since the beginning of the 1970s, it is only in recent years that recognition of the international nature of environmental problems has achieved a large media and diplomatic dimension. This largely followed and reflected public opinion in OECD countries: polls, for instance, show the great importance given to international environmental issues compared to more national or local ones. (Table 24)

Thus, over the last twenty years progress with regard to international environmental issues has mainly taken the form of development of international environmental law and adoption of related bilateral and multilateral agreements such as those concerning trade in flora and fauna, sea pollution, transfrontier pollution, international movement of hazardous wastes, and protection of the ozone layer. The actual impacts of these agreements on the state of the environment obviously depend on the adoption of effective national and international mechanisms for implementation and, further, on the length of time needed to see implemented measures translate into environmental improvements.

The challenge in the 1990s will be:

- To ensure that such agreements are effectively translated into environmental realities;

- To supplement existing agreements with new ones on emerging issues such as climate change, and, more broadly, with quantified targest and appropriate liability rules;

- To promote the integration of environmental concerns into trade and aid policies and practices, in order to ensure sustainable development of the planet Earth and a fair share for all regions and countries of the world in that development.

REFERENCES

OECD (1978), *Legal Aspects of Transfrontier Pollution*, Paris.

OECD (1979), *Environmental Protection in Frontier Regions*, Paris.

OECD (1981), *Transfrontier Pollution and the Role of States*, Paris.

OECD (1981), *Compensation for Pollution Damage*, Paris.

OECD (1982), *Combatting Oil Spills*, Paris.

OECD (1982), *The Cost of Oil Spills*, Paris.

OECD (1985), *Transfrontier Movements of Hazardous Wastes*, Paris.

CONCLUSIONS ON THE STATE OF THE ENVIRONMENT

Over the past two decades governments have formulated policies, passed laws, and created new institutions to control pollution and manage natural resources. Industry has introduced changes in products and production processes, and stepped up efforts to conserve resources. In the OECD's pluralistic democracies and market economies, it is no surprise that this has happened largely in response to public awareness and persistent demands for a better environment. Co-ordinated opinion polls carried out in the late 1980s in the United States, Japan and 14 European countries showed clear public support for environmental protection, even at the expense of reduced economic growth.

How effective have all these efforts been in improving the environment? This Secretariat report addresses that question and relates the state of the environment to economic growth and structural changes in OECD countries.

The report is based on the work of the OECD Group on the State of the Environment. It draws on the OECD environmental database as well as on other expertise and scientific evidence accumulated by the OECD. It also uses information from national reports on the state of the environment.

On the basis of this assessment it is now possible to:

- Review the environment today to assess the progress achieved since 1970 and identify the problems on the agenda of the 1990s;
- Conclude that achieving sustainable development will require changes in environmental policies and economic structures as well as effective responses to the international issues.

A special assessment is also made concerning the overall *state of environmental information*.

1. THE ENVIRONMENT TODAY

Progress

OECD countries have made progress in dealing with a number of the most urgent environmental problems identified over the last two decades. The following achievements are detailed in the report:

- Reduction of urban air pollution by sulphur dioxide, particulate matter and lead;
- Reduced pollution of waterways and lakes by organic substances through the extension of treatment of household wastewater and industrial effluents;
- Virtual elimination of significant pathogenic microbial contamination of drinking water supplies;
- Decreased *accidental* oil inputs to the oceans as a result of the reduced frequency of large shipping accidents and spills;
- Increases in the area of protected land and habitats, such as parks and refuges, throughout OECD countries;
- Increased forest resources, in area as well as in the volume of timber stock, in almost all OECD countries;

- Better protection and management of a number of game species, and growing populations of several threatened species of flora and fauna;
- Improved collection, disposal and recycling of municipal waste;
- Reduced release into the environment of certain persistent chemicals, such as DDT, polychlorinated biphenyls (PCBs) and mercury compounds.

The full scale of this progress becomes clearer if the improvements in the state of the environment are assessed in the light of the deterioration that would have occurred had nothing been done: for example, while Japan's GDP grew by 116 per cent, its SO_x emissions were reduced by 80 per cent; in the USA GDP grew by 68 per cent, while its SO_x emissions declined by 27 per cent; and in OECD Europe GDP grew by 59 per cent, but SO_x emissions fell by 42 per cent. Also in some cases, progress already achieved will be taken further as delayed benefits of past policies materialise.

The progress achieved has not been unduly expensive. The direct cost of anti-pollution policies is estimated to range from 0.8 to 1.5 per cent of GDP, while available estimates of the resulting reduction in the damage caused by pollution are significantly higher. The effects on overall prices and economic growth are limited but those on total employment are beneficial in several countries. In more advanced countries, the structure of spending on the environment has shifted markedly, with operating costs accounting for a higher share and capital expenditure a lower one.

This progress must, however, be qualified:
- Progress often remains insufficient and needs to be *consolidated*: for example, while the proportion of people in OECD countries served by wastewater treatment plants has increased from 33 per cent to 60 per cent, 330 million people are still not served at all;
- Progress is *unevenly distributed* among OECD countries: for example, southern European countries have often started later with their pollution abatement efforts.

Remaining problems

The environmental problems of today, as identified in the report, are mostly problems remaining from the *unfinished agendas of the 1970s or 1980s*. The relatively slow pace of progress in dealing with and solving them can be partially explained by two sets of factors:
- Certain weak and inefficient aspects of environmental policies;
- The close interdependencies between the state of the environment and the state of the economy, nationally and internationally.

Atmospheric problems

Evidence of the adverse health, ecological and economic effects of atmospheric pollution is now abundant and has generated the following acute concerns at city, national, continental and world levels. This reflects:
- *Urban air pollution* by NO_2, photochemical smog and fine particulates;
- *Large-scale pollution* problems resulting from the long-range transport of air pollutants such as photochemical oxidants and acidic compounds, despite reduced SO_x emissions;
- Growing concentrations of CO_2 and other greenhouse gases and their *potential global impacts* on the climate, on the sea level, and on world agriculture;
- The release of fluorocarbons and other halogenated alcanes into the atmosphere and their effects on the stratospheric *ozone layer*;
- The human intake of *toxic pollutants* (e.g. cadmium, benzene, radon, asbestos), not only through air but also through food and drinking water;
- Exposure to *pollution inside* vehicles, homes, and commercial and industrial buildings.

Water

As far as water pollution is concerned, the major problems are:
- Pollution of *ground waters*; once perceived as invulnerable to contamination and a precious reserve of clean water, ground waters have deteriorated because of salinisation, diffuse pol-

lution sources such as urban runoff, nitrogenous fertilisers and pesticides used in agriculture, and seepages from contaminated industrial sites and dump sites;

- Pollution of *waterways* and some *coastal areas* by nutrients, and pollution by metals and synthetic organic compounds accumulated in sediments;
- Eutrophication of a number of *lakes* and acidification of lakes in sensitive areas;
- *Drinking water* quality: whereas microbial pollution has been largely overcome, chemical pollution remains a matter of concern when raw waters containing organic substances, nitrates or heavy metals have to be used to produce drinking water which, even after treatment, contains chlorinated organic substances, nitrogenous compounds or metals;
- Risks relating to *floods, droughts and accidental pollution* which threaten, for instance, the sustainable development of agriculture and the continuity of water supply to households in a number of countries;
- *Oil inputs* to the oceans from continental sources such as rivers and coastal activities as well as from routine maritime transport.

Waste

Waste produced in OECD countries has continuously grown in quantity and complexity. Industry is, and will continue to be, the principal source of waste in terms of both quantity and toxicity. Although progress has been made in treating hazardous waste, much remains to be done, such as:

- Cleaning up abandoned *contaminated industrial sites* and hazardous waste dumps, as well as establishing new treatment and disposal facilities;
- Avoiding *marine dumping of hazardous wastes* and offshore incineration;
- Implementing effective accident prevention and control procedures covering the national and international *transport of hazardous substances*;
- Developing liability, insurance and compensation for damages.

Noise

An estimated 16 per cent of the inhabitants of OECD countries – some 130 million people – are exposed to *"unacceptable" levels of noise* (over 65 decibels on a daily outdoor basis). About 400 million people suffer "acoustic discomfort" (over 55 decibels on a daily outdoor basis). Progress made in reducing aircraft noise has been offset by increased noise from cars, goods vehicles and motorised two-wheel vehicles, so that transport is still the main source of noise.

A number of problem areas remain:

- The spread of urban "grey areas", where the noise environment is neither satisfactory nor unacceptable;
- The spread of noise over time (later in the evening, at night, at the week-end) and space (into rural and hitherto unspoilt areas);
- Reducing multiple-exposure to various noise sources: at home, at work, in vehicles.

Land

The land is exposed to a variety of environmental hazards:

- Soil degradation occurs in OECD countries as a result of *pollution* caused by: deposition from short- and long-distance transport of air pollutants, such as acid compounds and heavy metals; spreading of poorly treated sludge; inadequate disposal of solid and hazardous wastes from landfills and abandoned industrial sites; intensive use of agro-chemicals such as certain pesticides;
- Soil degradation in OECD countries also occurs in *many other forms*: erosion by water and wind, desertification, salinisation and waterlogging, ground subsidence, soil compaction and soil loss through the conversion of farmland to urban uses;
- Land is subject to increasing competition from various human activities: agriculture and forestry, industry, energy facilities, urban sprawl, tourism and mining. Despite the use of environmental impact assessment procedures, there is considerable concern about the impact of development on *critical areas* such as coastal regions and wetlands, good quality farmland and designated areas like national parks and natural reserves;

- Land use is a major determinant of the level of risk associated with *natural hazards*. While prevention and mitigation policies have helped to decrease the death tolls from natural disasters significantly, the accumulation of capital assets in disaster-prone areas, sometimes encouraged by subsidised insurance schemes, has already led and will continue to lead to an increase in the damage caused by natural disasters.

Forests

Most of the forests in OECD countries have a higher ecological stability than those in other regions of the world, but from an environmental standpoint a number of problems have appeared which call for greater vigilance in the years to come:

- Regional and global *atmospheric problems* (long-distance pollution, greenhouse effect, etc.) are likely to have impacts which are not well understood as yet but may be extensive;
- *Various types of pressure on forests* can occur: pressure from pollutants, forest fires, invasions by harmful insects or epidemics of cryptogamous diseases; the introduction of tree species from areas with different climatic conditions without sufficient experimentation; pressure from the demand to clear forest land for urban, industrial, commercial or leisure development or for transport infrastructure;
- The growing demand for industrial roundwoods will probably create pressures to make the most productive forests more productive still through the use of *artificial and intensive techniques*, emulating to some extent the development of the agricultural sector;
- In many countries outside the OECD area, particularly tropical ones, the current state of forest resources is a cause for real concern. In a number of those countries, the area and quality of forest resources are declining rapidly. Among the numerous causes is the harvesting of valuable woods from wet *tropical forests* part of which is exported to OECD countries.

Wild life

The main threats to the world's wild life can be summarised as follows:

- Numerous *plant and animal species* remain endangered and the numbers that are threatened are even larger; some species have become extinct while awaiting classification. These problems largely reflect the loss of habitat as well as pollution effects felt directly or through biomagnification;
- *Trade in endangered species* continues to be an issue, requiring more adequate regulation and more effective policing of illegal trading;
- The increasing intensity of resource *harvest practices in international waters* is causing concern, particularly where significant resource wastage is involved or endangered species are affected;
- *Genetic diversity*, including the genetic foundations of crop plants, livestock and fish stocks, is declining; there is a potential for harm to ecosystems by altered microbes and other modified plants and animals.

The extent of all these problems varies greatly between different OECD countries. Emissions of major air pollutants are higher (in absolute figures as well as in emissions per unit of GDP or per capita) in North America than in Europe, and are higher in Europe than in Japan. Water treatment is more developed in North America than in Japan and in Europe as a whole. The proportion of the population exposed to high traffic noise is lower in North America than in Europe, and lower in Europe than in Japan. Within Europe itself, the endowment in water resources, forest resources and "tourism" resources varies greatly as between Nordic and Mediterranean countries; energy resources similarly vary considerably from one country to another. The differences in the scale of environmental problems faced in the various OECD regions and countries essentially reflect differences in population density, economic growth and structures, the pattern of agricultural, industrial, transport and energy activities, endowment in natural resources, climate, and the efforts made to combat particular threats to the environment.

2. TOWARDS SUSTAINABLE DEVELOPMENT

In the 1990s OECD countries will thus have to face more intractable problems than those solved in previous decades and most of those problems are left over from the past. To tackle them effectively, the report stresses that:

- Environmental policies based on national regulations and technological progress must be pursued, but with *renewed determination and innovation*;
- A second level of action will also be required, taking full account of the *economic and international* dimensions of environmental problems.

In other words, the challenge of the 1990s will be not only to strengthen and adapt environment policies but also to bring about *changes in OECD economies* that will make sustainable development a reality, nationally and internationally, by the beginning of the 21st century.

A new challenge for environmental policies

To find effective solutions to the many remaining problems identified above will necessitate both continuity and innovation in environmental policies. While delayed effects from the environmental policies and agreements already adopted can reasonably be expected to show through in the coming years, current evidence suggests that the implementation of these existing measures will need to be further strengthened. In a number of cases, environmental progress requires not only a reduction in the yearly output of pollution, but also reductions in the backlog of *pollution accumulated in the environment* over several years. *Inadequate pricing of natural resources* is leading to inefficient use of these resources; water, for instance, is underpriced in most OECD countries. Moreover, some environmental initiatives will need to be reoriented and targeted at *clearer national and international goals* in order to achieve sustainable development.

Changes in substances of concern

Whereas action to date has concentrated on a limited set of "traditional" pollutants, more sophisticated methods of measurement and analysis have led to the gradual identification of a *wider range of substances* – in air, water and/or soil – that are potentially damaging to human health and to the environment. These include a broad spectrum of organic substances, metal pollutants and fibres, including asbestos.

About 100 000 *chemical compounds* are in current commercial use, and several thousand new chemicals are manufactured and brought to market each year. As regards the introduction of new industrial chemicals, OECD countries have established notification mechanisms for assessing the potential risks of new chemicals before they are put on the market. However, many of the chemicals already in use before the adoption of such mechanisms have not been subjected to risk assessment and there is often insufficient information on them. This has prompted co-operation among OECD countries to investigate the characteristics of mass-produced chemicals.

Whereas the emission of pollutants from point sources such as the chimneys of industrial plants or municipal sewage outlets has tended to decline, emissions from *diffuse sources* have generally increased. For example, surveys have demonstrated that in many areas ground water is contaminated by nitrates and pesticides used in intensive agriculture, by urban run-off and by seepages from abandoned contaminated sites.

Better integration within environmental policies

People's exposure to pollutants has been studied and treated in a compartmentalised way, to some extent with good reason. There is, however, growing evidence that *multiple exposure* to several contaminants through eating, drinking water and breathing may also produce unsuspected health problems. In addition, the cumulative exposure to noise from road traffic as well as from machines at work, from leisure equipment and from household appliances needs to be considered in a more integrated way.

Further, pollution abatement policies have mainly focused on outside environmental conditions which relate to effects both on man's health and on ecosystems. There is increasing evidence, however, that people's exposure to pollutants occurs largely *inside* homes and commercial and industrial premises as well as inside vehicles. Exposure to radon is an example.

There is an increasing awareness that the traditional approach of dealing with problems in only one medium at a time, such as air or water, may not be the most efficient way of dealing with all pollution problems, and may lead to *"cross-media" pollution*. It may simply result in the transfer of the pollutant from one medium to another; it may fail to take account of the physical, chemical, biological and commercial cycles that can affect the pollutant; or it may not adequately consider the multiple paths of exposure that can combine to create human health and environmental risks. Soil, surface waters and ground water may be polluted by acid deposition or by other forms of air pollution transported over long distances or by mismanaged hazardous waste dumps. Soil and ground water could be polluted by the inappropriate spreading on land of sludges produced in wastewater treatment.

Policy *integration* and new strategies are thus needed to deal with issues of multiple exposure, "inside" pollution and "cross-media" pollution. This calls for a better balance between prevention and cure, and will also require the co-operation of national and local environmental administrations as well as the co-operation of enterprises and citizens.

Adjusting economic structures

During the 1970s and 1980s OECD countries experienced more or less continuous economic growth, totalling 116 per cent in Japan, 71 per cent in North America and 59 per cent in OECD Europe. The rate of economic growth had a major influence on the state of the environment, and it will continue to be the major determinant of the intensity of pressures on the environment.

Whereas the environment was once seen as a free and largely unmanaged resource, there was a shift in the 1970s and 1980s towards a more active management of pollution and natural resources. However, economic forces have often eroded the benefits of environmental regulations and technological progress rather than playing the environmentally positive role that they can play when, for instance, prices reflect the true cost of pollution or the full value of natural resources. The *key challenge* for the 1990s is *to bring about cost-effective solutions to environmental problems through the structural adjustment of OECD economies*. Achieving sustainable development is a major task, which will require governments, enterprises, households and the international community to work together.

This 1991 State of the Environment report reviews the effects of *structural changes* in several key economic sectors on the state of the environment. Adjustments have been quite significant and successful in industry as a result of environmentally positive structural changes. Significant adjustments to environmental concerns have taken place in the transport sector as well, but they have been largely counter-balanced by the growth effect, particularly of road transport. Similarly, adjustments in the energy sector benefited from a context of relatively slow growth in energy requirements, but fuel substitution effects tended to diversify rather than reduce environmental impacts. The agricultural sector woke up to environmental concerns in a context of growth and intensification of agricultural practices. These lessons from the past show that structural changes provide both opportunities and challenges for the environment. They demonstrate that, *to achieve a successful transition towards sustainable development, the integration of environmental policies within sectoral policies and within economic decision-making in general is indispensable.*

Industry

Over the past 20 years, industry in OECD countries has undergone structural changes of considerable significance for the environment. These include: the relative decline of the most polluting sectors (iron and steel, non-ferrous metals, cement) and the emergence of innovative sectors (electronics and telecommunications, data processing and transmission, chemicals, biotechnology, and new materials) with new kinds and degrees of pollution problems; obsolescence of old equipment accompanied by the modernisation of plant and equipment, leading to higher productivity and cleaner processes; the rise of non-material investments; and the globalisation of industrial markets. Even though industry continues to account for a large proportion of overall pollution, there has been a tendency for industrial pollution to decline gradually.

Nonetheless, the current situation leaves a number of challenges for the 1990s:

- Although OECD countries now have greater control over the quantities of resources used and pollutants emitted by industry, they will have to deal with environmental pressures arising from continuing industrial growth, and absorb marginally higher costs for each unit of pollution eliminated or waste treated;
- OECD countries will also have to face types of *industrial risk* that will be far more complex to manage: risks inside and outside industrial premises from new technologies and plant accidents, the cumulative effects of widely disseminated or trace pollutants and the unforeseeable repercussions of inadequate treatment of toxic waste;
- The *transformation of production systems* should be used to accelerate and bring benefits to the environment (with more effective recycling, for instance), as industry, science and technology work more and more closely together;
- OECD countries should draw the benefits from the development of an industrial sector engaged specifically in the *business of environmental protection and safety*, as well as from the introduction of more and more "clean" products.

This prospect makes it necessary to step up the monitoring of high-risk industrial installations and integrate environmental considerations into the formulation of business strategies   concerning for instance research, investment, the choice of products and raw materials, siting policies – at the earliest possible stage.

Transport

Over the past 20 years the transport sectors of OECD countries have considerably expanded their infrastructures, while vehicle stocks and traffic volume have risen sharply. Some structural changes have helped to mitigate the environmental effects of these developments: they include the adoption of motor vehicle standards and technology relating to air and noise, new infrastructure design and integration in the environment, motor vehicle fuel efficiency and fuel quality, transport systems management, speed limits and public transport development. But there are significant variations between countries and regions in the extent to which these policies have been implemented.

At the beginning of the 1990s, however, and despite this progress:

- The contribution from the transport sector to total emissions of *air pollutants* is both higher than in the past, and high compared to the contributions from other sectors;
- In *urban areas*, people are exposed to high levels of ozone and noise, and inside their vehicles they are subjected to high levels of pollution from traditional air pollutants;
- *Regional and global pollution problems*, to which the transport sector contributes substantially, are of growing concern;
- The stock of vehicles and the related *traffic volumes grow continuously*, leading to excessive levels of traffic congestion in urban areas and around major air hubs. In particular, there has been a rapid increase in the number of diesel vehicles, including heavy-duty trucks.

Against this backdrop of environmental damage combined with congestion and financial constraints, the development of the sector will be sustainable if, and only if, transport and environmental policies are better integrated. This implies, above and beyond rigorous implementation of the legislation and measures adopted, a need for:

- *Slowdown in the growth of demand*, particularly for road freight and passenger transport, and an increase in the shares of more environmentally friendly modes;
- *Technological progress* in the short and long terms to achieve very quiet, very clean and very energy-efficient vehicles;
- Development of a *sound economic approach* based on the polluter pays principle, reducing overall subsidies and adapting charges and taxes on vehicles, fuels and the use of vehicles to ensure that their use is consistent with environmental and economic efficiency.

Energy

The once close relationship between economic growth, energy demand and environmental effects has been considerably modified in OECD countries: while the GDP of OECD countries has increased by 72 per cent since 1970 and their energy requirements have grown by only 30 per cent, some forms of pollution have increased to a lesser extent (a growth of 15 per cent for CO_2 emissions and of 13 per cent for NO_x emissions) or even have been reduced (by about 38 per cent for SO_2 emissions).

Structural changes in the economies of OECD countries, changes in energy prices and the resulting structural changes in the energy sector itself have played a major role in reshaping this relationship:

- *Technologies* needed to meet certain environmental concerns, such as sulphur control in the context of coal or oil use, have been mastered and widely, although not yet fully, implemented;
- Improvements in the *energy efficiency* of OECD economies have been achieved (25 per cent overall), particularly in the years after the oil shocks 1973 and 1979. Although this progress did not extend to all countries nor continue into the latter part of the 1980s, it helped to limit the total yearly emission of pollutants. Energy conservation is still the most cost-effective solution for reducing the adverse environmental effects of energy, and there is considerable potential in this regard at the OECD level;
- The growing reliance on *indigenous sources of energy* (up 38 per cent) located in OECD countries or adjacent marine areas brought an increase in various environmental impacts such as those associated with oil, coal and nuclear energy production;
- *Shifts in energy use*, mainly from oil to coal and nuclear energy, have changed the type, location and extent of the environmental impacts of the energy sector, with both positive and negative effects.

In the 1990s, therefore, OECD countries will have to contend with major environmental issues related to energy production and consumption of a markedly changed nature:

- Concerns with traditional *atmospheric pollution* arising from the combustion of fossil fuels remain at local and regional levels (urban smog, acid rain), but are supplemented by;
- Concerns with global atmospheric problems relating to *greenhouse gases* such as CO_2 and with their potential impacts in terms of climate changes, further sea level rise, modified water cycles and effects on agriculture and forestry;
- Risks relating to the various stages of the *nuclear fuel cycle* and problems connected with the disposal of high-level radioactive wastes for which long-term policies have yet to be implemented;
- Risks relating to the extraction, transport and use of *fossil fuels*, such as risks to coal miners, and others relating to the production, transport and refining of oil, such as oil spills.

The magnitude of the energy sector's environmental impacts will largely depend on the rate of economic growth, on developments affecting the supply of energy resources such as oil, and on efforts by government, industry and households to save energy and implement cleaner and safer technologies.

Agriculture

The agricultural sector in OECD countries has experienced persistent imbalances between production and demand in the last 20 years. The result has been growing surpluses of temperate foodstuffs and declining producer prices in real terms. In most OECD countries this led to a reappraisal of agricultural support policies in the latter part of the 1980s. The accompanying structural changes have had far-reaching implications for the environment: increasing vertical integration of the food sector; initially a slight and then a more marked decline in the land area devoted to food production; the increasing intensity and specialisation of food production; the emergence of a more environmentally friendly agriculture; and the internationalisation of food markets. Although agriculture has had a long positive association with the environment during this century, its environmental impact has tended to be increasingly negative over the past two decades, a trend that only began to moderate in the late 1980s.

In the 1990s, growing world population pressures and rising demand for foodstuffs in developing countries will increase the pressure on agricultural land resources both in developing countries and in the OECD, which is likely to remain a significant exporter of agricultural products. These developments have some major implications:

- OECD countries will have to face the consequences of *fertilizer and pesticide residues* in foodstuffs and in water supplies; although the effects on human health are not fully understood at present, pure food and water will be important issues for all countries of the OECD, but even more acute for regions where production intensity is high or will further increase;
- On a regional and local scale, OECD countries will have to ensure that the effects on agriculture of pollution and resource use by both agricultural and non-agricultural activities will not compromise *sustainable agricultural development* in larger areas through, for example, water scarcity or soil erosion;
- More broadly, OECD countries will need to better understand the potential implications for agricultural production of changes in temperature and precipitation regimes which might result from global atmospheric problems, and the related potential changes in national food balances and international trade;
- The process of *agricultural transformation* in OECD countries should accelerate, doubtless in a direction more favourable to the environment, with more environmentally conscious agricultural practices, growing demand for healthier food, and an increasing role for farmers not only in maintaining landscapes, rural ecosystems, and a genetic pool of plant and animal varieties, but also in developing rural tourism activities on marginal land.

This prospect makes it necessary to integrate the environment into agricultural policies and practices, by preventing and controlling pollution, accentuating and enhancing the positive role of agriculture for the environment, and adapting agricultural support policies to take appropriate account of environmental concerns.

Forestry

As a result of forest management policies, the forest resources of the OECD as a whole are actually increasing: both the stock of timber and its average annual growth have increased during the past 20 years. This will continue, unless pollution or climate changes occur on such a large scale as to upset the ecological equilibrium of forest ecosystems.

However, the massive deforestation that is taking place in tropical areas has very grave consequences for the countries concerned – erosion, disturbance of water regimes, disappearance of biotopes and species, wasting of economic resources, destruction of traditional lifestyles. It also has consequences on a worldwide scale – decline of the global forest resource potential at a time when world demand is expected to increase. Above all, this deforestation will aggravate global climatic problems, for the tropical forests play a vital role in biosphere mechanisms both as a stock of carbon (which their destruction would release into the atmosphere in the form of CO_2, thus intensifying the greenhouse effect) and as a regulator of the planet's radiative and water balance. The disappearance of tropical forests could modify the pluviometric regime of very extensive zones.

The national and global implications of deforestation, given the strength of economic and ecological interdependencies, justify the concern to *preserve the tropical forest* area. This goal can be pursued in two ways: protection of existing valuable tropical forests and development of highly productive artificial plantations in all the regions of the world with real forestry potential. Such plantations would help meet the foreseeable worldwide demand for wood and reduce pressure on protected and less intensively managed forests. *Sustainability of forest resources* could be achieved *on a worldwide scale and on an equitable basis* for all concerned. Thus, the major challenge in preserving forest resources in the years to come is to extend the principles of forest management and sustainable development to the entire planet. These principles have been applied to a greater or lesser extent in OECD countries' forests for a long time, and have contributed to an increase in their forestry resources. OECD countries bear a major share of the responsibility for safeguarding the future of the world's forests, since they are the major consumers and importers of wood.

CONCLUSIONS ON ENVIRONMENTAL INFORMATION

Progress Made

Over the past two decades, environmental information and reporting has progressed in OECD countries.

Environmental monitoring and environmental data collection have gradually developed and been consolidated to support the definition and implementation of specific environmental policies, to provide a general picture of the environment, and to better identify pressures on it. The stage of development reached today by environmental monitoring and data collection varies however, among Member countries, in terms of: means; coverage; techniques and methods used; the degree of dissemination and adaptation to decision-making; and institutional arrangements.

Treatment and analysis of environmental statistics has improved; compendia of environmental data have now been published once or more or less regularly in 17 OECD Member countries: Canada, the United States, Japan, Australia, Austria, Denmark, Finland, France, Germany, Ireland, Italy, the Netherlands, Norway, Portugal, Sweden, the United Kingdom and Yugoslavia, and for the European Community.

National reports on the state of the environment have been published yearly in the United States (since 1970), Japan (since 1969), France, Portugal and Spain only, but have been published at least once in most OECD countries and by the European Community. Recently, a prospective state of the environment report was issued in the Netherlands. The OECD itself has published reports in 1979, 1985 and 1991.

Some methods and techniques relating to environmental information have progressed: remote sensing techniques, using satellites and information treatment capacity at relatively low costs, have begun to be applied to the monitoring of land use changes. Resource accounting has been developed and tested, for example, in Norway and France, to assess the stock of natural resources such as water, forest, energy, land and fish. Other technical developments (micro-computer, electronic information networks, geographical information systems) have been used for environmental data transfer and processing, and applied to air pollution or flood monitoring and alert systems.

International environmental statistics emerged in the 1980s and international comparability of data has progressed; international classifications and nomenclatures have been established, for example, for land use and protected areas by the UNECE and the IUCN. OECD efforts to develop a core set of environmental data using a commonly agreed questionnaire and other international data led to publication of an OECD compendium of environmental data in 1984 (pilot version), 1985, 1987, and 1989.

Towards a Second Generation of Environmental Information

Environmental information in the 1990s will have to adapt to a new context which shapes the demand for environmental information:
-- Changing environmental policy priorities reflecting, above all, the international, intersectoral and economic dimensions of sustainable development;
-- Increasing demands for reliable, harmonised and comparable environmental information from governments, business and the public;
-- Progess with regard to scientific knowledge and to measurement and information technology.

This calls for progress in new directions, as well as consolidation of the existing environmental information systems.

Monitoring systems, although often very useful for research purposes, too often lead to situations of being "data rich and information poor." They need to be reassessed and made more responsive to new policy priorities. This will require correcting the gaps, imbalances or weaknesses in the coverage of these systems; promoting more "integrated" approaches such as multiple exposure and biological monitoring, and health effects monitoring; improving the quality and comparability of results; disseminating and making better use of monitoring results for decision-making; better co-ordination of monitoring carried on by central and local bodies, public agencies and private firms, research institutes and universities; making monitoring efforts more cost-effective and financing them with a proper mix of public and private funds.

The quality of existing data needs to be improved, to ensure inter alia statistical reliability, annual updating, continuity of time series, and proper geographical disaggregation. Their international comparability must also be further developed by using international definitions and classifications as far as possible, strengthening the quality of national contributions to international efforts, and further co-ordinating international work on environmental information.

A number of gaps in environmental statistics and information remain to be filled with regard to:
-- The condition of soil resources and of the marine environment, of species and their habitats as well as biodiversity itself;
-- The trends in the physical stocks of natural resources and their economic value;
-- Health, ecological and economic risks relating to long-term pollution; for example, cumulative exposure to substances that may give rise to genetic changes, cancer or birth defects; or the ecological, economic and social risks associated with atmospheric problems, such as those from increases in CO_2 and other greenhouse gases in the atmosphere;
-- Economic data such as data on environmental expenditures, on environmental damages, and on the economic significance of environmental policies;
-- Environmental aspects relating directly to economic and sectoral policies such as agricultural, industrial, transport, energy and tourism policies.

Increased attention to the intersectoral nature of environmental issues and to their international dimension leads to a need for environmental indicators to integrate environmental and economic decision-making nationally and internationally. These indicators need to provide aggregate, policy-relevant, analytically sound and measurable information. More specifically, sustainable development requires strengthened capabilities within and among countries:
-- To better assess environmental performance in terms of environmental quality itself, of achievement of national environmental goals and of implementation of international commitments;
-- To integrate environmental concerns in sectoral decision-making; and

-- To improve environmental accounting.
This includes adjustments through environmental satellite accounts of the System of National Accounts, and development of natural resources environmental accounts so as to better assess stocks, and changes in stocks of natural resources. Such work needs to be made compatible at an international level.

Better reporting of countries' environmental performance and their contributions to international environmental progress (e.g. transfrontier pollution, management of global commons and regional seas, trade, aid) should build on this information. Periodic assessments of the state of and trends in the environment are to be supplemented by other forms of assessment such as environmental outlooks or reviews of countries' environmental performance, which can be related to environmental quality levels, national goals and international agreements.

Some institutional adjustments aiming at improving the quality, independence and relevance of environmental information have taken place, or are being proposed, such as the "European Environment Agency," the "US Bureau of Environmental Statistics," or the "French Environmental Institute." Determined action is needed to overcome institutional, administrative and financial barriers to the development of better environmental information.

The provision of environmental information and its improved dissemination have become a major environmental action in itself. It is needed in order to address environmental issues in their economic and international context. It is needed simply in order to fulfil the public "right to know" in democratic societies.

Consumption and time-use patterns

Other structural changes have occurred during the past two decades. The population of OECD countries has grown by 116 million inhabitants, but declined from 19 to 16 per cent of the world population; it has become richer and older, and the size of households has declined dramatically. Consumption patterns have become increasingly dependent on packaged goods, durable goods and the automobile; consequently, they have generated more waste and pollution and generally consumed more natural resources, such as oil, water and wood. Time-use patterns have been marked by a rapid increase in leisure and tourism activities; this has been partly beneficial for the environment, by stimulating improved protection of the natural environment, landscapes, historic sites and wild life in a number of countries, but it has also generated increased pressures (air pollution, water pollution from sewage, littering, environmental restructuring with second homes and tourism-related buildings and infrastructures), often concentrated in environmentally sensitive areas such as lakes, seashores and mountains.

The likely continuation of these trends through the 1990s and beyond has several implications for the environment and for future environmental policies:

- Despite the slowdown in demographic growth, the inhabitants of OECD countries will continue to place a major strain on the world's resources and on the state of the environment through increased consumption and their use and disposal of final products. Consequently, a critical issue is how to prevent the general increase in incomes from being transformed into *environmentally harmful consumption patterns* and instead to encourage people to adopt environmentally friendly consumption patterns and ways of life;
- The socio-demographic development of OECD countries seems to encourage the preference for cars over other modes of transport. The growth in private transport will lead to, among other things, increased congestion but will at the same time have the effect of dispersing leisure activities and related environmental problems;
- The impact of tourism on physical resources and the environment is substantial and is expected to increase. But since a high-quality environment is an essential prerequisite for tourism, there are growing doubts about the *tourism industry's capacity for sustainable development*. This issue is of crucial importance for Mediterranean countries in particular.

The international context

Today, OECD countries represent only 16 per cent of the world's population and 24 per cent of its land area; but their market economies account for about 72 per cent of world gross product, 78 per cent of all road vehicles, and 50 per cent of global energy use. They generate about 76 per cent of world trade, including 73 per cent of chemical product exports and about 73 per cent of forest product imports. They also provide 95 per cent of bilateral development assistance. Given world economic and ecological interdependencies, the environmental and economic state of OECD countries influences and is influenced by non-OECD countries, including Eastern European countries, dynamic Asian economies and developing countries.

A growing number of environmental issues are international by nature. Firstly, some problems relate to *cross-border pollution*. Among these are long-range pollution, the management of international river basins, the international transport of hazardous wastes, and risks associated with installations located close to international frontiers.

Secondly, some problems concern regional or global commons. They they cannot be resolved without concerted action on the part of OECD countries. This applies not only to *planet-wide problems*, such as the protection of the stratospheric ozone layer and potential climate changes as a consequence of CO_2 and other greenhouse gas emissions, but also to issues like the management of *regional seas* such as the Baltic Sea, the Caribbean Sea, the Mediterranean Sea, the North Sea and the Arctic Ocean. Some of these problems have already been addressed at international level by means of bilateral or multilateral agreements. However, the full-scale implementation of these agreements and the wish to address other pressing international pollution issues make it necessary to deal with pollution problems at both national and international levels and to monitor national and international progress.

Thirdly, a number of environmental issues are trade-related. OECD countries account for a large part of world *trade* in chemicals, automobiles and other products which can indirectly cause pollution, and in natural resources such as forestry products or endangered species of wild flora and fauna. In many cases, trade and the trade-related policies of industrialised countries affect the use of natural resources in both developing and developed countries.

Fourthly, environmental problems in non-OECD countries, whether in the developing world or in central and eastern Europe, for instance, need to be handled in conjunction with *bilateral and multilateral aid and financing*. In the last 10 years, both development assistance agencies in OECD Member countries and multilateral financial institutions have progressively assessed the potential environmental impacts of traditional development aid projects, financed specific environmentally beneficial projects, and stimulated the capability of recipient countries to deal with environmental issues.

Although some interest was apparent as far back as the early 1970s, it is only in recent years that recognition of the international nature of environmental problems has acquired a large media and diplomatic dimension. In OECD countries this trend largely followed and reflected public opinion; polls in the early 1980s, for instance, showed the great importance already attached to international environmental issues compared to more national or local ones.

Hence, over the last 20 years progress on international environmental issues has essentially taken two forms beyond general co-operation on environmental research and information (see Conclusions on Environmental Information): development of *international environmental law* and adoption of related *bilateral and multilateral agreements*. Such agreements concern, among other things, trade in flora and fauna, marine pollution, cross-border pollution, international movement of hazardous wastes, and protection of the ozone layer. The actual impact of such agreements on the environment obviously depends on the adoption of effective national and international mechanisms for their implementation and also on the length of time needed for these measures to translate into environmental improvements.

The international challenges in the 1990s will be:

- To ensure that such international agreements are effectively translated into environmental realities;
- To supplement existing agreements with new ones on emerging issues such as climate change, and to back them up with appropriate quantified targets and liability rules;
- To monitor improvements in the international environment and the contributions of different countries and regions of the world;
- To promote the integration of environmental concerns into trade and aid policies and practices;

in order to ensure the planet's sustainable development and a fair share in that development for all regions and countries of the world.

LIST OF THE MEMBERS OF THE GROUP ON THE STATE OF THE ENVIRONMENT

CHAIRMAN: MR. P. ROSS

AUSTRALIA	Ms. L. HINGEE Mr. W.S. McNAMARA	NETHERLANDS	Mr. R. FREDRIKSZ Mr. R. HUETING Mr. P. KLEIN
AUSTRIA	Mr. G. SCHNABL Mr. G. SIMHANDL	NEW ZEALAND	Mr. N. FRASER
BELGIUM	M. R. BRULARD M. S. KEMPENEERS	NORWAY	Mr. F. BRUNVOLL Mr. O. LONE
CANADA	Mr. A. JOLICŒUR Ms. A. KERR Mr. K. O'SHEA Mr. P. RUMP Mr. S. SEGARD Ms. L. WHITBY	PORTUGAL	Mme. G. BORREGO Mme. L. GOMES M. L. GOULAO Mme. N. MIGUENS M. P. NUNES LIBERATO
		SPAIN	M. D. ARANDA M. J. MARQUEZ LEON M. J. SOLANA
DENMARK	Mr. J. SCHOU Mr. E. VESSELBO		
FINLAND	Mr. H. SALMI Mr. H. SISULA	SWEDEN	Mr. C. BERNES Mr. S. NYSTROM Ms. I. OHMAN
FRANCE	M. M. FORTIER M. G. GUIGNABEL Mme. A. LE MEUR M. J. L. WEBER	SWITZERLAND	M. M. KAMMERMAN M. A. RIST
		TURKEY	Ms. S. GUVEN Ms. N. FEYIZOGLU Mr. H. KASNAKOGLU Mr. K. TEPEDELEN
GERMANY	Ms. U. LAUBER Mr. E. MAEGELE Mr. P. ROEMER Mr. K. TIETMANN		
		UNITED KINGDOM	Mr. P. MacCORMACK Mr. C. MORREY
ITALY	M. C. CONSTANTINO M. C. MUSCARA M. L. SABATINI M. P. SOPRANO	UNITED STATES	Mr. P. ROSS Mr. J. SHEERIN Mr. T. TITUS
JAPAN	Mr. Y. KIMURA Mr. Y. MORIGUCHI Mr. T. MORITA Mr. N. TANAKA	CEC	Mr. J. ALLEN Ms. G. HILF Mr. R. UHEL

OECD SECRETARIAT
M. C. AVEROUS

Consultants: Mr. J. BOWERS, M. P. CHAPUY, Ms. K. DOLAN, M. J.P. HANNEQUART, Mr. M. IWATA, Ms. J. JÄGER, Mr. B. JOHNSON, Mr. B. KENNEDY, M. D. LARRÉ, M. N. LEE, Mme. M. LINSTER, Ms. B. LÜBKERT, Mr. T. McRAE, M. P. MIRENOWICZ, Mr. J. De MONTGOLFIER, Mr. K. NEVALAINEN, Mr. S. NILSSON, Mr. N. SHELTON, M. J. THEYS, Ms. J. VINKE, Mr. D. ZOELLNER

WHERE TO OBTAIN OECD PUBLICATIONS – OÙ OBTENIR LES PUBLICATIONS DE L'OCDE

Argentina – Argentine
Carlos Hirsch S.R.L.
Galería Güemes, Florida 165, 4° Piso
1333 Buenos Aires   Tel. 30.7122, 331.1787 y 331.2391
Telegram: Hirsch–Baires
Telex: 21112 UAPE–AR. Ref. s/2901
Telefax:(1)331–1787

Australia – Australie
D.A. Book (Aust.) Pty. Ltd.
648 Whitehorse Road, P.O.B 163
Mitcham, Victoria 3132   Tel. (03)873.4411
Telex: AA37911 DA BOOK
Telefax: (03)873.5679

Austria – Autriche
OECD Publications and Information Centre
Schedestrasse 7
5300 Bonn 1 (Germany)   Tel. (0228)21.60.45
Telefax: (0228)26.11.04

Gerold & Co.
Graben 31
Wien I   Tel. (0222)533.50.14

Belgium – Belgique
Jean De Lannoy
Avenue du Roi 202
B–1060 Bruxelles   Tel. (02)538.51.69/538.08.41
Telex: 63220   Telefax: (02) 538.08.41

Canada
Renouf Publishing Company Ltd.
1294 Algoma Road
Ottawa, ON K1B 3W8   Tel. (613)741.4333
Telex: 053–4783   Telefax: (613)741.5439
Stores:
61 Sparks Street
Ottawa, ON K1P 5R1   Tel. (613)238.8985
211 Yonge Street
Toronto, ON M5B 1M4   Tel. (416)363.3171

Federal Publications
165 University Avenue
Toronto, ON M5H 3B8   Tel. (416)581.1552
Telefax: (416)581.1743

Les Publications Fédérales
1185 rue de l'Université
Montréal, PQ H3B 3A7   Tel.(514)954–1633

Les Éditions La Liberté Inc.
3020 Chemin Sainte–Foy
Sainte–Foy, PQ G1X 3V6   Tel. (418)658.3763
Telefax: (418)658.3763

Denmark – Danemark
Munksgaard Export and Subscription Service
35, Norre Sogade, P.O. Box 2148
DK–1016 Kobenhavn K   Tel. (45 33)12.85.70
Telex: 19431 MUNKS DK   Telefax: (45 33)12.93.87

Finland – Finlande
Akateeminen Kirjakauppa
Keskuskatu 1, P.O. Box 128
00100 Helsinki   Tel. (358 0)12141
Telex: 125080   Telefax: (358 0)121.4441

France
OECD/OCDE
Mail Orders/Commandes par correspondance:
2 rue André–Pascal
75775 Paris Cedex 16   Tel. (1)45.24.82.00
Bookshop/Librairie:
33, rue Octave–Feuillet
75016 Paris   Tel. (1)45.24.81.67
                        (1)45.24.81.81
Telex: 620 160 OCDE
Telefax: (33–1)45.24.85.00

Librairie de l'Université
12a, rue Nazareth
13090 Aix–en–Provence   Tel. 42.26.18.08

Germany – Allemagne
OECD Publications and Information Centre
Schedestrasse 7
5300 Bonn 1   Tel. (0228)21.60.45
Telefax: (0228)26.11.04

Greece – Grèce
Librairie Kauffmann
28 rue du Stade
105 64 Athens   Tel. 322.21.60
Telex: 218187 LIKA Gr

Hong Kong
Swindon Book Co. Ltd.
13 – 15 Lock Road
Kowloon, Hongkong   Tel. 366 80 31
Telex: 50 441 SWIN HX
Telefax: 739 49 75

Iceland – Islande
Mál Mog Menning
Laugavegi 18, Pósthólf 392
121 Reykjavik   Tel. 15199/24240

India – Inde
Oxford Book and Stationery Co.
Scindia House
New Delhi 110001   Tel. 331.5896/5308
Telex: 31 61990 AM IN
Telefax: (11)332.5993
17 Park Street
Calcutta 700016   Tel. 240832

Indonesia – Indonésie
Pdii–Lipi
P.O. Box 269/JKSMG/88
Jakarta 12790   Tel. 583467
Telex: 62 875

Ireland – Irlande
TDC Publishers – Library Suppliers
12 North Frederick Street
Dublin 1   Tel. 744835/749677
Telex: 33530 TDCP EI Telefax : 748416

Italy – Italie
Libreria Commissionaria Sansoni
Via Benedetto Fortini, 120/10
Casella Post. 552
50125 Firenze   Tel. (055)645415
Telex: 570466   Telefax: (39.55)641257
Via Bartolini 29
20155 Milano   Tel. 365083
La diffusione delle pubblicazioni OCSE viene assicurata dalle
principali librerie ed anche da:
Editrice e Libreria Herder
Piazza Montecitorio 120
00186 Roma   Tel. 679.4628
Telex: NATEL I 621427
Libreria Hoepli
Via Hoepli 5
20121 Milano   Tel. 865446
Telex: 31.33.95 Telefax: (39.2)805.2886
Libreria Scientifica
Dott. Lucio de Biasio "Aeiou"
Via Meravigli 16
20123 Milano   Tel. 807679
Telefax: 800175

Japan – Japon
OECD Publications and Information Centre
Landic Akasaka Building
2–3–4 Akasaka, Minato–ku
Tokyo 107   Tel. (81.3)3586.2016
Telefax: (81.3)3584.7929

Korea – Corée
Kyobo Book Centre Co. Ltd.
P.O. Box 1658, Kwang Hwa Moon
Seoul   Tel. (REP)730.78.91
Telefax: 735.0030

Malaysia/Singapore – Malaisie/Singapour
Co–operative Bookshop Ltd.
University of Malaya
P.O. Box 1127, Jalan Pantai Baru
59700 Kuala Lumpur
Malaysia   Tel. 756.5000/756.5425
Telefax: 757.3661
Information Publications Pte. Ltd.
Pei–Fu Industrial Building
24 New Industrial Road No. 02–06
Singapore 1953   Tel. 283.1786/283.1798
Telefax: 284.8875

Netherlands – Pays–Bas
SDU Uitgeverij
Christoffel Plantijnstraat 2
Postbus 20014
2500 EA's–Gravenhage   Tel. (070 3)78.99.11
Voor bestellingen: Tel. (070 3)78.98.80
Telex: 32486 stdru   Telefax: (070 3)47.63.51

New Zealand – Nouvelle–Zélande
Government Printing Office
Customer Services
33 The Esplanade – P.O. Box 38–900
Petone, Wellington
Tel. (04) 685–555   Telefax: (04)685–333

Norway – Norvège
Narvesen Info Center – NIC
Bertrand Narvesens vei 2
P.O. Box 6125 Etterstad
0602 Oslo 6   Tel. (02)57.33.00
Telex: 79668 NIC N   Telefax: (02)68.19.01

Pakistan
Mirza Book Agency
65 Shahrah Quaid–E–Azam
Lahore 3   Tel. 66839
Telex: 44886 UBL PK. Attn: MIRZA BK

Portugal
Livraria Portugal
Rua do Carmo 70–74
Apart. 2681
1117 Lisboa Codex   Tel. 347.49.82/3/4/5
Telefax: 37 02 64

Singapore/Malaysia – Singapour/Malaisie
See "Malaysia/Singapore" – "Voir "Malaisie/Singapour"

Spain – Espagne
Mundi–Prensa Libros S.A.
Castelló 37, Apartado 1223
Madrid 28001   Tel. (91) 431.33.99
Telex: 49370 MPLI   Telefax: 575 39 98
Libreria Internacional AEDOS
Consejo de Ciento 391
08009 –Barcelona   Tel. (93) 301–86–15
Telefax: (93) 317–01–41

Sweden – Suède
Fritzes Fackboksföretaget
Box 16356, S 103 27 STH
Regeringsgatan 12
DS Stockholm   Tel. (08)23.89.00
Telex: 12387 Telefax: (08)20.50.21

Subscription Agency/Abonnements:
Wennergren–Williams AB
Nordenflychtsvagen 74
Box 30004
104 25 Stockholm   Tel. (08)13.67.00
Telex: 19937 Telefax: (08)618.62.36

Switzerland – Suisse
OECD Publications and Information Centre
Schedestrasse 7
5300 Bonn 1 (Germany)   Tel. (0228)21.60.45
Telefax: (0228)26.11.04

Librairie Payot
6 rue Grenus
1211 Genève 11   Tel. (022)731.89.50
Telex: 28356
Subscription Agency – Service des Abonnements
4 place Pépinet – BP 3312
1002 Lausanne   Tel. (021)341.33.31
Telefax: (021)341.33.45
Maditec S.A.
Ch. des Palettes 4
1020 Renens/Lausanne   Tel. (021)635.08.65
Telefax: (021)635.07.80
United Nations Bookshop/Librairie des Nations–Unies
Palais des Nations
1211 Genève 10   Tel. (022)734.60.11 (ext. 48.72)
Telex: 289696 (Attn: Sales)
Telefax: (022)733.98.79

Taiwan – Formose
Good Faith Worldwide Int'l. Co. Ltd.
9th Floor, No. 118, Sec. 2
Chung Hsiao E. Road
Taipei   Tel. 391.7396/391.7397
Telefax: (02) 394.9176

Thailand – Thaïlande
Suksit Siam Co. Ltd.
1715 Rama IV Road, Samyan
Bangkok 5   Tel. 251.1630

Turkey – Turquie
Kültur Yayinlari Is–Türk Ltd. Sti.
Atatürk Bulvari No. 191/Kat. 21
Kavaklidere/Ankara   Tel. 25.07.60
Dolmabahce Cad. No. 29
Besiktas/Istanbul   Tel. 160.71.88
Telex: 43482B

United Kingdom – Royaume–Uni
HMSO
Gen. enquiries   Tel. (071) 873 0011
Postal orders only:
P.O. Box 276, London SW8 5DT
Personal Callers HMSO Bookshop
49 High Holborn, London WC1V 6HB
Telex: 297138 Telefax: 071 873 8463
Branches at: Belfast, Birmingham, Bristol, Edinburgh,
Manchester

United States – États–Unis
OECD Publications and Information Centre
2001 L Street N.W., Suite 700
Washington, D.C. 20036–4095   Tel. (202)785.6323
Telefax: (202)785.0350

Venezuela
Libreria del Este
Avda F. Miranda 52, Aptdo. 60337
Edificio Galipán
Caracas 106   Tel. 951.1705/951.2307/951.1297
Telegram: Libreste Caracas

Yugoslavia – Yougoslavie
Jugoslovenska Knjiga
Knez Mihajlova 2, P.O. Box 36
Beograd   Tel. (011)621.992
Telex: 12466 jk bgd   Telefax: (011)625.970

Orders and inquiries from countries where Distributors have
not yet been appointed should be sent to: OECD Publications
Service, 2 rue André–Pascal, 75775 Paris Cedex 16, France.
Les commandes provenant de pays où l'OCDE n'a pas encore
désigné de distributeur devraient être adressées à : OCDE,
Service des Publications, 2, rue André–Pascal, 75775 Paris
Cedex 16, France.

OECD PUBLICATIONS, 2 rue André-Pascal, 75775 PARIS CEDEX 16
PRINTED IN FRANCE
(97 91 01 1) ISBN 92-64-13442-5 - No. 45323 1990